Real World ICT

for AS and

2nd Edition

Clarke Rice
Karen Ward
Keith Redfern

Colourpoint
Educational

© Rice, Ward, Redfern and Colourpoint Books 2009

First published by Colourpoint Books 2004
This edition 2009
Fourth Impression

Designed by April Sky Design, Newtownards
Printed by W&G Baird Ltd, Antrim

ISBN 978 1 904242 94 9

COLOURPOINT EDUCATIONAL

Colourpoint Educational
An imprint of Colourpoint Creative Ltd
Colourpoint House
Jubilee Business Park
21 Jubilee Road
Newtownards
County Down
Northern Ireland
BT23 4YH

Tel: 028 9182 6339
Fax: 028 9182 1900
E-mail: info@colourpoint.co.uk
Web site: www.colourpointeducational.com

Clarke read Computing at the University of Ulster and entered teaching via industrial experience in software engineering, completing his PGCE at the Queen's University of Belfast. He now teaches ICT and Mathematics and lives on the north coast of Northern Ireland with his lovely wife. When he is not teaching, Clarke enjoys reading, quizzes and playing Badminton.

Keith read Electrical and Electronic Engineering at the Queen's University of Belfast and has gained over 11 years experience in the software development divisions of various telecommunications and security companies. When he is not programming, Keith's hobbies include mountain biking, hill walking and triathlons.

Karen read Modern History at the Queen's University of Belfast followed by an MSc in Computer Science and Applications at Queen's. She went on to complete her PGCE at the University of Ulster. She now teaches GCSE and A Level ICT. While not teaching, Karen enjoys spending time with her husband and children, shopping, walking her dog and listening to music.

Contents

Authors' Preface

Authors' Preface

This book is written for the ICT teachers in Northern Ireland and their students. We hope that our teaching colleagues will use it to encourage others to develop our shared interest in ICT and Computing. We hope that students will use it as a starting point to explore an ever-expanding field of knowledge, leading to further study and a rewarding career.

Thanks are due to the teachers and students who took time to read and comment on early drafts of this work. Thanks are especially due to Margaret McDonnell and the ICT students at Loreto College, Coleraine. Thanks also to those who encouraged our early interest in Computing: Keith Hill (now of Omagh Academy); Richard Clingan and John Ryan of the Royal School, Dungannon; the lecturers of the University of Ulster at Coleraine and the Queen's University of Belfast. Thanks also to our families (especially, Alison Rice, Winston Ward and Ruth Redfern) who gave us time to research and develop this book.

To students:

Our world changes at a fast pace: much of that change is due to the use of ICT, which has made some aspects of society unrecognisable when compared to 50, or even 10 years ago. Therefore, unlike some other subjects, ICT is not a static body of knowledge but changes rapidly. Indeed, these changes prompted an extensive revision of the CCEA ICT A Level and an extensive revision of the first edition of this book only a few years after its publication. However, a good knowledge of the fundamentals of ICT will equip you for your future use and understanding of technology, regardless of how it develops.

The fact that you have chosen to study ICT at A Level suggests that you seek more information than is required of an end user. To that end, we encourage you to open your mind to what ICT is used for and the ways in which it functions. Develop an understanding of the subject that goes beyond an exam specification, so that you may see where the material presented here applies to the 'Real World' of ICT. Read ICT magazines and web sites; explore the operation of your PC; stretch your knowledge and abilities; experiment and be bold.

Amoeba Antiques

Throughout this book, a number of ICT concepts are described through the fictional firm *Amoeba Antiques*, formed through the merger of a group of antique stores and an antique warehousing firm: one based in Scotland, the other in Ireland.

While Amoeba is fictional, the scenarios presented are not. Many of their modes of operation can be seen through publicly available information regarding a number of organisations. The companies who have inspired the **positive** side of Amoeba are listed below, in alphabetical order. Many other organisations employ similar methods. The companies who inspired our examples of how **not** to operate – *Mauvaise Antiquité*, *Gormless Gauges* and *National ISP* – are purposely left anonymous.

+ Amazon – http://www.amazon.co.uk

+ ASDA – http://www.asda.co.uk

+ British Telecommunications – http://www.bt.com

+ Fujitsu – http://www.fujitsu.com/uk

+ Laura Ashley – http://www.lauraashley.co.uk

+ Marks and Spencer – http://www.marksandspencer.co.uk

+ Royal Mail – http://www.royalmail.com

+ Sainsbury's – http://www.sainsburys.co.uk

+ Tesco – http://www.tesco.co.uk

+ Wesley Owen – http://www.wesleyowen.com

Real World ICT on the web

An accompanying web site containing additional material, such as a glossary and tutorials, is available at **http://www.colourpoint.co.uk/extra/realworld**

To Colourpoint

None of this would have been possible without the advice and guidance of the people at Colourpoint. Thanks are especially due to our editor, Wesley Johnston, for co-ordinating this project.

CR, KR & KW
March 2009

AS Module 1: *Components of ICT*

Introduction

Computers have affected the world in many ways, from household chores to human communication. Students growing up in the early 21st century take for granted many tools that have only became commonplace in the past few decades. Consequently, the world that the readers of this book inhabit is in many ways very different to the one that their parents, or the authors of this book, grew up in.

Module 1 examines the basic components of the Information Systems that permeate our world together with how these systems have affected society. It also explores how the computer systems that today we take for granted are built. Many of these topics are further developed later in the course.

As a student of ICT, the reader should not rely solely on this book for information on the impact of ICT on our lives. Other sources should be consulted in order to keep informed on a topic that is constantly expanding. For example: ICT magazines; television and radio programs such as BBC's *Click* (News 24) and *Digital Planet* (World Service radio and podcast); and web sites such as *slashdot.org*. Examining other sources will help to develop a wider knowledge and understanding of ICT and its relevance in the real world beyond the course specification.

The book has been written to follow the CCEA course specification, for the benefit of students and teachers. Hence some topics, such as the Internet, are considered in several chapters. These chapters have been carefully designed to make sense whether they are read in the order presented in the specification or if the chapters relating to a single topic are read together.

AS MODULE 1 SPECIFICATION MAP
How this book relates to the CCEA specification

Content....	...is covered in Real World ICT 2nd Edition by:
1.1 Data and information	Chapter 1: Data and Information
1.2 Hardware and software components Input and Output	Chapter 2: Hardware: Input Devices and Chapter 3: Hardware: Output Devices
Storage	Chapter 4: Hardware: Storage Devices
Processor	Chapter 5: Hardware: Central Processing Unit
System Software	Chapter 6: Software: System Software
Application Software	Chapter 7: Software: Application Software
Open source software	Chapter 8: Software: Open Source Software
1.3 Network Communication	Chapter 9: Local and Wide Area Networks and Chapter 10: Internet Technology
1.4 Applications of ICT The use of ICT in a range of areas	Chapter 11: Emerging Technologies and Chapter 12: Health, Safety and Legal Issues
The Internet	Chapter 13: The Consequences of the Internet
The consequences of the use of ICT for individuals, organisations and society Security issues, including disaster recovery	Chapter 14: Factors Affecting ICT
1.5 Developing ICT applications	Chapter 15: Developing ICT Applications

CHAPTER 1
Data and Information

1.1 Introduction

Information is communicated in a variety of ways. In an increasingly media-saturated world, people make the decision on whether to pay attention to information or ignore it almost constantly.

For example, at the time of writing the author is surrounded by the following sources of information:

+ the radio in the background;
+ icons on a PC screen which indicate incoming mail and instant messaging;
+ what can be seen through the window;
+ a mobile phone on the desk;
+ a flashing red light on an answering machine.

What people do with information on offer depends on the context in which it is received. The flashing red light on the answering machine is currently being ignored because the message has already been heard, but has not yet been deleted for a particular reason. The radio will be ignored until the hourly news is broadcast. If a message is received on the instant messaging client it will probably be responded to, but this depends upon who the sender is. If an e-mail is received it will be read eventually, but perhaps not immediately. If the phone rings it will probably be answered, although caller identification allows it to be ignored if appropriate.

Thus the context in which data or information is received has a strong bearing on how it is treated. Indeed, context is often vital for understanding. For example 'red light' means nothing unless the source of the red light is known – whether it is on an electronic device, the back of a car, or on a set of traffic lights.

The data and information in our world are also of varying quality. Often people choose to accept or question it because of its source. For example, if a tabloid newspaper carried an article 'Rock Star ate my gerbil!', how many people would believe it without asking questions? If the same story appeared on the BBC or ITN evening news, how many people would believe it? Indeed, if this appeared on a web site, how many people would automatically believe it? Thus both information and its source must be taken into account when it is being evaluated.

The work of any user of ICT will be more productive if they can be sure they are using trustworthy data and accurate programs that produce reliable results. These are all factors that lead to 'high quality' data.

The quality of data is also affected by standards within ICT. Many nation-specific standards, such as those relating to measurement, connecting cables, and connecting telephones exist today because of the way in which different countries developed. Because of such issues, international bodies, such as ISO, exist to promote uniform standards throughout the world and the easy transfer of data and information between countries. The role of such bodies is explored towards the end of this chapter.

1.2 The Characteristics of Data, Information and Knowledge

This section is about the **understanding** (knowledge) placed on **information** when it is presented as **data** in a **specified context**.

Definition

Data – Raw facts and figures at the input stage before it is processed into a meaningful form, with no explicit meaning of their own. Data cannot be understood without a context.
For example, 'red light' means nothing without a setting.

Information – Data that has been processed into a form that has meaning and is useful. This data has been placed in a context and can be understood. Processing could involve performing calculations on the data, sorting it or even grouping or organising the data in a certain way.
For example, 'red light on the back of the car in front of me.' The 'red light' is data but the context is that the light is on the back of a car.

Knowledge – Applying rules to information to make decisions.
For example 'red light on the back of the car in front of me', tells a driver to slow down. Their mental understanding of what the red light means and its consequences is knowledge. In addition to understanding that they should slow down when they see the red light, they know if they do not then certain consequences will follow.

Take a different example. '42' on its own is *data*, because this figure is meaningless when out of context. '£42.00' on a bank statement is *information* because it is meaningful. "If I only have £42.00 in my bank account, I haven't got enough money to pay my bills" is *knowledge*.

Definition

A **knowledge worker** is a person whose specialist knowledge makes them an expert in their particular field. This knowledge may be based either on facts that can be written formally and taught to others, or on experience – something that cannot easily be taught.

A **knowledge base** is a computer system which holds knowledge (facts plus consequences) about a particular area. This knowledge is often held in the form of IF… THEN type rules.

For example, a medical knowledge base may contain:

> IF a patient is anaemic
> > AND has high blood pressure
> THEN avoid certain drugs.

A share-dealer's knowledge base may contain:

> IF Company X announces a huge profit
> > AND we have enough money
> THEN buy shares in Company X.

Alison is a *Knowledge Worker* for Amoeba Antiques. That is not her job title – her actual job title is *Head of Retail Operations*. Like many people in similar jobs, Alison relies on the knowledge and experience she has gained through many years' work. Such skills cannot be taught simply by reading books or attending courses.

In her day-to-day work, Alison investigates new product lines for Amoeba. This includes both the current interests of the public and what they may be interested in, in the near future. For example, if a 100-year-old table is sold in a televised auction for a large amount of money, Alison's experience will tell her whether it is worth commissioning reproductions of that same table for sale to the public.

Those who work with Alison are responsible for making this information available to her before such an auction takes place so that she can act in advance: a table like the one auctioned is more likely to sell the day after the auction than a month after. Members of Alison's team also source antiques at auctions to be re-sold in their shops.

Alison has a highly pressurised job and mistakes happen. Delivering the goods that customers want can be worth millions of pounds to Amoeba but ordering goods that customers have no interest in can cost millions. For this reason, it took Alison many years to learn her trade fully and it will take any successor many years to be as good as Alison.

Because of the competitive nature of her business, Alison cannot ask competitors for advice. She must depend on those around her. However if Alison is off work for any reason the knowledge she carries in her head is not available, and while her trainees may be good, they do not have the same degree of accumulated knowledge and wisdom.

As Amoeba expands, Alison spends more time travelling. She feels that time spent waiting in airports is time wasted. Yet she has no choice since the growth of operations around the country means she feels she often has to be in two places at once.

Amoeba have asked *Erudite Software* to help their situation. Alison has read articles about *Knowledge Bases* and *Expert Systems* that have been developed for doctors, lawyers, engineers and other knowledge workers. She feels that such a system would be of huge benefit to Amoeba as it would allow her trained staff to access her accumulated knowledge from anywhere in the world. This would allow her to spend more time directing operations. *Erudite* have developed such systems before but because each of their systems is specially designed for a particular customer, the costs are high.

Amoeba Antiques

Task

You have been asked to write a one-page report on Alison's behalf, to be presented to Amoeba's Board of Directors.

You should outline the benefits such a system will bring to Amoeba as well as the costs. In addition to the material presented here, your report should draw on external sources of information such as periodicals and web sites.

1.3 Direct and Indirect Data Sources

Data is derived from difference sources. It can be collected either **directly** or **indirectly**.

Definition

Direct data is data that has been collected from a source document for a specific purpose to enable decisions to be made.

Indirect data involves the use of data for a purpose other than that which it was originally collected and intended for.

Examples of Direct Data

+ In a supermarket a bar code scanner will read the bar code on a product (this is the source document). The bar code is read for the specific purpose of obtaining the product code so that the price can be obtained from the product database for the person to be billed.

+ In many colleges, pupil attendance is recorded on a data collection sheet by a teacher for the specific purpose of keeping a record of who is present/absent on a particular day.

+ In a greenhouse, temperature and humidity sensors are used to capture data from within the greenhouse environment for the specific purpose of controlling the environment within the greenhouse and keeping it stable.

Examples of Indirect Data

+ Census figures which are used by education authorities in planning how many teachers to have in schools;

+ Credit agencies that build a profile of a person's finances from several different sources, such as banks and lending firms.

+ A bank that builds up a list of customers who may respond to advertising for a loan. This uses that bank's own data, originally collected for a different purpose.

Advantages and Disadvantages

Direct Data	Indirect Data
The information collected will be **relevant**. The information collected is exactly what the organisation wants and will not require additional processing to filter out irrelevant information.	The information may contain **irrelevant** material. Additional processing to filter out irrelevant material will increase processing time and data collection costs.
The information collected will be **complete**. The information collected should include everything the organisation needs and time will not have to be spent gathering information from additional sources.	The information may be **incomplete**. Additional time or money will have to be spent adding to the data collected.

Direct Data	Indirect Data
The information collected will be **up-to-date**. The information will be collected at the time it is required. It will not be obtained from an organization who may have collected the information at a previous time giving the opportunity for the data to become out of date.	It will be **difficult to know how up-to-date and accurate** the original data was. For example people change address often causing personal information to become quickly out of date.
The information will be **accurate** as it will be collected directly from the source and input immediately, thus reducing the margin for error.	
Data collection will be **costly**. The organisation collecting data must pay all the costs related to collecting it ie hardware, software and personnel.	**Cost**. The organisation wanting information may only pay a fraction of the original cost of collecting it. **Time**. The organisation wanting information will not have to spend time directly collecting the information.

Companies sharing data – direct and indirect data sources

Amoeba Antiques

Amoeba go to a lot of trouble to retain customer loyalty. They offer a reward scheme which records how much each customer spends and what they are spending it on. This is similar to the 'loyalty cards' offered by many supermarkets. Amoeba can use direct data from tills to monitor what goods each shop is selling, who is buying them and to enable automatic re-ordering of goods.

The same data becomes an indirect data source for Amoeba when customer purchase reports are produced to support direct marketing. For example, if a customer regularly buys small tables from Amoeba warehouses it is likely they will have an interest in special offers on tables, so they can be sent advertising material for these products. If the same person has never bought a china tea set from Amoeba, it is unlikely that they will be interested in special offers on these products, so they will not be sent such material.

Other companies are also interested in what Amoeba sells through their High Street outlets and can use Amoeba as an indirect data source.

These include Nifty Nappies who became interested in Amoeba after Amoeba started selling reproduction Victorian cots. Nifty's managers believe that most people who buy a cot through Amoeba's High Street outlets either have a baby or know someone who has a baby. For this reason Nifty will specifically target these people rather than randomly mailing a wider group of people. Under the conditions of the Data Protection Act (see chapter 5), Nifty are allowed to use information from Amoeba as an indirect data source. They can combine this with information from other retailers, for example supermarkets and chemists, and thus target a large proportion of the parents of newborn babies in the country.

Task
There are examples of direct and indirect data as used by Amoeba in this section. What other examples of direct and indirect data can you think of?

1.4 The Quality of Information

Quality refers to how useful the information in a particular setting is considered to be. Information that is considered to be of **high quality** (useful) in one setting may be considered to be of **low quality** (not useful) in another.

Organisations spend large amounts of money maintaining and ensuring the quality of their information. If information loses quality, it ultimately translates to a loss of profit or a loss of relations with other organisations. However, information that is of high quality ensures accurate decision-making and can also be sold as a valuable commodity.

Information that meets some of these factors may fail to meet others. For example an **accurate** financial report may fail to be **presented effectively** because a mass of figures on a page make it difficult to read.

Five main factors affect the quality of information. Information should be:

Accurate — Information should be error free in order to prevent poor decisions being made and a loss of confidence in the source of the information. Transcription errors should be avoided where possible.

Up-to-date — Information should be up-to-date at the time it is presented in order to ensure the correct decision is made. It should not reflect a previous state of affairs.

Complete — The information should include everything the organisation needs to make good decisions. Therefore the information needs of the user must be investigated thoroughly and considered carefully during the design of the computer system. The queries and related criteria being used to extract information must be designed to meet the user's complete information needs.

Relevant — Only relevant information should be supplied. Again, the information needs of the user must be investigated thoroughly and considered carefully during the design of the computer system. The queries and related criteria being used to extract the relevant information must be designed appropriately to select only the required data. It is important to avoid irrelevant information as this may lead to time being wasted or 'information overload' resulting in the user missing vital facts.

Presented effectively — The information should be presented to the user by the system in an appropriate format. For example, it should be readable, uncluttered and if necessary summarised. The user's information needs must be considered when designing the report, graph or table that will present the information. Sometimes a graph or chart may be a better way of presenting information than giving a list of figures. Any use of coding used should be explained with a key.

Consider these factors in relation to (i) a school textbook and (ii) a supermarket:

Factor	School Textbook	Supermarket
Accuracy	Before a book is published, it is important to know if sales will be of a sufficient level to cover the production costs. Imagine the consequences for the publisher if a decision made to produce a book hinged on a wildly inaccurate sales estimate.	Before ordering a product, the managers need know if it will sell. Suppose 40% of a store's customers were thought to have children under 2 years old and a large part of the store was refurbished to sell nappies and baby clothes. Imagine the consequences if the figure was actually found to be 0.40%.
Up-to-date	What would be the effect if an examining board re-organised the specification but the authors ignored the changes? What would be the effect if a thirty-year-old manual about the public telephone network was used as the main source material in a section about computer networks?	It is vital that goods are re-ordered as soon as they are needed to ensure stock is always on the shelves. Imagine the consequences if stock levels were only checked once per week – and hence goods ordered only once per week.
Completeness	Imagine the consequences if a GCSE class used only one textbook which did not cover all of the course specification.	Imagine the consequences if the re-ordering system failed to record stock from certain suppliers or failed to record sales from certain cash tills.
Relevance	Those presenting information must keep to the point. For example, if this book spent several pages describing the intricacies of the circuitry on an Intel *Pentium*™ processor, it would have little relevance to the purpose of the book and only distract the reader from what *is* relevant.	Suppose the store manager asked for a report on the sales of canned goods, and was given a list of every can sold detailing the product, the customer and the time and date sold. The information is complete and accurate but is not relevant in this context.

Factor	School Textbook	Supermarket
Effective Presentation	Even the most valuable information is useless unless it is presented in a form that people can read and understand. Imagine the impact if the authors of a textbook did not divide the text into paragraphs or illustrate their points with diagrams. Suppose the authors of an ICT book assumed everyone reading it already had a high level of ICT knowledge – would all readers be able to understand it?	If the sales figures for a particular product were to be presented in order to identify trends, it could be done in a number of ways. Figures 1.1 and 1.2 show two different examples of ways to present the data. One is much more effective and useful than the other.

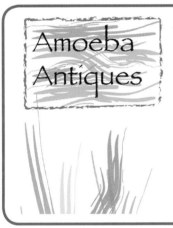

Amoeba and declining information quality

Alison, the head of Retail Operations at Amoeba, has a number of people working for her. One of their duties is to make surveys of auctions, sales from the warehouses to independent shops, and sales through Amoeba's own stores. With this information they then decide which products are worth investing in. Since these decisions drive Amoeba's profit, it is vital to the company that the information used by Alison's staff is up-to-date and accurate.

Alison has noticed that some members of her team are becoming lazy in their approach to sales analysis. This has resulted in problems that she is concerned about. Regardless of the people responsible, Alison feels that these issues should be addressed in conjunction with all the staff in her department.

Task

Based on material in this section, prepare a clear, concise and accurate report on information quality and its relevance to Amoeba Antiques, to be presented to the rest of your class.

The report should address the following issues:

+ What is meant by 'quality of information'.
+ Why information must be of a 'high quality' and the consequences if it is not.
+ The different types of data used by Amoeba – specifically, direct and indirect data.
+ The costs Amoeba must meet to maintain the quality of its 'information'.

The report itself should be of a 'high quality'.

Effective or not? The two reports shown in Figures 1.1 and 1.2 present the same data. Which do you think is more effective at illustrating the trends in sun-cream sales?

Week Starting:	Sales (1000s):	Week Starting:	Sales (1000s):	Week Starting:	Sales (1000s):	Week Starting:	Sales (1000s):
5 Jan	0	5 Apr	50	5 Jul	158	4 Oct	200
12 Jan	0	12 Apr	52	12 Jul	200	11 Oct	150
19 Jan	4	19 Apr	58	19 Jul	230	18 Oct	58
26 Jan	1	26 Apr	60	26 Jul	249	25 Oct	26
2 Feb	3	3 May	62	2 Aug	380	1 Nov	3
9 Feb	4	10 May	62	9 Aug	420	8 Nov	18
16 Feb	9	17 May	58	16 Aug	400	15 Nov	12
23 Feb	10	24 May	68	23 Aug	380	22 Nov	2
1 Mar	14	31 May	70	30 Aug	410	29 Nov	3
8 Mar	16	7 Jun	80	6 Sep	380	6 Dec	1
15 Mar	40	14 Jun	92	13 Sep	360	13 Dec	0
22 Mar	45	21 Jun	100	20 Sep	300	20 Dec	0
29 Mar	42	28 Jun	112	27 Sep	300	27 Dec	0

Figure 1.1: Sun-cream sales throughout all branches, 2003.

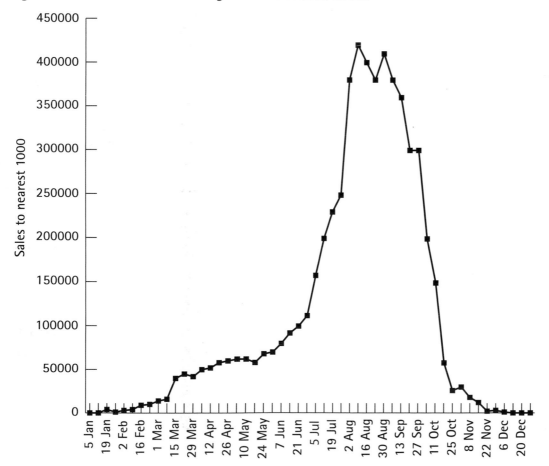

Figure 1.2: Sun-cream sales throughout all branches, 2003.

17

1.5 Sources and Types of Error in Data Capture

So far we have examined **how** data is stored without regard to its accuracy. However a number of ways that errors can occur that compromise the accuracy of the data stored in a system.

Transcription Errors

Transmission errors are data entry errors made by humans or by optical character recognition programs in copying data from source (often paper) to destination. Human transcription errors can be caused by things like pressing the wrong key on a keyboard, by striking two or more wrong keys, or misreading source material. Electronic transcription errors are usually the result of scanned printed matter being incorrectly converted – often because it is crumpled or not clearly printed.

Transcription errors can be further categorised into **substitution, transposition** and **omission** errors. Some transcription errors can be detected using spell-checking programs. However, many transcription errors, particularly those involving numeric data, are difficult or impossible to detect without some further checking, such as check digits (further below).

Omission errors occur when information is left out. While some of these can be detected by spell-check programs, others may be difficult or impossible to detect without further checks. For example:

+ Postcode: *BT45 5S* (wrong) instead of *BT45 5SE* (correct)
+ Name: *Kith* (wrong) instead of *Keith* (correct)
+ Book title: *The Curious Dog in the Night Time* (wrong), instead of *The Curious Incident of the Dog in the Night Time*

Substitution errors occur when information appears to be complete, yet is the incorrect information. For example:

+ Postcode: *BT46 5SE* (wrong) instead of *BT45 5SE* (correct)
+ Name: *Keitj* (wrong) instead of *Keith* (correct)
+ Book title: *The Curious Incident of the Cat in the Day Time* (wrong), instead of *The Curious Incident of the Dog in the Night Time*

Transposition errors are slightly different from substitution errors in that the correct information is entered, but is reversed or mixed up in some way. For example:

+ Postcode: *BT45 5ES* (wrong) instead of *BT45 5SE* (correct)
+ Name: *Kieth* (wrong) instead of *Keith* (correct)
+ Book title: *The Curious Incident of the Night in the Dog Time* (wrong), instead of *The Curious Incident of the Dog in the Night Time*

Transmission Errors

Transmission errors are caused by machine failure in transmitting data accurately from one piece of hardware to another. Transmission errors can arise from interference on the network. This is usually in the form of electrical noise but the end result is that some **bits** get corrupted and binary zeros get turned into binary ones etc, or the complete message becomes unrecognisable.

Transmission errors can be detected by parity checks, described later in this book.

1.6 Data Validation and Data Verification

Because errors will happen, reasonable steps must be taken to limit their impact. There are two aspects of this process: **verification** and **validation**. Both are essential as verification may identify an error that validation may miss and vice versa.

Definition

Data verification is usually performed by a human. Its purpose is to check that data being input has been accurately transferred from the source document to the computer. The data may be input twice, or the user could confirm that the data is accurate by performing a comparison of the data on screen against the original source document.

Data validation is performed by a computer program by performing an automatic check on data after it has been input to ensure that it conforms to a pattern or set of rules. The purpose of validation is to ensure that the input data is reasonable, complete, sensible and within valid boundaries.

Verification

When a human operator or Optical Character Recognition (OCR) reader is used to copy data into a computer system, verification checks can ensure that it has been accurately transferred. Verification will detect, for example, if a fault has occurred in the OCR process or the human has made a mistake while entering the data.

However, verification checks do not guarantee that the data is factually correct. If the source of data is incorrect then the erroneous data will be transferred and may pass a verification check despite being incorrect. Therefore data verification must be accompanied by data validation.

For example, if a human age is written on a document as 6809 it will be accurately typed into a computer system as 6809. While this may be wrong, there is no guarantee the human transcribing it will realise – for example, if they are coming to the end of an eight hour shift and are too tired to notice that the data they are copying makes no sense. Furthermore, if OCR is used, the error definitely will not be noticed at this stage.

Data can be verified by:

+ **Double entry.** Data is keyed twice, with the computer only accepting the data for processing if the two versions are identical. This method has an obvious overhead with the work effectively having to be done twice, but it is highly reliable. Nevertheless the mistake will not be detected if the error is keyed in twice. An example of double entry is when network users change their password, they are required to type in their new password twice to verify it.

+ **Proof reading.** This is a visual check made by the operator to compare entered data with the original source document. This method is relatively easy to implement but some errors may still get through, as operators can make mistakes in the cross-checking. Another example is to read back details just taken from a customer, or sending printouts of the data that has been entered back to the customer and asking them to confirm the accuracy of the data. A third form of verification is the **dialogue box**. Here the user must confirm whether or not the data, or the action about to be taken, is correct by clicking on the appropriate button (figure 1.3).

Figure 1.3: An example of data verification via a dialogue box.

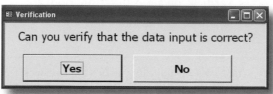

Validation

The purpose of validation is to ensure that data which has been input is reasonable, complete, sensible and within valid boundaries.

Above we saw how data representing a human age of 6809 years could pass a verification test. However this data would not pass a validation test, as it is not sensible or reasonable for what it is trying to represent. Other examples of data that should not pass a validation test would be a telephone bill of £80,000 for a residential customer or a football match attendance of 49,600 people when the capacity of the stadium is 38,500.

However it is important to remember that validation is **unable to stop all errors** from occurring. It will accept data which is **valid** but which is not **accurate**. For example a validation check for a person's age could be applied to accept numbers within a range of 0 and 130 years. However if a person's age is input as 34 rather than 43, then the input is accepted and deemed as valid despite being inaccurate. No amount of validation would be able to detect this error.

A computer can be programmed to automatically carry out data validation according to rules for the data that is entered.

Data can be validated by a:

+ **Range check.** This ensures that a value falls within a particular range by specifying an upper and lower boundary. Data values falling between these limits is deemed valid. If the data entered does not fall between these boundaries, it is not accepted and an error message is displayed. The check on the human age above is an example of a range check. Note that range checks are usually only used on numeric or date data types. A variation on the range check is the **limit check**, in which only one boundary is specified. For example a bank-balance may have a lower limit of -£1000, to prevent a customer becoming very overdrawn.

+ **Presence check.** Sometimes called an **existence check**, this ensures that important data is not omitted by alerting the user if an input field is left blank or null. For example it would be essential that a new employee's National Insurance Number is input to a payroll system.

+ **Format check.** This ensures that entered data matches a preset layout, such as the number and type of characters to be accepted. For example a car registration number or a postcode uses a defined number of characters and numbers in a regular combination and would be appropriate for such a check.

+ **Type check.** This ensures that data is of a particular type specified by the programmer. For example, 'age' is numeric, 'name' is text.

+ **Length check.** This makes sure that data is of a specified length. For example, credit card numbers are sixteen digits long and account numbers are eight.

+ **Lookup table.** Data is validated by making sure that it the same as one of the entries in a list or table of acceptable values. For example, the rating of a new DVD must correspond with an existing rating found from the list of possible ratings such as '18' or 'PG' (figure 1.4).

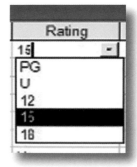

Figure 1.4: A lookup table being used to validate the rating of a new DVD.

+ **Batch total.** Batch totals are applied to groups of data and used to make sure that the data entered is correct by checking the original batch total against a recalculated total. A mismatch between totals indicates an error. There are two types of batch total:

  + A **control total** is the sum of values in a specific field in a group of records. A control total is meaningful in some way, for example the total value of all bills issued in one day. The process is as follows:

    1. The control total is calculated manually before the data is entered and saved along with the data input.

    2. When the file is to be processed the computer recalculates the control total based on what was entered. This total is then compared with the original stored check digit.

    3. If the two values match then it is likely (although not certain) that the data was input correctly. If, however, the two totals do not match then a mistake has obviously been made when entering the numeric data.

  + A **hash total** is an arbitrary total that has no meaning and can only be used to validate the integrity of input data, for example a sum of account numbers or phone numbers. A hash total is calculated in the same way as a control total. Correct comparison of the original hash total to a recalculated total provides assurance that data was input correctly (figure 1.5).

Account Number	Customer Name	Telephone Number	Bill Amount
034672	Mr. S Black	02890324567	£34.99
034732	Mrs. R Grey	02893467542	£98.00
034871	Mrs. G Green	02894234587	£73.50
034231	Mr. R Green	02890765452	£150.45
138506		11568792148	356.94
Hash Total		Hash total	Control Total

Total value of bills

Figure 1.5: Example of hash totals and a control total being used in order to validate accounts information.

+ **Check digit.** This is an extra digit appended to the end of a number and which has been created from a calculation based on the other digits. It allows the number to be 'self-verifying'. Once the number and the check digit have been input into the computer, the digits are used to recalculate the check digit and compare it to the check digit that was input. If the two do not match then an error is detected. Check digits provide a way of trapping transcription and transposition errors and are useful where it would be easy to incorrectly copy across a large number of digits such as an account number or product code. For example when a bar code belonging to a product is scanned the check digit is automatically recalculated.

By the way...

Check Digits and ISBNs

A check digit is calculated from numeric data. Some mathematical algorithm is applied to the data to produce an additional digit. For example, a check digit could be calculated by repeatedly adding all the digits of a number until one digit is left. So if the original data is 4759, the check digit is obtained by: 4+7+5+9 = 25 and then 2+5=7. This number would become 47597. On entry, the first four digits are used to re-calculate the check digit. Suppose the person entering the data typed 47567. The check digit would be calculated as 4+7+5+6 = 22 and then 2+2 = 4. Since the **input** check digit and the **calculated** check digit do not agree we know that a mistake has been made. This simple system, however does not detect data transposition errors – if 45797 was entered in place of 47597, no error would be detected as the input data will give a 'correct' check digit.

A more complex check-digit system is *Modulus-11*, which was used with ISBNs until January 2007. In this system a check digit is calculated from original data by the following method.

1. Multiply the right-most digit by 2, the next by 3, the next by 4 and so on.

2. Add the results of these multiplications together.

3. Divide the total by 11.

4. Subtract the remainder from 11.

5. The final answer is the check digit, unless:

    (a) the final answer is 11, in which case the check digit will be 0;

    (b) the final answer is 10, in which case the check digit will be X.

For example, to calculate the check digit for a pre-2007 book which had an ISBN of 189893810:

1. multiply the right-most digit by 2, the next by 3, the next by 4 and so-on:

1	8	9	8	9	3	8	1	0
10x	9x	8x	7x	6x	5x	4x	3x	2x
10	72	72	56	54	15	32	3	0

2. add the results of these multiplications together:

    10 + 72 + 72 + 56 + 54 + 15 + 32 + 3 + 0 = 314

3. divide the total by 11:   314 ÷ 11 = 28 remainder 6

4. subtract the remainder from 11:   11 – 6 = 5

Thus the check digit is 5. Hence the ISBN number, including check digit is 1898938105. *Material discussing the similar Modulus-10 system (used with ISBN numbers since 2007) is available at* www.colourpoint.co.uk/extra/realworld

Task

This method is not limited to ISBN numbers.
Calculate a Modulus-11 check digit for (a) 4589 (b) 14789 (c) 4778963

Prove by the Modulus-11 method that the check digit (ie, the last digit) of the following pre-2007 ISBN number is correct: 1904242227.

1.7 The Costs of Producing Information

Collecting information and keeping it up to date is expensive, since a lot of time and resources are required for the task. The costs involved in keeping information up to date are called the **overheads.** There are three categories of overhead: **hardware, software** and **personnel**.

Hardware Overheads

The following hardware would have to be purchased or leased:

+ Computers and their peripherals will be required by employees. These may include:
  + Direct data entry devices for data input, for example **Optical Mark Recognition** (OMR), Optical Character Recognition (OCR) or key-to-disk;
  + Storage media, including online storage and data backups;
  + Printers to output the information as a result of data processing. Printers will also have associated running costs such as paper and toner.
+ Network hardware such as a server will be required to store and process data. Additional hardware will be needed to construct a **Local Area Network** (LAN) or connect to a **Wide Area Network** (WAN). Choosing a WAN will then result in bills from a telecommunications company.

Software

+ **Applications software** will be needed by employees to query or otherwise make use of stored data. The software may have been purchased 'off-the-shelf' or it may be custom-built software.
+ **Systems software**, such as an operating system, will obviously be required.
+ Each computer making use of software must have the necessary licenses in order to comply with copyright legislation.
+ There will be a cost to **upgrade** the software as it becomes out of date.

Personnel

+ Data collection incurs costs in terms of the staff who have to be paid to produce, send out and collect the information.
+ Technical staff will be required to maintain the hardware and software, for example an ICT manager or ICT technician.
+ Experts will need to be hired to train staff in how to use the software.

1.8 Finding, Selecting, Exchanging and Managing Information

An organisation may obtain data from many sources and must have a set of procedures in place to manage large volumes of information. Data can be obtained from a variety of sources. These include:

Surveys. Provided the survey is designed well, so as to eliminate vague questions such as "What do you think of our response time?", surveys allow data to be collected from large numbers of people in a straightforward way. Good questions, such as "Is our response time (a) better than expected (b) as fast as expected or (c) slower than expected?" allow data to be more readily entered into a database and analysed in a more precise manner. Note that if a survey is used as an indirect data source, the survey may not ask for the information the new data users would like.

The Internet allows data to be published, transferred and accessed very quickly. The disadvantage is that this same potential for speed can lead to people skipping the important process of editing and checking, leading to poor quality (ie false) information. It is often difficult to tell how 'expert' the author of a web site actually is, and there is a temptation to plagiarise the resources of the Internet.

CDs can be used to disseminate data in a more secure manner than using the Internet (provided the CD is not lost). They became popular due to their large capacity, but have the disadvantage that they cannot be updated or edited. Although a travelling salesperson may be able to use a secure Internet connection to access company data, if they are away from Internet access, a CD may be a useful alternative source of data.

Once the data is found, some sort of selection (what is useful and what is not) must take place. For example, an education authority using census returns as an indirect data source will have to ignore much of what was returned (they are interested in numbers of children in certain areas but not the names on the forms, for example). A data source is often combined with many others to build up a full picture of what is going on (such as, census figures, immigration statistics and primary school trends being used by an education authority to plan secondary-level schooling). If many data sources are combined, data items that are duplicated by the various sources must be appropriately filtered from future use.

Over time, any organisation will gather and produce a considerable amount of data. All of this must be managed effectively. In a non-ICT environment, it would be normal for much unused paper to be disposed of at appropriate intervals. Today's processing technology means that there is often an expectation that more data can be processed and presented to managers: while this may aid decision making, it also has the effect that much duplication and inconsistency may accidentally occur. Data users may become reluctant to discard even seemingly mundane e-mails and forms, 'just in case', and the ability to store huge capacities of data may be counter-productive unless it is managed effectively. Version control of software similarly presents a challenge to organizations, in ensuring that individuals amending a particular document do not produce contradictory revisions and to make sure that the most up-to-date version of documentation is in use.

Consider a typical school. Before the widespread use of ICT, a whole school register would be taken each morning and teachers would maintain their own class register. The whole school register only existed in the general office and the class-register only existed in the teacher's briefcase. Class marks would be recorded by the teacher and would only be centrally reported at infrequent intervals. While there may have been a desire to centrally monitor the attendance of certain individuals on a period-by-period basis or monitor their marks for every homework and test, etc, this was often not easily achievable. Software such as *Capita SIMS* allows all marks, attendance, timetables and comments on a student's effort on a per-period basis to be entered to a central database, allowing for easier access to data that builds up a picture of all students' progress and behaviour. While such solutions are effective, they may create extra work for teachers if school management insists that every piece of data generated must be centrally recorded, logged and analysed. With any information system, the ability to analyse data quicker and more completely than before only leads to greater efficiency and savings of time and effort if data is not produced and analysed simply for its own sake. There is therefore an onus on management to decide what information is useful and should be recorded and also to decide how it should be recorded and managed. From a user's perspective, it is preferable to store information in a single database, or in a place that is centrally indexed, although this may present security issues (see Database Management Systems in Chapter 16).

Amoeba and Document Control Issues

Ben, a new recruit within Amoeba's software development department found the volume of information he was expected to be aware of a challenge. He describes his situation below.

Within Amoeba, it is normal to communicate with colleagues through e-mail. However on a busy project one person might e-mail you several times in one day. I recently got an e-mail from one person saying "Earlier problem solved – disregard previous e-mail". However, this was the fourth e-mail they had sent me that day and all three before it had described different problems. It didn't help that the first problem, to do with our web site had been sent to six people at 9.02am. At 9.10am, Adam replied to all six of us to say he had fixed the problem. At 9.12am, Emma replied to the lot of us to say she couldn't find the problem (presumably she had not read Adam's e-mail). At 9.15am, Leah replied to Emma's e-mail to say she thought it might be related to another intermittent fault. In this case, a problem-tracking system that allowed faults to be centrally logged and marked as open or closed issues, with a note of who was dealing with them would have helped. It was the sheer volume of information, some of low quality, that led to Emma and Leah's confusion.

Some of our documentation is circulated on CD, in encrypted form, within our department and can only be opened on-site. This is because of security issues that prompted Amoeba to restrict the likelihood of documentation being transmitted to unauthorised users. This seems sensible but imagine my frustration after spending several days working from a software design document, only to find that the requirements had changed and I was working to a design that was now obsolete. If we even had a networked resource to say what date the current version of the document was created on, I could have avoided the problem.

1.9 Standards

In everyday life, a **standard** is a set of rules that are agreed within a community so that people within that community can work together effectively. Examples of standards in everyday life include:

- Driving on the left-hand side of the road in the UK and Ireland. Imagine the chaos if there was no standard in place here.

- The use of 240 volt electricity and three-pin plugs in the UK and Ireland. Imagine the problems that would occur if each manufacturer set their own standards, that were not compatible with each other (as happens with the fittings on many mobile telephone chargers).

- The use of a standard system of weights and measures to replace older systems that varied between countries. Before standardisation, a mile was 1609m in England, 2240m in Ireland, 1814m in Scotland, or anything between 1000 and 10,000m depending on where else you were. Similar confusion existed concerning other units of measurement.

In ICT, a number of standards are used to ensure effective communication and sharing of data. Some of these are informally agreed by ICT users as the accepted way to do things (**De Facto** standards) while others are enforced by a governing body of some sort (**De Jure** standards). The role of De Facto and De Jure standards is discussed below.

Standards Within the ICT Industry

Since 1996, **Universal Serial Bus (USB)** has become the De Facto standard for attaching peripheral devices to a computer. While no government or agency has ruled that USB is 'correct', the wider ICT community has agreed, through the widespread adoption of USB, that it offers a sensible and efficient way to connect devices. Before USB, there was one type of connection for printers, several connection types for keyboards and mice, yet another for modems, etc. This forced PC vendors to offer PCs with a wide variety of connections on the rear which may not all have been used. The design of USB was agreed by a large number of vendors who set aside company-specific interests to agree a standard that the entire industry would benefit from. One key consequence of this standard is the large number of new devices that were invented to take advantage of USB, such as USB flash-memory drives.

The history of **Apple** provides a contrasting example of the use of standards within the computing industry. Until the 1990s Apple were reluctant to allow other companies to adopt their design, which resulted in users of Apple computers often having no choice but to use Apple peripherals and software. In contrast, IBM permitted any other company to develop a PC or associated hardware and software to the specification IBM had laid down. These companies were free to use the operating system IBM had commissioned (Microsoft DOS) or another compatible operating system (such as Digital Research's DR-DOS). The terms 'IBM Clone' and 'IBM compatible' were used to describe these machines and their associated software.

Apple's approach led to much fewer issues of compatibility for users of Apple hardware, but while many users felt that Apple's PCs were easier to use and of a higher standard than the IBM-compatibles, the fact that IBM-clones were significantly cheaper and allowed greater choice of hardware components and software, led to IBM-clones dominating the PC market.

By the 1990s, the PC market had standardised on IBM compatible machines while Apple's *Macintosh* was restricted to a niche market. The advent of Microsoft's *Windows 95*, that incorporated many of the software advantages developed by Apple, ensured the IBM-clones' dominance of the PC market – indeed, the term 'Personal Computer' is often associated with these machines alone.

The IBM-PC and its successors are thus a De Facto standard. This means that there is no legal requirement to use these devices but they are a standard that people have informally agreed to use. Although IBM are no longer a large retailer of PCs and the technical specifications of the early IBM PCs have been largely superseded, IBM's original standards defined a developing industry for several decades to come. Today, Intel and AMD set standards for PC processors and Microsoft effectively define software standards. However, the need for 'backwards compatibility' with older hardware and software means that IBM's original standards have continued to be influential.

Because IBM allowed anyone to develop compatible equipment, a wide range of uses were devised that IBM themselves never originally envisaged. These uses include the first IBM-clone laptop (developed by Compaq in 1983), improvements to processors and graphics cards by various companies and eventually modern game consoles that use specialised PC-hardware.

USB and the IBM-compatible PC both highlight a number of advantages of the adoption of standards:

+ A wide number of vendors can build devices that are compatible with other vendors' devices. This can lead to the development of devices that the original vendor did not have in mind, such as the USB memory stick.

+ As a result, users are not restricted to a single vendor when purchasing new equipment or software.

+ If a user's preferred manufacturer stops supporting a product, open-standards allow anyone else to supply compatible equipment. For example, if Dell were to cease to supply printers, the users of Dell PCs would be able to acquire printers from other vendors.

+ Hence, users are not restricted to a single supplier and vendors are free to develop equipment that will work with other vendor's equipment.

ASCII

Within a computer, data is stored as a series of on/off signals. Humans often represent this in the binary (base 2) number system, viewing 'off' as 0 and 'on' as 1. In computers, each letter in a text file was originally represented by eight of these signals (today it is sometimes represented by sixteen). It was important for early networked machines to use an agreed format for representing characters to allow data to be shared between different types of computer: otherwise the signal sent as text by one machine could be misinterpreted by the receiver as, for example, a command to perform some totally unrelated action.

The **American Standard Code for Information Interchange (ASCII)** is the standard used on modern computers. As its name suggests, it was devised in the USA and originally had no provision for non-American symbols such as '£', or any text outside the standard 26-letter Latin alphabet, including accented characters and symbols used only in some languages (such as, the German 'ß' or Slavic 'Đ'), though such provision was added as the international use of ASCII grew. Within ASCII, each symbol is represented as eight bits: 'A', for example, is represented as 0100 0001 whereas the lowercase 'a' is represented as 0110 0001.

ASCII was not the only standard developed in the 1960s. **Extended Binary Coded Decimal Interchange Code (EBCDIC)** was a rival that also used eight bits per symbol. EBCDIC represented 'a' as 0101 0001. Hence an 'a' sent by an EBCDIC machine would be interpreted as 'Q' on an ASCII machine, while an EBCIDIC machine would interpret 0110 0001 (an 'a' in ASCII) as '/'. It was therefore important for the computing industry to standardize on a single format for representing text.

A key weakness of ASCII was that it was only originally designed to represent the English language and, although it was extended to incorporate other languages that use the Latin alphabet it was unsuitable for other alphabets. As a result, **Unicode** was designed to incorporate ASCII while allowing representation of numerous other writing systems. Unicode is a De Jure standard, governed by ISO (see later in this section), and is today used throughout ICT.

Word Processor Document Formats

While ASCII and Unicode are adequate for representing text, word processors must add information to a file to store information about fonts, graphics, etc. Until recently, it has been common in the design of word processors for each vendor to develop their own proprietary format. However this resulted in difficulties for users wishing to share data.

Now consider the previous paragraph. The text below shows part of how the word processor that was used to write it has encoded this paragraph. As can be seen, what the user sees on the screen is only part of the actual file.

```
<style:style style:name="P1" style:family="paragraph"
style:parent-style-name="Text_20_body"><style:text-
properties fo:font-weight="bold" style:font-weight-
asian="bold" style:fontcomplex="bold"/></style:style> ...
<text:h text:style-name="P1" text:outline-level="3">Word
Processor Document Formats</text:h><text:p text:
style-name="Text_20_body">While ASCII and Unicode are
adequate for representing text, word processors must
add information to a file to store information about
fonts, graphics, etc. <text:s/>Until recently, it has
been common in the design of word processors for each
vendor to develop their own proprietary format. However
this resulted in difficulties for users wishing to share
data.</text:p>
```

The data above is represented using the **Open Document Format (ODF)**, approved by ISO in 2006 as an international standard that would remove the problems caused by vendor-specific formats. At the time of writing, almost all word-processor developers have set aside their own formats in order to use ODF in new products. The notable exception to this is Microsoft who have developed their own similar, but incompatible, format called **Office Open XML (OOXML)**, represented, for example, by the .docx file extension. While ODF may be a De Jure standard, Microsoft's market share may mean OOXML, used in *Office 2007*, becomes a De Facto standard (as did the previous *Word 97* document format).

Similar issues exists in the realm of spreadsheets, graphics, etc. The Open Document formats for a number of applications are overviewed at http://en.wikipedia.org/wiki/OpenDocument .

A brief history of the confusing topic of word processor formats

By the way...

Early word processors used their own formats for encoding data. This meant that a user of *WordStar* may have had to save data as plain text to share with a user of *AmiPro*, and hence lose all the formatting within the file.

A number of solutions were developed. Over time, the developers of *AmiPro* studied documents created by *WordStar*, Microsoft *Word*, *Word Perfect*, etc., worked out how they worked and developed their own conversion tools, and vice-versa. This was not a precise science though, and an imported document often lost some of its formatting – for example, graphics were often mis-placed or mis-sized. A further development was **Rich Text Format**, designed as an industry standard format that any vendor could use – unfortunately the large files it produced prevented its widespread use.

In the early 1990s, Microsoft released *Windows 3.1*, along with version 6 of Microsoft *Word* which became a De Facto standard as many other rival products did not work effectively on *Windows*. In response to user expectations, most other companies incorporated the new document format used by Microsoft *Word* 6, associated with the .doc extension. *Word 97* (version 8) introduced a new format for storing data that, thanks to a huge market share, became a De Facto standard that other vendors had to study and incorporate into their products, as they incorporated the *Word* 6 format beforehand. This format also used the .doc extension, although earlier versions of *Word* could not open the file. At the time when many other vendors had fully figured out the *Word 97* format, and jointly developed the Open Document Format to allow easy sharing of data, Microsoft announced their own Office Open XML format (.docx), together with legal restrictions on other vendors' use of it!

For users, a common De Jure file format will result in convenience and an assurance that, many years from now, their documents will still be accessible by new products. This is not the case with proprietary standards that may only be supported by one vendor and even then not for an indefinite period– even a current version of Microsoft *Word*, for example, does not always perfectly import documents created by earlier versions of *Word* in the early 1990s!

The problems of 'legacy' data still existing in old formats is discussed in *Warning of data ticking time bomb*, BBC News online, 7 July 2007, via: http://tinyurl.com/2qv6ds

Protocols

A further use of standards is in **protocols**, or sets of rules, that govern the transmission of data. For example, rules such as as **HyperText Transfer Protocol (HTTP)** govern the use of the Internet. In simple terms, HTTP requires a client (such as a web browser) to identify itself to a server, then request data, and finally confirm receipt of the data.

HTTP uses rules that were developed between the 1960s and 1980s long before Microsoft *Windows* appeared. Microsoft's later products had to comply with the rules already in place or their devices would have been unable to communicate with others. Other protocols, such as the **Simple Mail Transfer Protocol (SMTP)** and **Wireless Application Protocol (WAP)** are De Jure standards, governed by ISO, and used by people today who had no involvement with their development. These timescales demonstrate that great thought must be given when developing a standard, to making it flexible enough to handle unforeseen uses that future generations will put it to. This is seen in the flexibility that allowed ASCII to evolve into Unicode and in the development of the **HyperText Markup Language (HTML)** and its derivatives.

Standardising Bodies

Within ICT and related industries there are a number of bodies who exercise a regulatory role. Some of these are sanctioned by national governments while others are drawn from the industries they regulate. Bodies you should be aware of are:

Postal, Telegraph and Telephone (PTT) Operators. A generic name given to regulators of communication in any country, responsible for traditional mail and electronic communications. In many countries the traditional postal service incorporated telegram (later, telephone) services and even broadcasting when these technologies were developed. In the UK, the **General Post Office (GPO)**, was formally split into **British Telecom (BT)** and **Royal Mail** in 1981. In due course other telecoms companies, such as mobile operators, moved into a market that had once been a state-owned monopoly. Today the **Office of Communications (Ofcom)** is the government body with oversight of telecommunications, standards in broadcasting and licensing of commercial broadcasters.

The International Telecommunications Union (ITU). This is a global body whose role is to standardise international telecommunications and broadcasting. Their roles include:

+ Ensuring that national telephone services can interconnect, hence allowing a telephone user in one country to directly dial another without requiring human operators. The data making up the call may pass through many nations.
+ Regulating the allocation of radio frequencies to ensure that broadcasters in one nation do not broadcast on the same frequency as a broadcaster in a neighbouring state and hence interfere with each other. In Northern Ireland, this means that BBC and RTÉ broadcasts are both available without their respective signals interfering with each other.

The International Organisation for Standardisation (ISO). The name 'ISO' is derived from the Greek word for 'equal'. ISO is made up of national standards bodies and makes decisions that affect many aspects of our lives. Although ISO is not appointed by governments and compliance with ISO is entirely voluntary, ISO standards are often given legal status in many nations. Since ISO came into being in 1947 they have retrospectively taken responsibility for many existing standards, such as defining units of time and measurement, to setting new standards, such as file formats for music CDs and word processors.

The British Standards Institute (BSI). This was founded in 1901 and is responsible for the 'Kitemark' that is used on many products to indicate they meet certain standards. While some BSI standards are not internationally used (such as BS 1363, which governs domestic electrical connections), a number of BSI standards have been adopted by ISO. BSI standards adopted in this way include:

- BS 5750 which describes manufacturing methods, including software development, that became ISO 90011.
- BS 7799 which describes practises relating to information security, and which has been adopted as ISO 17799.

The American National Standards Institute (ANSI). Founded in 1918, ANSI is the American representative within ISO. Its membership includes US Government agencies, academic bodies and industry. As with BSI, ANSI standards can be adopted via ISO as international standards. ANSI standards that have become worldwide standards via ISO include:

- Standards that define film and shutter speeds in cameras and are used throughout the photographic industry.
- 'ANSI C', a standardised version of the C programming language that is used throughout the software industry.

The International Electrotechnical Commission (IEC). This is an international non-governmental body that publishes and develops standards that are particular to electrical and electronic technologies (hence 'electrotechnical'). BSI and ANSI are both national representatives in IEC. IEC standards include:

- IEC 60027, describing the SI system of weight and measures.
- IEC 60608, which specifies how CDs operate.

The British Computer Society (BCS). BCS is the leading professional body for the IT industry in the UK, although it also has an international membership. BCS manages professional development programmes, such as ECDL and award 'Chartered Engineer' status within the computer engineering industry. The BCS also oversee standards in many Computing degree courses in the UK. The BCS has a number of local groups (see www.bcsbelfast.org) and special interest groups (including The Computer Art Society, the Law specialist group and the BCS-Women specialist group). The **Association for Computing Machinery (ACM)** is the American equivalent body and performs a similar role to the BCS.

The Institute of Engineering and Technology (IET). A similar body to the BCS, although membership is largely drawn from those working in electronics, as opposed to software development. Like the BCS, the IET provides professional development opportunities and encourages professionalism within its members. The IET also plays an important role relating to wiring standards, carrying on from one of its predecessors the **Institution of Electrical Engineers (IEE)**. Their American equivalent is the IEEE (see below).

The Institute of Electrical and Electronic Engineers (IEEE) is an international body of engineers, including computer engineers and computer scientists, as well as scientists from other disciplines. Although founded in the USA, their membership is now international. As with other bodies, they have a role in defining standards used across the world, such as the IEEE 802 set of standards that govern the protocols used in computer networks, and which includes standards jointly ratified with ISO.

Despite the large number of standardising bodies, they frequently work together when they have a shared interest in order to avoid creating contradictory standards. Likewise, professional bodies that may represent different groups within ICT will often work together to promote overall interests and professional standards.

Many readers of this book will be eligible for student membership of the BCS or IET and, depending on future career aspirations, would do well to consider these. When students graduate and commence a suitable career they will be recognised as Associate Members, later as 'full' members, Chartered Engineers, and perhaps 'Fellows', after a distinguished career.

Questions

1. Define the term knowledge. (2)
2. Define the term information. (2)
3. Define the term data. (2)
4. Using an example not mentioned in this textbook distinguish between data, information and knowledge. (6)
5. Define direct data. Support your answer with a real-world example. (2)
6. Define indirect data. Support your answer with a real-world example. (2)
7. Describe two advantages of using a direct data source. (4)
8. List three factors which affect the quality of information. (3)
9. A person fills out a membership form by hand when joining a gym. Describe two ways in which the quality of the completed membership form might affect the quality of the information produced. (4)
10. Name and describe three transcription errors. (6)
11. Explain what is meant by validation. (3)
12. Explain what is meant by verification. (3)
13. Describe two data verification checks. (4)
14. Why will data verification not detect all errors? Give an example. (3)
15. Name and justify appropriate validation checks for the following fields:
    i. Date of birth (2)   ii. Postcode (2)   iii. Quantity of stock to be ordered. (2)
16. What is the difference between a hash total and a batch total? (2)
17. In a bookshop, the old-style ISBN of a book is entered into the Point of Sale system as 0434003484. Is this accepted by the system? Show your working out. (4)
18. State and describe three factors that contribute to the cost of producing information. (6)
19. Describe two benefits of adopting standards. (4)
20. State and describe three standardising bodies. (6)

CHAPTER 2
Hardware: Input Devices

2.1 Introduction

Hardware is the physical elements of any computer system. It is a term used to describe the parts of a computer system that can be seen or touched. Hardware is used in all the operations of an information system, but it is useless without a set of instructions to control it. These sets of instructions are known as **software**. Hardware devices can be categorised by their operations.

+ Input
+ Processing
+ Output
+ Storage

Some devices, such as a mouse or monitor, are used for only one of these functions while other devices, such as touch sensitive screens and some joysticks, are used for a combination of functions. The relationship between human beings and computers is known as **human computer interaction (HCI)** which is discussed in Chapter 26.

The subject of hardware will be discussed over the next six chapters.

2.2 Keyboards

In its many different forms, this is the input device that many users will be most familiar with. Keyboards are still the most common method for entering text and numerical data. In addition, certain key combinations on a keyboard can be used to access commands in the computer, for example to access the Cut and Paste menu commands. Standard keyboards include alphanumeric keys, a numeric keypad, function keys and control keys. Smaller keyboards, such as those found on a laptop, may omit certain keys such as the numeric keypad. A keyboard is traditionally connected to a computer via a cable, though wireless connections are increasingly common.

Text and numerical data entered using a keyboard is often copied from a paper 'source document'. However, entering such data using a keyboard is labour intensive and unless the user has been trained as a 'touch typist' can be slow and prone to error. A keyboard will be used in conjunction with some form of pointing device as navigating around the screen or moving objects using cursor keys can be awkward and time consuming.

By the way... How does a keyboard work?

When a key is pressed, an electronic signal is sent to the processor which interprets the signal. Software then takes the appropriate action, for example making a letter appear in a word-processed document. This is the procedure when a user types Shift-B:

+ The keyboard has a small microprocessor within it that continuously monitors for key presses.

+ When a key press or a combination of key presses (in this case the shift key plus a letter) is detected, the ASCII (American Stand Code for Information Interchange) code specific to that combination of keys is sent to the processor.

+ If a 'b' on its own had been pressed the code 1100010 would have been sent to the processor. However, the shift key means that instead the code for 'B' (1000010) is transmitted.

+ This binary code is stored in a **buffer** (a temporary storage location used when data is being moved from one location to another) where it is transmitted **serially** (one **bit** at a time) to the CPU.

+ The character 'B' is then displayed on the screen and the buffer is emptied.

CL Sholes designed the **QWERTY** key layout in 1878 with the remit of preventing stuck keys on mechanical typewriters, by ensuring that the most commonly-used letters were spaced far apart. Technology has moved on and we no longer have the issue of stuck keys. However this keyboard layout remains simply because people are used to it. There have been some attempts to revise the keyboard layout, such as August Dvorak's 1936 design that allows for less finger movement when typing but these have not met widespread acceptance.

Because the QWERTY keyboard is designed around the frequency of certain letters in English, a different layout is often adopted in non-English speaking countries. France uses the AZERTY keyboard, while Germans will be used to using the QWERTZU layout.

Concept Keyboards

Instead of the usual keys, an overlay sheet containing different pictures is placed on top of a touch sensitive pad. The user indicates input by pressing one of the pictures. Related software then interprets the input. It can be used:

+ to help people with physical disabilities.

+ in young children's **Computer Based Learning** systems.

+ fast food restaurants or bars where there is need for quick, efficient input of menu choices. It has the advantage of having a water and dirt resistant surface.

With a concept keyboard it is possible to change the overlay to provide a different set of pictures. A concept keyboard can only be used when all the inputs are anticipated and the range of options is small.

Figure 2.1: A concept keyboard (left) and an alternative keyboard (right) with keys arranged into curves.

Alternative Keyboards

These are designed around the form of the human body, for example having split or curved keyboards to minimise wrist and arm strain.

Repetitive Strain Injury (RSI) is often associated with poor keyboard design or poor seating. A traditional QWERTY keyboard forces a user to rotate their forearms so that the palms are down and lift their middle fingers so that all four can touch the keys, which is not a natural body movement. Alternative keyboards have been designed to alleviate the likelihood of such injury, and my include some or all of these features:

- **Split keyboard**, which straighten the wrists by increasing the distance between the left and right sides of the keyboard and by rotating the keys to align them to the forearms.
- **Tented keyboard**, which is tilted up at the centre to reduce forearm rotation.
- **Alternative key positions** arranged into curved rows in concave wells, instead of horizontal rows, to allow the fingers to straighten more.

Conduct some research into alternative keyboards. What are the specific problems they are attempting to address? What different designs have been developed?

T a s k

2.3 Pointing Devices

A number of devices can be used to move an on-screen pointer, for example to select or move icons. The most common of these is the mouse. Other pointing devices include: the joystick, trackpoint, trackball, touch screen and graphics tablet.

Mouse

The mouse, like the keyboard, is amongst the most widely used input devices. It became popular with the **Graphical User Interface** of Apple's *Macintosh* in 1984.

A mouse consists of a small body that can fit in the palm of the hand. and requires a flat surface. By moving the mouse around the surface the user can direct a pointer or cursor on the computer screen. It usually has two or more buttons positioned on the front which, when used with software that supports them, may allow the user to draw, erase or move objects and select menus or text for formatting. Some feature additional buttons that can configured to trigger other functions. One example is the **scroll wheel** used to navigate through a word processing document or a web page.

By the way...

How does a mouse work?

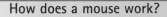

When the mouse is moved on a flat surface a small ball underneath the mouse moves. Sensors detect the movement in two directions (horizontally and vertically) and convert the movement into an analogue electrical signal. The analogue signals are converted to binary via an **analogue to digital converter** and input to the computer which takes the appropriate action, for example by moving the pointer on the screen. The clicking of the button likewise generates a binary signal which is interpreted by the computer.

Optical mice contain an LED instead of a ball. The light reflected off the surface on which the mouse is placed is picked up by a sensor. When the mouse is moved, the sensor detects differences in the reflection and translates this into an indication of the direction of movement.

Advantages of mouse input

+ Movement and control of the pointer within a Graphical User Interface is more straightforward than using keyboard shortcuts or cursor keys.
+ It is much easier to produce drawings using a mouse than a keyboard.

Disadvantages of mouse input

+ Mice cannot be used for text input.
+ A reasonably flat surface is needed beside the computer
+ Mice are very susceptible to dust and dirt which makes them function incorrectly, or cause the on-screen pointer to jump rather than move smoothly.
+ Using a mouse for long periods of time leads to repetitive strain injury (RSI).

TrackPoint™

Laptop computers may not always be used where desk space is available, and therefore require alternatives pointing devices. One such device is the **TrackPoint** (or 'pointing stick' or 'nipple'). A small knob found in the middle of some keyboards that works like a very short joystick. Pressing it toward or away from you or from side to side moves the pointer on the screen. It uses virtually no extra space and requires minimal movement of the hands from the keyboard. TrackPoint is a trademark of IBM.

Figure 2.2: A laptop computer equipped with both a TrackPoint and a touch pad.

Touch Pad

This consists of a touch sensitive pad that senses the position and movements of a finger or a stylus. Finger-presses are interpreted as button clicks. There may also be dedicated buttons that are used to carry out some of the more complicated mouse actions, such as scrolling. Some people find a touch pad difficult to use as it can be too sensitive and movement may feel less natural than a mouse.

Trackball

A further alternative is a **trackball**. The user controls cursor movement with a touch of the finger on a tracker ball which remains in one place. The trackball is useful when there is limited desk space on which a mouse can be moved. It also allows for highly accurate cursor movements and is used in many CAD applications.

Joystick

Joysticks are popular for games rather than windows-based interfaces. Joysticks are also used in aeroplanes, specialist cars, robots and wheelchairs. The 'shaft' is moved about a central axis and the movement is detected by sensors, which converted it into digital data and pass it on to a processor. Instead of representing movement, the data represents precise X and Y coordinates which are used to determine the position of the pointer on the screen. Buttons are usually added to a joystick to provide additional functionality depending on the software in use.

Touch Screen

Touch screens allow users to interact with a computer by touching icons or menu options on the display: here the 'pointing device' is the human finger. Touch screens are ideal where the user must select from menus so they are often used, for example, in information kiosks, tourist information points or **point of sale** terminals in restaurants. Touch screens can also be used in systems designed to help those who have difficulty operating a mouse or keyboard. Very small touch screens are used in **Personal Digital Assistants (PDAs)**, using a stylus in place of the human finger. Many PDAs also incorporate handwriting-recognition software, thus allowing the user to 'write' on the screen with the stylus.

Touch screens are well suited to the public environment as they require no previous experience or training as the user simply selects a valid option from the menu provided. More control can be exercised over what options are available to a user as it is easy to 'hide' options that are irrelevant and therefore reduce the potential for invalid input. Although a touch screen is expensive, it may be preferable to a keyboard and mouse in a public place as it is takes up less space, is easy to keep clean is and less likely to be stolen or damaged. However touch screens are not suitable for use over a long period as significant pressure is required and the non-flexible screen can place stress on human fingers.

Figure 2.3: A trackball (top), joystick (middle) and touch screen (bottom) are all pointing devices.

©iStockPhoto

How does a touch screen work?

A series of horizontal and vertical infrared beams are directed across the screen, underneath a protective membrane. When the user touches the relevant menu option or icon on the screen, they break a horizontal and vertical beam. The touch screen will detect determine the exact coordinates of the finger (and hence of the mouse pointer) which is interpreted as a 'click' at that point.

Graphics Tablets

Also known as digitising tablets or digitisers, these consist of a flat surface containing a touch-sensitive membrane which detects the location of a specially designed stylus. As the stylus is moved across the pad, the movement is interpreted by software as a drawing, which appears on the computer screen. The harder the user presses on the stylus, the thicker the line drawn on the screen. Each point on the tablet always represents the same fixed point on the screen, in contrast to the position of a mouse which can be picked up and set down somewhere else.

A puck, which features a transparent centre with cross-hairs for pin-point accuracy, can be used instead of a mouse. Graphics tablets are useful where drawings must be entered with a high degree of accuracy. Using the stylus is a very natural method of drawing lines and shapes. Various templates can be used with the graphics tablet: the template can be laid on the tablet allowing the user to select pre-defined shapes (for example, common electrical symbols) which then appear on the screen to be included in a drawing. The size of a graphics tablet can vary – anything from the size of a book, to the size of a desk, depending on the application.

Graphics tablets may be used:

+ Within **Computer Aided Design (CAD)** applications.

+ In tracing hard-copy drawings.

+ In art applications, where the use of a mouse is not considered precise enough.

2.4 Document Readers

A number of methods can be used to automate the input of printed data, such as:

+ Optical Character Recognition (OCR)
+ Optical Mark Recognition (OMR)
+ Magnetic Ink Character Recognition (MICR)
+ Bar Code Scanners

Optical Character Recognition (OCR)

OCR is the recognition of hard-copy by a computer. In most cases the characters will be printed but recognition of handwriting is also possible.

Initially, OCR operates like a scanner. A light is shone on the characters and the scanner senses the reflected light from the characters. Software then analyses the reflection and determines the shape of each character. Next, the OCR software compares the shape of each character with a database of stored shapes. Each shape is then interpreted as a character, or rejected. Finally, a digitised representation of the scanned document is saved as a text file and can be edited further.

OCR has a wide range of applications, including:

+ Converting old printed documents, written before computers were invented or widely available, to digital form.
+ Postal sorting by using OCR to read postcodes and sorting post automatically. Although faster than if done by entirely manual methods, this method relies on legible, ideally printed, postcodes on envelopes.
+ The input of turnaround documents such as electricity and telephone bills.

Recognition of characters involves complex image processing algorithms and rarely achieves 100% accuracy so manual proof reading is recommended. It is essential that the document is clear of creases and smudges to prevent further inaccuracies. A major problem for OCR has been human handwriting. While regular fonts such as Times New Roman and Arial can be interpreted with a high degree of accuracy, human handwriting is less predicable – for example one person's '5' or '7' can be another's 'S' or 'T'.

Optical Mark Recognition (OMR)

OMR is used to read marks made by a person in preset positions or boxes on a specially designed form. The mark is made using a pencil or black pen. OMR readers reflect light against the form, which is reflected where no mark is present. The pattern of reflected light is compared to a stored template.

This system is used in applications where there are a restricted number of possible choices, such as:

+ Marking multiple-choice exams.
+ Noting the responses on survey forms.
+ Choosing lottery draw numbers.
+ Completing school attendance sheets.
+ Recording meter-readings.

Figure 2.4: A player making precise marks on a lottery ticket with a pencil which will then be processed via OMR.

OMR systems are expensive to set up: there is the cost of specialist hardware and OMR sheets must be printed to a high specification. OMR can eliminate transcription errors provided the instructions given to users are clear and the user puts their mark in the correct place and does not mark anywhere else. Also, crumpled forms often have to be manually entered, as the OMR system may not be able to distinguish between proper marks and folds OMR is useful when there is a high volume of forms to be processed in a short time.

Magnetic Ink Character Recognition (MICR)

MICR is a character recognition system that uses special magnetised ink.

Characters, written in a special font, are told apart through their magnetic fields. MICR is used almost exclusively in the banking industry where it is used to print details on cheques to enable fast processing. Usually, the cheque number, the branch sort code and the account number are printed in MICR-readable ink.

MICR has the advantage of being fast and minimises human errors. It is difficult to forge cheques as the special magnetic ink is difficult to reproduce accurately. Furthermore the characters can be read even if the cheque is crumpled, dirty or smudged.

Figure 2.5: Magnetic ink in use on a credit slip.

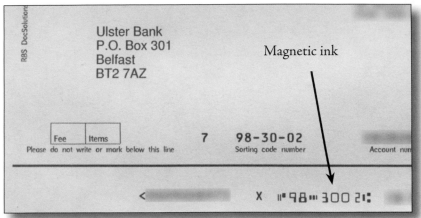

Ulster Bank
P.O. Box 301
Belfast
BT2 7AZ

Magnetic ink

Fee | Items
Please do not write or mark below this line

7   98-30-02
Sorting code number

Account nu

X   ⑈98⑈300 2⑉

MICR cannot, however, read the amount on a cheque as this is not written with magnetic ink and human interaction is still needed for this task. The use of MICR may become less common because the use of cheques by customers is in decline with many large stores no longer accepting cheques as a method of payment, due to the growth in the popularity of credit and debit cards.

Bar Code Scanners

Bar codes represent a binary number as a series of thick and thin black lines. The number is usually printed in human-readable form underneath. They are usually printed on or attached to an object so that it can be identified.

Data is captured by shining the light from a 'wand' or special bar code scanner onto the bar code. This light is reflected differently by lines than gaps, and this light is detected by photoelectric cells to produce an electrical signal. This signal is decoded by the scanner to produce a number, which is transmitted to a computer where it may be used for further processing, for example to look up a price.

Bar code scanners have a variety of applications:

+ Item tracking. Bar codes attached to objects can be used to track their movement, for example products in a warehouse or luggage in an airport.
+ Retailers use bar codes to identify the price of a product at the checkout and record how many items of each type have been sold.
+ In libraries bar codes are used to both identify members and the books they are borrowing.

There are four items of information on the bar codes used in the commercial European Article Number system (despite its name, this is an ISO-approved international system):

+ The first two digits indicate the product's country of origin.
+ The next five digits represent the manufacturer's code.
+ The next five digits represent the product and package size, but not the price.

♦ The last digit is a check digit, which is calculated from the other digits in the code and ensures that the bar code is keyed in or read correctly (see section 1.6).

The use of bar codes greatly reduces data entry time as a code or price does not have to be entered manually. This in turn reduces the potential for transcription errors as there is less human involvement. Bar codes are durable in rough environments, such as warehouses, where a label may be read many times. They are quick to create as they can be printed in an office without the need to use a commercial printer. One example of this is the weigh scales in supermarkets which print labels for customers when they weigh fruit and vegetables.

However, bar codes are limited to applications where the data to be stored can be represented in numerical form. Occasionally a bar code cannot be read correctly (perhaps it has been torn badly) and the operator will have to input the code manually which can increase data entry time. This is why the number represented by a bar code must also be printed in human-readable form underneath.

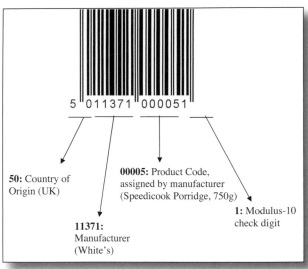

50: Country of Origin (UK)

00005: Product Code, assigned by manufacturer (Speedicook Porridge, 750g)

1: Modulus-10 check digit

11371: Manufacturer (White's)

Figure 2.6: Example of a bar code from an item in a supermarket. How much information does it contain?

2.5 Speech Input

Speech input, or **voice recognition**, can be used on a PC to dictate text, or as an alternative method of inputting commands. Other devices, such as car entertainment/control systems, security systems and toys, use speech input. Many telephone-based computer systems, such as banks and couriers, use speech input methods so that customers can interact with the system using the telephone.

A word is spoken into a microphone which is connected to the **sound card** of a PC, which converts the signal from analogue to digital form. Software then compares the digitised signal with a database of digitised sounds seeking a matching word or phrase. If no match is found the user will be asked to repeat the word. If the word is found, then the appropriate action is carried out. For example, the word may be displayed in a word processing package or a command is carried out.

Currently, speech recognition systems require a period of training to adapt to an individual's voice, and the reliability is still far from perfect. One important benefit of speech input is that it can help people who have visual or mobility restrictions but can still communicate verbally. Furthermore speech recognition can reduce the impact of health problems associated with computer use, such as repetitive strain injury. Speech input is a fast method of input for people who do not have well developed keyboard skills.

Key disadvantages of voice input are that there is a certain degree of error and even small changes in the user's voice, such as having a cold, can affect the system's accuracy. Also, a system designed for general use by many people, such as a directory enquiries voice recognition system, may not be suitable for people with broad accents.

2.6 Card Readers

A **magnetic stripe** (or **strip**) is a short length of magnetic tape sealed into the surface of a ticket or card. The stripe can contain up to 220 encoded characters of information to identify the ticket/card, or its user. This information can then be read, or new information written, each time it is 'swiped' through an appropriate device.

Uses of magnetic stripe cards include:

+ Bank cards that use a magnetic stripe to store the customer's account details.
+ Security systems where people swipe a magnetic card through a reader to gain access through special doors.
+ Phone cards use the stripe to store the amount of credit left on the card.
+ Automated car park systems that store the time of entry on a magnetic stripe.

Disadvantages of the magnetic stripe are that it has a limited storage capacity, that the card can be rendered useless by bending it or exposure it to magnetic fields and that it is relatively easy to copy the data from it.

©iStockPhoto

Figure 2.7: Modern credit cards, or smart cards, feature a small embedded computer chip.

Smart Cards

A card technology that overcomes these weaknesses is the **smart card** – a plastic card with a small embedded computer chip. Unlike a magnetic stripe, the smart card can be programmed to perform tasks and store information. Instead of swiping the card, you plug it into a reader

Smart cards can store millions of characters of data, rather than the limit of 220 with magnetic stripes, and are more reliable. Because the data is encrypted, they are more difficult to forge, and are compatible with portable electronic devices such as mobile phones, **personal digital assistants** (PDAs) and PCs.

Smart cards have many uses, including:

+ Pay TV, where subscribers can activate a channel by inserting a smart card into their digital receiver.
+ All-purpose student ID card, which can be used as 'electronic money' for vending and laundry machines, as a library card, or as a meal card.
+ More modern chip-and-pin credit/bank cards which offer better security.

2.7 Sensors and Data Logging

Sensors are used by computers to detect changes in various physical quantities, such as temperature, air pressure, electromagnetic fields, noise levels, sound, light etc, which are input directly into a computer via an interface. They are particularly useful for applications which are either too dangerous, or too tedious, for a human being to record data. They can operate 24 hours per day, 365 days per year. The use of sensors and feedback permits a much quicker reaction time than could be achieved by a human recording and processing data.

Data logging is the recording of data gathered via sensors over a prolonged period. Once it has been recorded, the data can be downloaded into a computer package such as a spreadsheet for analysis.

Examples of data logging include:

+ measuring temperature in a heating system. When the temperature falls below a certain preset level, the boiler can be activated.
+ recording the number of people passing through a turnstile. This is useful in situations where it is necessary to know the precise numbers of people in a shopping centre or stadium for safety reasons.
+ measuring and logging the build-up of pressure in a volcano. In this case, it is simply too dangerous for a human to do this work.
+ recording conditions on another planet, such as composition of the soil on Mars. At the present time, it is too expensive, impractical and dangerous to send a human.

Feedback

Feedback is the use of a system's output as a further input. This is a common feature of control systems, such as cruise-control systems in cars, or systems that regulate the temperature of a room. The operation of a feedback system follows four stages that are continuously repeated.

+ Data arrives as input.
+ The input data is compared with some predetermined value (processing).
+ Output devices are instructed to perform some action as a consequence.
+ The results of these actions then form the next set of input data (feedback).

Consider an oven that is set by the user to a temperature of 200°C. A control system within the oven is designed to ensure that the temperature remains within a narrow range of values close to the desired temperature, for example 197°C to 203°C. A number of temperature sensors within the oven supply input data to a microprocessor which will compare the actual temperature with the acceptable range of values and turn the heating elements on or off accordingly. The temperature sensors then detect the effects of these output decisions as new input data which are then processed as before. This process continues for as long as the temperature is set.

Other common feedback-control systems include:

+ the cruise control system in a car. The driver sets a desired speed, which a control system then regulates.
+ automated navigation, or 'autopilot', on aeroplanes and ships. The actual speed and direction of travel of the craft is compared to the desired speed and direction, as set by the pilot or captain, and corrected if necessary.

Many feedback systems that rely on sensors also make use of **actuators**. For example, in a greenhouse control system, sensors detect temperature and humidity. If it is too warm, actuators are used to open windows. Feedback (via the sensors) is used to determine when the temperature has fallen to an acceptable level, at which point the windows are closed, again using the actuators.

Definition

Closed-loop feedback is used in systems that require no user intervention once the system is operative. That is, once it is installed the system will look after itself until it is deactivated. Examples of this include:

+ an environmental control in a greenhouse that maintains temperature and humidity levels without intervention;

+ an automated shelf-loading system in a warehouse that places items on a shelf, determining their position via sensors without human input.

Open-loop feedback is used in systems that require human intervention after output has been generated. The system will take no further action until intervention is received. Hence the 'output' generated may simply be to sound an alarm and wait for the user. Examples of this include:

+ a burglar alarm that remains active and waiting for human intervention once it has been triggered;

+ a computer game, such as chess, that takes turns with the player. In this example the output is the move made by the chess game, after which it waits for the player to respond.

Task

Examples of an oven, a car's cruise-control system and automated navigation were given in the text above. Would each of these be described as an open-loop or a closed-loop system? Justify your answer.

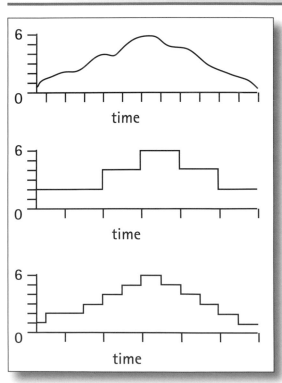

Figure 2.8: Graphs illustrating the conversion of an analogue input (top) to digital (middle, bottom) input.

Analogue to Digital Conversion

Many signals generated by sensors are **analogue** in nature, ie consist of data that can be represented using an infinite range of values. However, because computers must represent data using a finite number of 1s and 0s, analogue input signals must be converted to digital form before they can be processed.

A sensor (or transducer) converts an analogue signal, such as temperature, into an analogue electrical voltage, which can be fed into an analogue to digital converter. The analogue data is then converted by a process called **sampling**: at fixed intervals the analogue signal is compared to the nearest equivalent on a digital scale and that approximation is recorded. An example is shown in figure 2.8. The first graph represents a voltage (in the range 0-6V) over a period of time. The two graphs below it show the digital equivalent with a coarse sampling method (middle) and a finer sampling method (bottom). The finer the sampling method used, the closer the resemblance between the digital values and the original analogue signal. However finer sampling methods also require more storage space for the digital values.

Analogue to digital conversion is used anywhere that analogue data must be input into a computer. For example recording the human voice, logging temperatures or inputting an image with countless shades of colour.

Digital Images

An analogue image contains millions of subtle changes in shade and texture. To record all of these accurately in a digital file would requires huge amounts of computer memory which may not be practical, for example if an image is to be downloaded over the Internet. Image compression allows the user to sacrifice some quality, either in terms of resolution or quality of colour, in return for an acceptable file size. Figure 2.9 shows an original image that is then compressed by two different methods to greatly reduce the file size. Both of the compressed images convey the original image in an acceptable way.

  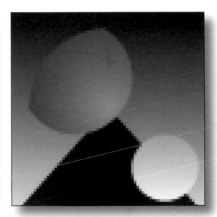

Figure 2.9: An original image (left) compressed by two different methods: reduction of the number of colours used (centre) and a reduction in resolution (right).

By the way...

Digital broadcasting

At first glance, the suggestion of a broadcasting method that reduces the number of distinct colours on a television screen may seem like a bad idea. Yet, digital broadcasting makes for better pictures!

All broadcasts are liable to interference. Unfortunately, with analogue broadcasts it is difficult to correct errors. Suppose the value of 1 volt is transmitted, but due to interference 0.875 volts arrive – the receiving device does not know if the signal is intended to be 0.875 volts or not. In a digital system, if there were only two values in use (0 and 1) and 0.875 was received, the receiver would determine that 1 was intended. Hence a signal can be restored to perfection despite interference, provided the interference is not too severe. Using a system that allows for higher graphics resolution than traditional broadcasts and for images in millions of colours, viewers tend to notice far better pictures with digital than with analogue. This is discussed further in Chapter 11.

2.8 Applications of Input Devices

Many different input devices are available. Some are more suitable for particular applications than others. Some have been designed for particular applications. It is therefore essential that the user chooses the correct input devices for each application.

In **retail** applications, two of the most important things to consider are speed of input and the potential for errors to be made by the user. For example, in supermarkets it is essential that product details are input and reliably as quickly as possible. In this application, a bar-code reader will be the primary means of instead of a keyboard, which is slow and cumbersome in this context. However, it is possible that bar code labels may be damaged (eg by being torn or scratched) so most supermarket checkouts will still have a keyboard as an auxiliary input device. The same is true for devices that read magnetic-stripe or chip-and-pin credit cards, where the preferred input device is supplemented by a backup numeric keypad.

It is for the same 'speed of input' reasons that concept keyboards or touch screens are often used in supermarkets, particularly to input the details of vegetables (pressing one button is quicker than typing "onion"). OMR is used in many shops for inputting details of lottery tickets. In this application, speed is not the only consideration, because it is essential that a person's numbers are recorded absolutely accurately. Imagine the argument if a person thought they had won the lottery, but discovered that their entry was invalidated because the shop assistant had entered the numbers incorrectly. The ATM has become a standard tool in **banking**, and combines user-friendly card input for speed and security with and a simple keypad for the user to enter a PIN and confirm choices. Because ATMs are exposed to the weather all day and night, and may be subjected to vandalism, they are made of extremely durable materials.

Manufacturing workers in factories may not be skilled computer users or have the time to use a keyboard, so concept keyboards or touch-screens may be used for entering details of components moving past on a conveyor belt. In many cases, these devices are connected to sensors, such as scales, so that, for example, the worker can record information about the type and weight of a joint of meat simply by pressing a button to identify the type of meat being weighed. Input devices with more options, such as keyboards, will be used for more complex work, for example a supervisor wishing to query information on new orders or the state of the production schedule. Input errors are usually alerted visually (for example by flashing the screen for a second, or lighting an LED) since the beeps favoured by desktop PCs are impractical in noisy environments.

Medicine has been responsible for driving the development of many new technologies. In order to reduce the need for to invasive surgery, **endoscopes** have been developed to allow a doctor to place a camera deep inside a patient's body with minimal injury. The same tube containing the camera can be equipped with small pieces of surgical equipment that can be used for reasonably complex procedures, such as removing small cancer polyps in the intestine. To free up staff and to alert doctors of problems more quickly, many sensors are used in hospitals, for example to measure heartbeat, blood pressure and temperature. These devices monitor and record the data quietly, but will sound alarms if the values exceed acceptable limits.

Modern **schools** utilise many different technologies. **Interactive whiteboards (IWBs)** are both input and output devices. A data projector aimed at the board is used to output the desktop of a PC. The screen itself contains sensors which accurately record the position of a special pen which is then input back to the PC instead of a mouse. As with other applications, consideration must be given to the choice of equipment. For example, some projectors may contain noisy fans that are a distraction, and some teachers may prefer to write on IWBs with conventional marker pens when interactive output from a PC is not required.

Document readers are common in education. OCR may be used to input typed documents to save space and time, while OMR forms may be used for class registrations and for multiple-choice exams. These forms of input are quick to process. In science and technology classrooms, a range of sensors are used for inputting experimental data while **actuators** may be used to control a mechanical device (such as, opening a valve to control the flow of liquid after a certain pressure has been achieved in an experiment).

2.9 The Future

The development of input technology is far from over. Many new input devices with exciting potential are under development, as suggested by the articles below.

By the way...

Bionic Man: For the first time in 20 years, John German can peel a banana or open a can of pop with ease. Best of all, he can hold his daughters' hands without squeezing them too hard. German, 40, is one of 11 people in the world who has received a revolutionary new prosthetic arm called the "iLimb" – which is basically a bionic arm... With the iLimb, German, a Marquette native who lives in Pennsylvania, has five individually powered fingers and is able to control the pressure of his grips – characteristics that no other prosthetic he's tried has had.

From *The Mining Journal*, 7th September 2007, via http://tinyurl.com/2ltsr3. Such systems use actuators to control fingers and sensors and feedback to regulate pressure. See also www.touchbionics.com

Changing room mirror that gives fashion tips: A mirror has been invented that gives fashion tips while you are trying on clothes in a store. But unlike a human, the Magic Mirror knows what suits you and never gets bored. Once the mirror sees what you have tried on, it will then suggest matching items... The mirror reads a bar code on each item before displaying information about it on a built-in screen.

From *The Daily Telegraph*, 7th June 2006, via http://tinyurl.com/34hgnf

Get ready for the smart shopping basket: We are all familiar with the hassle of unpacking a supermarket trolley at the cash till. But in a few years' time, shoppers could be able to simply walk past a check-out which will automatically recognise the goods and debit your account. While this may sound like science fiction, the technology to do this already exists... [Radio Frequency Identification (RFID)] works much like a bar code, but instead of having to be passed in front of a scanner, tiny transponders send out radio signals. Each tag is unique so any one item, be it a pack of razor blades or a shirt, can be tracked individually, all the time and just about anywhere. Some experts predict this technology will become commonplace over the next decade or so. At present, it is too expensive to put on individual products and instead big companies use it to track shipping pallets. But as with everything in the tech world, the trend is towards smaller and cheaper devices.

From *BBC News Online*, 27 October 2003, via http://tinyurl.com/3238q4

Questions

1. Explain how the following input devices work:
   (a) keyboard
   (b) mouse
   (c) touch screen
   (d) OMR   (3 each)
2. Name three alternatives to a mouse (3)
3. Name and justify applications for the following input devices:
   (a) Joystick
   (b) Graphics tablet
   (c) Voice recognition
   (d) bar code   (2 each)
4. Describe the difference between smart card and magnetic stripe technology, suggesting a use for each. (4)
5. State four uses of sensors (apart from those given in the text), providing a justification for each. At least two of your examples should use data logging. (4)
6. What is OCR? What is the main weakness of OCR? (2)
7. A company proposes to use speech recognition systems to allow or deny access to its building. Describe two problems with this approach. (4)
8. State and describe three situations where analogue-digital conversion is required. (6)
9. Describe the advantages of digital input compared to analogue input. (2)
10. Describe the disadvantages of digital input compared to analogue input. (2)

CHAPTER 3
Hardware: Output Devices

3.1 Introduction

Output devices are used when a computer system is presenting information either to the user or to another electronic device.

As with input devices, there is a wide range of output devices, designed for many applications. Some are designed to appeal to a wide variety of users while others are designed for specialist uses.

3.2 Printers

Printers are used when a 'hard copy' (ie, physical copy) of information is needed from a computer. They come in a variety of shapes, sizes and abilities so to decide which type of printer to buy, the user must take several factors into account, including initial cost, running costs, speed, quality and colour. There are several printer technologies to choose from.

Dot Matrix Printers

These use a 9 or 24 pin head which is controlled from the computer and strikes a ribbon soaked in ink against a page repeatedly as the page scrolls through (see figure 3.1). While cheap to buy and run, their output is of low quality and they are noisy. By passing **multi-part stationery** through the printer, a single print-head can be used to strike several layers of carbon-paper to make multiple copies of the information. This is particularly useful in places such as a warehouse, where, for example, the white top sheet may go to the customer, the yellow second sheet to the sales department and the blue sheet to the production department. Examples of uses include ATM machines, shop receipts and printing invoices.

Thermal Printers

These work in a similar way, except that the pins make a mark by burning the image into the paper rather than using ink. While they do save ink, they need special paper. Some fax machines and cash registers use this method.

Ink Jet Printers

Sometimes called 'bubble jet' printers, they work by forcing small droplets of ink through nozzles onto the page, building up an image one line at a time in a similar way to dot-matrix printers. They are often used at home because they are cheap to buy, quiet, and can produce reasonably good colour output. Some printers use a single ink cartridge with all three colours in it, while the more expensive ones use a cartridge for each colour plus a black. Many models of ink jet printer are now

Figure 3.1: A close–up of the head of a dot matrix printer, and example output.

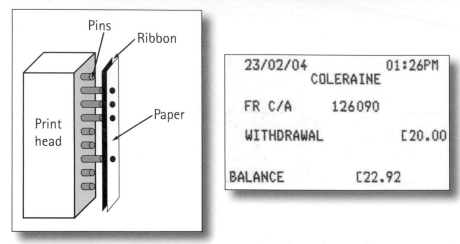

designed to print directly from a memory card, without the user having to turn the computer on.

They are not suited to large-scale use as running costs can be high compared to laser printers: ink cartridges can run out quickly and their replacements can be expensive. For example, the cost of printing a high-quality A4 colour photograph can range from 50p to several pounds, depending on the ink-jet printer. Their speed also varies: a fast printer can print five pages of plain black text per minute, while a complex combination of text and colour can take several minutes for a single sheet.

Laser Printers

Most common in office environments, laser printers use a cartridge filled with **toner** (a black powder which is converted into ink by heating it). A laser then 'draws' the image to be printed onto the outside of a **drum,** which leaves an electric charge in the shape of the image to be printed. The toner then sticks to the electric charge, so that when the drum is rolled over the paper the toner is transferred to the page. The page is then heated to **fuse** the toner onto the page permanently.

Colour lasers use one drum for each colour. Both laser printers and their toner are expensive to buy, but they are faster and produce a better quality result than ink jets do. However because toner cartridges tend to last much longer than ink jet cartridges (several thousand pages as opposed to several hundred), their unit cost per page is lower. A basic laser printer typically costs around £200.

Figure 3.2: Examples of an ink jet printer (left) and a laser printer (right).

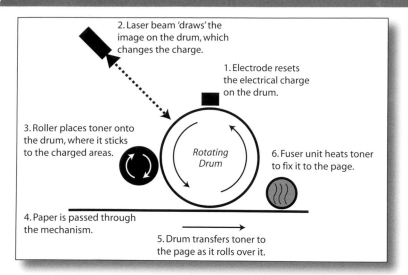

2. Laser beam 'draws' the image on the drum, which changes the charge.

1. Electrode resets the electrical charge on the drum.

3. Roller places toner onto the drum, where it sticks to the charged areas.

Rotating Drum

6. Fuser unit heats toner to fix it to the page.

4. Paper is passed through the mechanism.

5. Drum transfers toner to the page as it rolls over it.

Figure 3.3: The mechanism found inside a typical laser printer.

Plotters

Plotters are used when accurate, high definition hard copy is required. They are used by art/design businesses, map makers, architects and engineers. Plotters are often used when very large pieces of paper are required but where the cost of a laser printer that can cope with these is prohibitive. Plotters that print on smaller page sizes have been made largely redundant by improved laser printers. Figure 3.4 shows an A3 plotter, but many plotters can cope with A0 or even larger sizes.

Plotters use one or more pens that can be raised, lowered and moved over the printing media to draw graphics or text. The printer head assembly is attached to a horizontal bar. The pen can be moved horizontally by moving the printer head along the bar and vertically by either moving the bar (stationary page plotter) or the paper (rolling page plotter). Combinations of horizontal and vertical movement are used to draw lines and curves in a single action. This is in contrast to printers which can only simulate lines by printing a closely spaced series of dots. Real time direct control of the drawing arm is possible whereas with a laser printer the page image is transferred to the printer buffer before printing commences.

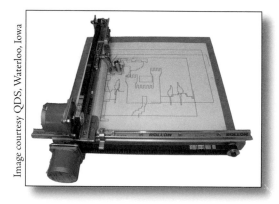

Image courtesy QDS, Waterloo, Iowa

Figure 3.4: A typical plotter.

Combined Input and Output: the Fax machine

Facsimile (Fax) Machines scan a hard copy of a document as input and transmit it to another location for printing, via the telecommunications network. Many businesses consider fax machines a vital tool and may take it for granted that business partners use them too.

A fax machine scans a paper document line by line from the top to the bottom of the page. Each scan line is divided into pixels and the scanner decides

By the way...

whether each pixel is black or white. From this, a low-resolution image file is created. The document is then transmitted via the telephone network to the receiving fax machine. At the receiving fax machine the data is decoded, uncompressed and reassembled into the scanned lines of the original document and is printed.

See also: *Connected Earth – Modems and Faxes*, via http://tinyurl.com/35llws

Many PCs are equipped with a **fax modem** and appropriate software. From the user's perspective, fax software is represented as an alternative printer (enter the recipient's number and press 'print'), thus eliminating the need to scan a hard copy into a fax machine. The receiving fax modem automatically answers the telephone and stores the fax on the PC's hard disk. The fax can then be viewed on screen. The advantage of such a system is that the faxes may be stored for future reference and do not need to be stored in a physical filing system.

Because a fax is simply a picture of a page, it is not possible to transfer a fax of some text directly to a word processing package without using OCR software. Their low image quality is a consequence of being originally designed to work with traditional PSTN (telephone) technologies.

Figure 3.5: Text and an image before (left) and after (right) being faxed.

3.3 Visual Display Units (VDUs)

Instead of creating a hard copy of an image, VDUs, or **monitors**, provide a **soft copy image,** ie one that is non-permanent. VDUs receive input via a **graphics card**, a special-purpose device connected to the motherboard of a computer.

Cathode Ray Tubes (CRTs)

Until the mid 2000s, CRTs were used with the majority of desktop computers, although recently their use has declined in favour of LCD monitors. These screens provide a high resolution and have historically represented colours more accurately than LCD displays.

The monitor contains three electron guns located at the rear of the monitor; one for each of the primary colours of light. The inside of the screen is coated with tiny red, green and blue phosphorous dots. Electron beams generated by the electron guns are directed at the phosphorus dots, which lights up and create the image. As the image has to be sharper than on a TV, monitors typically have a larger number of smaller dots. Virtually all CRTs produced today are colour, so they are almost as cheap to manufacture as monochrome screens.

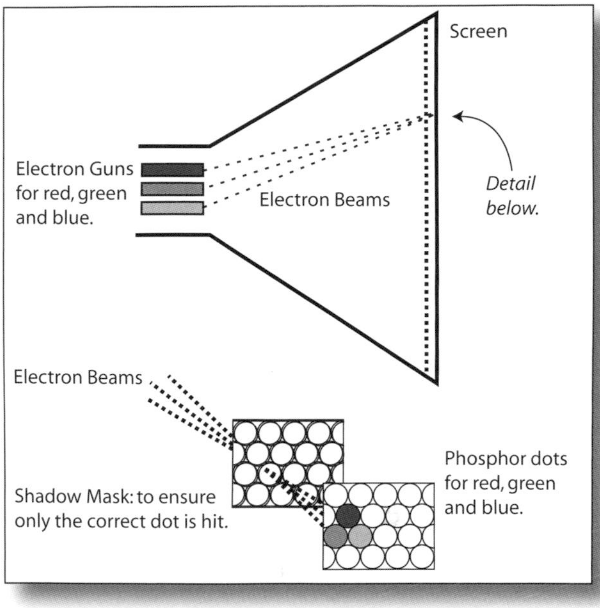

Phosphorus dots remain lit for only a fraction of a second after being activated, so the electron beam has to repeatedly scan the screen (televisions have a refresh rate of 25 Hz while a monitor operates at between 50 and 100 Hz). Lower refresh rates lead to a noticeable flicker which is the effect seen when the dots are not being re-lit often enough. Flickering has been linked to headaches and even epileptic fits.

Figure 3.6: Diagram of a typical CRT monitor.

Liquid Crystal Displays (LCDs)

LCD screens are used on calculators, laptops and more recently with desktop PCs because they take up less space, generate less heat and use less power than a CRT, so can run from a battery. Modern LCD screens are almost as effective as CRT. Instead of an electron gun, each pixel consists of a small area of liquid crystal lit from behind. By varying an electrical current through each pixel, the amount of light that passes through it can be varied. Because each pixel remains continually lit, LCDs do not produce a flicker and so are less likely to cause eyestrain. A disadvantage of LCDs is that the viewing angle is more limited, so that the image can be difficult to see from particular angles. In addition, their colour reproduction is still not as precise as a CRTs making them less suitable for graphic designers who need consistent and accurate colour reproduction. The price of LCDs has fallen to the point that they make up the majority of monitors supplied with PCs.

Thin Film Transistor (TFT) technology is an improvement over earlier generations of LCD that and better image quality. Early LCD displays are often difficult to read from a distance or a sharp angle. TFT addresses this problem, making them particularly suitable for televisions and public displays.

Data Projectors

A data projector is used to display output on a large screen. They are used where a standard monitor would not be large enough, for example for presentations to a group of people, or to create a *home cinema* experience. The data projector is connected directly to the computer via the computer's video output port. A remote control can be used to control focus and image size.

There are two types of projector technology. **LCD projectors** use a high intensity bulb to illuminate a transparent LCD panel. A lens is used to project the LCD's image onto a screen. **Digital Light Processing (DLP) projectors** use a panel covered with tiny mirrors to create the images to be projected. This system produces greater contrast and deeper blacks than LCD projectors and can be seen clearly without dimming the lights in a room, unlike LCD projectors.

A limitation of data projectors is that the bulbs are expensive and have a limited life span and the fans that cool the bulbs can be noisy.

Interactive Whiteboards

These devices are versatile presentation tools which are touch sensitive and can be connected to a data projector and computer. The display from the computer monitor is projected onto the whiteboard but instead of controlling the computer through a mouse, the user can control the cursor, and hence different application programs, by touching the sensitive screen with a special **magnetic pen**. The whiteboard has a number of electrical circuits behind its surface which are affected by the pen's magnetic field, and can determine its position.

Using special software a user can draw virtual 'ink' on the screen. This is particularly useful in a school setting where teachers can use the whiteboard as an electronic flip chart and save complicated diagrams or mathematical derivations for future reuse or printing. Handwriting recognition software is often included so that users can enter text using the magnetic pen.

3.4 Sound Output

Sound can be produced by most home computers and is used in many ways, for example in games, multi-media presentations and as 'alert' noises. A PC needs a **sound card** to convert digital sound data into analogue electrical signals that can be sent to speakers.

Speech synthesis software can be used to convert text into speech. Such a system contains a database of words and their sounds, which are retrieved when a word is to be spoken. Sometimes, however, unknown words are encountered. These may be broken up into a number of syllables and each syllable is then played separately.

While the speech output may sound monotonous, some systems attempt to add 'stress' to syllables, to try to sound as close to human speech as possible. For example, such a system would break the word *Ananova* into syllables and pronounce *an-a-no-va*, but if given different dictionaries or training it may pronounce *AN-a-no-va* or *an-a-NO-va*, depending on the accent of the human trainer.

Speech synthesis has a wide range of uses beyond home PCs, for example:

+ Automated telephone systems present a range of options to users via synthesised speech ("press 1 to do this, press 2 to do that").
+ Directory enquiry services often use synthesised speech to read numbers to customers.
+ Providing an audible warning for car drivers, such as "Seat belt not on" or "Fuel levels low" or for pilots, such as "Pull up".
+ As a substitute for speech in the case of some handicapped people – famously Professor Stephen Hawking.

NASA

Figure 3.7: Professor Stephen Hawking

3.5 Output Between Electronic Devices

Computers often send data to, or receive data from other devices. Traditionally, some sort of copper cable is used but today there are many alternatives such as fibre-optics, infra-red signals and radio. Many of these are used in computer networking and are discussed in more detail elsewhere in this book.

Methods of transmission between electronic devices include:

+ A single copper cable, used in **serial transmission**, transfers a single **bit** at a time. Serial transmission is usually used when transmitting data over long distances because bytes will arrive in the same order as they are sent.

+ Several copper cables running together can be used for **parallel transmission**. This is used to send one byte at a time over a short distance. Because data bits can become unsynchronised when cables go round corners (see *By the way...* overleaf), parallel transmission is not suitable over long distances. Parallel transmission is often used to connect printers to PCs.

+ Due to their cost, **fibre-optic transmission** is only practical in applications where large volumes of data are transmitted over large distances. Many Wide Area Networks rely on this technology because it is capable of handling a much greater volume of data than other methods.

+ **Infra-red transmission** has been used for many years for television remote controls, but it is increasingly popular for connecting peripherals, for example connecting palm-top computers to keyboards.

+ **Radio signals** are also growing in popularity for short-range transmission. A popular use is in communicating between devices in warehouses, where a lot of movement takes place and wired transmission facilities can be impractical. Radio is also a popular way up setting up 'wireless' Local Area Networks in many businesses and homes. The major drawback of radio over any other transmission media, is security. Unless precautions are taken (for example, encryption), any device within a reasonable distance could potentially receive and decode transmissions.

3.6 Other Output Devices

There are many other output devices apart from those detailed above. The student should take time to research the many other ways in which computers can produce output data, including:

+ **Light Emitting Diode (LED)** which are used, for example, on petrol gauges to tell the driver they are about to run out of fuel, or many devices to indicate that a mains electricity supply is connected.

+ **Dot-matrix screens** used, for example, in railway stations to announce departures or on motorways to provide information to drivers via overhead displays.

+ **Braille** output devices, used by visually impaired computer users. They convert text to Braille by raising or lowering a series of pins which the user can read by touching them with their fingers.

By the way...

Serial v Parallel transmission

Consider the serial cable in figure 3.8. Data arrives in the order it was sent, regardless of the length of cable.

1 0 0 1 0 1 1 1 ————————————— 1 0 0 1 0 1 1 1

Figure 3.8 (above): Data in a serial cable arrives in the order in which it was sent.

Figure 3.9:

Top: Data in a parallel cable also arrives in the order in which it was sent, provided the cable is straight.

Bottom: If the cable is not straight, then over time the data becomes skewed.

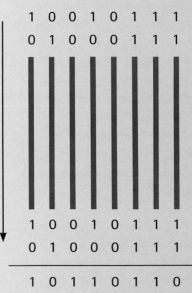

If data is sent in parallel and the cables remain straight, data likewise stays in order because data in each cable travels at the same speed as shown in figure 3.9 (top).

If the cables are not straight, then over time the data will become skewed. Like athletes running around a bend, the athlete in the outside lane has a far greater distance to travel than the athlete in the inside lane. Hence data arriving with the receiver is corrupted as shown in figure 3.9 (bottom) because bits from one byte get mixed up with the previous or next byte. In this example all data following the inside line has arrived before the outside line has delivered anything.

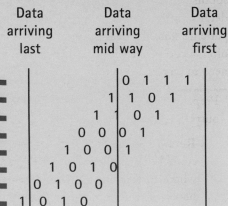

3.7 Applications of Output Devices

As with input devices, thought must be given when choosing an output device to ensure that it is capable of doing the job required, yet is not inappropriately complex for the standard actually required.

In **retail** settings, thought is often given to the quality that is really required of the output. For example, receipts can be printed on low-cost dot-matrix or thermal printers may be used for receipts because it will only read a few times and does need to be either durable or attractive to look at. Similarly, labels used to record the weights of bagged goods (such as delicatessen produce) can be cheap and printed on low-cost labels since they will only be needed for the few minutes until the customer pays. These printers use so little ink that they will run for long periods without running out.

In **manufacturing** settings a similar approach may be taken. However, in these harsher environments it may be necessary to use thicker or more durable paper to prevent data loss. **Actuators** are used to carry out tasks automatically in response to computer output, for example by opening the ventilators in a factory whenever the temperature reaches a certain level.

In **banking**, many ATM machines use monochrome CRT screens for displaying information. Such screens become burnt with a bank's logo because this image is often displayed statically for hours at a time and as a result, modern ATMs use cheap flat-screen displays, as well as screen-savers. Because they can be subjected to temperatures well below freezing, and may be attacked by vandals, these screens have to be designed to be much more durable than the screens used on a typical laptop computer.

In **health**, ultra-sound scanners are used to examine inside limbs and joints without an invasive procedure. Obviously it is essential that the medical practitioner can see the results of these scan. Because the data has no associated colour, they are usually attached to a monochrome VDU and fairly basic printer, since no more sophisticated output is possible from these devices. GPs use PCs to record patient details and a high quality laser printer for formal letters, which may be kept in patient's notes for many years. On the other hand, cheap dot matrix printers are often a good choice for prescriptions since they are only used for a short time and need to be printed quickly in batches.

Task

Prepare a presentation or word-processed report describing the input AND output devices used in the applications below. A few suggestions are given.

+ **Retail.** How is data input at tills? How is it output? What sort of devices could be used to scan cards where wires are impractical – eg in a restaurant where customers have full table-service? How do you avoid long queues for people purchasing lottery tickets?

+ **Manufacturing.** As a product moves through a factory, how can its progress be tracked? If a company wanted to transmit an order, how could a paper-based form be used?

continued overleaf...

Task

+ **Banking.** A wide variety of card and printed input and output is used here, all of which are described above. How are cheques printed in banks, and how can they be input quickly?

+ **Health.** How can staff monitor and record heart rate, temperature, etc? How might an automated system deliver medicine at a controlled rate, once a nurse has inserted a line into a patient's arm? What sort of input devices allow a brain or stomach to be examined without surgery?

+ **Education.** What sort of input devices can be used for the daily registration of students? What methods can be used if a teacher does not have immediate access to a PC? What new technologies are used in the classroom alongside blackboards and photocopiers? If a teacher wants to compile an examination paper without photocopying parts of past-papers or re-typing them, what can be done?

Questions

1. Copy and complete the following table:

Type of Printer	How it works	Advantages	Disadvantages	Example use
Dot Matrix	(3)	(2)	(2)	(1)
Ink Jet	(3)	(2)	(2)	(1)
Laser	(3)	(2)	(2)	(1)
Plotter	(3)	(2)	(2)	(1)

2. How does a cathode ray tube build up a colour image? (3)
3. How does a liquid crystal display build up a colour image? (3)
4. Describe two advantages of an LCD display when compared to a CRT display. (4)
5. Describe the operation of an interactive whiteboard. (3)
6. Describe the production of speech output. (3)
7. Describe how output is produced using a data projector. (4)
8. State and describe three methods of transmitting data between devices with an advantage and disadvantage of each. (4 each)

CHAPTER 4
Hardware: Storage Devices

4.1 Introduction

Storage devices are a vital component of any information system and can be broken into two main categories:

Internal memory: holds application programs that are running and data in use.

External memory (or **backing store**): holds data and programs permanently for future use, without the need of a power supply.

Definition

While **internal memory** is chiefly associated with the CPU (see Chapter 5), it is discussed here to compare and contrast it with backing store, and hence develop an appreciation of the need for external memory.

4.2 Internal Memory

Internal memory holds all programs and data that are currently in use, and is thus sometimes called **working memory**. It is needed because a processor chip cannot directly access data held in backing store. The two main types of internal memory found on a PC are **Random Access Memory** and **Read Only Memory**.

Random Access Memory (RAM)

RAM holds components of the operating system in use as well as application programs and data. It is said to be **volatile** because its contents can be changed and are lost when power is removed from the system. Hence data must be transferred to backing store after use, otherwise it will be lost. Increasing the amount of RAM can often drastically improve a PC's performance. This allows more data to be held in RAM and hence reduces the time spent moving data between RAM and backing store (see Chapter 5).

Read Only Memory (ROM)

ROM is non-volatile, ie its contents may be read but cannot be changed. ROM is a suitable storage medium for any application that never requires programs to be altered or where the time required to transfer programs and data from backing store to main memory is not acceptable. One common use of ROM is storing the instructions needed for loading the operating system from backing store into RAM when a PC first starts up (the **Basic Input Output System** or **BIOS**). It is also used for storing programs in an **embedded system**, such as the control program for a washing machine or microwave oven. The only way to change a program in ROM is to replace the ROM chip. In many systems, this is not practical and hence alternatives such as **EPROM** may be used (see below).

As well as RAM, there are two other types of **volatile** internal memory.

 * **Cache** is a small and expensive, but very fast, memory holding recently or frequently accessed data. Its cost prevents it being used for all RAM.
 * **Complimentary Metal Oxide Semiconductor** (**CMOS**, pronounced see-MOS) is a volatile medium used to store date and time information, as well as setup information on a PC. CMOS uses a re-chargeable battery to preserve its data after mains power is switched off.

By the way... Basic Input-Output System (**BIOS** pronounced Bye-Oss) – built-in software that controls the most basic operations of a computer such as the keyboard, screen and disk drives. Its main task is to find, load and execute the operating system which is usually stored on the computer's hard disk. The BIOS is stored on a ROM chip that comes with the computer, to ensure it cannot be damaged by disk failures, although some modern computers use a flash memory chip which can be updated.

Other than ROM, there are three other types of **non-volatile** internal memory.

 * **PROM – Programmable Read-Only Memory** manufactured blank and programmed once at a later stage, after which it becomes ROM. PROM is used for applications where the mass-manufacture of ROM is not practical, such as research and development work.
 * **EPROM – Erasable Programmable Read Only Memory** is similar to PROM but can be erased and reprogrammed when removed from the device. When operational inside a device, EPROM functions like ROM storage.
 * **EEPROM – Electrically Erasable Programmable Read Only Memory** functions in a similar way to EPROM, except that a special electrical signal can erase the contents while it is still within the device. EEPROM is sometimes pronounced as "E-squared PROM" to avoid confusion with EPROM`.

Although the content of ROM is intended to be permanent, EPROM and EEPROM allow it to be changed in a limited way. This is important in applications where the benefits of ROM are needed, but where it is possible that the contents of ROM may have to change in the future. One example is in telephone exchange equipment, which uses ROM that often has to be re-programmed remotely. This can be achieved with EEPROM, saving both money and time. Other examples include computers in cars and mobile phones, which can be upgraded or moved to

By the way... **Wait a minute – if the contents of RAM is lost when the power is switched off, how come my word-processed document re-appeared even though there was a power cut and I hadn't saved it?** Be thankful for modern applications! Only a few years ago if a user forgot to save their work and there was a power cut, everything would have been lost because the document was held in RAM. Today a modern application can automatically save data to backing store at set intervals, if this option is activated. This does not do away with the good practice of purposely saving your work at intervals.

a different network by the same method. **Flash** memory, used with **USB memory sticks** (or **pen drives**) and in mobile phones is a high-speed variation of EEPROM that writes several bytes of memory simultaneously. Conventional EEPROM only writes one byte at a time.

By the way...

The use of RAM and ROM in a typical PC

When a PC is first switched on, its RAM is blank. None of the programs it needs, including the operating system are loaded. Therefore a **boot sequence** is followed.

1. Power is turned on.

2. The BIOS program is automatically copied from ROM to RAM.

3. BIOS scans disk drives to search for an **operating system**, such as Microsoft *Windows* or *Linux*. The floppy disk or CD drives are searched before the hard disk to allow the user to bypass any pre-installed operating system if desired.

4. Once an operating system is found, it is copied into RAM.

5. Once it is in RAM, it is executed and control of the PC is given to the operating system.

6. The operating system will then load a number of **utilities**, such as anti-virus software and communications software.

7. Once boot-up is complete, the user can launch application programs, eg a word processor, which are copied from the backing store into RAM and then executed. Any user data, eg a document, is also copied from backing store into RAM as necessary.

8. Any files the user creates or modifies must be copied from RAM to backing store so that they are not erased when the system is re-started.

4.3 External Memory (Backing Store)

External memory holds data and programs permanently for future use, without need of a power supply. Typical uses include:

+ Storing a copy of systems software and various applications programs on a PC's hard-disk.

+ Storing users' data between work periods.

+ Storing backup copies of the data held on a PC's hard disk in case of failure.

+ In the distribution of software, which is normally via CD-ROM or DVD.

The choice of external device depends on a number of factors that determine how suitable it is for an application. These factors include:

+ **Capacity**. While a 3½ inch floppy disk was highly suitable for distributing software in the 1980s today many applications would require hundreds of such disks to store them.

- **Portability**. For example, if a user wants to transfer a document between PCs a USB memory stick may be the best choice.
- **Whether it can be over-written**. For example, if a student wants a permanent record of their work, a CD-R may be a good choice since it cannot be written over by accident.
- **Compatibility with other machines.** Sharing data with users of older PCs is difficult with new types of storage media, such as DVDs. Hence older media such as floppy disks are still sometimes an appropriate choice.
- **Robustness.** A student, for example, should consider whether a portable computer is an appropriate device to store in their school bag.

The most common types of backing store media are **magnetic media** (tape and disk), **USB Flash** and **optical media**.

Magnetic Tape

This has a similar structure to a VHS video tape but has enormous capacity, often reaching 800 gigabytes. Data is copied to tape **sequentially** by playing it from the start. Magnetic tape has a very low cost per unit of storage and is compact making is very suitable as a **backup** medium. Some enterprises use one or more **tape drives** (or **tape streamers**) in a single unit to copy the entire contents of servers' hard disks at regular intervals, and can build up thousands of terabytes of data on tapes. The key disadvantage is that searching for files can be time-consuming since the tape must be played from the start until the desired file is found.

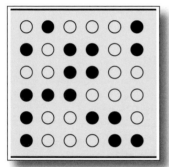

Figure 4.1: Data is stored on magnetic tape as a series of north/south (shown as black/white) polarised spots.

Magnetic Disk

As with tape, binary data is represented as polarised spots of magnetic data. However a disk is circular, so the spots form concentric circles called **tracks**. Regions of the disk are split into **sectors**. A **read-write head** is used to detect the 0s and 1s on the surface of a magnetic disk. When the disk is formatted, the operating system numbers the sectors and tracks and creates an index (effectively a map of the disk) so that they can be located and allocated to individual files.

Figure 4.2: Tracks and sectors on a hypothetical magnetic disk.

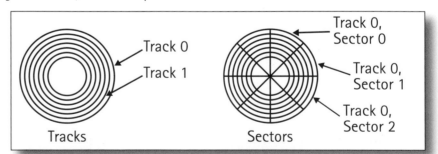

One type of magnetic disk is the floppy disk which is a flimsy disk of magnetic material housed inside a plastic case. When inserted into a disk drive, the protective flap on the case is pulled to the side by the disk-drive to allow a read/write head to access the disk. Although the case and flap exist to provide protection to the fragile disk within, floppy disks are quite fragile unless carefully handled. The 3½ inch **high density** floppy disk is re-writable but can be write-protected and has a formatted capacity of 1.44MB. A floppy disk does not continually rotate within the disk drive, so the disk has to speed up to operating speed before data can be read off or written to the disk. They are no longer widely used with modern PCs as they have too little capacity and a data transfer speed which is too slow for most users. Applications of a floppy disk include backing up small files or transferring them from one computer to another.

A number of improvements to floppy disk technology appeared in the 1990s, now largely eclipsed by USB memory sticks. These included Zip disks with 100, 250 and 750MB capacities and Jaz disks with a storage capacity of up to 4GB. Both of these required a different drive from the normal floppy disk drive.

Hard Disk

The purpose of a hard disk is to permanently store

+ the operating system
+ applications programs
+ the majority of a users' data files.

Figure 4.3: A typical hard disk, here seen removed from the PC it would normally be attached to.

Hard disks are usually fixed inside a PC and have a sealed, rigid case containing a number of disks (**platters**) on a spindle (see figure 4.4). As with floppy disks, each disk surface is divided into tracks and sectors. Tracks that are above each other on different platters are called **cylinders**. A series of read-write heads move across the platters simultaneously. When a file is larger than the capacity of a single track, the operating system will store it in tracks within the same cylinder, rather than spreading it across tracks on the same platter, in order to reduce movement of the read-write heads, thereby minimizing access time. Unlike a floppy disk or optical disk no time is wasted waiting for disks to reach operating speed since the disks rotate continuously.

Figure 4.4: The structure of a hard disk.

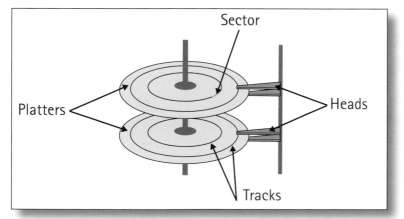

To access data, the read/write head first moves to select the correct platter and track. As the disk rotates the correct sector will pass under the read-write head and the data can then be read or written.

Hard disks do not have to be inside a PC. Portable hard drives are increasingly popular and are particularly useful for backup purposes. Hard disks have the fastest data transfer speeds of all backing store devices and offer a large storage capacity.

Hard disks provide a cost-effective form of read/write memory. While the capacity of hard disks continues to increase dramatically the cost per unit storage continues to drop. For example, in mid 2007 a new hard disk with a capacity of 80GB was cheaper than a 2GB disk sold in 1997. One disadvantage is that the failure of a hard disk will stop a PC from functioning and data may not be recoverable.

Task

Examine the figures below which show the average size and cost per gigabyte of hard disks from 1996 to 2006. What does this tell us about the development of ICT? Why did users in 2006 find that they still ran out of disk space as easily as they did in 1996? *(Figures 1996-2004 from IDC. 2006 Colourpoint.)*

	Average Hard Disk Size	Cost per gigabyte
1996	600MB	£76
1998	4GB	£16
2000	10GB	£2.97
2002	40GB	£0.90
2004	80GB	£0.43
2006	250GB	£0.24

4.4 USB Backing Store Devices

A **memory stick** (also referred to as a **'pen drive'**) is a small device, typically a few centimetres long, that holds a large amount of memory. The largest drives available in 2007 had a capacity of 16GB. Once inserted into the USB port of a PC the data can be accessed by the user in much the same way as data on any other removable media, such as a CD-ROM. Most modern operating systems allow immediate use of USB memory sticks without the need to install drivers, although drivers are required on older systems such as Windows 98.

Memory sticks use **flash memory**, which is a type of EEPROM. This is the same technology that allows hardware such as digital cameras to store pictures when the power is turned off. Unlike magnetic or optical disks, flash memory has no moving parts and is therefore quite robust. It can be used to store data files, programs etc, and can be write-protected to prevent data being accidentally deleted.

Despite providing a cheap and robust portable storage medium, USB memory devices can fail if they are not used properly. For example if they are unplugged while data is being written they can short-circuit and have their contents erased.

4.5 Optical Storage

Optical storage disks are made up a series of tiny pits arranged in a spiral pattern that radiates out from the centre of the disk towards the edge. Data is read by spinning the disk and shining a fixed-position laser at it. The light is reflected in a different way if it hits a smooth part than if it hits a pitted part of the disk (figure 4.5) . In this way, the difference between a 1 and a 0 can be discerned.

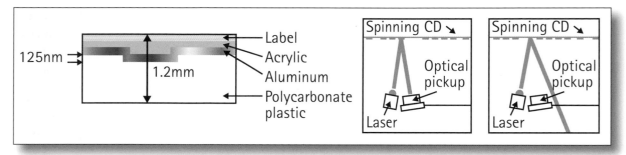

Figure 4.5: Cross-section of an optical disk (left) and how a laser is reflected.

There are a number of types of optical disk:

+ **CD-ROM** disks ("Compact Disk, Read-Only Memory") have been used to distribute music since the early 1980s and have since become a popular storage media for computer data. CD-ROMs are portable, have a high capacity (720MB) but must be treated with care as they can scratch easily and can't be modified.

+ A **CD-R** disk ("Compact Disk, Recordable") is like a CD-ROM except that it can be written to once only. It is popular with PC users as a backup medium, and for distributors of low-volume software who cannot justify using expensive CD manufacturing facilities. A CD-R disk is written by using a laser set to a higher-than-normal power and is an example of **Write Once, Read Many (WORM)** storage.

+ A **CR-RW** disk ("Compact Disk, Re-Writable") contains a middle layer that can be written to, erased, and re-written as many times as the user desires. CD-RW is practical for backing up files or for transporting files between PCs. CD-RWs are not practical for music CDs as their structure, which varies slightly from CD-ROM and CD-R, cannot be read by many older CD music players.

+ **DVD-ROM** disks ("Digital Versatile Disk, Read-Only Memory") use similar, but more advanced, technology than a CD-ROM, allowing them to store 4.7GB while a double-layered DVD surface can store 8.5GB, and a double-layered double-sided DVD can store 17GB.

+ **DVD-R** ("DVD-Recordable") and **DVD-RW** ("DVD-Re-Writable") disks follow a similar principle to CD-R and CD-RW, with a capacity of 3.9GB and 2.6GB respectively. DVD is popular as a distribution medium for movies because its capacity allows room for extra material, alternative soundtracks etc, and because it does not deteriorate in the way VHS tapes do. DVD recorders for home televisions are popular. DVD is also popular for distributing large pieces of software, such as encyclopedias that contain large quantities of video and images. DVD-RW drives are supplied with new PCs as standard. With the size of hard disks growing along with the amount of data users now have, DVD-R have replaced CD-R as the backup medium preferred by PC owners.

+ **High Definition** disks offer further increases in capacity, with particular benefits in improving the resolution of recorded films or in games, although improved televisions that support the technology are needed before users can benefit from this. The standard in this area is the **Blu-ray disc**. A rival to

Blu-ray, **HD DVD**, had a maximum capacity of 30GB but did not gain wide support from publishers or consumers and was withdrawn in 2008. Blu-ray systems are so-called because they use a blue laser whereas conventional DVDs and CDs use red. Blue light's shorter wavelength makes it possible to store more information (54GB when using two layers within the disk, enough for 9 hours of high definition video or 23 hours of standard video). Blu-ray disks with capacities of 100GB and 200GB are currently being researched, with these capacities achieved by using four and eight layers respectively. In comparison to DVD, Blu-ray discs offer improved interactivity, such as more options for moving between scenes or versions of a film. Users can also connect to the Internet to download subtitles and other 'interactive' movie features. As with CDs and DVDs, a wide range of formats (such as ROM/R/RW) have been developed. Blu-ray players are backwards-compatible with DVD and CD disks. The following formats are part of the Blu-ray disc specification:

+ BD-ROM: read-only format for software, games and movie distribution.

+ BD-R: recordable format for High Definition Television (HDTV) recording and PC data storage.

+ BD-RE: re-writable format for HDTV recording and PC data storage.

Questions

1. What is the difference between RAM and ROM? (2)
2. State how a computer may use ROM, justifying your choice. (2)
3. Describe EEPROM, stating a use for it in modern electronic devices. (2)
4. What is the purpose of internal memory? (2)
5. What is the purpose of external memory? (2)
6. State an advantage, a disadvantage and an application for each of:
   (i) Hard disk (ii) Magnetic tape (iii) USB (iv) DVD (v) Blu-ray disc. (15)
7. Describe how data is recorded and read by a DVD. (3)
8. Describe how data is recorded and read by a hard disk drive. (3)
9. Name and describe three generations of optical disk, stating their capacity and comparing their uses. [12]

CHAPTER 5
Hardware: Central Processing Unit

5.1 Introduction

The Central Processing Unit, or **CPU**, is the most important piece of hardware in any computer system. It controls all input and output and performs all calculations.

The CPU has three main components:

+ **Control Unit (CU)**, which controls other hardware devices and software. The CU performs the **Fetch-Decode-Execute cycle**;

+ **Arithmetic and Logic Unit (ALU)**, which performs calculations, comparisons of values and Boolean (true and false) operations;

+ **Immediate Access Store (IAS)**, which holds data and programs currently in use.

On some devices the components of a CPU may be housed inside a single chip, while in other devices the CPU may actually be made of separate components. For example, in a PC a single chip usually houses the CU and the ALU while the IAS consists of a number of RAM chips. The CU/ALU functions are combined on commercial products, such as Intel's *Pentium* processors and AMD's *Athlon* processors. The relationship between the components of the CPU and other devices is shown in figure 5.1.

Figure 5.1: The components of the CPU in relation to other devices. Arrows represent the flow of data. Dotted lines represent control signals sent between the CU and other devices.

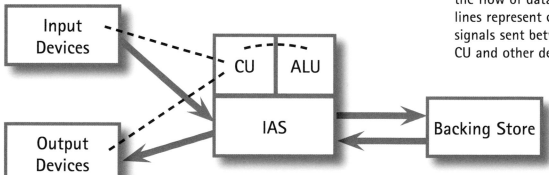

5.2 The Fetch–Decode–Execute Cycle

The Fetch-Decode-Execute Cycle describes the operation of the CPU when it is executing (running) a program. A program is made up of many instructions that are sequentially fetched, decoded and then executed. This process is sometimes simply known as the Fetch-Execute Cycle.

Although most users are unaware of it, all programs, from word processors to games, are made up of a series of simple instructions called **machine code** that must be followed in order for the program to work. Because the instructions are stored as a series of numbers (each representing a different instruction like 'add' or 'store') humans are only able to write the very simplest of programs in this form. Therefore, programmers write the **source code** of programs in either text-based **third generation languages** such as *C* or *Java*, or a diagrammatic **visual programming language** such as *Dephi* or *Visual Basic*. In either case, it is ultimately translated into machine code, the format that the CPU can understand. On a Microsoft *Windows* PC, these are often referred to as **.exe** files because of the file extension they use. The equivalent in *MacOS* is **.app**.

When a program is executed, the machine code is copied into the computer's internal memory. Each instruction is placed at a different location (**address**) which is uniquely numbered. For example the first instruction of a program may be at memory address 1000, the second at 1001, and so on. Care must be taken by programmers to ensure no two programs try to use the same portion of memory. If they do the program or even the entire computer may 'crash'.

The process of executing the series of instructions that make up a program is known as the **Fetch-Decode-Execute Cycle** which breaks into three main phases:

+ **Fetch** – an instruction is copied from memory into the **control unit**;
+ **Decode** – the meaning of the instruction is determined;
+ **Execute** – the appropriate action is taken or calculation performed.

This cycle is repeated for each instruction. To carry out this cycle, the control unit contains a number of extremely fast memory stores called **registers**. Some of these include the:

+ **program counter**, recording the address of the next instruction to be executed;
+ **current instruction register**, which holds a copy of the instruction being decoded or executed at that point in time;
+ **memory address register**, which records the source address of data to be transferred in from memory, or the destination address of data to be transferred out;
+ **memory data register**, which stores data that is to be copied to memory or has just been copied from memory.

Example of the Fetch–Decode–Execute Cycle in Action

Consider a computer whose memory contains the following items:

Address	Contents	Meaning of contents
5	0000 1111	The number 15
6	0000 1001	The number 9
7	0100 0001	The number 65
1003	0110 0111	Load contents of memory location 7
1004	0110 0101	Add contents of memory location 5
1005	1001 1000	Copy data to memory location 8

We will now consider what happens as the computer executes the program using the Fetch-Decode-Execute Cycle. The PC cannot tell whether a particular piece of data in memory is just data or actual program code, so it is initially pointed to address 1003 by the operating system and commences execution here.

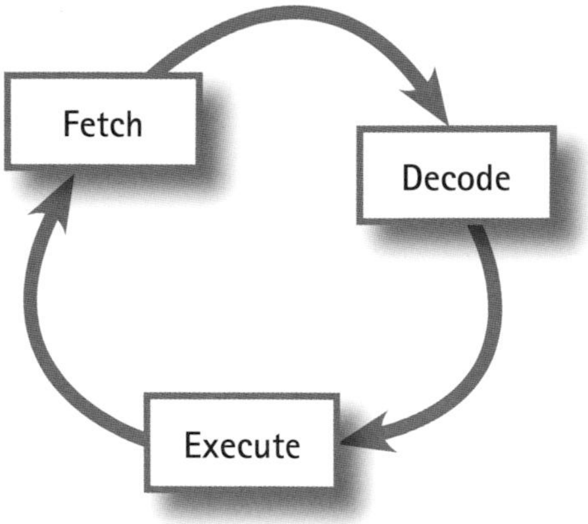

Figure 5.2: The Fetch-Decode-Execute Cycle.

Fetch

1. The program counter is initially 1003, so we need the instruction at this address.

2. The memory address register is set to 1003 by copying the value from the program counter.

3. The contents of memory address 1003 is fetched and placed in the memory data register.

4. This is then copied to the current instruction register.

5. The program counter is incremented by one.

After what may appear to be quite a long-winded process, the instruction is now ready to be decoded and executed.

Decode

1. The purpose of the contents of the current instruction register is decoded. It means 'bring in contents of memory location 7'.

2. Therefore, the memory address register is set to '7' ready to get that piece of memory.

Execute

1. The contents of the address pointed to by the memory address 7 is fetched and placed in the memory data register.

2. The memory data register now contains the number 65.

This Fetch-Decode-Execute Cycle is repeated *ad infinitum*. The next instruction will be interpreted as adding a second number to the first one and then the next instruction will copy the result to a new location in memory. All mathematical operations are performed by the **arithmetic and logic unit** (see below). Note that the CPU executes the instructions as it finds them, regardless of whether they make sense or not. Even one mistake by the programmer can result in data being stored in the wrong place, data being deleted or nonsensical instructions being carried out.

Task

Continue writing out the Fetch-Decode-Execute cycle for the next two instructions in the program.

Demonstrate by this method that the contents of memory address 8 at the end of the process will be 80.

This process will repeat until the program reaches an instruction that means 'stop', or if the operating system halts the program. If the power remains available, no programs crash, and nobody halts the program, this Fetch-Decode-Execute Cycle will continue for ever.

5.3 The Arithmetic And Logic Unit

The Arithmetic and Logic Unit (ALU) performs three types of operation:

Calculations

Mathematical operations such as addition or multiplication.

Logical Comparisons

The ALU can compare data items such as numbers, letters, or special characters to see if they meet a particular condition. The ALU can compare two values to determine:

- if they are equal,
- if one value is less than another,
- if one value is greater than another.

This is useful when a piece of code is to be executed if only a certain condition is met, for example:

IF A > B THEN do X
ELSE do Y

Logical Functions

These are based on **Boolean** algebra. Boolean algebra is used to compare numbers that can only be 1 or 0, which are usually used to mean 'true' and 'false'. There are three **basic** types of Boolean function:

- The OR function states: "if any of the input values are 1, the output is 1; otherwise the output is 0."
- The AND function states: "if both input values are 1, the output is 1; otherwise the output is 0."
- The NOT function uses a single input and states: "the output value is the opposite of the input value."

5.4 The Immediate Access Store

Immediate Access Store (IAS) is often referred to as **Random Access Memory** (**RAM**), which is the technology chiefly associate with it. This name reflects the fact that data can be read from anywhere in IAS without going through all memory addresses in sequence. IAS has two functions:

- To temporarily store programs (instructions) currently being executed by the CPU. These include both active application programs and parts of the PC's operating system.
- To temporarily store data that is either currently being processed by the CPU, that has just been input and is awaiting processing, or has just been processed and is waiting to be output.

Data and programs are preserved on backing store when they are not being used or when the computer is off. However, it is not possible to run programs or process data unless they are in IAS. Therefore, all program instructions and data that the CPU is working with have to be copied to main memory initially.

Because each instruction is brought into the CU, then sent out to IAS after executing each instruction, a lot of processing time can be saved if frequently-used data is held in a faster type of IAS known as **cache memory**. For example, a user's instant messaging client or e-mail client may reside in 'ordinary' RAM while the kernel of the operating system and the GUI may be stored in cache memory. Although it would seem like a good idea to use cache instead of RAM, due to the speed diffrence, this is impractical since cache is much more expensive to manufacture than conventional RAM.

Read-only memory (ROM) is used to store the BIOS. ROM is not volatile, which makes it suitable for storing bootup instructions (used when the computer first starts up). ROM and cache are both described in more detail in section 4.2.

Questions

1. Name the three main components of the CPU and describe their purposes. (9)
2. Describe the Fetch-Decode-Execute cycle. (3)
3. Name and describe three components of the Control Unit. (6)
4. Name and describe three functions of the Arithmetic and Logic Unit. (6)
5. What does Immediate Access Store do? (2)

CHAPTER 6
Software: System Software

6.1 Introduction

Software is the name given to the programs, or sets of instructions that are carried out by hardware. There are two main types of software that you should have experience of and be able to understand:

1. **System software** (this chapter)
2. **Application software** (in the next chapter)

Note: As well as studying the theoretical material in this section, readers should gain practical experience in the use of a wide range of software packages and become familiar with the advanced features of a PC's operating system. A range of excellent tutorials are available in the form of books and web-based resources.

Definition

Systems Software refers to programs that enable the computer to function effectively, to interact with the user, to communicate with hardware and to manage the demands made upon hardware by applications software.

Systems software can be further broken down into:

- **Operating systems** to control the hardware and co-ordinate other systems software as well as manage applications software.
- **Utility programs** to perform often repeated tasks: for example anti-virus software and **drivers** to manage hardware devices.
- **Library programs*** to perform tasks needed by several other pieces of software: for example a spreadsheet, word processor and e-mail client which all share program code in the same **Dynamic Link Library**.
- **Translators*** that convert programs written by the user into executable form understood by the operating system and hardware .

*While included here for completeness, these were not part of the CCEA specification at the time of writing.

6.2 The Operating System

Definition

The **operating system,** or **OS**, is a program. It is essential for a computer to operate. It performs four main functions:

- It controls and coordinates the operation of hardware.
- It provides a platform for application software to run on.
- It organises files on disk.
- It provides a user-interface to enable the user to run applications software, save files, communicate with peripherals etc.

A component of the operating system known as the **kernel** must be held in the computer's working memory (also known as **immediate access store**) at all times. The kernel is responsible for managing the computer's resources (the CPU, main memory, storage devices, input/output devices and communication devices). Other components of the operating system are loaded into memory as they are required Common operating systems include Microsoft *Windows*, *Linux* and *MacOS*.

Common Operating Systems

By the way...

+ **Disk Operating System (DOS)** was a **command-line** operating system popular on IBM-compatible PCs until the mid 1990s. Microsoft originally produced *Windows* as a **graphical user interface** (**GUI**) for their version of *DOS* in 1985 but it did not gain popularity until the 1990s.

+ **Windows 95** replaced *DOS* and used a GUI by default instead of as an add-on. As corrections were made and new features added, *Windows 95* was superseded by versions of *Windows 98* and *Windows ME* ('Millennium edition'). This product range is no longer in development.

+ **Windows NT** ("New Technology") is a totally different product from the *Windows 95* family, despite what the name and similar user interface suggests. Inspired by an earlier OS used on Digital's *Vax* servers (*VMS*), *Windows NT* was designed to be more stable than the *DOS/Windows 95* product line, making it more suitable for commercial use, and particularly on servers. *NT* 5.0 was marketed as *Windows 2000*, *NT 5.1* as *Windows XP* and *NT 6.0* as *Windows Vista*. A number of customised versions of the *Windows NT* product line are available for particular uses, such as *Home Edition*, *Media Centre Edition* and *Windows Server 2008*.

+ **Windows Compact Edition (aka Windows CE and Windows Mobile)** is a much smaller member of the *Windows* family used on hand-held devices. As with *NT/95* it looks similar to other *Windows* products but has a different architecture. *PalmOS* and *SymbianOS* are also popular on hand-held devices like PDAs and mobile phones.

+ **MacOS** was launched in 1984 as a GUI operating system for Apple's *Macintosh* range of computers. Although extremely popular in some niche markets, particularly graphic design, it has never been used on more than 10% of computers. In 2000 *MacOS X* was launched, a completely rewritten and very stable system built around a version of *Unix* called *FreeBSD*.

+ **Unix** is popular on large servers because of its efficiency and stability under heavy workloads. It was originally developed by AT&T in the early 1970s. Users of *Unix* were encouraged to customise it to meet their own needs – if a feature a user wanted was not available they would develop it themselves.

As a result, many different versions of *Unix* now exist including *FreeBSD*, *Sun Solaris* and *HP-UX*.

- **Linux** is a *Unix*-like operating system, originally developed in the early 1990s by Finnish student Linus Torvalds as a hobby. *Linux* became popular with other hobbyists and went on to gain much popularity in commercial applications and in running web servers. *Linux* is also gaining popularity on desktop PCs.

The chart below shows how the usage of some operating systems has changed over time. As can be seen, there have been many changes in the operating systems used with microcomputers, because hardware has developed so rapidly. Note, however, that there has been relatively little change in large systems, because in these applications hardware is often used for several decades. It is not unusual to discover a late 1970s *Vax* system in use today and a large percentage of servers today are still *Unix* or *VMS* based.

*Windows NT and derivatives, such as Windows XP, Windows Vista, Windows Server 2003 and Windows 7

Decade	Large servers	Small–medium servers	Microcomputers (later called PCs)
1970s	Unix, VMS (late 1970s)	VMS, Unix	CP/M, a fore-runner of DOS
1980s	Unix, VMS	VMS, Unix	DOS, MacOS
1990s	Unix, VMS	Unix, Linux, Windows NT	DOS, MS Windows 95/98/ME, MacOS
2000s	Unix, VMS, Linux, Windows NT*	Linux, Windows NT*	Windows NT, Linux, MacOS

6.3 Functions of an Operating System

The OS and Hardware

It is the responsibility of the operating system to manage all the computer's hardware and ensure effective communication between devices. As all hardware is controlled by the CPU, and the CPU can normally do only one task at a time (see Types of Operating Systems, below), the operating system must schedule the CPU's time between various hardware and software components.

Because a computer has many hardware components, often made by different manufacturers, the operating system relies on a **device driver** (a special utility program) to allow it to communicate with each hardware device. The driver will translate messages from the operating system into messages that the hardware device can understand, and vice versa. Device drivers are specific to a particular operating system so if you change from one operating system to another a different set of hardware drivers will be required.

Sometimes the device drivers in common use at the time are supplied with the operating system. However the operating system will not normally understand newer hardware, such as new type of printer built after the operating system was installed. For this reason, the device driver is usually supplied on disk with the hardware, or is downloadable from the manufacturer's web site.

The OS and Other Software

Most modern computers can run several programs at once. As well as the operating system and utility programs, there are the user's own programs such as word processors and spreadsheets. All these programs need to be held in **main memory** to enable the CPU to access it. All programs in memory must be organised in a logical fashion so that they don't conflict with each other. The operating system is responsible for allocating space (in the form of one or more memory **blocks**) in main memory to each program, as needed, and records where various programs and data are held. The operating system ensures no two programs can use the same area of memory or hardware device at once, preventing a **clash** that would corrupt data.

Although the CPU may appear to be processing several tasks at once, it is only ever working on one task at a time. Under the direction of the operating system, the CPU rapidly switches between running processes to give the illusion of performing tasks simultaneously. This is called **multitasking**.

Of course, as programs are loaded into memory it is conceivable that the computer could run out of main memory. The operating system provides a solution to this problem called **virtual memory** (or **virtual RAM**), which is invisible to the user. Under this system, each program is assigned the same amount of memory in a **page**. A program may not need an entire page worth of memory: in this case, the rest of the page is left empty. When there is not enough memory in the system, pages are **swapped** out of main memory when not in use, and moved into virtual memory, an area of the hard disk allocated to this purpose. Other pages are then swapped into the space that was left.

Suppose we have 32MB of RAM and five programs. Under this system, each page is 8MB in size. When programs A, B, C and D are loaded, each is given an 8MB page which is stored in main memory. However, when program E is loaded, there is no memory left. So the page from the **least-recently-used** of the first four programs (say it is program A) is copied out into virtual memory and program E can then use the space cleared. When program A is next needed, it is swapped again with the least-recently-used of the other four programs. This process continues as each program is used, allowing 40MB of virtual memory with only 32MB of actual memory. (A modern PC may have 1024MB of RAM, but dozens of programmes running. Hence RAM runs out and Virtual RAM is still needed.)

Virtual memory is not without its problems. If a lot of programs are running together on a PC, and the user switches between programs, the user may sometimes notice a delay. This is caused by the operating system swapping memory pages to and from virtual memory. This is why adding memory to a PC can improve its performance. **Thrashing** is caused when there is excessive use of virtual memory, and so much time spent transferring data to and from virtual memory that the system effectively comes to a halt.

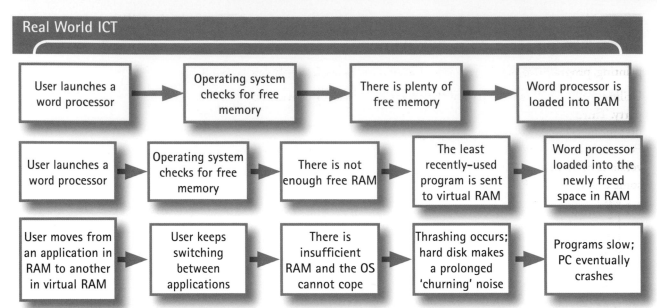

| User launches a word processor | → | Operating system checks for free memory | → | There is plenty of free memory | → | Word processor is loaded into RAM |

| User launches a word processor | → | Operating system checks for free memory | → | There is not enough free RAM | → | The least recently-used program is sent to virtual RAM | → | Word processor loaded into the newly freed space in RAM |

| User moves from an application in RAM to another in virtual RAM | → | User keeps switching between applications | → | There is insufficient RAM and the OS cannot cope | → | Thrashing occurs; hard disk makes a prolonged 'churning' noise | → | Programs slow; PC eventually crashes |

**Figure 6.1 (above):
Three possible scenarios
of memory use in a PC.**

Figure 6.1 shows three possible scenarios of memory use.

The OS and Organising Disk Storage

Like main memory, files stored on disk must be stored in a logical way to allow them to be located at a future date. For this reason, a disk is divided into **partitions**, then **tracks** and finally into a series of uniquely numbered **clusters**. A special database system is used to record which clusters are used to store each file. A single file may not be stored in one location, but may be broken over several locations depending on where there is space. The physical operation of disks was discussed in more detail in Chapter 4.

While the operating system tracks files by their cluster, this bears little resemblance to the user's view of file storage. A user perceives their system as having a number of **drives**, which are broken into **directories** and **sub-directories** (or **folders** and **sub-folders**) as shown in figure 6.2. These are designed purely to help the user to organise files, and does not affect where they are stored on the surface of the disk. So while it may appear to the user that all the files in 'My Documents' on a *Windows*-based PC are held together, in reality they will be stored in various places, catalogued by the File Allocation Table.

Figure 6.2: Windows Explorer is used to view directories.

The OS and the User

An interface is where any two systems meet. Therefore, the **user interface** is where the computer system and human meet. Modern user interfaces are part of the operating system and present an abstract, logical view of the system that is far removed from physical reality. Users send commands via menus, observe programs running in windows and organise files into folders, none of which are anything more than virtual representations generated by the computer to map to the user's way of thinking. User interfaces are discussed in more detail in Chaper 26.

The OS and Utilities

A utility is a program used by an operating system to perform often-repeated tasks. Examples of utility programs are those that list files on disk, programs to manage printing, programs to manage communications and anti-virus software.

Utilities can be provided as part of the operating system or provided by a third party. Third party companies often develop utilities to provide functionality not present in the operating system, although the functionality may be added later. For example, *Windows XP* includes a firewall, a feature not supplied with earlier versions of *Windows* but instead provided by third-party utilities. Figure 6.3 shows some examples of utilities.

(a)

(b)

(c)
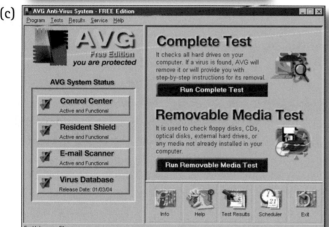

(d)
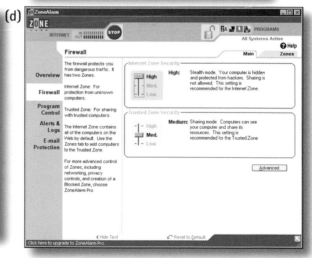

6.4 Multiprogramming, Multi-Tasking and Multi-User OS's

There are many operating systems, and each is suited to a particular task. When a systems analyst recommends a solution to a problem, an operating system is often chosen as part of the solution. The choices usually are:

+ an 'off-the-shelf' operating system, such as Microsoft *Windows*, which does not require modification.

+ an off-the-shelf operating system, such as *Linux*, that allows extensive customisation. For example, the control system of many power stations and the BT *Home Hub* both use modifications of *Linux* that are suited to their needs.

+ a purpose-built operating system, which may be needed for specialist hardware such as VCRs or telephone exchanges.

Figure 6.3: Utilities provided with an OS (Windows XP), (a) Windows Explorer (b) System Tools; and some provided by third parties, (c) AVG Anti-virus and (d) ZoneAlarm firewall utility.

Operating systems are categorised by their capabilities, which may be one or more of the following:

+ single-user, single-task operating systems
+ multi-tasking operating systems
+ multi-user operating systems

Single-User, Single-Task Operating Systems

This is a system that is designed to be used by one person at a time. The operating system is responsible for interacting with one user and will load and run one program at a time. The *PalmOS* for Palm hand held computers is an example of a modern single-user, single-task operating system.

Multi-Tasking Operating Systems

Multi-tasking systems appear to run many tasks simultaneously. Although only one program is actually being executed at any one moment, the processor rapidly switches between tasks via **timeslicing** (see below) to give the impression that many programs are being executed at once. The user can switch between one program and another without having to close the first program down, for example running a query on a database in one window while using a word processor in another window.

Early multi-tasking systems (sometimes known as **multiprogramming** systems) used **co-operative multi-tasking** to move between programs. Each program used the CPU for as long as it needed and would voluntarily give CPU time to other programs when waiting for input or output. However this did not always lead to the most efficient use of CPU time because tasks could be designed to monopolise the CPU.

Modern multi-tasking systems (sometimes called **timeslicing** systems) use **pre-emptive multi-tasking** whereby all programs in use are allocated a regular time slice of CPU time, strictly managed by the OS. Modern single-user PC operating systems, such as Windows *Vista*, use multi-tasking to allow the user to switch between applications. Many multi-user systems adopt the same concept.

In **timeslicing**, a CPU's time is divided into **time-slices**, during each of which it concentrates on a particular task. Since a CPU can perform billions of calculations per second, each time slice is only a tiny fraction of a second in duration. Nevertheless, a piece of hardware that needs to get the urgent attention of the CPU before its next turn can send an **interrupt** signal to override the time sharing.

For example, suppose there are five processes running on a computer (A, B, C, D, E) one of which is the operating system itself. The operating system will schedule each program to give it an appropriate amount of time. For example, if all programs are considered equal they could be processed like this:

Time slice	1	2	3	4	5	6	7
Process	A	B	C	D	E	A	...

At the end of time slice 1, the state of process A is saved in main memory. Process B is then loaded into the CPU from memory, worked on for a period and then it too is saved. Process C is then loaded, and so on.

However, if for some reason process A is considered more important than the rest, it may be given extra time, although all other programs still get a chance to run, like this:

Time slice	1	2	3	4	5	6	7	8	9	10	11	12
Process	A	B	A	C	A	D	A	E	A	B	A	...

The switching between processes happens so fast that the user does not notice and instead perceives several programs running simultaneously.

Multi-User Systems

This type of operating system allows two or more users to communicate with the computer at any one time. Each user interacts with the computer via a **terminal** (which must have, at the minimum, a keyboard and VDU). Each user is given a time slice, during which processing can be carried out. By rotating the CPU's time around the terminals on the system and processing in short bursts, each user has the impression that they are the sole user of the system. However this type of system stops working well when there are too many users on the system – a large workload may make the system noticeably slow for all users.

A common example of a locally-accessed multi-user system is a games console, which can have several players' handsets plugged in at once. However such systems often work by giving the users **remote** access. Two examples of remote access multi-user systems are:

+ An airline's booking system which allows many travel agents to access the central computer simultaneously via remote access.

+ Internet games which allow many people to play different games at the same time, all controlled by a central computer which uses multi-tasking to control the different processes related to each game and multi-programming to run several games at once.

Today, a dumb terminal emulator program can be used on a PC to access a remote machine, often via a **telnet** system where keystrokes are sent to the remote machine and output sent back. The first image in figure 6.4 shows a telnet window on a PC being used to access an Internet chat room . The second image in figure 6.4 shows a draughts game being played from a remote games server. As well as making sure each player sees appropriate output, many games of draughts have to be managed at once, as well as many other games (such as chess, backgammon, etc).

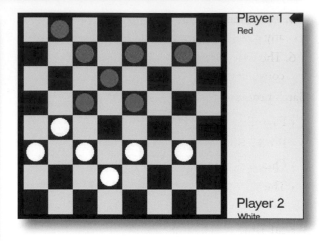

Figure 6.4: Two examples of dumb terminal systems that access a remote computer: a chat room being accessed via telnet (left) and a draughts game being played with a remote user (right).

6.5 Batch Processing and Real Time Transaction Processing

Section 6.4 showed how systems may be categorised according to their modes of operation. It is also possible to categorise systems by the way in which their data is processed.

Batch Processing

In **batch processing**, all input happens together, then all processing together, then all output together. For example an electricity company may collect meter reading OMR forms over a period of days. Then they are scanned at once and then all the bills are calculated and printed.

Each piece of input data, such as a single OMR form, is called a **transaction**. These are collected together to form a **transaction file** which is then processed. Batch processing is very useful for high-volume applications which require the same processing to be performed on every transaction and where an immediate response is not essential. Furthermore, batch processing does not require human intervention once processing has started with the result that data can be processed in an off-peak period making efficient use of computer time and resources. A limitation of batch processing is that as the inputs are gathered over a period of time and then processed at a later date, stored data becomes ever more out of date as time elapses since the last processing run.

The typical steps to creating the transaction file for batch processing are as follows:

1. The input data is collected.
2. The input documents are put into batches and control and hash totals are calculated manually for the batch.
3. The batch of data is keyed in and stored as a transaction file.
4. The batch of data is verified as it is keyed in the data a second time. If any errors are discovered corrections are made.

5. The batch of data is then validated via programmed validation checks. Again, any errors are corrected.

6. The valid data is now held on a transaction file and is ready to be processed at a convenient time.

Batch processing systems are particularly useful for these applications:

+ Payroll;

+ Production of bank and credit card statements at the end of each month;

+ Quarterly production of gas, electricity and telephone bills;

+ The marking of multiple choice examination papers.

Real Time Processing

In **real time processing**, input is processed and acted upon immediately. Real time processing is used in **mission critical** applications where no delay in processing can be tolerated, such as automatic pilot systems, safety systems in cars and control systems in power stations.

Real time transaction processing is similar to batch processing except that the whole input-process-output cycle is completed for each transaction before the next transaction is processed. It differs slightly from pure real time processing in that a delay of up to a few seconds is usually acceptable between the transaction taking place and the files being updated.

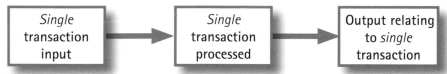

In real time transaction processing, the processing is immediate because it is vital that data files are updated to reflect the current situation so that they can influence future transactions. As a result, the records held are kept accurate and up-to-date and can be queried at any time to retrieve accurate information.

Real time transaction processing systems are used when real time processing is desirable, although not critical. They are particularly useful for these applications:

+ Library systems, where books borrowed are immediately recorded as being unavailable and on-loan to a particular person;

+ Retail systems, where users build up a 'basket' and then go to the 'checkout' option where the availability is confirmed in real-time.

+ Online booking systems, where the user will book several things at once (for example flights, hotel and car).

+ ATM machines where a withdrawal of cash is recorded immediately and the customer's balance is immediately updated to reflect the withdrawal.

Real time transaction systems are suitable for such applications because they provide immediate feedback. For example a person may have booked the last available room in a hotel, so this transaction must be input and processed before the next transaction is input, so that the next person who requests a booking can be told that there are no more rooms available.

Information overload

"Real time? Batch? Dumb terminals? Web browsers? Multi-user? I'm confused. All I want is an on-line retail system that will allow lots of people to browse and buy goods at the one time. And where we don't have the problem of two people being told they have bought an item when there is only one left in stock." Gail at Amoeba's warehouse is confused by all these terms.

Task

Martin, one of Amoeba's sales managers, has asked Gail to outline briefly the requirements for an on-line retail system. He wants her to investigate whether it should be *multi-user*, *batch*, etc. Prepare a report that briefly describes *how* operating systems function, explaining the key terms you have met so far in language that a non-IT specialist can understand. Then list the features that you think should be present in an on-line retail system for Amoeba.

Questions

1. Define systems software. (3)
2. Describe three tasks performed by an operating system. (6)
3. Describe the main features of each of the following operating systems:
   + single user (3)
   + multi-tasking (3)
   + multi-user (3)
   + batch (3)
   + real time (3)
4. State and justify an application for
   (a) a real time system (2)
   (b) a batch processing system (2).
5. Name three different operating systems. (3)

CHAPTER 7
Software: Application Software

7.1 Introduction

Unlike system software which exists only to manage a computer, **application software** is used to perform tasks that the user would want to perform even if there was no computer for them to use, such as writing a letter or presenting a graph. A **generic applications package** is not designed for one specific task, but for a range of functions. For example, a **word processor** can be used for writing letters, designing business cards, editing web pages etc.

The reader should ensure that they have experience using the software described in this chapter. Studying the theory is essential, but is not enough, and the course expects that students will use some of these packages to a high level of competency in modules 2 and 4. In addition, these packages will be encountered by students compiling a **Key Skill ICT** portfolio.

7.2 Generic Software Packages

A wide range of generic software packages are available.

Word Processors

Examples include Microsoft *Word*, Corel *WordPerfect* and *OpenOffice.org Writer*. These are some of the most commonly used applications on PCs. While they began as little more than 'glorified typewriters', many more features have now been added such as:

* inserting and moving text. Unlike a typewritten document, which cannot be modified, word processors allow repeated alterations to be made easily on screen.

* spelling and grammar checking. Users can have their work checked either when they are finished or as they type.

* graphics manipulation. Most allow graphics to be inserted into documents and some have simple graphics editing facilities to allow the user to make minor changes to an image, such as changing it from colour to black and white, or re-sizing it.

Database Management Systems (DBMS)

Examples include *Filemaker* and Microsoft *Access*. A database is a collection of related data. While simple databases can be built using a spreadsheet, purpose built database management systems exist to manage more complicated sets of data. It is normal for a DBMS to share data with spreadsheets in some way for statistical analysis. Databases are fully discussed in Chapter 16.

Spreadsheets

Examples include Lotus *1-2-3*, *Openoffice.org Calc* and Microsoft *Excel*. Spreadsheets are ideally suited for the manipulation of numerical data and are heavily used in finance and engineering. One advantage over pen-and-paper is their ability to generate graphs quickly and perform 'what-if' analyses. For example, a shopkeeper who tracks sales using a spreadsheet can see easily what would happen to his or her overall finances if prices or sales figures were modified.

Other examples of situations where spreadsheets are useful include:

- managing household finances and budgeting by tracking salary, standing order and expenditure information each month.
- recording marks in a school, and automatically assigning grades based on marks. An if-then-else formula can assign grades.
- a petrol station performing a 'what if' analysis. What would happen if the price of petrol was raised by 2p per litre, with the effect of losing 5% of customers?
- analysing and predicting statistical trends, such as predicting Northern Ireland's population in 2020 based on birth rates and immigration, in order to manage housing, schools etc.

Desktop Publishing (DTP)

Examples include Adobe *Pagemaker*, *Scribus* and Microsoft *Publisher*. There are many similarities between word processors and DTP packages. Originally, DTP packages were capable of graphics manipulation and varying page layouts whereas word processors were not. However the most obvious difference today is that desktop publishing packages deal with only one page at a time and do not automatically flow onto a new page, as it does in word processors. Rather, the user decides exactly where text will be placed on a page within a text box. DTP packages also allow much more versatile manipulation of graphics and text within a page. Modern DTP packages also have a number of built-in **assistants** to aid production of posters, greetings cards, banners, etc.

Presentation Software

Examples include Microsoft *Powerpoint*, *Openoffice.org Impress* and Lotus *Freelance*. Before these tools were used, speakers at meetings would have prepared a series of acetate slides or flip-chart notes which were cumbersome to change or difficult to read. Modern presentation tools allow the main points of a talk to be broken into a series of slides with sub-points. It is common to have each point appear separately either by manually advancing it with the mouse or make it proceed automatically as they speak. Unfortunately many users of presentation tools place too much emphasis on sound and visual effects, or overload the screen with information. A presentation should support what is being said rather than duplicate it.

> Prepare a presentation that compares and contrasts word processors with desktop publishing packages. Use a presentation package to create your slides.
>
> **Task**

Graphics Packages

Examples include *Paint Shop Pro*, Adobe *Photoshop*, *The GIMP* and *Paint .net*. As their name suggests, graphics packages allow the manipulation of images. From simple programs such as *Paintbrush* or Microsoft *Paint*, the field has expanded to include a vast array of features. They have enabled people who have difficulty using traditional artistic methods to become skilled artists. Even non-skilled users can make use of them, for example to remove 'red-eye' from photographs or even to add people who were not there. Advanced graphics packages are used increasingly in movie making: eg the ship in *Titanic* and special effects in movies such as *Spider-man*, *The Hulk* and series such as *Heroes* and *Doctor Who*.

> Assess the risks involved in giving people the ability to modify images so effectively.
>
> **Task**

Many of the tools in graphics packages mimic traditional tools used by artists and photographers, such as: drawing lines of varying thickness, smudging, spray-painting, collage layers, and altering brightness and colour levels. Figure 7.1 shows how a graphics package has been used to enhance the focus and brightness of a photograph from the 1930s.

Web Authoring

Examples include *Macromedia Dreamweaver*, *KompoZer* and *Microsoft FrontPage*. Ten years ago anybody wanting to create a web page had to write the HTML code manually. Today most word processors can directly convert their documents into HTML, but there are even more powerful tools that can add animation and other effects, such as *Macromedia Flash* (part of the *Dreamweaver* package).

Integrated Packages

Examples include *AppleWorks* and *Microsoft Works*. Instead of buying separate software from all of the categories above, some users prefer an integrated package which offers basic features from all of these applications. They usually lack the full range of features of the other packages, but are cheaper and are often sufficient for many users. Sharing data within an integrated package is easier and the interface is more consistent.

Figure 7.1: Paint Shop Pro has been used to improve the appearance of a photo from the 1930s which was originally out of focus.

Office Suites

Examples include Corel *WordPerfect Suite*, Microsoft *Office*, Lotus *Symphony* and *OpenOffice.org*. An alternative to an integrated package is an office suite that will typically include software in most of the above categories and the user can choose which to install (eg just the word processor and the spreadsheet). Unlike integrated packages, office suites are often a combination of stand-alone applications.

A major advantage of office suites is that all programs have the same look-and-feel and the same basic functionality. Hence once a person is used to one program in the suite they often have little difficulty getting to know the others. Combining several applications allows for functionality that is not available with the stand-alone applications. For example, Microsoft *Word* and Microsoft *Access* can function well alone, but together they provide features such as **mail-merge** (generating documents based on data in a database).

Other Features of Generic Software Packages

While the above discussion focused on types of software package, there are some major features found in many of these. Students should familiarise themselves with the practical use of these features.

Macros are used to perform a series of repeated tasks quickly in a particular sequence. Most packages will supply in-built macros though the user is free to add their own. For example, if the user of a word processor frequently changes text to Arial, 14 point, italic bold, they may record a macro with the four instructions. Rather than laboriously setting each style characteristic, the user simply highlights the text and runs the macro. As another example, a database user may frequently run three queries and then generate a report. Again, this process can again be replaced by a macro.

Queries are used in databases and spreadsheets to allow the user to interrogate data and only see records that match stated criteria. This is often preferable to displaying all records. The results of queries can be formatted via a **report**. Databases are fully discussed in Chapter 16.

Wizards are programs used to automate difficult tasks and often allow inexperienced users to produce high-quality work. Experienced users may also use a wizard to save time. A wizard will generally guide the user through a number of options, for example to create a greeting card or a special effect in a presentation.

Object Linking and Embedding (OLE) is used to insert data of one format into a file of a different format. For example, graphics can be inserted into text or a spreadsheet into a presentation. OLE can be performed in two ways.

In the first method, Object **Linking** does not put the actual graphic into the text. Instead, it stores the location of the graphic and this is re-located and re-inserted each time the document is opened. This results in a much smaller file size and it means that changes to the graphic are reflected in the linked document. However, if the location of the graphic is changed, the word processor may not be able to find it.

In the second method, Object **Embedding** creates a copy of the image within the document. This overcomes the problem of losing the original. However, if the original file changes this is not reflected in the linked file. In addition, file sizes can be much larger since copies of the linked documents are being stored inside them.

As part of a group, choose four related applications (one for each person) and prepare a short instruction manual using either a word processor, desktop publishing tool or web page authoring package. Your report should account for the differences and similarities between the packages. These packages can be part of a suite, or may be four packages that are used for the same, or similar, purposes.

7.3 Internet Software Prior to the World Wide Web

The Internet is a very important ICT tool for many business and private individuals. In the past decade, the widespread adoption of the **World Wide Web** (**WWW**) has transformed communication and research. It is important for the reader to understand that the Internet is **not** the same as the WWW so in this section we will first look at what the Internet was like prior to its development.

In the days before the WWW, the Internet was primarily a tool for academics to share information and was not as easy to use as it is now. If someone wanted to access data they had to know what remote server to contact and what files to ask it for. There was no concept of either 'surfing' or search engines, both of which are common today.

File Transfer Protocol (FTP)

FTP was a widely used tool and remains available today, though largely unknown to non-ICT specialists. FTP's origins lie in the days of text-based interfaces but today both GUI-based and WWW-based FTP software is available. Users of Microsoft *Windows* can access a **text-based FTP** program through the **command prompt**. The following example shows how text-based FTP may be used to download a copy of the *Mozilla* browser. Any retrieved files will be saved to the directory in use on the local PC – in this case C:\documents and settings\clarke.

Figure 7.2: The user interface of a text-based FTP system.

1. Type **ftp** at the command prompt and press return to start the software.

2. Type **open ftp.mozilla.org** to connect to the remote server. The server will acknowledge itself.

3. Type a username and password, in this case "anonymous" and your e-mail address respectively.

```
C:\ Command Prompt - ftp
Microsoft Windows XP [Version 5.1.2600]
(C) Copyright 1985-2001 Microsoft Corp.

C:\Documents and Settings\clarke>ftp
ftp> open ftp.mozilla.org
Connected to manna.mozilla.org.
220 (vsFTPd 2.0.1)
User (manna.mozilla.org:(none)): anonymous
331 Please specify the password.
Password:
230 Login successful.
```

4. Type **dir** to see list the contents of the remote directory. In this example, it shows one folder called "pub".

5. Type **cd pub** to enter the directory (fig 7.2).

```
ftp> dir
200 PORT command successful. Consider using PASV.
150 Here comes the directory listing.
drwxr-xr-x    3 ftp      ftp          4096 Oct 25  2005 pub
226 Directory send OK.
ftp: 61 bytes received in 0.00Seconds 61000.00Kbytes/sec.
ftp> cd pub
250 Directory successfully changed.
```

The text on the left of a directory listing – drwxr-xr-x 3 ftp ftp – refers to access rights. The first "d" indicates that this is a directory. The next three letters are the rights that the file's creator has, followed by the rights for users on this machine's LAN, and then the rights for everyone else. In this example, a user called **ftp** created the directories seen here and has read/write/execute access to the same, while both local and remote users do not have write access (to prevent vandalism or carelessness!).

By the way...

6. Using the same method we can enter the sub-directory **mozilla.org** then **firefox** and then **releases**. Type **dir** to get a listing of the directories here.

7. To find the most recent version of *Firefox*, we look for the most recent directory, which at the time of writing was **2.0.0.5**. Type **cd 2.0.0.5** to enter the directory.

8. Type **cd win32** to enter the directory for the Windows version, then **cd en-GB** to enter the directory for the UK English version. Type **dir** to see the contents.

9. To download the file, type the command **get** "**Firefox Setup 2.0.0.5.exe**" and after a short wait, the FTP client confirms a successful transfer. Check the local directory (in this case <u>C:\documents and settings\clarke</u>) and the file should be there. See figure 7.3 below.

Figure 7.3: Downloading a file using a text–based FTP system.

```
ftp> cd en-GB
250 Directory successfully changed.
ftp> dir
200 PORT command successful. Consider using PASV.
150 Here comes the directory listing.
-rw-r--r--    1 ftp      ftp          5819936 Jul 17 23:15 Firefox Setup 2.0.0.5.ex
e
-rw-r--r--    1 ftp      ftp              186 Jul 17 23:18 Firefox Setup 2.0.0.5.ex
e.asc
226 Directory send OK.
ftp: 170 bytes received in 0.02Seconds 10.63Kbytes/sec.
ftp> get "Firefox Setup 2.0.0.5.exe"
200 PORT command successful. Consider using PASV.
150 Opening BINARY mode data connection for Firefox Setup 2.0.0.5.exe (5819936 b
ytes).
```

Task

Use a text-based FTP system to download the latest version of the *Firefox* browser by the same method. This task may help you appreciate why computers were not widely used outside specialist fields until fairly recently!

GUI-based FTP is a significant improvement. It essentially works the same way as text-based FTP (the user is expected to know precisely what data they are looking for) but browsing is greatly simplified. On starting the FTP client, the remote host, username and password are specified by typing them into a dialog box. On connection to the server, the left-hand window shows the directory currently selected on the local machine while the right-hand window shows the remote machine. Files can be downloaded by double-clicking on folder and file names.

Figure 7.4: Downloading a file using a GUI–based FTP system.

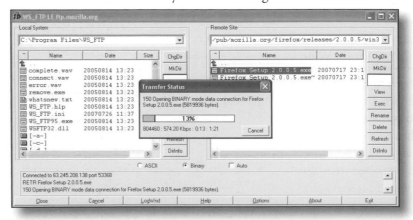

File transfer via the WWW is much simpler than either of these methods. The user simply clicks a link and waits for the download to complete. In addition, the web page containing the link can give more accurate descriptions of the file than the filename alone can provide. The screenshots in figure 7.5, show how servers can even be set up to detect the user's locality and hence offers software in the appropriate language. The main image is from a PC in Northern Ireland, while the small image is from the same web site, but captured in Brazil.

After clicking the 'Download Firefox – Free' link, the user is prompted to confirm the directory they want the downloaded file to be stored in. This process is much easier for the user than either of the traditional FTP methods described above.

E-mail Autoreplies

This system involved setting up an e-mail server to send a reply based on the subject line of the user's e-mail. For example, a university lecturer could ask his first-year students to e-mail him with the subject line REQUEST: FILELIST YEAR1. The server would respond by sending through information specifically for first year students, including details of further requests that they can make such as REQUEST: YR1 SAMPLE PAPERS to get sample examination papers. This system has mostly fallen into disuse since the widespread adoption of the WWW. However, in parts of the world where bandwidth is limited a textual e-mail-based service is still a viable method of using the WWW – see TEK, in section 7.8.

Figure 7.5: Downloading a file using a WWW–based file transfer system.

Telnet

Before the Internet was in widespread use, a number of information-sharing services used Telnet, a text-based service that allowed a user to connect to a remote multi-user server. No processing was done on the user's own PC (which was therefore acting as a **dumb terminal**). Rather, all input was sent to the server, processed and the text to be displayed sent back to the dumb terminal. As was common until the 1990s, these systems were entirely controlled by a keyboard, although many telnet-based information services have now been replaced by HTML interfaces.

7.4 The World Wide Web

As with many great ideas, the World Wide Web is so simple that a lot of people wondered why they hadn't thought of it first. The WWW was the first widely-used system to allow a remote user to open a series of files by selecting **hyperlinks** within those files. Suppose you have downloaded a standard text file via FTP and are viewing it. If you find a reference to another file that you want to look at, you would need to write down the file name, close the file currently open and use FTP software to retrieve the desired file before opening it.

However, the early WWW allowed users to read files using a text-based **browser**. They could select a filename using the cursor keys, press 'Enter' and have that file immediately opened. These 'selectable' pieces of text were called **hyperlinks** and created using the **Hypertext Markup Language (HTML)**. Web sites built to be compatible with **World Wide Web Consortium (W3C)** standards are still accessible to such text-based browsers, and these browsers still form the basis of systems used by audible screen readers and Braille interfaces: a vital consideration for web designers. The WWW quickly grew due to its simplicity of use, especially once GUI-based browsers such as NCSA *Mosaic* had been developed. In fact they have been so successful that other methods of requesting data are rarely used outside specialist fields. Despite the fact that FTP is technically more suitable for the transfer of large files, many novice users are unlikely to have used it and instead rely on HTTP instead.

Browser Wars and Non-Compliance

The W3C are the body responsible for administrating HTML standards. If a new feature is to be included, the W3C decide how this is to be done. For example, early versions of HTML did not support frames or tables, and as the use of the WWW grew the need for these features grew. The growing commercial interest in the WWW, and notably the rivalry between Netscape Communications and Microsoft, meant that rival browser developers did not wait for the W3C to ratify proposed additions to HTML, but instead implemented their own 'dialects' of HTML. As a result, a site built with HTML codes specific to Netscape *Navigator* did not display properly in Microsoft's *Internet Explorer (IE)*, and vice-versa.

In the space of just two years, 1997 and 1998, the commercial *Navigator* browser went from a dominant product to a minority one. The rapid decline was because an improved *IE* had been made available free of charge, and bundled with Windows. There was also a perception that *Navigator* did 'not work', as sites created with Microsoft's web authoring tool *Frontpage* used an *IE*-specific dialect of HTML.

Task	Research the second 'browser war', between *Internet Explorer* and *Mozilla*, which began around 2004. In what ways was this 'war' similar to the first one? In what ways did it differ?

The dominance of *Internet Explorer* (and an element of laziness on the part of some web developers) led to a situation where new web sites were only checked with *IE*. Because the WWW asks a browser to identify itself, some sites were even designed to inform users that they could not use the site if they were not using *IE*. Today, most web sites use **HTML 4**, a W3C approved standard which encompasses all the 'dialects' that appeared in the 1990s.

Users with Special Needs

A common design mistake made in the development of a web site, software, or piece of equipment is the idea that the world is full of 'people like us', ie they do not take into consideration users with different needs, such sight or mobility problems. Recent years have seen legislation in the UK to improve the accessibility of buildings but there is no comparable legislation covering software or hardware design.

In the same way, computers in the 1980s were only accessible to those who had good eyesight and who could use a keyboard. The invention of the graphical user interface greatly improved accessibility, but there was still a requirement for the user to be able to see and use a keyboard and mouse. Today, however, Braille and audio input/output devices allow users with sight problems to access textual data. Unfortunately web site developers have been slow to take these facts into consideration when designing web sites.

By contrast, the BBC News web site, news.bbc.co.uk, is an example of a page that is designed to be read aloud as well as viewed through a GUI. The textual version of the site shown when it is viewed in a browser such as *Lynx* (Figure 7.6) can be read aloud without confusion and the design of the menu allows it to be easily separated from the main text. The news story itself is only stored once, but good design means that it is made accessible to a range of devices in the most appropriate way.

 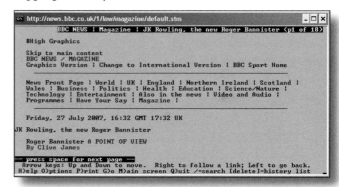

Figure 7.6: The BBC web site viewed in a conventional browser (left) and Lynx (right).

7.5 Web 2.0

At the time of writing, a buzz-word popular in the media is **Web 2.0**. Despite the name, this does not refer to a new World Wide Web. It is not a well-defined term, but rather refers to new generations of functionality (that did not exist when the WWW was first developed) which take advantage of the increased network bandwidth, faster processors more memory available in modern computers. Key concepts associated with the term Web 2.0 include:

+ Applications available via a web browser rather than being installed on a user's PC, such as *Google Docs & Spreadsheets* and the *Ajax13* word processor.

+ Web sites that are not static, but can be modified by users using **wiki** technology. The online encyclopedia *Wikipedia* is the most notable example of this. The concept has been adopted by many other sites, often devoted to special interest groups such as hobbies, sports, or TV programmes.

+ The ease of publishing content to the WWW, for example Google's *Picasa* photo organising software, that allows users to directly 'publish' a folder of photos from their PC to a web site, as illustrated in Figure 7.7.

+ Data downloads no longer restricted to a single server but following the **bit-torrent** approach where a user downloads small pieces of a large file from many sources simultaneously.

Figure 7.7: *Picasa* being used on a PC (top) and how the same content appears when published to a web site (bottom).

+ Concepts that could only exist on the Internet, such as online auctions (eg *eBay*) and Social Networking (eg *MySpace*, *Facebook*). The functionality they offer is not possible with other technologies, unlike word-processing or buying music, for example.

+ **Really Simple Syndication** (**RSS**) where updates to a site can be automatically sent to subscribers who have an RSS reader. RSS can also be used to embed sections of one site on another and is popular within Social Networking and blogging sites (eg *Blogger*, *Livejournal*). RSS is also used by many radio stations to distribute **podcasts**.

As Web 2.0 is not a static and well-defined concept, readers are encouraged to access online resources such as Tim O'Reilly's description of Web 2.0 (http://www.oreillynet.com/lpt/a/6228).

Task

The online encyclopedia *Wikipedia* has quickly become one of the most popular web sites on the Internet. What are the advantages of an encyclopedia that any user can edit? What are the disadvantages? To what extend should users rely on *Wikipedia*?

7.6 Web Authoring Software

The contents of the file used to store a web page is quite different from how it looks when viewed in a browser. Elements such as font, text size, hyperlinks etc are coded using a notation called **Hypertext Markup Language** (**HTML**). HTML is discussed in more detail in section 13.6. However, figure 7.8 shows an example of a simple web page shown as HTML and how it appears in a browser.

```
<HEAD>
<TITLE>My first web page</TITLE>
<HEAD>
<BODY>
<H1>Greetings...</H1>
<P>This is a <I>simple</I> page used to
demonstrate HTML
</BODY>
```

Figure 7.8: The HTML coding (left) for a simple web page (right).

Task

Using a text editor (such as *Notepad* on a *Windows* PC) type in the HTML code from figure 7.8 and save it as a file called **index.html**. View the file in a web browser by double-clicking the file icon. The HTML **tags** are indicated by angle brackets, and even a simple error can be enough to prevent the file displaying.

Now, change the **<BODY>** tag to read **<BODY BGCOLOR=FF5511>** and refresh the browser. What effect has this had? The first two digits FF are hexadecimal (base 16) numbers referring to the amount of red colour (in the range 00 to FF) while the next pairs refer to blue and green. Now, modify the line **<P>** to read **<P><FONT COLOR=FF77FF>**. What effect has this had?

As this example shows, the web browser must interpret the HTML tags in order to display what the creator intended. However the process of typing these commands for a large web site would be very time consuming. For these tasks, novice users instead use **WYSIWYG** ("what you see is what you get") **web editors**, which work in a similar way to a word processor. Although the web page and all its elements are edited at the same time on screen, the software saves it as an HTML file and separate image files that can be uploaded to the Internet. Common WYSIWYG web editors include Microsoft *Frontpage* and Adobe *Dreamweaver*. Figure 7.9 shows the *KompoZer* WYSIWYG web editor.

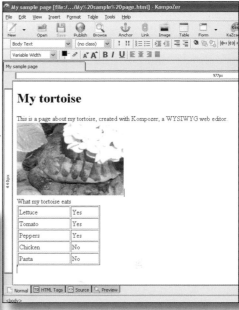

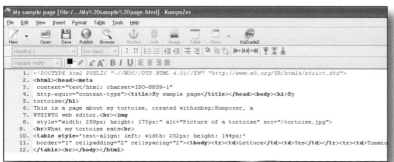

Figure 7.9: A web page being edited in KompoZer (above) and some of the HTML code generated by the software (left).

7.7 Web Browsers

In December 2007, the most commonly used web browsers were:

+ *Internet Explorer 7* (21.0% of users)
+ *Internet Explorer 6 or 5* (34.9%)
+ *Mozilla Firefox* (36.3%)
+ *Apple Safari* (1.7%)
+ *Opera* (1.4%)   Source: http://www.w3schools.com/browsers/browsers_stats.asp

In addition, a growing number of users access the WWW through other devices, such as games consoles and mobile phones. The Nintendo *Wii*, for example, allows users access the WWW via *Opera*. The wide variety of web browsers in use underlines the need for web developers to rigidly follow standards to ensure that all users of the WWW can access data. Since most browsers and sites today do follow these standards, the choice of browser is largely down to individual taste.

Nevertheless, non-standard features that are included in some web browsers may be useful for some developers. For example, *Internet Explorer* includes features that are designed for server versions of Microsoft *Windows*, and some designers will take advantage of these features to facilitate file transfer services without expecting the user to install extra software. This does, of course, depend on the user having a copy of *Internet Explorer*. Similar tools, allowing access to features of certain web-servers exist in other browsers.

Functions of a Web Browser

At a minimum, a web browser should display HTML pages and any linked graphics or audio. It should also allow the user to enter data for submission to a web site. However, modern browsers incorporate a large number of additional features. At the time of writing, these include the following:

Figure 7.10: Bookmarks in a typical web browser.

+ **Bookmarks** (called **favourites** in some browsers) allow a user to store a list of their favourite sites for easy access, rather than having to write out a list of web addresses. Bookmarks can usually be sorted into folders (Figure 7.10).

+ **Plug-ins** are extra programs that display data that is not in standard HTML format. Popular plug-ins include Adobe *Flash Player* and Adobe *Acrobat Reader*. Third-party plug-ins, often known as **widgets**, are also available for some browsers.

+ **Tabbed Browsing**. If a user is working between several web sites, the screen can becomes very cluttered with windows. **Tabs** (Figure 7.11) allow the user to open several pages inside the one main browser window. This was developed by *Opera* and later included in *Firefox* and *Internet Explorer 7*.

Figure 7.11: Tabbed browsing in *Opera*.

+ **Integrated e-mail / chat / RSS clients**. While these functions are available via stand alone programs, a number of browsers offer communications tools.

+ **Integrated web editing** is available in some packages, such as the full Mozilla Suite which includes an e-mail client (*Thunderbird*) and a web editor (*Seamonkey*) as well as a web browser (*Firefox*).

+ **Password management**. To prevent users forgetting passwords, a number of browsers ask a user, when they type password, if they would like it stored for later use.

+ **Download managers** allow a user to pause a download or resume a failed download to reduce frustration and allow very large files to be downloaded progressively. Figure 7.12 shows a number of completed downloads, one that has been paused and one in progress.

...	Name	Size	Progress	Time	Speed
	OOo_2.2.1_Win32Intel_install_wJRE_en-US.exe	108.8 MB	Stopped		27.6 KB/s
	winamp535_full_bundle_emusic-7plus.exe	8.3 MB	Done		24.2 KB/s
○	gimpshop_2.2.8_fix1_setup.exe	7.4 MB	19.7%	4:22	23.1 KB/s
	install_flash_player.exe	1.2 MB	Done		13.1 KB/s
	AdbeRdr810_en_US.exe	22.4 MB	Done		31.9 KB/s

Figure 7.12: The download manager in *Opera* showing a number of completed downloads, one paused, and one in progress.

+ **Pop-up blocking**. Pop-up windows appear automatically when browsing certain web sites, and are often perceived as a nuisance. Pop-up blockers, such as the *Google Toolbar* and the *Yahoo! Toolbar*) prevent such windows from opening, although they do notify the user in case they wish to over-ride the block. A number of browsers now include this feature as standard.

+ **Integrated search engine links** first appeared on toolbars, but most browsers now include this as a standard feature that users can customise.

7.8 Search Engines

Search engines are essential tools that allow WWW users to find relevant information in the vast arena of the Internet by entering key words or phrases that form the basis of a database query. The database in question is the search engine's catalogue of the entire Internet. At the time of writing, the *Google* search engine accounts for more searches than all other search engines combined. Google's dominance stems from its ease of use and quality of results. When it was launched, its rivals had large, complex interfaces that required users to refine their results until they found what they wanted. *The Wayback Machine*, at web.archive.org can be used to view old versions of these sites and study the development of their interfaces. *Google*, however, presented a non-cluttered interface with accurate results. Other examples of search engines are *Yahoo!* and *Ask.com*.

Although search engines usually return useful results immediately, most include a number of features that can be used to refine results. For example, the query **crisps +tayto** will search for crisps but insist that only pages containing the word 'tayto' are returned. Placing a request in quotes, for example **"cheese and onion"**, will search for this precise phrase, rather than pages that simply contain those words anywhere in the page. Most search engines include options to search for particular types of files (PDF, images etc), or limit the search to certain languages.

How a Search Engine Works

A search engine uses a huge database held on a central server. This database is a built up by a process called **spidering** or **crawling** where an automated web browser will visit a page and then visit every page it links to. Over time, the spider program will visit most pages on the Internet. As new web sites will have no links going to them, many search engines allow users to submit details of their site to allow it to be indexed. When a site is spidered, its content is **indexed** so that search terms can be compared to the contents of the page.

When a user performs a search the search terms are compared to the index of web pages that are stored on the server and results are returned in a ranked order. A site's ranking is influenced by factors such as title tag, keyword frequency, how many other sites link to it and how many people visit it (which can be used as measurements of a site's importance). Some search engines look at over 200 factors in order to rank a web site. Many search engines provide free toolbars that can be installed on a user's PC in order to personalise the service they provide by watching how the search engine is used. For example, if a user often opts for British-based sites and later searched for 'Newspaper', British newspapers may be promoted in the ranking for this user. Rankings determine the perceived quality of the search engine in the eyes of the user. In the same way, if a site ranked low down is visited often enough, the search engine will recognise that users perceive it to be important, and in future it will receive a higher rank. Hence the performance of search engines is affected by what users do with the results.

Ask Jeeves (now *ask.com*), founded in 1996, allows users to present queries in natural language (eg "Where can I buy Tayto crisps in England?") reflecting the growth in research to develop an interface that is closer to how humans think. This was reflected in the choice of mascot, a butler called Jeeves.

Specialist Search Engines

Search engines like *Google* and *Ask* search the whole WWW, but a number of special purpose search engines also exist. These include:

- **Meta-search engines**, such as *Dogpile.com*. These submit a single query to many search engines at once and combine their results in a single page. In the hypothetical example below, three search engines (SE1-SE3) provide different results for the word **crisps**. A meta-search engine combines results, and presents an average. Hence **Tayto** has an average place ranking of 2.67 here (1+4+3 divided by 3) compared to Pringles' average of 1.67 (3+1+1 divided by 3). This means that Pringles is presented before Tayto in the meta engine. A drawback of this approach is that it ignores the mechanism each search engine has used. Perhaps SE1 returned Tayto higher than others because it has a record of the user's search history and is giving results that are fine-tuned for them, or SE2 and SE3 may have highlighted Pringles because many users have chosen that site from search results in the past. SE1 may have taken account for the user being in UK and has reduced the importance of US-based Lays as a result.

SE1	SE2	SE3	Meta Engine
1st. Tayto	1st. Pringles	1st. Pringles	1st. Pringles
2nd. Walkers	2nd. Lays	2nd. Lays	2nd. Tayto
3rd. Pringles	3rd. McCoys	3rd. Tayto	3rd. Lays
4th. McCoys	4th. Tayto	4th. Walkers	4th. Walkers
5th. Lays	5th. Walkers	5th. McCoys	5th. McCoys

- **Sites that aggregate content**. Many popular sites have very little content of their own but will compile data from many other sites and present them in one place. Examples include:

  - Reference sites such as **answers.com**. A search of this site for **ice cream**, for example, will produce a large results page featuring descriptions of ice cream from a number of online encyclopedias, dictionary definitions of the term, recipes etc.

  - News sites such as *Google News*, present a summary of news headlines from a number of sources. This site can be customised by the user, allowing control over what sort of stories are shown and what sources are used. It can even be instructed to e-mail relevant stories to registered users.

- **Shopping comparison site**s such as *Kelkoo* allow users to search many shopping sites for a given product. The results are presented on a single page, listing many vendors and their price for the product. The same principle has been applied to travel (eg *Expedia*) and financial loans (eg *Money Supermarket*).

- **Sites that restrict content** to a particular subject area. *TorrentSpy*, for example, only searches for *BitTorrent* files while *Blogscope* only searches blogs. Northern Ireland's *PropertyNews.com* restricts results to local houses for sale, allowing users to specify criteria such as area, price and number of bedrooms.

✦ **E-mail based search engines**, such as *TEK (Time Equals Knowledge)*, which was developed at MIT for use in countries with low bandwidth. A user can e-mail a request to the TEK server, which carries out the search while the user is offline and e-mails data from the most relevant pages back to the user's server at a non-peak usage time for the user to access at a time convenient to them. See *World's poor to get own search engine*, BBC News online, 15th July 2003, via: http://tinyurl.com/2hmk54

Questions

1. Identify four features of a spreadsheet which make it useful for accounts purposes. (4)
2. Describe the steps involved in making a bar graph. (4)
3. Describe the difference between an office suite and an integrated package. (4)
4. Describe a wizard, stating an example of its use. (3)
5. What is a macro? (2)
6. Describe OLE. (3)
7. State two advantages to the user of buying off-the-shelf software. (2)
8. State two disadvantages to the user of buying off-the-shelf software. (2)
9. State two advantages to the user of buying tailor-made software. (2)
10. State two disadvantages to the user of buying tailor-made software. (2)
11. Describe the purpose of telnet. (3)
12. Describe two reasons for the availability of various browsers. (4)
13. What is HTML? (3)
14. Describe three main features of browser software. (6)
15. What is the purpose of a search engine? (3)
16. Describe how a search engine works. (4)
17. Identify and describe two specialist search engines. (6)

CHAPTER 8
Software: Open Source Software

8.1 Introduction

Open source software gives users the ability to modify a program's functionality in any way they please by editing, adding and removing components. **Closed source software**, by contrast, allows the user to run the software but not make changes to functionality, other than modifying options provided by the vendor.

The arguments presented by those in favour of open source software, and those against, are frequently impassioned. Indeed, the debate often hinges on the way in which particular firms operate rather than the merits of each approach. It is therefore essential for the student of ICT to be aware of both the advantages and disadvantages of each approach and the wider arguments involved.

8.2 Source Code

When a program is written, a programmer uses a programming language such as *Java* or *Visual Basic* to create source code. The source code is saved as an ASCII text file which cannot be executed until it is **compiled** and turned into **object code**. Object code is distributed to users in the form of executable files. Executable files designed for Microsoft *Windows* have a file extension **.exe.** Depending how a program has been designed, a single set of source code files can be compiled into a form that is suitable for *Windows*, a form suitable for *MacOS* and a form suitable for *Linux*. Or, the program may be designed to work exclusively with one operating system.

Some software developers allow the user to access the source code and even encourage users to modify it and share the results. This is the **open source** model of software development. By contrast, in the **closed source** model developers do not share source code with customers, who are thus not free to make significant changes to the functionality of the software.

Many of the world's largest software companies, such as *Microsoft*, *Corel* and *Adobe* follow the closed source model.

8.3 Closed Source – Advantages and Disadvantages

Disadvantages of Closed Source

+ **Vendor lock-in**. Closed source software typically uses a propriety file format. Because the details of this format are kept secret, anyone attempting to read the file must also buy a copy of the software. In addition, any user who keeps data in this format may be obliged to retain that product if they are to continue to access their own data. This also discourages them from switching to a different software package and helps to keep a customer base, and hence maintains a revenue stream for the vendor. For example, Microsoft *Office* uses a number of proprietary file formats to store application data.

+ **Requirement to upgrade**. Closed source vendors often rely on selling new versions of their product to generate a steady stream of revenue. Once every customer has purchased a copy of a particular package, developers add new features and improvements to convince users of the need to upgrade. With this pressure to remain 'up to date', many businesses feel forced to upgrade so that they can continue exchanging data.

+ **Restriction of sharing.** Critics argue that since it is perfectly normal for people to share objects such as newspapers or umbrellas, it is not right that **licensing** restrictions usually prohibit sharing software.

+ **Restriction of user freedom**. Closed source license agreements often state how the product may be used. For example, 'educational' versions of software are often available, but come with the restriction that they must only be used in an educational establishment. Using the same software for personal or commercial purposes is usually a breach of the license agreement.

+ **Users cannot learn how software works.** In other forms of engineering, it is normal for students to deconstruct (or **reverse engineer**) equipment to learn how it works and how to adapt and modify it. Closed source software prevents this, or at least makes it very difficult.

+ **Rushed development**. Closed source developers often work towards financially-determined deadlines and hence products may be released without thorough testing or with many mistakes still present. This leads to a cycle of upgrades and patches long after the product is released.

Advantages of Closed Source

+ **High budgets**. Because closed source software is usually part of a commercial project, large budgets are often available to hire skilled developers, equipment and conduct research and development. These budgets are derived from selling licenses to use the products and also on-going support contracts. In contrast, the majority of open-source projects have a lesser budget as they rely on selling support services. As a consequence, closed-source developers may have a larger budget to devote to research and development of new or improved products.

+ **Restriction of sharing**. Supporters argue that sharing software is not like sharing physical objects since sharing software creates a new copy that has not been paid for. They argue that it is thus a form of theft and therefore unethical. By preventing users from sharing software, the vendor protects its revenue stream and can remain in business to improve the software. If software was copied freely, there would be no motivation for the company to produce it.

+ **Protection of intellectual property**. When an engineering company develops a better version of an item, for example a car engine, it protects the design so that others cannot unfairly profit from the work. In the same way, many software development companies wish to keep their source code a **trade secret** to prevent others from profiting from their work.

+ **Criticisms are vendor-specific**. Supporters of closed source argue that many of the criticisms of the model result from the policies of individual companies. They argue that it is possible for a closed source company to be both 'friendly' and protect trade secrets.

By the way...

Free Beer versus Free Speech

Although these two terms may seem strange, they are often used to describe the differences between the two types of free software. The term **free-as-in-beer** describes products that are free to use but which the user may not modify or adjust, for example *Pegasus Mail*, *Opera*, Adobe *Acrobat Reader* and Microsoft *Internet Explorer*. The term **free-as-in-speech** describes products that the end user can do whatever they like with, including modifying it. There are no contractual restrictions over what the user does, similar to the idea of free speech. The developers of these may derive income through:

+ giving the software away free, while selling support services (eg *Opera*).

+ selling related products, for example Adobe *Acrobat* which is a version of *Acrobat Reader* with substantially more features.

Notable free-as-in-beer (free to use, closed source) products

Many readers will have used one or more of the products described below. What was the motivation for each developer to give the object code away for free, while keeping the source closed?

+ *Pegasus Mail,* developed and given away free by David Harris since 1990. Harris sells support services to business, as do other Pegasus users.

+ *Opera* began as a research project at the Norwegian state telecoms firm, supported by advertising, but now free. Income comes from related projects.

+ Microsoft *Windows Media Player* is free to use, but companies wishing to create files in this product's file format must pay for software to do this.

+ *AVG Anti-Virus* is a free, basic, anti-virus package. The developers, Grisoft, charge for versions with more features, and for support.

Notable free-as-in-speech (free to use, open source) products

+ The operating system *Linux* was originally developed by student Linus Torvalds in the early 1990s, and has been adopted for a wide variety of uses including mobile phones, MP3 players, cars, and games consoles. Versions have also been adapted for PCs both old and new.

+ *OpenOffice.org*, a competitor to Microsoft *Office*, is free to use. The first version for *MacOS* was compiled from the source code by volunteers, and named *NeoOffice*. While *OpenOffice.org* is now officially available on a Mac, *NeoOffice* remains as a fully compatible alternative.

+ **Mozilla *Firefox*.** When *Netscape Communications* lost the 'browser war', owners AOL opened access to the source code and formed the non-profit Mozilla Foundation, to ensure the *Netscape* browser survived.

8.4 Open Source – Advantages and Disadvantages

Disadvantages of Open Source

+ **Products can 'fork'**, leaving users confused. Rival groups of developers can take a product in separate directions, resulting in two incompatible products. For example, there are over a dozen different incompatible versions of Unix, though developers of these would argue that they are all fine-tuned to particular uses.

+ **Breach of patents**. Allowing anyone to contribute source code can leave room for breach of patents. At the time of writing, SCO were suing IBM for allowing material copyrighted by SCO, that IBM had legitimate access to, to enter open source projects. Microsoft have likewise taken legal steps to prevent *Linux* distributors from infringing its patents.

+ **Lower quality**. Because anyone can contribute to an open source project, quality control may be less robust than with closed source. While large open source projects such as *OpenOffice.org* do have controls to prevent vandals from contributing source code, smaller projects may suffer from this problem.

+ **Unreliable**. Some detractors argue that a free product implies that it may be unreliable, while a higher price implies better quality.

+ **Insecure**. Open source products may be insecure because hackers have easy access to source code to identify flaws.

+ **Distribution of benefits.** Some argue that it is unfair for companies to make money charging users for support, while the volunteers who contributed to the software development are unpaid.

Read more at these sites: The Free Software Foundation, www.fsf.org, responsible for the *GNU Public License*. The Open Source Initiative www.opensource.org. Eric S. Raymond's "The Cathedral and the Bazaar", via http://tinyurl.com/3qo8p.

By the way...

Advantages of Open Source

+ **Users are not tied to a particular vendor**. If a product becomes unavailable, users can go elsewhere and still access their data. Open source development encourages open standards, such as the **Open Document Format** which any developer can implement.

+ **Future resistant**. There is no single entity on whom the future of a product depends. If a closed source developer chooses not to develop a new version of a product for a new operating system, then that product ceases to be available and there is nothing that users can do, even if they have the skills to update the software themselves.

+ **Low cost**. Open source software is generally free to use, and even the cost of support may not be as much as purchasing closed source software.

+ **Security problems** are more likely to be found. Writers of open source products know that whatever they do will be scrutinised by others. This not only allows the detection of errors, but also allows their immediate correction and helps prevent malicious users inserting rogue code. Closed source software is not publicly scrutinised in the same manner.

+ **Users can share software freely.** There are no patent restrictions that inhibit how users may share software with one another.
+ **Users can use the product in any way they choose**. There are no licensing models that state how a user may or may not use a product.

Task

Compare the text of the **GNU Public License** (accessible from the *Free Software Foundation* http://www.fsf.org) to a license agreement from a piece of commercial (closed source) software. What are the main differences?

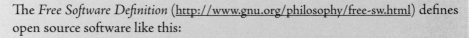

8.5 Digital Rights Management

Another manifestation of the open source / closed source debate is the issue of **Digital Rights Management (DRM)**. DRM is an initiative to restrict unauthorised use of copyrighted material, such as DVD movies or downloaded music in order to protect copyright and revenue. For example, if a user pays to download a music track to their PC, they may find that the file is 'locked' to that PC and cannot be used on other computers.

Many people in the open source community dislike this concept as they feel it restricts how users can access files they have paid for, in the same way that closed source software licenses can be restrictive. Opponents of DRM suggest that the technology goes much further than is needed to prevent copyright violation and that it affects the **fair use** of products that people have legitimately paid for.

Task

The *Free Software Definition* (http://www.gnu.org/philosophy/free-sw.html) defines open source software like this:

"Free software is a matter of liberty, not price. To understand the concept, you should think of free as in free speech, not as in free beer. Free software is a matter of the users' freedom to run, copy, distribute, study, change and improve the software. More precisely, it refers to four kinds of freedom, for the users of the software:

- *The freedom to run the program, for any purpose (freedom 0).*
- *The freedom to study how the program works, and adapt it to your needs (freedom 1). Access to the source code is a precondition for this.*
- *The freedom to redistribute copies so you can help your neighbour (freedom 2).*
- *The freedom to improve the program, and release your improvements to the public, so that the whole community benefits (freedom 3). Access to the source code is a precondition for this."*

Do you agree with this definition of "free software"? Assess the advantages and disadvantages of open source software.

Questions

1. Explain what is meant by 'Open Source' software. (3)
2. What is Closed Source software. (2)
3. State three disadvantages of closed source software. (3)
4. How might a closed-source vendor attempt to persuade consumers that open-source software is a disadvantage to their firm? (3)
5. What is 'free-as-in-beer' software? Give an example. (2)
6. Evaluate open source software. (4)

CHAPTER 9
Local and Wide Area Networks

9.1 Introduction

The earliest computer systems (see figure 9.1) were large machines confined to a room. Anyone who wanted to use it would have to physically bring their work to it and would be able to use the system only for a short time. There was no way to connect from a distance, and data was entered via switches or paper tape. In time, remote access systems were developed allowing a user to be at a dumb terminal. All processing took place at the remote computer and data was transmitted to and from the terminal.

US Army Photo

Digital Equipment Corporation

Figure 9.1: The ENIAC computer of 1946 (left) and a VAX terminal of the 1970s (right).

Eventually systems were developed whereby large computers could communicate with each other, and networks were born. Since then, the use of computers and networks has mushroomed and is now taken for granted. In this chapter you will look at the reasons for networks, their structure, their advantages and their disadvantages.

9.2 Why Create Networks?

Networks are immensely useful, from universities wishing to share research, to people wanting to play games. They have a number of key advantages for these tasks, as well as associated disadvantages:

Advantages of networking

+ Expensive resources can be shared between many computers, saving money:
  + All computers on a network can use a single printer.
  + Multiple computers can access the Internet via a single connection.
+ Software can be shared between network users:
  + A site license can be bought for all systems and applications software.
  + Sharing a program on a network allows for easier upgrading of the program as there is only one version of the software.
+ Files can be shared by many users:
  + Only one copy of the file needs to be stored.
  + The need to move disks back and forth between computers is eliminated.
+ Making backups is easy.
+ All users will be allocated a username and password.
  + Data can be centrally stored and, although a user can log on from any terminal, privacy and access rights can be enforced.
+ Communication is possible over a wide area with a network:
  + Users can access a database or web site on another computer.
  + Users can send e-mail or play 'networked' games with friends via the Internet.
  + Real time communication is possible with **instant messaging**.

Disadvantages of networking

+ A network can be expensive:
  + Network software will have to be purchased.
  + Network hardware devices such as cabling, routers and servers have to be purchased.
  + A network technician and network manager must be employed to maintain the network.
+ Viruses stored on one computer on a network can spread around the whole network and destroy data:
  + Anti-virus software must be installed and kept up-to-date.
+ Appropriate security measures must be in place to prevent unauthorised access.
+ There is an increased danger that centrally-stored files may be accessed, modified or deleted by unauthorised users.
+ Security measures are required, including the use of usernames and passwords, different levels of access and firewalls (see Chapter 13).
+ Companies can become heavily dependent on the network. For example, if the file server crashes, users may be unable to carry out their tasks because access to programs and data files has been lost.
+ Problems caused by the inter-working of pieces of network hardware and software can lead to failures in some (or all) of the network, depending on its design.

9.3 Types of Network

A network is a communication system that allows the transfer of data and sharing of hardware and software between two or more computers. Networks can be subdivided into **Local Area Networks** (or **LANs**) that connect computers within a single building, and **Wide Area Networks** (or **WANs**) that connect computers in several buildings, towns or even countries.

A **Local Area Network** *connects a group of computers, usually within one building.* It is used to share data and any device that is utilised by more than one person, such as a printer, fax, server or broadband connection. LANs are normally owned, controlled, and managed by a single person or organisation. The predominant mode of communication is physical cabling, usually a combination of fibre optic and copper cabling although there is a growing use of wireless devices in LAN environments. They will usually follow a bus, star, ring or bus/star composite topology (see section 9.4). Data is typically transmitted at 10 and 100Mbps (megabits per second).

A **Wide Area Network** *connects computers over a wide geographic area, such as several towns, using a variety of communications media such as telephone, radio or satellite.* Because of limitations due to distance, WANs carry data at a slower speed than LANs. Most WANs are not owned by any one organisation but exist under collective or distributed ownership and management. For example, a company WAN may rely on links hired from, or managed by, telecoms companies in several countries, or may use links owned by a partner company. Some WANs are made by connecting LANs in different buildings. The Internet is a huge collection of WANs and LANs joined together.

9.4 Local Area Network Topologies

Networks can be built following a number of designs, or **topologies**. There are many factors, such as those listed below, that need to be taken into account when choosing the most appropriate one.

- The purpose of the network (connecting two computers together as opposed to connecting two factories together).
- The cost of building (or hiring) and managing the network.
- The distance to be covered.
- Will there be a need for future network expansion?
- Is data security important?
- How important is it that the network can still operate when cable failures occur?
- Ease of identifying network problems when they occur.
- Will the data be random or generated at regular intervals?
- Speed required and amount of data to be transferred, ie, degree of bandwidth needed.

The three most common LAN topologies are **bus, ring** and **star**. Some large LANs may be a **bus-star** composite. Other less common topologies, such as **mesh**, also exist.

The Bus Topology

A **bus LAN** consists of a single **bus** cable, or **backbone**, to which all devices are attached, as shown in figure 9.2. A machine wishing to send a data packet will first check the backbone is currently free of transmission. If it is free, the data **packet** is injected into the bus cable where it travels in each direction along the wire until it reaches a **terminator** at the end. The terminator absorbs all the signals that reach it, thus clearing the network for new communication. As the data passes each device, an address in the data **header** is checked to see if that device is the intended target. If it is, the data is read; otherwise it is ignored. A bus network is **passive**, which means that once on the bus a data packet passes to the ends without any further action necessary. A data packet must travel to all devices as neither the packet nor the sending device know the location of the recipient.

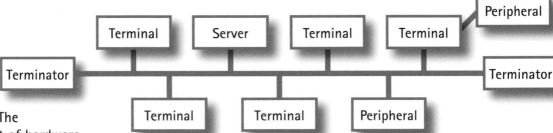

Figure 9.2: The arrangement of hardware in the **bus** LAN topology.

It is possible that two machines may transmit a message simultaneously, resulting in the two data packets **colliding**. A bus network detects collisions as 'garbled' data and the devices that sent the data will wait for a random period of time and attempt to transmit again. Hence the more traffic on the bus, the higher the chance of collisions. No single computer has overall control of a bus network. It is therefore sometimes described as a **peer-to-peer** network because no terminal is higher in status than others. Although the network may be have a file server, it serves data without 'controlling' the network (as in a **star** network).

Advantages of bus networks include:

+ It is cheap, as the only costs are network interface cards and minimal cabling.
+ If one of the workstations malfunction, the rest of the network is unaffected as is not necessary for any workstation to pass the data onto a recipient.
+ It is easy to add additional machines without affecting the existing network.
+ Gives good network service under light traffic loads.

Disadvantages of bus networks include:

+ The entire network shuts down if there is a break in the main cable.
+ It can be hard to trade where the damage to a cable is physically located.
+ Performance can degrade significantly under high traffic loads.
+ Data passes through all other devices, so is potentially insecure.

For the above reasons, the bus network topology is most suitable for situations where there are a small number of devices with light data traffic, for example in a small office situation.

Why is it so hard to diagnose the fault in a bus network?

With bus networks it is difficult to locate a faulty cable because the only symptom may be that all terminals have lost their network connection. The fault could lie on any cable between any device, which may be especially problematic if the cable is inaccessible, eg under the floor. Specialist equipment such as **sniffers**, that detect network traffic, may be connected in place of each terminal in turn, to find which portion of the cable is at fault.

By the way...

The Star Topology

A star network differs from the bus in that each terminal is connected directly to a **central node** by a dedicated cable as shown in figure 9.3. The central node is responsible for controlling the network. On small networks it may simply be part of a server or, on large networks, a hub dedicated purely to managing the network. Peripherals such as printers can be connected to terminals or directly to the network. The central node checks each device in turn to see if it wants to send data. When a data packet is sent from a computer, it is sent to the central node via a direct link. The central node in turn forwards the data packet on to the appropriate machine.

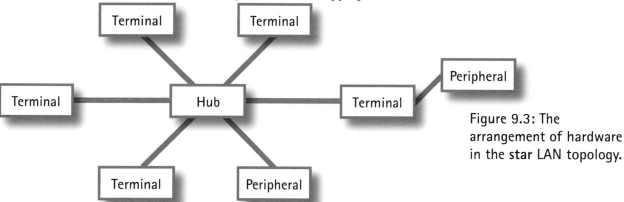

Figure 9.3: The arrangement of hardware in the **star** LAN topology.

Advantages of star networks include:

+ The failure of a single terminal will not affect the rest of the network and it can be traced fairly easily.

+ Extra computers can be added easily without disturbing the network – all that is needed is a free access point on the hub.

+ Collisions are greatly reduced since each computer has its own cable to the central node (in contrast to bus networks).

+ Transmission can be more secure as security schemes can be applied at the central node so that information is sent only from source to destination workstation (as opposed to all machines on the network).

Disadvantages of star networks include:

+ Failure at the central node can cause the entire network to become inoperative.

+ A large amount of cabling needs be used to connect all users to the central node and this can add greatly to the cost of the network.

+ Star networks require a central node (hub or switch; see section 9.5) which can be expensive.

The star network topology is most suitable for situations where there is a large number of computers with heavy traffic, or where a cable fault must not disable the entire network. It is also useful for evolving networks where devices are frequently added or removed.

The Bus/Star (Tree) Topology

As its name suggests, this is a mixture of the bus and star topologies. As shown in figure 9.4, a number of star networks are linked by a high-bandwidth bus backbone. The bus/star topology is most suitable for situations where there are a large number of computers grouped into a number of different functional groups. One star network is dedicated to each group and their server and data only enters the bus when it has to move between groups, such as sending e-mail or downloading data. The topology often makes use of the network's geography, for example one hub per floor and a bus cable to join floors together.

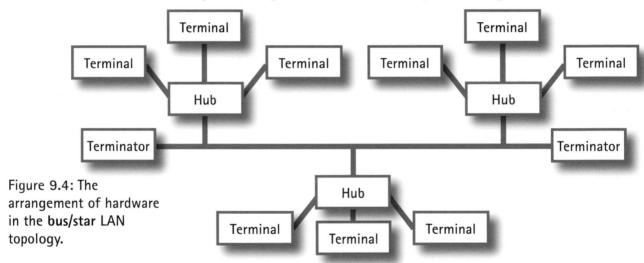

Figure 9.4: The arrangement of hardware in the **bus/star** LAN topology.

The Ring Topology

In the ring topology (also called **Token Ring**), as shown in figure 9.5, each workstation is on a ring onto which messages are placed – there are no terminated ends. A packet (called a **token**) continuously circulates the network by being passed from one terminal to the next around the ring. The token is generated by a machine that is identical to all others (except that it is the only one that can generate the token). If a particular workstation wishes to send data it waits until the token reaches it and then transmits the message by attaching the data and a destination address. The token then travels to the next workstation as before. If the message is intended for this workstation then it is received and the receiving computer acknowledges receipt by returning an appropriate message to the sender using the same token. The original sender then releases the token for use by the next computer, ensuring that no machine can monopolise the token. If a particular machine does not wish to send any data, it simply passes the token along.

Since machines must pass data on, even when they have nothing to send, rings are said to be **active networks**. Like bus networks, they are also called peer-to-peer networks since no device is in overall control.

Advantages of ring networks include:

+ Since all data travels in the same direction, and devices transmit in turn, the ring is predictable under heavy loads and can achieve high speeds.

+ Since each machine acts as a **repeater** (regenerating the signal as it is passed on) rings can be large.

+ As this is a peer-to-peer network there is no need for an expensive server.

+ It is not possible for one machine to flood the network with data, blocking others from transmitting.

Disadvantages of ring networks include:

+ The failure of a single device or cable will lead to total network failure.

+ Data passes through all workstations, which can compromise security.

+ Adding a device requires briefly taking the entire network off-line.

Figure 9.5: The arrangement of hardware in the **ring** LAN topology.

Why are ring networks so fast?

At first glance, it may appear that ring networks may be slow, as all devices must transmit in order and data may go only in one direction. But just like a one way system can improve traffic flow in a town centre, in a ring if all data is going in the same direction and at the same speed, then data can be sent as fast as the cable allows, safe in the knowledge that collisions will not occur. In addition, a second ring carrying data in the opposite direction can be added.

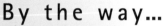

By the way...

File Servers

Many network topologies feature a **server**, which is a powerful computer with a fast processor, a large amount of RAM and backing storage, as well as a network interface card to access the network.

A server can have the following functions:

+ **It stores all programs and data**, including the network operating system, utility programs to manage the network and application programs. Each user can save and open their data files from any terminal on the network. In some networks, frequently-accessed programs (eg office applications) are stored on individual workstations to reduce the time taken to load these and to reduce server-load.

+ **Logs all file-accesses**, which in turn facilitates auditing and accounting (see section 19.2).

+ **It controls access to software and user data.** Each user will be allocated a unique user name and password along with an appropriate level of access.

+ **It provides a backup facility.** For example all user data may be automatically backed up to a remote hard disk or a magnetic tape cartridge at regular intervals to minimise loss of data.

9.5 Network Hardware

Networks are composed of a number of devices, each with a specific task to perform. For example, data on a school PC will typically travel via a network interface card, a cable and a hub to a server. By contrast, data on the Internet may travel via routers, gateways and fibre optic cables. This section looks briefly at various network hardware devices.

Task

Write a brief definition of each of the following devices (no more than two sentences) describing the device and its basic purpose.

Network Interface Card (NIC)

Figure 9.6: Network cards for (left) a traditional cable LAN and (right) a PCMCIA slot in a laptop.

The NIC provides the physical connection between the network and the computer workstation. Most NICs are internal, with the card fitting into an expansion slot inside the computer, and may be supplied with a PC or added at a later stage. Figure 9.6 shows examples of both.

Image courtesy LinkSys

Repeater

As electrical signals travel down a cable, their initially clean signal gets 'smeared' and indistinct with distance. After a certain distance the signal becomes too degraded to be decipherable. Thus every cable has a maximum length. The task of a repeater is to clean up the signal by regenerating it so it can pass along a further segment (figure 9.7). As it only passes the data on, it has no function in controlling the data. A good example of the use of repeaters would be in a LAN using a bus topology with **coaxial** cable. The repeater amplifies all the signals that pass through it allowing for the total length of cable on the network to exceed the limit that would exist for a single length of coaxial cable, as shown by figure 9.8.

Figure 9.7: The signal in a very long length of ethernet cable will become weak and distorted over time (top) unless a repeater is used to regenerate the signal part way along (bottom).

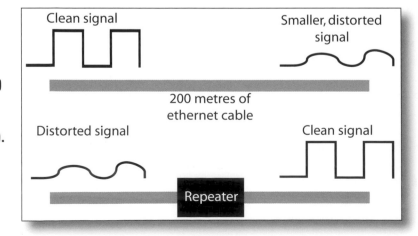

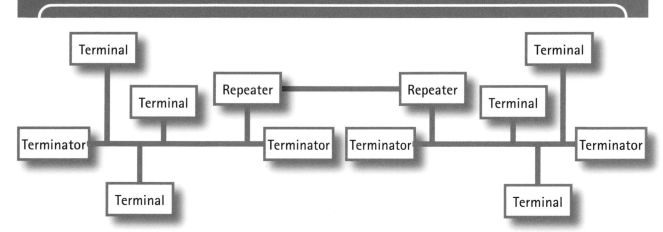

Figure 9.8: Example of a bus LAN extended with repeaters.

Bridge

A bridge is a special type of repeater which can be used to connect two or more LANs of the same type (ie LANs which communicate using the same protocol), although the cabling or the physical topologies can be different. A bridge is an 'intelligent' repeater because it controls the movement of data packets in a network by building an internal list of hardware addresses (**MAC address**) of the attached network devices on each side of it. When a bridge sees a data packet, it checks the packet's address against its internal list. Only if the destination address is on the opposite segment, or if the bridge doesn't have the address in its list, the bridge forwards the packet to the other network. This allows a large network to be broken into two smaller, more efficient, networks by controlling where the packet can go and hence preventing unnecessary traffic. A network with a bridge looks the same as the arrangement shown in figure 9.8, except that the two repeaters are replaced by a single bridge.

Router

A router is used to transmit data packets across the most efficient or cost effective route through a LAN or a WAN. It will translate information from one network protocol to another to allow connections between different types of network. Several routers connected to each other form a path between smaller LANs or WANs of differing topologies and media as shown in figure 9.9.

Routers select the best path to send a message based on the destination address and origin (hence their name). While bridges know the hardware addresses of all computers on each side of the network, routers know the protocol addresses (eg IP address) of computers, bridges, and other routers on the network. They communicate with each other to share information about the state of the network and build up a 'routing table' to allow informed decisions about which route to send data along based on current traffic levels. A router will send a data packet across an alternative link if the primary link is broken or busy. For example, if the very fast cables that go through the middle of Europe are under heavy loads, routers may direct data between UK and Germany via Scandinavia. This longer route avoids the 'traffic jam.'

Figure 9.9: A series of LANs connected by routers. If the connection between Router 2 and Router 3 becomes unavailable, then data can be sent via Routers 1 or 3 instead. The user should not notice a significant delay.

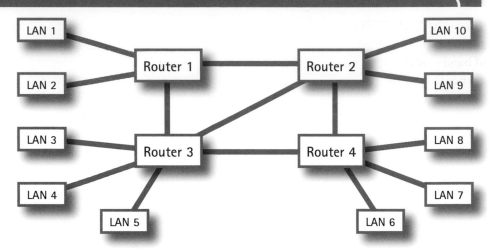

Gateway

A gateway is used when networks with different protocols need to communicate with each other: the gateway translates the data from one protocol to another and sends it on, using the network protocols of the destination network. They are commonly used to connect a LAN to a WAN. Gateways and routers may be combined as a single device.

Hub

A hub provides a central connection point for nodes on a Star LAN. Data arriving at the hub on one port is transmitted out via the other ports. Most hubs electrically amplify the signal as it moves from one device to another. Hubs will usually send data in several directions as they are not sophisticated enough to determine the precise destination of data. Hence hubs are suitable only in small networks as they create too much congestion in large systems.

Switch

A switch is an 'intelligent' hub which sends data packets straight to the destination, without being copied to all the computers. It will store the addresses of all devices that are directly or indirectly connected to it on each port. This increases network performance and offers greater security. A large LAN may have one or more switches connected to each other.

Firewall

A firewall may be a dedicated hardware device through which all network traffic passes, or it may be a program running on a network hub/switch. It analyses all data going in and out of the network to prevent unauthorised data entering or leaving the network. It does this by analysing each packet of data packet attempting to pass through the firewall and deletes it if it does not conform to predefined rules. It can act as a proxy server (see below) for applications by performing all data exchanges with the remote server on their behalf thus making devices inside the firewall invisible to outsiders. Firewalls may be used to prevent the illegal transfer of data, such as attempts by 'hackers' or viruses to send data out from the network.

They may also be used to block data transfers that are legal but which network administrators have deemed unsuitable, such as streaming media (which takes a lot of bandwidth) or data from web sites that contain unsuitable content (for example, a school's firewall). Figure 9.10 shows how a hardware firewall is used.

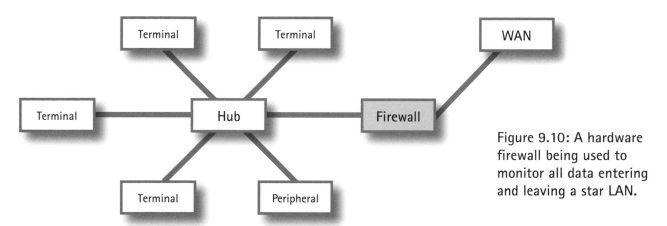

Figure 9.10: A hardware firewall being used to monitor all data entering and leaving a star LAN.

Making PCs invisible

By the way...

Each device on the Internet has a unique **Internet Protocol (IP)** address. It is possible to determine the time taken for data to travel between devices by using commands such as **ping**. A 'live' device will respond to this sort of request while off-line devices cannot respond. Devices behind a firewall will simply ignore unsolicited data from other machines, hence appearing offline. Figure 9.11 shows (left) a web server being 'pinged' with the time taken for the message to find it displayed and (right) another machine known to be online, but behind a firewall. In the latter case, when pinged it appears not to exist. See also Virtual Private Networks in section 10.6.

```
C:\WINDOWS>ping www.colourpoint.co.uk
Pinging colourpoint.co.uk [216.122.83.88] with 32 bytes of data:
Reply from 216.122.83.88: bytes=32 time=211ms TTL=237
Reply from 216.122.83.88: bytes=32 time=192ms TTL=237
Reply from 216.122.83.88: bytes=32 time=192ms TTL=237
Reply from 216.122.83.88: bytes=32 time=190ms TTL=237

Ping statistics for 216.122.83.88:
    Packets: Sent = 4, Received = 4, Lost = 0 (0% loss),
Approximate round trip times in milli-seconds:
    Minimum = 190ms, Maximum = 211ms, Average = 196ms
```

```
C:\WINDOWS>ping 162.11.64.111
Pinging 162.11.64.111 with 32 bytes of data:
Request timed out.
Request timed out.
Request timed out.
Request timed out.

Ping statistics for 162.11.64.111:
    Packets: Sent = 4, Received = 0, Lost = 4 (100% loss)
Approximate round trip times in milli-seconds:
    Minimum = 0ms, Maximum = 0ms, Average = 0ms
```

Figure 9.11: A server being successfully 'pinged' (left) and an attempt to 'ping' a machine behind a firewall (right).

9.6 Other Network Software

As noted above, a firewall can be implemented in software as well as hardware. Two other pieces of software that are often found in networks are:

Proxy Server

A proxy server is a program that sits between a client program (typically a web browser) and an external server (such as a web server). The software may be incorporated into a hardware firewall and monitors all requests being sent to the external server, or that come in from the Internet connection. A proxy server has many functions, which the user may not notice – unless data is blocked:

+ It may act as a **caching proxy** by storing a copy of all information that passes through. Thus, when one user requests, say, a web page, the proxy server first checks to see if it already has an up-to-date copy of that page without needing to access the Internet. If it cannot provide the page it passes the user request on to the actual server. This improves performance as the web page is available immediately. For example, if one user within the Northern Ireland schools' WAN (provided by **C2K**) accesses http://www.bbc.co.uk/news at 8.20 am, they are the first user of the day to access that site and will get a 'fresh' copy from the BBC, which is stored in the cache. The next few hundred users (who may be in other schools) will receive a copy from the cache. In the case of frequently-updated sites, the proxy will make periodic checks to the web server in question.

+ They can provide **additional security**. They can be placed within network firewalls to allow users to access the network, but without giving them full direct access. In this configuration, terminals communicate with the proxy server, but it is the proxy server that contacts the remote network location on behalf of its clients. Filters and rules can be applied at the proxy server to allow only certain information to be received, as all requests have to go through it, for example to prohibit users from accessing certain web sites. Another benefit of this is that it stops the remote network location from knowing the addresses of the user making the request for the information – thus restricting the possibility of malicious sites directly attacking a user's PC.

CD Server

CD servers provide accelerated, concurrent CD/DVD sharing in network environments. They enable administrators to create an **image** of many CDs or DVDs onto a hard disk. From the user's machine, the image looks like a CD/DVD on the network. However, data is accessed from the hard disk, a much faster storage medium. Some CD servers or DVD servers can store the contents of over 500 CDs or 76 DVDs on a network appliance. The advantage of this is that many users can concurrently access the data, which may be a backup disk, third party software, clip art, company archives etc. Security can be added to restrict access.

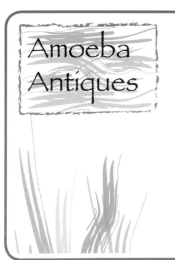

The development of LANs and WANs at Amoeba

When Amoeba first put networks into its offices, cabling was quite expensive. In addition, there was very little traffic on the network in comparison to today's systems. Their Northern Ireland office thus had a single bus LAN with six PCs connected to it. Most data was stored on the server, so since all processing took place on the PCs, most of the data on the network was going either to or from the server, with intervals between this activity.

The Scottish office used a different system – this was one legacy of Amoeba having been two separate companies – and was equipped with a series of **dumb terminals** that had no processing power of their own. As a consequence, the bus network in operation here had a regular stream of data: input from the dumb terminals being sent for processing; output from the server being sent back to the terminals for display.

In due course, a **leased line** connected the two operations. Employees in Northern Ireland could access the Scottish server via a **remote login**. Through running a **telnet** program, they could force their PC to behave like a dumb terminal. Figure 9.12 illustrates this: the document is being processed on the PC while the window is a telnet session. All data input for this is sent to the server for processing and output data for display is sent back. This data is not processed locally.

As the software development operation in Belfast grew, this section of Amoeba required its own file server. Initially this was added to the bus network they had, as shown in figure 9.13.

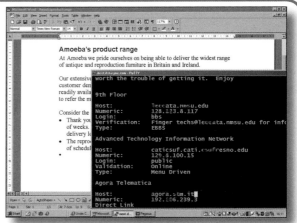

Figure 9.12: Telnet in use.

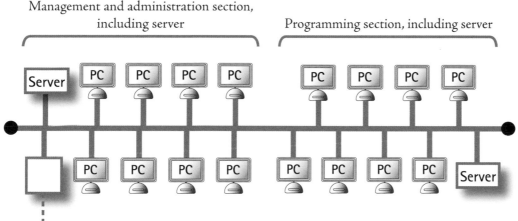

Management and administration section, including server

Programming section, including server

Connection via ISP to Scottish office

Figure 9.13: The initial arrangement for the new file server for the programming section at Amoeba.

This led to significant problems. The volume of traffic on the network caused by the software development section was such that other users of the network were affected. This happened because data packets on a bus network will travel the full length of the cable before the terminators at each end destroy them. Thus a lot of traffic that was intended only for the programming section slowed the network down for everyone.

The initial solution to this was to break the network into two **segments**, connected by a **bridge**. This meant that data relevant to each segment stayed in that segment. If a data packet in one segment was addressed to a device in the other, the bridge would pass it on. The bridge was later replaced by a **switch**, which connected the LAN segments and also connected to Amoeba's ISP.

Over a period of time, several more segments were added to cope with an increased volume of staff. In the late 1990s, the use of bus networks became problematic. As the World Wide Web became more useful to Amoeba, and as staff used it to listen to streaming radio stations, so the volume of traffic on the network grew at a huge rate. As many employees used the Internet, and thus the

network, simultaneously, this increased the chance of collisions. Because many people on the same segment in Amoeba were causing an almost continual stream of data, so the number of collisions multiplied rapidly.

At first, the use of a hardware **firewall** eased the problem. All Internet traffic must pass through this device, which was configured to reject streaming media. This caused some problems as sometimes streaming media was useful for work purposes, but it was a generally acceptable solution. Even with streaming media removed from the equation, the growth of use of the WWW caused a serious problem.

Short of reducing the segments to only two or three PCs, a bus network solution would be difficult to use in the long-term. As a consequence, a series of star networks was developed. Because Amoeba's offices are quite large, the use of a single huge star network would be difficult to realise. To illustrate this, an over-head view of their office is shown in figure 9.14.

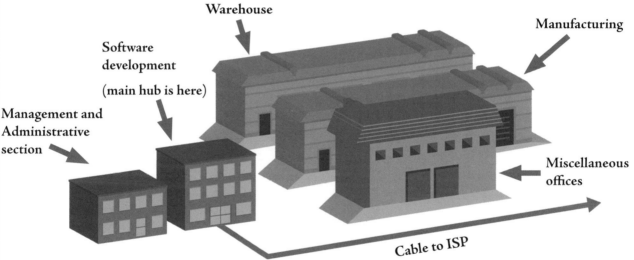

Figure 9.14: Layout of Amoeba's office complex.

The separate *Warehouse*, *Manufacturing* and *Miscellaneous Offices* sections were connected via underground cabling leading to hubs, which in turn lead to LAN segments. The main building is divided into a number of segments, all connecting to a centrally placed hub.

There are many PCs in each of the remote buildings. If a single huge star LAN were used, each PC would require a copper cable to be linked back to the main building which would not be practical. In addition, if more PCs were added, more copper cabling would be needed between the buildings which could lead to a lot of trench digging.

To simplify this, a fibre optic cable was installed from the main building to each remote building. Likewise, fibre optics connected the main hub to each floor in the software development and administrative blocks. Each fibre optic cable connected to a hub to which local devices connected via twisted-pair cable. Effectively, this led to a 'star network of star networks'.

Task

Based on the information you have been given above, draw a diagram to illustrate the new network layout at Amoeba Antiques.

Questions

1. Describe two advantages offered by networks. (4)
2. Describe two disadvantages offered by networks. (4)
3. Describe the main features of a WAN. (4)
4. What is a LAN? (2)
5. Describe the main features, with the aid of a diagram, of four common LAN topologies. (3 each)
6. Describe an advantage and disadvantage of each LAN topology. (8)
7. Name and describe four different devices that are used to connect networks and/or network segments. (3 each)
8. What is the purpose of a firewall? (3)
9. Describe the operation of a proxy server. (3)

CHAPTER 10
Internet Technology

10.1 Introduction

Having studied the technology behind LANs and WANs, this chapter examines the technology behind the Internet itself. For the final point in the specification (below) readers should review the discussions on Internet software in Chapter 7, since there is a degree of crossover between these two areas of the specification.

10.2 Electronic Mail

Electronic mail (e-mail) is a system that allows users to send messages between each other via computers on a network. Messages can be sent between different networks, but some companies have e-mail systems that are entirely internal. An e-mail may be a simple note typed by the user as a text file that their e-mail client can open, but it can also contain an **attached** file intended for some other application. Word documents, images, music files and PDFs can all be sent in this way. Many companies and businesses make extensive use of e-mail because of its speed and reliability. An e-mail can travel the world within seconds, whereas the same message could take a few days if sent by post. This has led to the postal service being dubbed 'snail mail'.

A major advantage of e-mail compared to telephones or fax machines is that the receiving device does not need to be online when data is transmitted. E-mail messages are stored on a server until the recipient downloads them via an e-mail client. Nowadays, many e-mail accounts are WWW-based. There are several benefits from such a service. Users of WWW-based e-mail can access mail from any device with a web browser, such as a PC or mobile phone (instead of being restricted to a single PC with a suitably configured e-mail client). In addition with traditional client-server e-mail, once an e-mail is downloaded to a PC it can only be accessed at that machine whereas web-based e-mail servers store e-mail on the server until the user deletes them.

Broadcasting is a term used to describe the process of sending the same e-mail to many users at once. A user might use this function to contact all of their friends and relatives on a particular mailing list. A company might do so to notify all of their employees or a particular department of a closure or a change in emergency procedures.

An e-mail has a **header** and a **body**. The header contains a wealth of important information. It gives the name and e-mail address of the sender along with those of the recipient(s), and the time and date that the message was sent. In the subject line the sender can type a phrase or short message summarising the content of their message. A server will add other information to help process the message as it is transmitted, but in most cases this will be hidden from the reader.

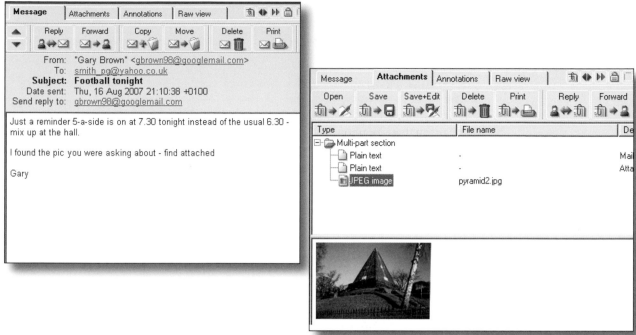

Figure 10.1: An e-mail displayed in an e-mail client (top left). Clicking to view the attachments (top right) shows that the body contains an image as well as the message itself. The third view (bottom) shows part of the "raw source" of the e-mail when it is displayed as text. Only the first part of the text is visible here – the rest is explained on the following pages.

The **body** of the e-mail is the text that the user has sent. The body may also contain attachments that the e-mail client displays as separate files. The Multipurpose Internet Mail Extensions (MIME) standard allows a body to contain plain text and other data that the receiving client interprets appropriately. Anything that is not plain, unformatted ASCII, including HTML and graphics, is sent as a MIME attachment. Figure 10.1 shows an e-mail displayed in three different ways.

The Full Headers of a Typical e-mail

The e-mail presented above is typical of how an end-user views an e-mail. A great deal of additional header information is added by various devices along the route from sender and receiver. Here, it is from a PC e-mail client via an ISP to Google

Mail and then on to Yahoo! Mail. Each device indicates the time it received the e-mail and also what time zone it is in. Most devices append their data to the top of this file when they receive it. Therefore, this is in reverse chronological order. *Note that the headers shown below include additional text not visible in figure 10.1.*

> **X-Apparently-To: smith_pg@yahoo.co.uk via 217.146.182.18; Thu, 16 Aug 2007 13:10:52 -0700**
> **X-Originating-IP: [64.233.182.190]**
> **Authentication-Results: mta299.mail.mud.yahoo.com from=gmail.com; domainkeys=pass (ok)**

This information was added by a Yahoo! server when the e-mail arrived in the recipient's mailbox. It shows the address of the receiving computer, where it got it from and confirmation that it genuinely did come from Google Mail.

> **Received: from 64.233.182.190 (EHLO nf-out-0910.google.com) (64.233.182.190) by mta299.mail.mud.yahoo.com with SMTP; Thu, 16 Aug 2007 13:10:51 -0700** *....and several similar lines....*
> **Received: by nf-out-0910.google.com with SMTP id c10so205816nfd for <smith_pg@yahoo.co.uk>; Thu, 16 Aug 2007 13:10:50 -0700 (PDT)**
> **Received: by 10.78.165.16 with SMTP id n16mr785780hue.1187295049911 ; Thu, 16 Aug 2007 13:10:49 -0700 (PDT)**

These headers trace the route that the e-mail took from the sender to the recipient. The third part has an IP address beginning 10.x.x.x showing that this part of the journey was on a private network, probably within Google Mail's servers.

> **Received: from ?192.168.1.65? ([81.151.132.188]) by mx.google.com with ESMTPS id f6sm2959329nfh.2007.08.16.13.10.43 (version=SSLv3 cipher=OTHER); Thu, 16 Aug 2007 13:10:47 -0700 (PDT)**

This identifies the IP address the e-mail originates from (81.151.132.188), which refers to a domestic DSL LAN. 192.168.1.65 identifies the PC within that house. The time it was received is also noted: 13:10 Pacific-Daylight-Time, or, 20:10 GMT.

> **From: "Gary Brown" <gbrown98@googlemail.com> To: smith_pg@yahoo. co.uk Date: Thu, 16 Aug 2007 21:10:38 +0100**

This header information is usually displayed for the recipient, and identifies the sender and when the e-mail was sent.

> **MIME-Version: 1.0 Content-type: Multipart/Mixed; boundary=Message-Boundary-5180**

Identifies the mail as being in MIME format, so the receiving client knows to display attachments appropriately.

> **Subject: Football tonight Reply-to: gbrown98@googlemail.com Message-ID: <46C4BD4E.25387.2A3730@garybrown98.gmail.com>**

Gives the subject line of the message, and the address that replies should be directed to. The second line is a unique identifier added by the sender's server.

> **X-Confirm-Reading-To: gbrown98@googlemail.com**
> **X-pmrqc: 1**

```
Return-receipt-to: gbrown98@googlemail.com
Priority: normal X-mailer: Pegasus Mail for Windows (4.41)
X-Antivirus: AVG for E-mail 7.5.484 [269.11.19/955]
```

These contain general information, such as the fact that the sender has asked for a receipt of message delivery, an indication of the message's priority, the name of the program that sent it and the fact that it has been scanned for viruses.

```
--Message-Boundary-5180
Content-type: text/plain; charset=US-ASCII
Content-transfer-encoding: 7BIT
Content-description: Mail message body
Just a reminder 5-a-side is on at 7.30 tonight instead of the usual 6.30 - mix up
at the hall.  I found the pic you were asking about - find attached.
Gary
```

Identification of the start of the body and what sort of data is in it. The body text then follows it (ie the message that the sender actually typed).

```
--Message-Boundary-5180
Content-type: text/plain; charset=US-ASCII
Content-disposition: inline
Content-description: Attachment information.
The following section of this message contains a file attachment prepared
for transmission using the Internet MIME message format. If you are using
Pegasus Mail, or any other MIME-compliant system, you should be able to
save it or view it from within your mailer. If you cannot, please ask your system
administrator for assistance.
---- File information ----------
File: pyramid2.jpg
Date: 16 Aug 2007, 21:07
Size: 46339 bytes.
Type: JPEG-image
```

This lets the recipient know that what follows is an attachment generated by the sending client, formatted as 'plain text'. This is a throwback to the days when many e-mail clients did not support attachments, and so any attached files would be displayed as ASCII 'gibberish' which the user would have to manually transfer into a text editor and save with extension **.jpg**. It is good practice to retain this format in case the recipient is using an old machine.

```
--Message-Boundary-5180 Content-type: Image/JPEG; name="pyramid2.jpg"
Content-disposition: attachment; filename="pyramid2.jpg"
Content-transfer-encoding: BASE64
```

This identifies the attached file and its type.

```
/9j/4AAQSkZJRgABAQEBLAEsAAD2wBDAAUDBAQEwUEBAQFBQU
GBwwIBwcHBw8LCwkMEQ8SEhEPRETFhwXExQaFRERGCEYGh0dHx8
fExciJCIeJBweHx7/wBDAQUFBQcGBw4ICA4eFB.....
```

This ASCII, which would continues for around 15 pages if shown in full, is interpreted by the receiving device as a JPEG image and displayed appropriately.

E-mail Clients and Protocols

E-mail clients are programs that run on a PC and communicate with a remote server to download and upload messages. There is no requirement for sender and recipient to use the same client. The most commonly used protocols are:

+ **Post Office Protocol 3** (POP3): to download mail from a server to a client. This is suitable for users who only download e-mail to a single PC.
+ **Internet Mail Access Protocol** (IMAP): in contrast to POP3 allows a temporary copy of an e-mail to be downloaded to a client but a permanent copy remains on the server. Suitable for those who access e-mail from several PCs.
+ **Simple Mail Transfer Protocol** (SMTP): to upload mail from client to server.
+ **Messaging Application Programming Interface** (MAPI): a proprietary standard used between the Microsoft Exchange server and the Microsoft Outlook client to provide similar functionality to IMAP.

Almost all e-mail clients and e-mail providers (such as ISPs) allow users a choice of IMAP or POP for accessing mail. They also support SMTP for uploading mail. With the exception of IMAP, the above protocols can be freely implemented by anyone designing an e-mail client or server.

*Note that some books classify e-mail clients as **utilities** rather than **applications** because of how they originated. E-mail was once a simple tool using the sendmail command in Unix. E-mail clients later developed into text-based tools such as Pine. Modern graphical e-mail clients included Mozilla Thunderbird, Pegasus Mail and Eudora. Some e-mail clients, such as Microsoft Outlook, also contain calendar software.*

Modern e-mail clients do much more than the simple sending and receiving of messages. The main features of an e-mail client include:

+ Sending and receiving e-mail via **several different accounts**, sometimes from different providers.
+ **Filtering** e-mail based on content, for example moving messages with a particular subject line into a different folder to either highlight them or prevent them disguising more urgent messages.
+ **Spam filtering**, to remove unwanted 'junk' e-mail messages. Early ones searched for certain key words commonly found, while more recent ones use Bayesian spam filters, named after the mathematician Thomas Bayes.

Task Use the WWW to research Bayesian spam filtering. How does it work? Why is it more effective than searching for key words?

+ **Sorting and searching** e-mails based on content, date or sender.
+ Managing **address books** so that the user does not have to remember everybody's e-mail address, but can simply type their name instead.
+ Managing distribution lists where the user can set up a list of people's e-mail addresses and then type a single phrase (eg 'Football Team') and the e-mail will automatically be sent to everyone in the list. People can be added to the list manually or, in some systems, automatically.

E-mail clients should not be confused with web-based e-mail accounts offered by systems such as Yahoo! or Hotmail. Users of web-based accounts will often have access to online services, such as Instant Messaging, file sharing and games.

Advantages of e-mail include:

+ Communication is much quicker than traditional postal services.

+ Saved e-mail provides an accurate record of communication.

+ Correspondents have more time to consider the wording of replies than a telephone conversation offers.

+ Correspondents do not need to be online at the same time, so communication does not require people to be available at exactly the same time.

Disadvantages of e-mail include:

+ Security can be a concern as it is very easy to accidentally (or deliberately) send confidential material. Some businesses limit employees to sending and receiving messages internally.

+ Once an attached file such as an important contract document is e-mailed changes can be made to it. This can lead to data inconsistency as many contradictory versions of the same file may exist.

+ Spam e-mail can become a burden, and can also leave users vulnerable to phishing: the name given to scams whereby an e-mail or web site masquerades as a legitimate company to trick a user into revealing personal data such as credit card details (see figure 10.2).

+ People can receive multiple messages per day: it is possible for an employee to receive hundreds. This can lead to 'information overload'.

+ Users may also waste company resources by sending e-mail of a frivolous nature.

From: "Royal Bank of Scotland" <corporateservice.refAA9960728981865.ib@rbs.co.uk>
To: "Clarke_rice"
Subject: The Royal Bank of Scotland: necessary to be read!
Date sent: Wed, 08 Aug 2007 23:55:47 -0400

Dear Royal Bank of Scotland customer,

The Royal Bank of Scotland Customer Service requests you to complete Digital Banking Customer Confirmation Form (CCF).

This procedure is obligatory for all customers of the Royal Bank of Scotland.

Please select the hyperlink and visit the address listed to access Digital Banking Customer Confirmation Form (CCF).

http://sessionid-553311.rbs.co.uk/customerdirectory/direct/ccf.aspx

Again, thank you for choosing the Royal Bank of Scotland for your business needs. We look forward to working with you.

Figure 10.2: Part of a typical phishing e-mail that has actually nothing to do with the Royal Bank Of Scotland. The hyperlink is usually fake (when the mouse pointer is placed over it the URL http://sessionid553311. rbs.co.uk.userport.li/ customerdirectory/direct/ ccf.aspx is revealed).

10.3 Video Conferencing

Video Conferencing allows people to see and converse with each other in real time via screens, cameras and microphones. It is typically delivered through a dedicated high bandwidth communications line. The end result is not unlike using a webcam or videophone, though it offers much higher image quality. A video conference can be restricted to two parties, or it may involve several parties, the main benefit being that it is time effective as it dramatically reduces the need to travel. A well-organised video conference can link representatives from several continents without them having to leave their respective offices.

Figure 10.3: Examples of the image quality that could be expected from video conferencing (top) and a webcam (bottom).

Video conferencing is also popular in universities as it allows students on different campuses to organise seminars, tutorials, workshops etc, without having to meet in person. Similarly, such systems could allow schools with small class sizes or a lack of suitably qualified teachers to offer subjects which would not be feasible otherwise. Such systems are already used in remote locations such as the Australian Outback, where they previously used two-way radio for the same purpose.

While video conferencing requires expensive technology to ensure a high quality of image and sound, webcams and videophones allow simple one-to-one meetings at a much lower cost for those occasions where image quality is not vital. Figure 10.3 illustrates the difference in image resolution that would been seen in video conferencing (top) and a webcam (bottom). In addition, the video refresh rate in a webcam system is greatly reduced, typically to around four frames per second while video conferencing allows a refresh rate similar to a television screen.

Advantages of video conferencing include:

+ Valuable time and money are not wasted on travelling to meet other people.
+ Unlike e-mail or text-based forums, users can see each other, allowing body language to be read.
+ Video conferences can be recorded, forming an accurate record of business meetings which can be preserved for further assessment.
+ In an educational setting, regular talks or presentations that do not require physical interaction can accommodate a range of students from a range of locations. This allows one teacher of a minority subject to teach to pupils from many different schools.

Disadvantages of video conferencing include:

+ The necessary equipment, combined with the fact that higher video and sound quality requires higher bandwidth, results in significantly greater costs.
+ Certain aspects of a physical meeting, such as shaking hands, cannot be replicated. This can sometimes be a barrier in building trust.
+ Relevant documents cannot be physically passed around a table.
+ The informal aspect of traditional meetings, such as talking over a meal, is lost.
+ If the technology fails, the meeting is potentially over.

10.4 Mobile Telecommunications

Mobile telephones provide a wide number of benefits to businesses and to private individuals in many scenarios. In the West, it is now taken for granted that most people will own one. In parts of the developing world, 'mobiles' have become the standard expression of telephone services, due to the ease of setting up a wireless network compared to the difficulties in setting up a wired network.

The mobile telephone was initially developed as a device for making voice calls without restricting the user to a hard-wired socket. It provides more functions than traditional voice calls, hence the growing use of the term **telecommunications** (communications over distance) in place of telephone (speaking over distance) to describe the features offered by this technology.

Features of Mobile Telecommunications

Mobile phones offer a number of features related to traditional voice calls:

- Directory and Caller ID;
- Short Messaging System (text messaging);
- MMS (Multimedia Messaging Service);
- Video Calling;
- Voicemail.

In addition, mobile telecommunications often offer features that are not explicitly related to traditional voice calls such as Internet access, cameras, radio, television, MP3 music players, road maps and *Bluetooth* and *WiFi* connectivity. The availability of these services is often dependent on what 'generation' their equipment belongs to, as discussed later.

Directory and Caller ID: Mobile phones, like some land lines, allow users to store an address book of contacts. Instead of keying in a full phone number, users browse this directory with a menu-driven interface to select the person they wish to call. The user can customise this function by tagging a particular ringtone or image to each of the contacts in their address book. When a call is received, the caller's name and number are displayed on-screen.

Short Messaging System (SMS) is a popular method of sending information to a friend where a lengthy call is not needed. One message may contain up to 160 characters. While modern phones allow users to enter longer messages, they are actually split over several individual messages (and charged as such). SMS is also used to provide premium rate services, such as entering television competitions, and the delivery of content via Extended Messaging Service (EMS). For the latter, the user sends a SMS message to an advertised number, whereupon they are charged at a premium rate and receive data (ringtone, wallpaper, theme, game etc.) in return. However, more recent technologies, such as MMS and WAP, offer the functionality of EMS and may eventually replace it completely.

Multimedia Messaging Service (MMS) is an enhancement over traditional SMS, allowing the transfer of longer text messages, images and short video clips. In Immediate Delivery MMS, the message is downloaded to the receiving phone without the user being prompted. In Deferred Delivery MMS, the user is informed a message is available for download from the network's servers. This benefits users who are billed by the amount of data downloaded since they can choose to ignore messages they don't want to pay for, such as advertising.

Video Calling offers similar features to webcam-based video conferencing (ie a two-way low-bandwidth link where it is sufficient for people to see each other, but where high-quality image resolution and a fast frame rate are not essential). It has been technically possible for many years, but the price of suitable equipment and the availability of sufficient bandwidth throughout telecoms networks has delayed widespread availability.

Voicemail is a development of the traditional answering machine that automatically answers a telephone, except that the message is saved on the network provider's server. In most cases, the network provider will text the user to remind them that there is a message waiting. Unlike a traditional answering machine, voicemail can record a message while a caller's phone is in use. Voicemail can usually be accessed even if the user has no mobile network coverage by calling a special number and entering a PIN. This makes voicemail popular in business.

Internet Access: Many third generation mobile phones (see 'By the way', below) have similar WWW access to a PC, although **web accessibility** (see Chapter 7) is an important consideration for designers because of a phone's hardware limitations. Many sites support **Wireless Application Protocol (WAP),** an alternative to HTTP for mobile devices that ensures sites are accessible with a tiny screen and keypad. WAP files are saved separately from their HTTP equivalent and due to the screen size large files are impractical. However WAP is suitable for many uses such as checking e-mail, news headlines or transport timetables. WAP devices access HTTP sites through services such as *Opera Mini* or Google *Mobile*. These store a large HTTP page on a remote server and reformat it for display on a WAP screen, transferring it to the mobile device in small sections at the user's request.

Camera Phones are a common form of mobile phone and have a resolution comparable to low specification digital cameras. While they may not have the storage capacity of a dedicated camera, extra memory cards can be purchased to slot into the phone. Camera phones allow easy transmission of still images or short motion-picture clips via MMS. There are various practical uses of this function; for example an engineer may send images of equipment to help diagnose a technical fault, but most people use them to take photographs of their friends.

Radio and Television: Radio has been available via mobile phones for some time, by adding a DAB (Digital Audio Broadcasting) or FM (Frequency Modulation) tuner to the handset. Television services are also available on suitably equipped handsets. The range of channels available depends on the mobile phone operator and the fees being paid by the user since there is currently no mobile phone equivalent of *Freeview* television. Mobile phones rely on a separate broadcast signal and, at present, there are a number of mutually incompatible standards in this market. Such services are tailored to the needs of mobile users and include on-demand video news headlines (eg from BBC News) and radio programmes (eg Channel 4 radio). **Podcasting** may also play a role here, where users have recorded content 'pushed' directly to a mobile phone, instead of transferring from a PC to an MP3 player.

By the way... **Generations of Mobile Phones**

The services available to a user depend on which 'generation' they subscribe to:

+ **'Zeroth' Generation (0G).** Developed since the 1940s, these services used unsecured radio broadcasting, and were often used in rural areas where a wired network would be too costly. This ancestor of modern services was wireless, but handsets required mains electricity or a large battery.
+ **First Generation (1G).** The first commonly available service in the UK was developed in the 1980s. The mobile handsets used large batteries that required frequent charging. For this reason, early models were often confined to cars.
+ **Second Generation (2G)** originally offered similar functionality to 1G, but used digital transmissions that could be encrypted. SMS was first possible

with 2G (though not widely available at first). '2.5G' is a marketing term that describes later 2G phones offering some services associated with 3G (eg WAP and image transmission). These are possible because of changes in how 2G services send data (**packet switching** having replaced **circuit switching**). Because rivals do not usually share facilities, one operator may offer excellent coverage in a region while another's is poor. The shorter transmission range of 2G, when compared to 1G, makes this more obvious to users.

+ **General Packet Radio Service (GPRS).** This is the packet switching technology associated with 2.5G mobile phones. GPRS can be used for services such as WAP, SMS and MMS though may be expensive to use, as many providers charge per megabyte, unlike the flat rate offered with ADSL broadband or 3G mobile services. GPRS adapters can be used to give Internet access to laptop PCs.

+ **Third Generation (3G).** This offers higher bandwidth than 2G and allows services such as streaming video. In many countries, 3G uses a different set of radio frequencies than 2G, so new transmitters must be built. As a result, a 3G customer may not have access to 3G services outside high population areas, which are usually given priority in the allocation of transmitters. Many 3G networks transfer customers to a 2G network if they move outside 3G transmission range.

Related Devices

A wide range of devices related to mobile telephones are available. For example, **Personal Data Assistants (PDAs)** which are a development of the personal organiser, which was itself a development of the written diary. The PDA offers the facilities of a palm top computer such as office applications, e-mail and web browsing. A number of such devices are designed to synchronise to a desktop PC, such as cross referencing calendar entries or updating word processed documents. Popular PDAs include smartphones such as the RIM *BlackBerry*.

10.5 Equipment Needed to Access the Internet

A PC cannot connect to the Internet without specialist hardware and software:

Hardware	Software

+ Computer
+ Modem / ASDL Adapter / Broadband Router
+ Telephone line.
+ Hardware connecting computer and phone line:
  + 56k Modem (dial-up)
  + ISDN adapter
  + ASDL adapter (direct connection to broadband)
  + Network Interface Card in PC to connect to ASDL router (if several devices share a broadband connection).
	+ Dial-up software to connect to the Internet Service Provider (ISP), provided by the ISP or the OS.
	+ A web browser such as *Internet Explorer* or *Firefox* to display web pages.
	+ An e-mail package such as Pegasus *Mail* or Microsoft *Outlook*.
	+ A news reader to participate in newsgroups, such as *Xnews*.
	+ An FTP client such as *WS-FTP*.

Task	Research three ISPs and compare the services that each provides.

There are a number of alternative methods of connecting to the Internet. The most commonly used are dial-up, ISDN and ADSL (broadband).

Traditional dial-up connections

These require a **modem** to communicate over analogue phone lines by converting the computer's digital output to analogue form for transmission and back to digital at the receiving end. The word 'modem' is short for **mo**dulate-**dem**odulate. Modems can be external (connected to the computer's serial port) or internal (located in one of the computer's expansion slots). Modems have a maximum bandwidth of 56 kilobits per second. The PC dials a phone number provided by the ISP which connects it to a remote server and hence to the Internet, as shown in figure 10.4.

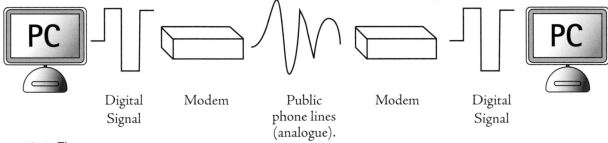

| Digital Signal | Modem | Public phone lines (analogue). | Modem | Digital Signal |

Figure 10.4: The operation of two modems to transfer digital signals over an analogue public phone line.

Advantages of dial-up connections include:

+ Available to anyone with a telephone line.
+ Useful for an occasional Internet user who does not want a monthly contract.
+ Broadband is not available in some rural areas so dial-up may be the only option.

Disadvantages of dial-up connections include:

+ Slow transmission speed which can make the transfer of files extremely laborious, and the time spent online can be expensive.
+ The phone line cannot be used for the Internet and for calls at the same time.
+ At peak times the connection will be even slower, or perhaps not available at all, as all modems at the ISP can be engaged.

Integrated Services Digital Network (ISDN)

ISDN passes a computer's digital output along a digital line. Instead of a modem, an ISDN adapter is used. Basic ISDN has a speed of 64kbaud though faster ISDN services are offered in multiples of this, such as ISDN-2 (2x64 kbaud) and ISDN-4 (4x64 kbaud). Many ISPs are phasing out the fibre-optic based ISDN now that broadband ADSL services of comparable speed are available through phone lines.

Advantages of ISDN include:

+ Higher bandwidth, allowing better transmission of graphics and sound.
+ The Internet can be used at the same time as the telephone.
+ Unlike ADSL providers, ISDN providers usually offer the same upload and

download speed to consumers. This can be important to businesses who transmit a lot of data, such as web hosting services.

Disadvantages of ISDN include:

+ The hardware required for ISDN must be installed by an engineer.

+ ISDN requires fibre-optic cables, which also need to be installed.

+ The development of ADSL has reduced the support for ISDN. Therefore, commercial offerings are often much slower than ADSL. Domestic ISDN is being withdrawn from service.

+ On a monthly basis ISDN can work out more expensive than dial-up access.

Asynchronous Digital Subscriber Line (ADSL)

Often referred to as **broadband**, ADSL carries a number of different signals (eg audio and video) simultaneously over a single communications link. The bandwidth available to subscribers is determined by proximity to their local telephone exchange and can vary from 512 kbps to 24 Mbps. Subscribers to an ISP with dedicated digital networks (eg a cable TV operator) can enjoy higher speeds than subscribers connecting via telephone lines.

Advantages of ADSL include:

+ Compared to dial-up or ISDN, fast access speeds are possible, which enables large files to be transferred and downloaded quickly.

+ Online gaming is only possible using a broadband account.

+ It is possible to simultaneously make telephone calls, send e-mails, send and receive faxes, and access the Internet via a single phone line.

+ A broadband account can be permanently connected to the Internet with no per-minute billing and no danger of blocking incoming phone calls.

+ There are no additional dial-up charges as a fixed monthly rate is charged.

Disadvantages of ADSL include:

+ A permanent connection makes a computer more susceptible to viruses. A firewall and antivirus software should be in place and updated regularly.

+ Broadband is not yet available in all rural areas as not all parts of the PSTN (Public Switched Telephone Network) are suitably equipped.

+ Actual speeds of connection are very much dependent on factors such as the number of people online at a given time or the distance between the PC and a telephone exchange. These can dramatically effect the actual connection speed.

+ An ADSL adapter is required for a single computer, but the user needs a broadband router and Ethernet LAN cards for each additional PC.

+ Upload speed is often much less than download speed (eg 256 kbaud compared to 2 Gbaud). Few users may notice this discrepancy, however, as most use their broadband for downloading files.

+ Most broadband accounts are 'capped', meaning that the user has a limited monthly usage allowance and can be penalised if they exceed this. Accounts with an unlimited monthly usage are available, but they are more expensive.

10.6 Internet Protocol (IP) Addresses

An Internet Protocol (IP) address uniquely identifies any device connected to the Internet. Data is transmitted as **packets**, containing data in the 'body' and the IP address of the sender and receiver in the 'header'. Large items of data are split into several packets that are re-assembled by the receiving device. **Routers** that join networks together use IP addresses to identify where data should be sent to. The protocols governing data transmission prevent devices that are not addressed in the header from accessing the data, although many applications encrypt data in case this security feature has been disabled on some network devices.

The IP address is usually written as four sets of numbers in the range 0 to 255. For example, *213.171.219.239*. IP addresses map onto a **Fully Qualified Domain Name (FQDN)** written in a form that is more familiar to web users (in this case, *www.colourpoint.co.uk*). In decimal form, the number 255 seems strange, although it makes perfect sense in binary: *1111 1111*, or 2^7. Viewed in binary, more detail can be revealed from an IP address. Our above example, *213.171.219.239* is *1101 0101. 1010 1011.1101 1011. 1110 1111* in binary.

Networks are assigned a range of IP addresses that may belong to one of five **classes**, depending on how many devices are within the network:

Class A networks have IP addresses beginning with *0*. The next 7 bits identify the network. Hence these networks have IP addresses beginning in the range *0000 0000* to *0111 1111* (or, with IP addresses *0.x.x.x* to *127.x.x.x*). For example, IP addresses beginning *0100 0111* (with IP addresses *71.x.x.x*) will all belong to one particular Class A network. The last 24 bits identify any machine within a network (16,777,215 possibilities in total, per network).

Class B networks have IP addresses beginning *10*. The next 14 bits identify the network. Hence these have IP addresses beginning *10 00 0000. 0000 0000* to *10 11 1111. 1111 1111* (or, with IP addresses *128.0.x.x* to *191.255.x.x*). The last 16 bits identify a machine within a network (65,535 in total).

Class C networks have IP addresses beginning with *110*. The next 21 bits identify the network. Hence these IP addresses begin with *110 0 0000.0000 0000.0000 0000* to *110 1 1111.1111 1111.1111.1111* (or, *192.0.0.x* to *223.255.255.x*). Any class C network has a maximum of 256 devices.

Class D networks have IP addresses beginning 1110 and are reserved for 'multicast' networks where many devices receive the same data, such as Internet Relay Chat (IRC) systems. A multicast network's IP address will therefore begin with anything from *1110 0000* to *1110 1111* (or, *224.x.x.x* to *239.x.x.x*). An IP address in this case identifies a group of devices subscribing to a particular multicast network and each individual machine will also belong to a Class A-C network and have a unique IP address.

Class E networks have IP addresses beginning *1111* (*1111 0000* to *1111 1111* or, *240.x.x.x* to *255.x.x.x*). These are not normally used, however, and are reserved for experimental purposes. A number of other IP addresses are also reserved for special purposes. For example, all devices identify themselves as 127.0.0.1 as well as their 'real' IP address (the computing equivalent of 'me' versus your real name).

192.168.x.x is also reserved for special purposes, such as Virtual Private Networks (see below).

Once the Class of network and the network itself have been identified, the rest of the IP address can be further subdivided by network administrators to identify particular groups of devices.

Copy out the IP address for *www.colourpoint.co.uk* as it appears in binary (see above). Then, using the information in this section determine if this address belongs to a class A, B, C, D or E network. Then identify the **bits** that refer to the network, and the **bits** that refer to the particular machine.

T a s k

Virtual Private Networks (VPNs)

It would be virtually impossible to assign a unique IP address to every device on the Internet. There are a number of ways to sidestep this problem, including VPNs which have the added advantage of bringing security benefits.

This section is being written on a desktop PC with an IP address of 192.168.1.65. The laptop nearby is 192.168.1.64, yet many readers of this book will have PCs with the exact same IP addresses. This is because these IP addresses have been allocated by the author's local hub as part of a domestic LAN. Meanwhile, the hub has an IP address of 81.151.246.33, which is the IP address remote servers will use to identify any machine within the LAN. Through a process called **Network Address Translation**, the hub will convey data to the correct machine. While the hub's address is allocated by an ISP and may change next time it is re-booted, the IP addresses within the VPN remain static.

A number of sets of IP addresses have been reserved for private network use, including 10.x.x.x (Class A), 172.x.x.x (Class B) and 192.168.x.x (Class C) and a network administrator will use whichever is appropriate.

IPv6

While the current 32 bit version of IP addressing (IPv4) will run out in due course, an alternative that is gradually being adopted is IPv6. This uses 128 bits to identify machines, or approximately 3.4×10^{38} in total. Theoretically, this is enough to allow each man, woman and child on Earth to have billions of devices connected to the Internet.

10.7 Protocols

A **protocol** is a set of standard rules that describes how data is transmitted. It must be followed to ensure that transmitted data is received and understood at its destination. Protocols allow machines of different standards (such as speed or operating system) to communicate. Protocols determine:

+ The cabling used and the standards for physical connection.
+ The mode of transmission, ie in **full duplex** mode or **half duplex**. In the latter case the protocol must allow determination of which device has control of the communications link.

+ The speed of transmission, usually determined by the slowest machine.
+ The data format.
+ How each device indicates that it has finished sending or receiving a message.
+ The error checking and correction used in the network.

As stated earlier, when data is transmitted, data is broken into a series of **packets** that are made up of the data plus a **header** containing information such as the address of the sender and receiver. The following terms should be understood:

+ **Packet:** a unit of transmitted data, constructed of data and a **header**.
+ **Transmission:** the act of sending data.
+ **Sender:** a machine that sends data.
+ **Receiver:** a machine that receives data.
+ **Header:** the part of a packet of data that includes:
  + the destination of data;
  + the source of data;
  + **cyclic redundancy check** or **CRC** (a checksum): information added to a packet header by the sender to allow a receiver to error-check received data;
  + packet number (a single piece of data may be split over several packets – it is important they are re-constructed in order).

A simple model for a packet of data being transmitted on a network is thus:

Data	CRC	Packet no.	Sender IP	Receiver IP

The Need for Protocols

As has been explained, protocols are a set of rules governing data transmission that allows devices of different speeds and operating systems to exchange data. For two machines to communicate they must follow an agreed set of rules, such as the **Hypertext Transfer Protocol (HTTP)** used with the World Wide Web. Protocols are not limited to machines on the Internet: those on a LAN communicate through the Ethernet protocol and mobile phones use guidelines such as **Short Message Service (SMS)** protocol.

Many protocols on the Internet were established when most web servers used the Unix operating system. When other servers connected to the Internet, they had to follow procedures that already existed, whether or not they were Unix based. Although the majority of devices now employ other operating systems, the same rules remain. Anyone attempting to alter them would lose access to the rest of the Internet.

The Open Systems Interconnection (OSI) Seven–Layer Model

As networks developed, so a number of differing protocols were developed. A drawback of this was the difficulty of connecting networks using different protocols. To unify these, the **OSI seven-layer model** was proposed. This model provides a framework that all protocols must work within. It is based on the concept of **packet switching**, in which large pieces of data are divided into small packets for transmission. These packets are then sent separately across the network, being directed on their journey by routers, which determine the optimum path to their destination where they are reassembled into the correct order.

Within the OSI model seven **layers** of header information are added to each packet of data to be transmitted. The sending device adds this information in a particular order and transmits the data. The receiver removes this header information in the reverse order, leaving the original data. As well as the data itself, the seven layers are:

Layer	Description
Application	Represents the services that directly support applications such as software for file transfers, database access, and electronic mail.
Presentation	Manages security by providing services such as encryption, and compresses data so that fewer bits need to be transferred on the network.
Session	Establishes dialogue control between the two computers in a session, regulating which side transmits, when and how long it transmits for.
Transport	Handles error recognition and recovery. It also re-packages long messages when necessary into small packets for transmission and, at the receiving end, rebuilds packets into the original message. The receiving Transport layer also sends receipt acknowledgements.
Network	Addresses messages and translates logical addresses and names into physical addresses. It also determines the route from the source to the destination computer and manages traffic problems.
Data Link	Packages raw bits from the Physical layer into frames (logical, structured packets for data). This layer is responsible for transferring frames from one computer to another, without errors. After sending a frame, it waits for an acknowledgement from the receiving computer.
Physical	The actual stream of bits along some physical medium. This layer defines how the cable is attached to the network adapter and what transmission technique is used to send data over the cable.

TCP/IP (Transmission Control Protocol/Internet Protocol) is used to transmit actual data packets on the Internet. The protocol implements the part of the OSI model responsible for transmitting data between LANs and WANs (ie the **Transport** and **Network** layers of the model) regardless of the type of hardware and software being used. The remaining layers of the OSI model are governed either by the application or the Ethernet network being used:

OSI seven layer	TCP/IP equivalent
Application	Application (eg telnet, ftp, e-mail)
Presentation	Not Defined
Session	Not Defined
Transport	Transport control protocol (TCP)
Network	Internet protocol (IP)
Data Link	Data Link (decided by the Ethernet in use)
Physical	Physical (decided by the Ethernet in use)

The operation of TCP/IP is shown in figure 10.5. The **TCP layer** breaks the data from the end user into packets of fewer than 1500 characters. Each packet is given a 'header' that contains information about how they should be reassembled at the destination. A checksum is also added to validate the accuracy of the transmission. The **IP layer** labels each packet with the correct destination address using Internet Protocol. The IP layer then is responsible for routing the individual packets from the sender to the recipient across the WAN.

When data is received at the destination it is processed in reverse order (ie the arrows in figure 10.5 are reversed) and header / trailer information is removed at the appropriate layer. TCP will recalculate the checksum to verify the accuracy of the data: if a data packet shows a discrepancy it is discarded and a request is sent for that packet to be transmitted again.

Figure 10.5: The progressive formation of an Ethernet data frame as it passes down through the layers of the TCP/IP model.

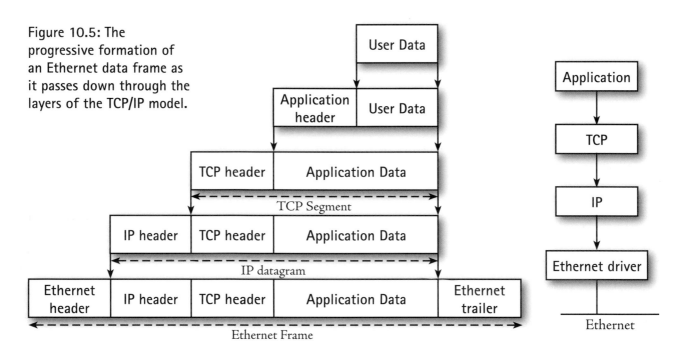

10.8 Definitions of Networking

Many concepts familiar to students are changing. While **LANs** and **WANs** were defined in section 9.3, their distinction is blurring in that neighbouring buildings can now be connected to a single LAN via wireless technology. While this type of network may once have been called a WAN, it is less clear-cut if the buildings are, for example, a house and garage. While students should be familiar with LAN/WAN as the main types of computer network and know the standard definitions for them, the following should also be known:

+ **MAN: Metropolitan Area Network**, *a small WAN that is optimised to connect computers within a city or large campus, usually characterised by the use of fibre optic cables*. Readers of this book who have access to cable television may well access the Internet via a MAN that was developed in the early 1990s at huge expense because of the cost of laying cables. Wireless technologies such as **WiMax** allow Internet providers to enable access for an entire city from a single transmitter. **WiFi** provides 'hotspots', such as in airports or hotels, to allow any traveller to access the Internet with little hassle and without cabling. It is likely that in time the term 'MAN' will become chiefly associated with these city-wide wireless networks. WiFi and WiMax are fully discussed in section 10.10.

+ **PAN: Personal Area Network**, *a network of devices within a few metres of each other and close to a person, usually communicating wirelessly.* One example is **Bluetooth** devices (see section 10.10) which connect mobile phones to earpieces, or PCs to peripherals. Wireless PANs are also used in short range transmitters that connect games consoles to controllers, while wired PANs connect entertainment devices such as iPods and camcorders.

+ **PSTN: Public Switched Telephone Network**, the traditional land line network dedicated to voice, such as BT in the UK. PSTN operators have accommodated non-voice data for several decades on an ageing copper-based network and have spent huge sums of money upgrading to fibre optic-based technologies. PSTN operators are starting to use **WiMax** technology to overcome a lack of sufficient bandwidth for many users (see section 10.10).

10.9 Cable Communication Technology

Four major types of cable are in use in networks today:

Cable	Maximum segment length	Maximum nodes per segment	Advantages
Thick Coax	500m	100	Good for backbones
Thin Coax	200m	30	Cheapest system
Twisted Pair (shielded and unshielded)	100m	1024	Easy maintenance
Fibre optics	2000m	1024	Best between buildings, massive bandwidth.

Coaxial cable (coax) is similar in construction to a TV aerial cable (figure 10.6). It consists of a central copper wire to carry the signal with a polyurethane coating and a layer of braided copper insulation. This insulation reduces, but does not eliminate, electrical interference. Commonly referred to as **Thin Ethernet,** it is a cheap and easy way to connect workstations that are relatively close to one another and is thus good for small networks. It is known for sending a strong signal and is generally used in bus topologies. Connections are generally easy to install, by disconnecting two cables that are joined together and inserting a 'T-piece' in place of the connector which plugs into the rear of a PC. The bus topology makes it difficult to isolate problems and thus **unshielded twisted pair** has become more common.

Unshielded twisted pair (UTP) and shielded twisted pair (STP). With UTP small copper cables are twisted to help cancel out electromagnetic interference from sources such as nearby cables. There are five grades with one being the lowest. The tighter the twisting, the higher the transmission rate and the greater the cost. UTP's lack of shielding results in a high

Image from Harting Technology Group

Image from Toptronics

Figure 10.6: Coaxial cable (top), and a typical Ethernet connection (bottom).

degree of physical flexibility but also makes it susceptible to radio and electrical interference. UTP is the most popular form of LAN cabling because it is the cheapest to install, and can handle high-speed data. A low-grade form of UTP (Category 3) is used for telephone cable while higher-grades of UTP (Categories 4 and 5) are used for LANs. The extra cost of fitting Category 5 over slower alternatives is negligible, so it can be installed even if a network doesn't need that level of bandwidth right away. STP, or Category 1, wiring is a more expensive form of UTP with a higher resistance to interference because of its extra shielding. The cabling and connectors used with UTP closely resemble standard telephone cabling and collections.

Fibre optic cable (figure 10.7) carries enormous amounts of data in the form of light pulses. It is very thin, light and flexible and is virtually immune to electrical interference. It is capable of very high bandwidths, in the order of several Gbps and requires repeaters only every 60 miles, compared to 3-4 miles for copper cable. It is thus mainly used for long distance, high bandwidth communications like cable TV, and 'backbone' connections between cities. It is difficult to 'tap' a fibre optic cable since cutting the sheathing will immediately disrupt the flow of data, making it popular for high-security communications such as banks. It can be used

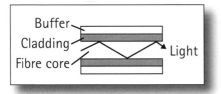

Figure 10.7: Fibre optic cable operates by the principle of total internal reflection.

in explosive or flammable atmospheres, for example, in the petrochemical industries or munitions sites, without any risk of ignition. In addition as fibre optic cable is not made from copper wire it will not corrode. Fibre optic cable is more expensive per metre than copper due to the cost of equipment to convert the light signals into pulses of light, more specialised installation and repair and the difficulty in locating the position of a break in the fibre. However, it is still cheaper per megabyte of data.

ISDN technology was discussed in section 10.5 of this book.

10.10 Wireless Communication Technology

Wireless technologies are becoming increasingly popular., and include:

Bluetooth

Bluetooth is an example of PAN technology, and is most associated with connecting mobile phones to earpieces or sharing data between handsets. A Bluetooth network may consist of a 'master' device with seven other connected devices, plus up to 255 devices in 'standby' mode. The master can deactivate an active device at any time so that a standby device can be activated. Early concerns that Bluetooth lacked security and could easily be 'hacked' have been addressed and the technology is considered to be as secure as other networking systems.

The invention of Bluetooth has allowed small, cheap transceivers to be put into many types of device, such as laptops, hand-held computers and PDAs (to reduce their dependence on wired networks), devices like games consoles (to connect controllers) and for connecting home PCs and printers. Bluetooth in homes performs a similar function to WiFi (see below), using the same broadcast frequencies but with a different protocol. Unlike ZigBee (see below), Bluetooth is designed for continual transmission with low power use. It has a bandwidth of 3Mbps, although a faster, more efficient version is currently in development.

Advantages of Bluetooth include:

+ Ad hoc networks are easy to set up;
+ Wireless devices, such as mobile phones, can share sound files, videos, images etc without being charged by a network.

Disadvantages of Bluetooth include:

+ Security remains a concern in cases where developers have been lax when implementing their software. Also, even novice users have the ability to manually alter security settings, which is potentially dangerous.
+ Distance is restricted to 10 metres in the most common devices ('class 2'). Therefore, Bluetooth is not suitable for replacing wired Ethernet in many settings. (Class 1 devices have a range of 1m while Class 3 devices, designed for an industrial setting, have a range of 100m.)

ZigBee

ZigBee is another example of PAN technology but, unlike Bluetooth, is designed for devices such as sensors or remote control devices, that transmit at intervals rather than continuously and which previously used infrared or wired connections. ZigBee can be arranged as a **mesh** and consists of three types of device, or **node**:

+ **ZigBee Co-ordinator (ZC)**. Forms the root of the network and may facilitate a link to other networks. There is only one ZC per network. It may be an independent device or it may be physically connected to the device(s) it controls, such as a burglar alarm or home entertainment system.
+ **ZigBee End Device (ZED)**. Transmits data to its parent node, and is normally in a passive state. As a result, ZEDs are cheap to manufacture and have a long battery life. A typical ZED may be a remote control or sensor.
+ **ZigBee Router (ZR)**. As in other network types, the router passes data between devices. This can extend the scope of the network by allowing ZigBee End Devices to be placed outside the range of the ZC. A ZR may also be connected to a device controlled by the ZigBee network, such as a stereo or light, and will rely on mains power. In case of a ZR failing, any ZED should be within range of several routers to take advantage of the mesh topology.

Figure 10.8 shows the arrangement of a typical ZigBee network. Note that distant ZEDs are usually within range of several ZRs in case one fails – this is particularly important in applications such as alarm systems.

Examples of the use of a ZigBee network are:

+ **A domestic alarm system**. Battery-powered sensors (ZEDs) throughout a house are connected to a central mains-powered hub (ZC) via routers (ZR) on each floor, which extend the hub's range. No network cabling is necessary. The routers incorporate mains-powered motion sensors. Sensors are also positioned in lamps and appliances. If a window or door is opened the sensor sends a signal to the hub. The hub returns a confirmation message to the sensor which then deactivates. If the alarm has been set to 'on', the hub triggers an alarm via a ZigBee signal. The alarm is mains-powered and includes a ZR. In an extension of this system the controller could remotely activate lamps, televisions, etc at random intervals, to create the impression of occupation.

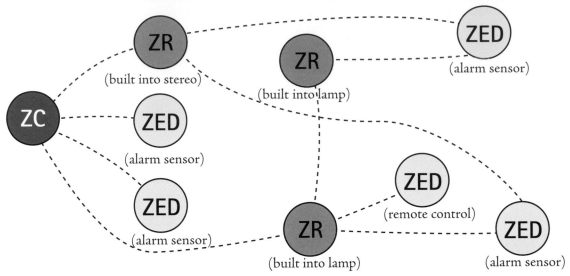

Figure 10.8: Example
ZigBee network with
wireless connections shown
by dotted lines.

+ **A home entertainment system.** A traditional IR remote control requires a clear line of sight to the device. A ZigBee-based system incorporating ZRs into entertainment devices (to extend the ZC's range) and ZEDs into remote controls allows any device to be controlled from anywhere in a house. A person could position speakers, incorporating ZRs, throughout their house while a ZC is built into a downstairs entertainment centre with ability to play MP3s, CDs or the radio. ZED-based remote controls allow the downstairs music system to power speakers anywhere in the house.

Advantages of ZigBee include:

+ In contrast with Bluetooth or WiFi, ZigBee can connect thousands of devices.
+ ZigBee consumes little power: batteries have a life span of several years.
+ Routers allow a ZigBee network to be extended over a large distance.
+ If one router fails, signals can be re-routed through the network.

Disadvantages of ZigBee include:

+ Mains-powered devices require battery backup in critical systems, eg security.
+ While ZEDs are relatively cheap, other devices in the network are not. A ZigBee-enabled home entertainment or automation system, for example, is significantly more expensive than traditional alternatives.
+ The technology is not yet widely supported.

WiFi

WiFi is the name given to the wireless Ethernet LANs that are now common in many homes. Indeed, readers may be regular users of devices such as a BT *Home Hub*, which allows several devices to share a single broadband connection. The devices connected to a WiFi LAN may be traditional computers, their peripherals or other devices such as those designed for streaming live radio.

WiFi base stations can support a maximum of 32 devices. Their range is hotly debated, but it is most likely that it is between 30 and 100m. This makes them ideal for domestic situations and small offices, but unsuitable for a large campus. Although it is illegal under the *Wireless and Telegraphy Act* to use a wireless broadband facility without the bill payer's permission, many networks will allow any passer-by to connect to them. One way of preventing this is to use **Wired Equivalent Privacy (WEP) decryption keys**. The user can allocate one when setting up a PC, which must be provided by any external device thereafter. A number of methods for bypassing this security measure have been published, and in turn enhancements to WEP have been developed to improve WiFi security.

WiFi devices use more power than PAN devices, which can be a drawback for users of laptop PCs with batteries. However, the same users benefit from having Internet access anywhere in their home, rather than just within reach of a telephone socket.

Advantages of WiFi include:

+ Ethernet LANs can be set up without cables.
+ Can be used to extend the range of a LAN within a building and its surroundings, allowing the use of hand-held devices (eg scanners in a warehouse).
+ WiFi hubs can act as hardware firewalls, giving an extra layer of security.
+ Cafés, airports etc can create WiFi 'hotspots' to attract customers.

Disadvantages of WiFi include:

+ If security is not properly configured, then theoretically anyone within a close enough radius can access sensitive data.
+ WiFi transceivers may drain batteries in portable devices very quickly.
+ As radio transmissions are affected by factors such as the weather, devices on the edge of a hub's range may be disconnected, unless repeaters are used.
+ There are health concerns about long-term exposure to WiFi signals. While some trials are under way, there is no conclusive evidence of risks.

WiMAX

WiMAX (Worldwide Interoperability for Microwave Access) offers a longer range than WiFi - up to 30 miles if a fixed device is used or 3-10 miles for mobile devices. This is the range associated with a MAN. In some sources, the term MAN has come to refer specifically to WiMax rather than a fibre optic or copper network. The chief advantage of WiMax is that it offers network access to devices in a large area with no need for cables. This has several benefits:

+ A town can gain Internet access from a single WiMax hub. This is especially useful in remote locations where traditional PSTN services are not available.
+ The 'last mile' of a PSTN network is often copper cable, especially outside of population centres. WiMax is one option for providing high bandwidth access without having to remove and replace cabling.
+ Entire cities can be turned into 'hotspots', allowing either free or paid access to anyone. This would allow a conurbation to have a series of connected hotspots.

GPRS

GPRS (General Packet Radio Service) is used by 2G mobile telephones to send non-voice data. To use GPRS, a user first connects to the data terminal at the service provider. Once connected, the user can access the Internet and download files such as web page or e-mail, and upload information, for example through an instant messenger service. Data is broken into packets which are uploaded or downloaded during predefined time slots. When finished, the user disconnects. The user is usually charged per megabyte of data. GPRS is a more efficient use of bandwidth than traditional voice channels since the packet nature means that the channel does not need to be in use continuously. Although the most common uses are to facilitate data transmission via SMS, MMS and WAP, GPRS can also be used to give laptop PCs Internet access when outside a WiFi hotspot. However, as WiFi and WIMAX grow, the usefulness of GPRS may diminish, as will the use of GPRS to send files between phones in close proximity (being replaced by Bluetooth). For more details about SMS and mobile telecommunications see section 10.4.

By the way...

These web pages contain further reading on topics covered in this chapter:

"Britain 'failing' net speed tests", BBC News, 2 Aug 2007
http://tinyurl.com/yrfno4

"Teachers Voice Fears of Wi-Fi Health Risk", Daily Telegraph, 24 Apr 2007
http://tinyurl.com/22htdd

"Bridging an African digital divide", BBC Click, 7 Sep 2007
http://tinyurl.com/2ff4uc

Questions

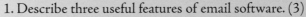

1. Describe three useful features of email software. (3)
2. Name three essential hardware components required for video conferencing. (3)
3. Evaluate whether the introduction of video conferencing would be beneficial for a multi-national company. (5)
   Discuss the hardware requirements for video conferencing. (6)
4. Compare e-mail and mobile telephony in relation to the transmission of text, voice and graphics. (6)
5. With the aid of a diagram, describe the hardware a home PC needs in order to connect to the Internet. (6)
6. What is 'broadband'? (2)
7. Describe two benefits of using broadband. (4)
8. Explain the parts of an IP address. (2)
9. What is the purpose of a protocol? (2)
10. Describe the main features of TCP/IP. (4)
11. What is PSTN and what does it stand for? (2)
12. Identify three features of twisted-pair cable. (3)
13. Describe three benefits of fibre optic cable. (6)
14. What is 'ISDN'? (2)
15. Define the following terms: (a) MAN (b) PAN (c) PSTN (2 each)
16. Give applications of Bluetooth, Zigbee, WIFI and WIMAX. (4)
17. Evaluate the operation of communication technology including Bluetooth, Zigbee, WIFI, WIMAX. (12)
18. Managers within a supermarket can make use of Internet access. How might the Internet benefit the managers in terms of (a) communication, (b) information searching and (c) information dissemination? (3 each)

CHAPTER 11
Emerging Technologies

11.1 Introduction

This section focuses on fairly new technologies that are shaping the way ICT is used. Many people are unaware of the true impact of ICT, largely because it has developed gradually over time, rather than changing dramatically overnight. Some readers will already appreciate just how different their world is from the one in which their parents grew up; others may find it bewildering when their parents describe the technology they grew up with such as '45rpm vinyl', 'AM radio' or television with only three channels. It is important that we appreciate the speed with which technology advances, not least because the devices and gadgets that are considered ultra-modern today will seem dated to the next generation.

Advances will continue after the publication of this book. The reader is advised to consult relevant journals and web sites to ensure that they are up-to-date with current developments in this area.

11.2 ICT and the Government

Governments have traditionally been large-scale ICT users. This has been necessitated by the huge volume of data that they process, eg census data. Many governmental ICT systems are comparable to those in the private industry, such as the databases and infrastructure of *HM Customs and Excise* and the *Driver and Vehicle Licensing Agency*. Of more relevance to students is the *Classroom 2000* system, which has a similar scope to many private companies: it connects hundreds of LANs, thousands of PCs with similar configurations, manages WWW and e-mail access, and retains backups of data for tens of thousands of users.

The course specification highlights three areas of ICT where computer systems are of particular interest because of the developing technology they use: National Identity Cards, passports and traffic control. Unlike other aspects of government ICT, these were not technologically possible until comparatively recently.

National Identity Cards

Unlike many European Union states, the United Kingdom currently does not have a **National Identity Card (ID card)** system, although there have been proposals to implement this for several years. Proponents of the system point to the many types of identification that citizens currently possess (eg passports, driving license, National Insurance cards) and suggest that a single national identification database could combine these items. Other suggested benefits include:

+ Protection from identity theft.
+ Easier travel within Europe without a passport.
+ Easier validation of identification (eg for new employees or migrant workers).
+ Improved national security.

However, detractors argue that cards are unlikely to prevent either terrorism or identity fraud. They point out that these crimes still occur in states that have ID cards. It has been suggested that the proposed all-in-one national database may be too complex to function effectively, and that having the information from many governmental departments in a single place will pose an excessive security risk should the information be accessed by unauthorised persons. Furthermore, there are concerns that civil liberty may suffer by giving central government access to civilians' data, and that the system could therefore be abused.

Under current plans, the data that may be held in the ID card register includes:

+ **Personal information:** Full name; other names by which person is or has been known; date and place of birth; gender; addresses of principal UK residence and all other residences, in the UK or elsewhere;

+ **Identifying information**: a photograph of head and shoulders; signature; fingerprints; other biometric information;

+ **Residential status**: nationality and, if applicable, a description of a person's entitlement to remain in the UK;

+ **Personal reference numbers**: National Identity Registration Number; the number of any ID card issued; National Insurance number; the number of any relevant immigration document; the number of their UK passport and any passport issued by another country; the number of any document that can be used by them instead of a passport; the number of any identity card issued by another country; the number of any work permit; any driver number given by DVLA; the date of expiry of any document described above;

+ **Record history**: any previous information held on ID cards and particulars of any changes made to it; date of birth;

+ **Registration and ID card history** of data or confirmation of data held here; other details, such as the reason for any omission from the information recorded here; the number of any ID cards issued to a person; whether these cards are in force (and why they are not, if applicable); the particulars given on an application of every person who has countersigned an application by the holder for an ID card;

By the way...

See these web pages which contain addition information on ID cards:
UK Identity and Passport Service: www.ips.gov.uk
The Problem With ID Cards at no2id.net: http://tinyurl.com/2s27lk
What Data Will ID Cards Store, BBC News Online: http://tinyurl.com/a3uft

+ **Security information**: a PIN to be used for making applications for information recorded in his/her entry; a password or other code to be used for that purpose or particulars; questions and answers to be used for identifying a person seeking to make such an application or to apply for a modification of that entry;

+ **Records of provision of information**: particulars of every occasion on which information contained in the individual's entry has been provided to a person; particulars of every person to whom such information has been provided; other particulars, in relation to each such occasion, of the provision of the information.

Task

Research current opinions on ID cards on the Internet. Then, either:

+ Prepare a report or presentation in favour of ID cards, outlining their strengths and challenging any perceived weaknesses in the scheme, or:

+ Prepare a report or presentation against the introduction of national ID cards, highlighting weaknesses or drawbacks in the scheme and challenging any perceived benefits of it.

Passports

Until recently, the passport was simply a paper booklet issued by a government to certify a person's citizenship. It was extremely time consuming for border control workers to check them against lists of suspicious persons. In contrast, modern communication systems provide the means to immediately carry out such checks.

The text of a modern UK passport (figure 11.1) is designed for easy recognition by OCR systems at border control, while lamination makes it difficult to manually alter the documents. A new system was introduced on modern biometric passports to make forgery and fraud more difficult (see the UK Identity and Passport Service's overview of biometric passports, at www.passport.gov.uk/general_biometrics.asp). A number of pieces of personal information are encrypted on a microchip. To access this data, an identification key (similar to a Hash Total) is calculated from the passport holder's personal data. Therefore, whoever is accessing the chip must have physical access to the passport.

Facial biometrics play an important part in recognising passport holders and preventing forgery. The photograph submitted to a passport agency must conform to certain regulations, such as its size and the distance the subject is from the camera. A number of statistics are determined from this, such as length of the person's mouth and distance between their eyes. These are compared to a photograph of the person that is taken at Customs, so an impostor can be readily identified.

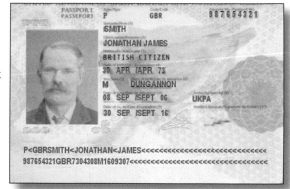

Figure 11.1: Top: personal data recorded on a standard UK passport. The identifying information in a form readable by humans is encoded on a microchip on the next page. The copper coil (bottom) magnetically induces a current, enabling the chip to transmit a low range signal to officials at border control who can check that the printed data has not been modified.

143

Traffic Control

Modern traffic light systems allow a single **Traffic Signal Controller** (control unit) to direct the traffic flow at many junctions. They usually operate continually, are reliable, can be programmed to take account of differing situations, and can be co-ordinated to improve traffic progression through several junctions in built up areas. The purpose of installing traffic signals is to improve safety and maximise the efficiency of the road network.

By the way...

Traffic Signal Controller

A Traffic Signal Controller (TSC) is a microprocessor unit which processes data from traffic sensors and, working within preset parameters, adjusts signal timings at a junction. In large towns, this is independent of human control, though it can be reprogrammed by replacing PROM chips.

Traffic lights in large cities, together with electronic signs on incoming motorways may be centrally monitored and controlled to ensure an efficient traffic flow and, as circumstances dictate, divert vehicles away from busy or congested areas.

The simplest form of traffic control uses predetermined fixed times. Vehicles entering the junction from each arm are given a specific period of 'green time' that has previously been calculated by traffic engineers. The engineers' calculations are based on the observation of traffic flow over a period of time. Engineers will calculate the green times considering the average daily traffic flow, and apportion more 'green time' to the busiest roads. The key drawback of these systems is that they are unable to respond to any deviations from the traffic flow for which they were programmed (figure 11.2). For example, signal timings designed for school traffic may still follow those patterns during school holidays and weekends.

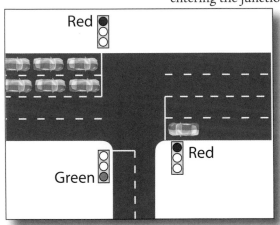

Figure 11.2: in this example, preset fixed timing fails to respond to a sudden surge in traffic on the main road, giving a green light to an empty road while congestion builds up.

More advanced traffic light systems use traffic detectors laid under the road surface (visible as lines in the Tarmac). In these **Vehicle Activated (VA) systems** the TSC is programmed to vary the length of green time given to any road depending on the number of vehicles detected.

In these systems the engineer will calculate the minimum and maximum green times based on traffic flows observed at the junction. For example, a road may have a maximum green time of 25 seconds, regardless of traffic flow, and a minimum green time of 7 seconds. As vehicles pass over detectors, the minimum green time is extended by 1.8 seconds per vehicle until the designated maximum green time is achieved. At this point, another arm of the junction will receive a green light.

Fully co-ordinated **Urban Traffic Control (UTC)** systems are often used in cities. The traffic lights at each junction are linked and co-ordinated to optimise timings to improve traffic flow through the city's road network. These systems include a number of pre-programmed **Signal Time Plans (STPs)** that are designed for certain predictable traffic conditions such as:

+ Peak traffic flow (more vehicles at some times than others).

+ Tidal traffic flow (more vehicles heading out of the city in the evening).
+ Off-peak traffic flow (very low traffic levels during the night).

STPs can be programmed to accommodate traffic flows affected by special circumstances such as major sporting and recreational events in a city. For example, STPs operate at the Lodge Road Roundabout, Coleraine for the *North West 200*. Vehicles travelling to concerts at Belfast's *Odyssey Arena*, are similarly controlled by STPs. Overhead signs change the speed limits to maximise the amount of traffic that can use the road, but human operators can override these, for example to alert drivers to dangerous fog or a crash ahead.

In the event of an emergency, humans may override the whole system. Police or UTC control centre workers can switch all lights to red to let emergency services pass, or manually direct traffic in the case of an accident or equipment failure.

Toll Roads increasingly make use of ICT. The toll booths on the M50 motorway in Dublin were replaced with an automatic barrier-free system in 2008. In this system, vehicles do not have to stop; instead cameras mounted on cameras read the number plates of the passing vehicles and automatically charge the toll to a person's account. If the person does not have an account (eg a visitor) they must instead pay the toll via a web site during the next twenty four hours. An associated system automatically sends out fines and, if necessary, legal enforcement notices to those who do not pay. A similar system has operated in central London since February 2003 where motorists pay to drive their vehicles into the very centre of the city. Discounts are available for residents, while taxis, buses, motorbikes, bicycles, alternative-fuel vehicles and the emergency services can all enter free of charge.

Figure 11.3: Vehicles on the main road have a green light while vehicles coming from the feeder road have a red light. Consequently, pedestrians who want to cross the feeder road are automatically given a 'green man' signal without the need to press any buttons.

11.3 Advertising

Advertising has changed significantly with the growth of ICT. Consider the typical advertising most people experienced in the 1970s, compared with the kind that they experience today. Figure 11.4 compares the two periods. While advertising media available to companies have changed dramatically, the proportion of a company's money available generally has not. Advertisers must make more efficient use of their budget to have the same impact.

In some cases, companies who had a large advertising revenue entirely to themselves (for example, ITV) are forced to share this with others. In this instance, ITV have to find other means of attracting advertising, such as their relatively new

Method	1970s	Modern
Billboards	Static posters	Static or rotating posters: TFT displays are becoming widespread
Sports events	Static hoardings	Static or animated hoardings, eg during football matches
TV and radio	Adverts during commercial breaks on a small number of channels	Eye-catching adverts in breaks on multiple channels; users can often fast-forward through them if programmes have been recorded. Animated logos can attract viewers' attention
Newspapers	Sales of newspapers high; static adverts	Sales of newspapers lower; ads must be eye-catching and are more often printed in colour. Ads appear on online editions.
Direct mail	Mailings to previous customers, or people in lists from other companies	More targeted mail possible via more sophisticated databases; but e-mail makes unwanted 'spam' advertising more likely
Text messages	Did not exist	Messages to people who have purchased tickets both before and during an event (eg "quote this code for half price merchandise")
Web sites	Did not exist	Adverts taken out on web sites likely to attract people with similar interests to the product

Figure 11.4: Simple comparison of advertising in the 1970s and today.

web site. In other cases, new media has led to a more efficient way of contacting customers. For example, supermarket chains will send known previous customers printed catalogues, while 'potential' customers receive a leaflet and an invitation to view a web site to view products, find out about promotional offers etc. Loyalty cards are an extremely useful way to monitor a customer's shopping habits. It is no accident that people receive coupons for alternatives to products that they already buy regularly. A few years ago, all customers would have been sent a leaflet for all promoted items, whereas now they would rarely receive such generic mailings.

The growth of new media types has also led to an increase in **advertising agencies**. Suppose the makers of *Acme Toothpaste* wanted to advertise their product on television in the 1970s. They would have negotiated with ITV's advertising managers for the times and prices of adverts. Acme would also have control over where their advert would appear. For example, they may not want an advert aimed at children to be shown during the breaks of a film aimed at adults. By comparison, smaller companies today may find it cost effective to employ an agency that will negotiate with a range of broadcasters. While this is a more efficient use of the company's time, they may have less control over where their advertisements appear. An advertiser may be able to specify inclusion on sports channels but not children's channels, or even ask for inclusion in certain types of programming, but the sheer number of broadcasters may make this impossible in some cases. Furthermore, in the 1970s it was possible for advertising executives to see exactly which programmes their adverts were placed in, but the number of channels nowadays makes this very difficult to check.

If they were placing an advertisement in the regional press, *Acme Toothpaste* would be pleased to see it near an article on a new dental surgery, but they would be less impressed if it was placed near a story on a group associated with extreme political views. In web-based media, it can be impossible to tell where advertisements will appear, due to the large number of sites available. To illustrate how this relationship can go wrong, in 2007 Vodafone and other companies agreed that their adverts could be used on the pages from the social network site *Facebook*. Unfortunately, their logo appeared alongside material advocating the right-wing British National Party. To avoid being associated with such a controversial political agenda, many companies withdrew their advertisements immediately. These examples highlights a number of the benefits and drawbacks of advertising in an environment dominated by ICT:

Advantages of advertising in an ICT-dominated world include:

+ Specialist broadcasters or web sites make it possible to target advertisements at particular demographic groups. A web site or television programme can be employed to reach a niche audience, but the large reach of the newspaper or soap opera will still be attractive to certain advertisers.

+ Customer databases can be searched so that people who are likely to be interested in a product can be targeted with advertising. Suppose a customer database had been used to determine the typical user of Acme Toothpaste was a female aged under 30, with young children, who reads the *Guardian*. Advertisements could be directed at media used by these people, eg the *Guardian*, TV, radio and web sites known to be used by twenty-something mothers. Users of rival products can be targeted in a similar way.

+ More eye-catching forms of advertising are possible. For example, billboards that rotate at set intervals can grab the attention of passers-by. Animated advertisements, such as those displayed on large pitch-side screens at sporting events, are not only visually appealing but also cost effective. It is cheaper to change the advert on a single animated display than a billboard, where the paper must be manually replaced.

+ Organisations can set up partnerships through new media, from which all parties benefit. Say, for example, that the BBC places a trailer for a new programme on a video site such as *YouTube*. The interested user is likely to spend more time browsing the site, but might also watch the full programme on BBC later in the week. Many independent musicians attract attention from major labels through promoting themselves on sites such as *MySpace*. Through this, the musician gains exposure while *MySpace* garners extra viewers.

Disadvantages of advertising in an ICT-dominated world include:

+ A filtering function in an e-mail client might mistake adverts for 'spam' messages and delete them. Because of spam, many users are sceptical about legitimate e-mail advertising and may often ignore it.

+ As many people are used to static billboard or newspaper advertisements, companies have to invest in more innovative methods to remain effective.

11.4 Travel and Holidays

It can be difficult to imagine or recall the time before budget airlines such as Easyjet existed. Easyjet was certainly not the first company to use computers, but they were notable for removing customers' dependency on travel agents. The ability to book flights online has had a significant impact on the Northern Ireland travel market.

Before the introduction of computers, a customer had to go to a travel agent to ask about the availability of flights and hotels. Any processing was done by post or by telephone. It was common for different travel agents to place multiple bookings with different representatives within an airline for the same seat. The issue of overbooking was partly solved when travel agents were given real time access (via dumb terminals) to airline computers. However, airlines continue to purposely overbook flights as it is normal for some passengers not to turn up on the day of departure.

Booking directly with the airline is cheaper for the customer, since they do not have to pay the travel agent's fees. However, if a holiday is booked with a travel agent there is a single point of contact should anything go wrong.

Imagine a typical holiday scenario: a family have booked a flight with Airline X from Belfast to Heathrow. From there they will fly onward to New York with Airline Y. If Airline X is delayed it may cause the family to miss their flight with Airline Y. This in turn will cause the hotel in New York to assume the family are not coming and therefore cancel their reservation. If the holiday was originally booked entirely through a single travel agent then it would be that travel agent's responsibility to amend bookings that were affected by the original delayed flight.

Before the use of the Internet it was *possible* to bypass travel agents by phoning airlines and hotels directly. However, the main disadvantage of this is the amount of phoning necessary before reservations could be made. For example, an individual may call a theatre in London to enquire about tickets for a particular date. They would then call an airline to check the availability of flights. Finally, they would call a hotel near to the theatre to book a room. Once they have established that their trip is possible, they may call the theatre to confirm, only to discover that the last tickets have recently been sold.

One of the benefits of the Internet is that many sites give anyone making an inquiry a grace period of time during which tickets are held for them. This allows the individual valuable time to simultaneously check the availability of all three sets of tickets by opening three web browser windows.

Holidays Then And Now

In this example, we look at a typical holiday in the 1980s and compare it with a holiday in the late 2000s. This will highlight the many ways in which ICT has affected all aspects of tourism from booking through to hotel services.

Booking in the 1980s: Just as they are today, 'package deals' were common in the 1980s, allowing customers to book a complete holiday through a travel agent from options listed in a brochure. Alternatively, customers could book flights, hotels and other components of a holiday directly. To do so, customers would have needed to find a list of hotels in the area they were visiting, and phone each one. Without a travel agent it may have been difficult to pay for services such as car hire or day trips in advance because many independent operators preferred payment in their local currency. While credit cards did exist, they were not as widely accepted.

Booking in the late 2000s: Today, many guidebooks are supplemented with web sites that include updates and other useful information that could not be included in the book. Web sites such as *TripAdvisor* allow travellers to share experiences with others. Many tourists feel comfortable using the Internet to book components of a trip from a variety of different providers. Because Internet booking reduces staff costs, many hotels and airlines offer discounted rates to those who book online. Nevertheless, some people remain concerned about Internet security, and worry that they will pay for a bus or hotel that they later discover does not exist. Booking and paying for services online reduces the amount of foreign currency that holidaymakers have to carry abroad. The growth of Electronic Funds Transfer, favoured by many small businesses, has made this approach commonplace. Even when abroad, international banking systems allow most tourists to access their bank accounts from ATM machines as if they were at home.

Baggage Management in the 1980s: Until fairly recently, airports relied on manual baggage processing. After checking-in, a label was attached to each bag with its destination. It was then moved via a conveyor belt to a baggage control area where workers sorted them and transferred them to the appropriate plane. Human error made it easy for bags to be lost or put on the wrong plane.

Baggage Management in the late 2000s: When bags are checked in they are given a bar code label or RFID tag (see section 11.6). They are then passed onto a series of conveyor belts that automatically direct the bag to the departure gate for the appropriate aeroplane by using actuators to control automated arms that push bags on and off the belts. The conveyor system allows the location of any bag to be followed in real time. While mistakes do happen, they are less common and are often caused by human error, such as a failure to properly attach a label. For more information on this technology, see the article on How Stuff Works, via http://tinyurl.com/6y2puj

Task

Heathrow Airport Terminal 5 in London opened in March 2008. It was equipped with a state-of-the-art computerised baggage control system such as that described above. However, within hours of opening the system had to be shut down and over 28,000 bags failed to make it onto the correct flight. Conduct some research on the Internet to find out exactly what happened. Was the failure caused by technical or human problems, or both? What does this real world example tell you about the impact of ICT?

Hotel Services in the 1980s. Upon checking in, guests were given two keys to their room. If these were lost or accidentally retained, the manager may have had to use a master key and get new keys cut. Guests could charge meals or drinks from their mini-bar to their bill, but these were dependant on hotel staff accurately recording what the guest had purchased, and the guest giving the correct room number. Check out may have been time consuming as the bill had to be calculated and written or printed out. Fewer guests used credit cards, and cheques would have been much more common. Some hotels may have been wary of large cheques as there was no way of determining their validity until customers were long gone.

Hotel Services in the 2000s. Metal keys have now been replaced with magnetic-stripe key cards (figure 11.5) which can be used both to open the door of the room and to charge bills to the guest's account. Cards are automatically invalidated when the guest checks out and are worth so little that it does not matter if people lose or forget them. In rooms, many items in mini-bars have RFID tags to automatically inform the central computer when a drink is removed. The television may be used

Figure 11.5: A typical hotel magnetic-stripe card being used to open a hotel room.

to access pay-per-view entertainment, internet access or to check the balance on the customer's account. Because a customer will have logged their credit card details on checking in, checkout is a simple matter of checking the bill and confirming it with reception.

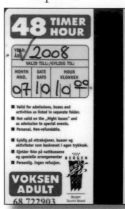

Figure 11.6: The Bergen Card. *Copyright Bergen Tourist Board, used with thanks.*

Tourist Attractions in the 1980s: Companies operating in the tourist sector try to encourage tourists to visit attractions other than those they initially planned to. In the 1980s, this was achieved by selling prepaid cards or books of vouchers that offered discounted rates when paying to enter an attraction. Customers who had purchased the book would then feel compelled to visit several attractions in order to feel that they had achieved value for money.

Tourist Attractions in the late 2000s: In many areas, voucher books have been replaced with a magnetic-stripe card that is used to allow access to attractions or to provide discounts. These cards are designed to fit conveniently inside wallets and is much less bulky than a book of vouchers.

11.5 Entertainment

Hardware

While there have been few radically new ideas in the entertainment industry during recent years, faster processing, increased bandwidth and cheaper hardware have brought changes to devices that have been available in one form or another since the 1970s.

The concept of **portable music** is certainly not a new one. The first portable tape player (1972) was succeeded by numerous similar devices, such as personal CD players. The main drawback was that their moving parts led to a very short battery life, especially when compared with modern MP3 players. Recent systems created by the likes of Apple and Sony are much more efficient, using **flash memory** instead of an internal hard drive, which means that they be used for even longer before needing recharged. Obviously, these devices are much smaller than personal CD players, so small that they could fit inside a shirt pocket, making them even more portable. They can store a large amount of music (currently, up to 40,000 songs), and transferring MP3 files onto these devices is straightforward. As a response to widespread copyright violations, **Digital Rights Management** is used with some download sites to restrict files to a few devices and may force files to 'expire' after a certain time.

Likewise, **portable video and television** is an old idea, though neither were that popular or successful until relatively recently. While hand held televisions have been in existence for some time, reception was generally poor and the screen size and resolution not of a high enough quality to benefit long periods of use. However, in the past few years there has been a marked increase in the technology. **MP3 and MP4** players are capable of playing video files, as are many modern mobile phones. The small size of new devices, coupled with improved battery life has made portable television and video more popular than before. Many channels are now offering their content for downloading or streaming directly from their counterpart web sites (see section 10.4 on mobile telecommunications).

DVD players / recorders have replaced traditional VHS video recorders in many households. They can be used to watch pre-recorded films and record television programmes. As DVDs are cheaper to manufacture and require less storage space than video tape, **Box sets** containing entire television series can be purchased. **Blu-ray** and **HD DVD** offer higher definition than conventional DVD, though as both are backed by rival studios, customers may not be able to find all of the films that they want to watch on their chosen formats. In 2008, manufacturers and retailers withdrew their support for HD DVD. Toshiba announced that they were no longer making HD DVD players, effectively rendering the format defunct. As they were only commercially introduced in early 2006, this should evidence the speed with which technology advances and changes within our current climate.

While DVD admittedly offers many benefits and therefore sells in great numbers, we must consider the fact that the **environment** is suffering as a result. This is due to the speed with which a large number of households have replaced perfectly functional VHS machines with DVD players, which in turn will be replaced by DVD recorders. It is also possible than many more households will replace their televisions with HD equivalents. The knock-on effect of this technological revolution is that refuse centres are often full of unwanted plastic machines that can not easily be recycled.

Digital Broadcasting

Digital Television has allowed a large increase in the number of channels available to users, compared to the five analogue-based channels received by most users in the UK a few years ago. Using the bandwidth that would have been allocated to a single analogue channel, a digital multiplex combines the signals of many channels into one. This is achieved through compressing the data to be transmitted. The bandwidth that would have been taken up by a second's worth of analogue BBC1 can hold a second's worth of compressed BBC1, BBC2, BBC3, BBC4, BBC News 24, BBC Parliament, BBCi, BBC Teletext and some BBC radio stations. At the receiving end, a digital receiver de-multiplexes the signal: it extracts the compressed channel the viewer wants to watch, decompresses it and sends a signal to the television. This explains the slight delay noticed between analogue and digital television sets showing the same program.

Digital television can be received in several different ways:

- **Freeview** broadcasts on the same UHF spectrum as analogue services. UK analogue services will be phased out gradually from 2008 (starting in Cumbria) to 2012 (ending in Northern Ireland). This will free up bandwidth for other services, and will remove the constraint on the number of channels available. Freeview offers around 40 television channels, along with radio and teletext services. All that is required is a one-off purchase of a **set-top box,** though many new televisions can be purchased with a built-in Freeview receiver. *Top-Up TV* also broadcasts on digital and offers a number of subscription services, though not all Freeview receivers are compatible with this. *Freesat* offers a similar service to Freeview, though with more channels via satellite. A number of European broadcasters can be viewed for-free or via subscription if appropriate equipment is installed.

+ **Satellite subscription services** in the UK are normally associated with *British Sky Broadcasting (Sky)*, although a number of foreign broadcasters can also be received via other satellite systems. Sky have a much greater bandwidth available than terrestrial broadcasters and in addition to their own channels, allow other providers (Setanta, MTV etc) to broadcast via their platform. Broadcasters who do not use Sky's satellite (eg BBC) may still negotiate inclusion on Sky's Electronic Programme Guide if their satellite is in a position where Sky's equipment will receive their signal. In addition to subscription services, a number of pay-per-view services exist (eg for sport or films) as well as non-subscription channels. Channels are encrypted to prevent unauthorised viewing. Receiving devices are updated via the broadcast system with decryption keys for subscription only channels.

+ **Cable television** is the primary method of distributing pay TV in some parts of the world, such as North America. In the UK, however, this service is rarely available outside large population centres because of the cost of cabling. Viewers of cable services benefit from the use of high bandwidth fibre optic equipment, which can also provide high bandwidth Internet access.

Advantages of digital broadcasting include:

+ A wider range of available channels.
+ Easy to browse channels that are themed by topic (sport, film, music etc).
+ Interactive services such as games, or voting for contestants on certain shows.
+ Many more sporting events can be watched live.
+ News and weather can be accessed on-screen at any time.
+ Offers a sharper signal than analogue.

Disadvantages of digital broadcasting include:

+ Some people live in remote areas still outside the digital 'footprint', so they are not yet able to receive digital programming.
+ Many services require subscription or pay-per-view fees.
+ Several Freeview channels do not start transmitting until early in the evening.
+ The need to replace equipment that may work perfectly well.
+ The unsightliness of digital adapters.
+ Digital television can be prone to lag, causing programmes to 'freeze'.

Computer Games

Computer games have been around almost as long as computers themselves, but have developed dramatically during the past few years. Text-based games, in which the user types commands in response to textual descriptions, came first, followed by graphical games. Initially, graphics were restricted to two-dimensional, basic animations, and sound effects were simple beeps. However, although graphics have advanced enormously as processing speeds have increased and costs have come down, the same basic problem-solving principle still remains in many games.

Some early text-based games were playable as single-user titles on computers such as the ZX Spectrum or could be played on multi-user systems as **Multi User Dungeons** (**MUDs**). These allowed several players at once within a shared environment. When a user logged off their character's status could be frozen and restored at a later time. The idea of a MUD further developed into graphical multiplayer networked games, such as *World of Warcraft* and *Second Life*. Such is the success of such online communities that 'virtual' properties can be worth considerable real world amounts and small 'economies' develop within them.

Figure 11.7: Manic Miner (1984) and Dizzy (1986). Both titles were very popular and have a number of WWW fan-sites which include playable remakes of the games.

Research the *Second Life* virtual world. How does it work? What ICT technology does it rely upon to function adequately? Why would the development of *Second Life* not have been possible in the 1970s? What social implications are there of this particular application of ICT?

Task

11.6 Shopping

Significant changes have taken place in shopping habits in recent decades, most obviously in the advent of Internet shopping. Some of these changes are related to developments in ICT while others are more closely related to changing business methods. For example, a modern supermarket's stock control systems are often linked directly to warehouses that in turn are linked to suppliers. Warehouse staff have a real time list of items in each supermarket that are out-of-stock and pack the delivery lorries appropriately. In turn, suppliers have access to trends and deliver goods appropriately. This provides a more efficient service for customers and, as fewer staff are needed to manually monitor stock levels, costs can be reduced.

As well as improving connections between suppliers and their customers, ICT also leads to improvements within a business. Within a warehouse, a crate of goods may be identified by a bar code. As a crate moves through the warehouse, a human worker scans the bar code and a central database system records which section of the warehouse it is stored in. This can be inefficient if a large number of crates must be individually scanned. In many instances, this has been replaced with **Radio Frequency Identification** (**RFID**) tags. RFID tags contain an antennae, transceiver and a microchip.

Passive RFID devices (as used in library books to determine those that have been properly checked out) contain no battery. A received signal must be strong to induce enough current for the transceiver to power up, determine an appropriate response and to transmit that response. **Semi-passive** RFID tags have a battery that powers only the microchip. **Active** RFID are fully battery powered and is suitable for devices that need to broadcast over a large distance or whose signal is liable to interference and hence a strong signal must be broadcast.

RFID does not need to be scanned in close proximity. RFID readers can operate up to a few metres from passive tags or around 500m from active tags. This allows many crates to pass through a door and be scanned together without any unpacking / scanning / repacking by humans. Indeed, some online shopping warehouses can remove humans almost entirely from operations:

+ A robotic device fetches the contents of an order, identifying each via RFID
+ Once the order is complete goods are put in a box on a conveyor belt to make their way to the packing area

Even in a conventional 'High Street' shopping environment, the traditional checkout can be removed if all goods carry RFID tags and customers carry a loyalty card that is used to identify themselves to their trolley. Goods placed in the trolley can be added to a bill automatically and the user's bank account debited. Any items taken off shelves but not placed in the trolley are still recorded as being in the shop and an alarm is triggered if somebody attempts to bring them past the exit. This may replace **Point of Sale** (POS) terminals, where a scanned bar code is compared to a database and the price retrieved. Readers may be familiar with **Electronic Fund Transfer at Point of Sale** (EFTPOS) which has replaced many used of cash.

As well as changes to the way physical shops operate, many areas of mail order shopping have been revolutionised by online retail. In traditional mail order, an order was posted, received at the warehouse a few days later, manually processed and, assuming it was available, received by the customer after a few weeks. Online retail allows customers to view live stock information and reserve goods in real-time. The delay of processing cheques is removed (as Electronic Funds Transfer takes its place) so a customer is able to place an order and receive immediate feedback on whether it can be fulfilled. Within the warehouse, processing and packing may be fully automated and a new order can be ready for couriers within minutes of being received. The customer can be e-mailed once it has been dispatched, and they can then track the order via the courier's web site. The way in which ICT has affected shopping is discussed further in Chapter 13.

11.7 Virtual Reality

Virtual Reality is a technology that allows a user to interact with an artificial environment in the same way that they interact with the real world. This requires the user to wear particular equipment which allows the user to experience the virtual world:

+ **Goggles with tiny inbuilt screens.** The images on each lens are slightly different to give the impression of depth. These goggles also have sensors that detect head and eye movement, so that the image presented to the user can be adjusted in real time.
+ **Speakers and a microphone** are also part of the headset, so the user can hear only the contents of the virtual world. A microphone allows their voice to be heard by other users who may be physically in a different town or country.

+ **Gloves with movement and pressure sensors** that detect the movement of the user's hands. The user can see their 'virtual hands' through the goggles and can therefore control objects in the virtual world. Because the gloves sense pressure, the user has to properly 'grip' virtual objects. The gloves also exert a force on the user's hand to properly simulate lifting objects. A full body suit can be used to give a more realistic experience and may control pressure, temperature and other sensations.

Uses of Virtual Reality

Due to the cost of equipment, virtual reality is still restricted to specialist fields. There are a number of reasons for this:

+ It is too expensive to practice a task in reality. Astronauts, for example, can use virtual reality to learn how to repair a satellite prior to going into space.

+ It is too dangerous to train on actual equipment. Trainee pilots can use as an aircraft cockpit simulator (figure 11.8) where, instead of goggles, the aircraft 'windows' are replaced with large VDUs.

+ In hazardous environments. There are many situations in which it would be desirable to control a robot from a distance, such as searching for mines.

Figure 11.8: An aircraft cockpit simulator uses virtual reality to replicate the view out of the aircraft's 'windows'.

+ To bring outside expertise. A surgeon can use virtual reality to perform surgery on a patient in a different continent, as if they were in the theatre.

+ Entertainment. Although the equipment is expensive, VR-based games are being developed and may become more common as time goes on. Users interact with virtual objects via an 'avatar' - a virtual representation of themselves.

Advantages of using Virtual Reality in training include:

+ No risk to human life.

+ No money lost as a result of damaged equipment.

+ The same scenarios can be repeated with exactly the same conditions each time in order to maximise understanding.

Disadvantages of using Virtual Reality in training include:

+ A false sense of security can develop, which can remain in a real situation.

+ Virtual Reality systems are complex to design and build, as thousands of rules and variables must be established.

+ A simulator may not be able to account for all possible scenarios.

See these web sites which contain more information on Virtual Reality:

Science, medicine, and the future: Virtual reality in surgery, at the BMJ web site, via http://tinyurl.com/39j7y7

Under the Knife... The Online Way , BBC News, 30th August 2007, via http://tinyurl.com/3aozl2

By the way...

Prepare a report assessing the advantages and disadvantages of using virtual reality to either (a) train pilots (b) carry out surgery.

Task

11.8 Computer Aided Design and Manufacturing

Computer Aided Design (CAD) is the use of a computer system to produce technical drawings for the design of a construction or engineering project. Examples include designs of circuit boards or an architect's plans for a building.

CAD is in widespread use because of the many advantages it offers over traditional design and technical drawing methods. In a traditional design environment **draughtsmen** had the job of creating scale drawings by hand. If any part of a design changed, then each drawing involving that component had to be redrawn. As with any manual process, this was liable to human error that may result from mis-measurement or carelessness. If such mistakes were not discovered until manufacturing had begun they could be very costly indeed.

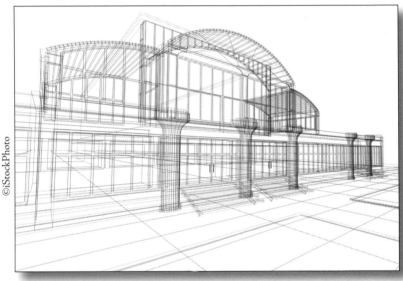

Figure 11.9: Left: An architectural draughtsman working on a design in the 1890s. Right: A design created using a modern CAD system.

By contrast, CAD software replaces desks, paper and pencils with a computer-based workplace. Modern draughtsmen and designers use graphics tablets and a stylus to draw designs with precision. Their drawings are represented as vector drawings within a CAD application. Rather than representing 3D objects in two dimensions, designers can work in three dimensions and rotate components to view them from all angles.

When designing components that are to be used together, the software can check that they will properly meet up before manufacturing, avoiding costly mistakes. Rather than drawing a series of progressively more detailed drawings, a designer can 'zoom in' to see a component in detail. Once a design is complete, a 'hard copy' can be produced in minutes with a laser printer or a large plotter.

In many manufacturing environments a transition has taken place over the last century towards fully automated manufacturing. In early production lines the workers involved in each stage of a car's manufacture became experts in just one job, but was very efficient at that job. This replaced traditional **craftsmen** who were responsible for all parts of a device's manufacture. This resulted in quicker and cheaper **mass production**. Robots eventually replaced humans in the production line, with the main advantage that they could perform the same repetitive task all day with the same level of competence throughout the day and no need for breaks.

Bitmap versus Vector

Bitmap graphics store an image as a series of numbers representing the colour required for each pixel (a single point on the image). When enlarged, a bitmap graphic appears as a number of blocks and is often described as being 'pixelated'. This loss of quality results because no data is stored about what exists between the pixels in the original image. **Vector** graphics use mathematical formulae to represent each line, so the quality of the displayed image depends only on the hardware used for display. Because graphics are stored as lines, rather than individual dots and curves, graphics can be enlarged with no loss of detail. This is more suitable for the line drawings used in the CAD design process.

The first two images below show a bit map image (left) and then enlarged (right) to show that it is made of pixels. No such problem occurs when a vector image (eg the *GIMP*™ logo) is enlarged (below). Note that the complexity of photographs means that it is not usually practical to store such images in a vector format.

Computer Aided Manufacturing (CAM) is the use of a computer system to control production in a factory, including the supply of components, planning and scheduling of production and the control of machinery used in the production process. In many cases a CAD/CAM system allows a seamless link between the design and production processes. In such systems, production lines can be re-programmed and re-tooled automatically and the necessary raw materials ordered and transferred from a warehouse automatically. The consequence of this is that in some environments it is now possible for a designer to submit a final design to a CAD/CAM system, which then appears at the end of the production line as a final product, with little human intervention on the way. Students of Technology and Design may be familiar with the CAD/CAM systems in schools that can turn a CAD design into a plastic or wooden prototype of an object via CAM (the full manufacturing process being too costly for most schools).

11.9 Smart Homes

A **smart home** automates many aspects of daily household management, such as closing blinds or locking doors. Current trends (eg media centres that combine the functionality of PCs, DVD players and televisions) suggest that in the future a Smart Home may consist of a number of distinct devices controlled via a single interface. Such an interface may be accessed via a networked television or PC, although individual devices could still be controlled in the usual fashion. For example, the central interface may be used to synchronise lights and central heating but if it gets dull, lights and heating could be switched on in the usual way.

Task

List all the electrical appliances or devices you have used at your home in the past week. Don't forget to include built-in devices such as lights or heating.

If you have completed the above task, it will illustrate just how many times an average user interacts with various devices in a typical home. While most homes have had central heating controlled by a timer for many years, many other daily interactions would benefit from ICT. For example, after leaving the house or going to bed, many of us worry that we have forgotten to either lock the front door or switch off a device such as a cooker. We may return home or get out of bed to double check. A smart home would remove this potential worry, but it is not the only way in which life would be made easier by a fully automated infrastructure.

A smart home could offer the following example daily routine. All these devices may use Zigbee or a wired network, except where indicated:

+ In the morning, centrally controlled heating systems activate half an hour before the user rises. This is according to a pre-decided schedule - weekdays are different from weekends. Curtains open a few minutes before the alarm sounds. Downstairs, coffee brews fifteen minutes after the alarm sounds, and windows open automatically for one hour.

+ If the occupants forgot to lock the doors when leaving, the smart home locks them automatically, but only if they have brought their keys. A system incorporating sensors at doors and a RFID keyring is used to monitor whether occupants are in or out. Even a pet may have a RFID tag on its collar, which could be used to activate the cat flap and deactivate the burglar alarm sensors.

+ The home's occupants also have a special 'key' used to enter their car. It resembles an ordinary keyring, but contains a RFID tag. The car's doors unlock if this key is within a metre's radius, and lock again when it is taken away. The presence of this RFID tag is also required before the car's engine will start. This is achieved by pushing an ignition button, instead of inserting and turning a traditional key.

+ A bar code scanning system in the refrigerator and cupboards logs the use of specific products and builds up a shopping list for automatic transmission to a local supermarket for delivery. This saves the owner the time and hassle of having to stop for groceries on the way home.

+ The occupants may log on to their home's control system from work: to turn on the oven, or turn on heating if they wish to deviate from the preset pattern. A digital video recorder (a TV receiver with an in-built hard disk) can be also accessed in this way if the user hears about an interesting programme.

- On arriving home, the occupants need not worry about lights or curtains which are each automatically activated when it becomes dark. Background music or radio stations can be activated on a room-by-room basis according to the preference of the occupant. These settings are stored on individual RFID tags, one for each member of the household. Music is stored in MP3 format on a central server. Preferred light levels and shower temperature can be adjusted in a similar way.

- If occupants are on holiday, the internal Zigbee network will activate lights, televisions etc to make it appear as if someone is at home.

> Assess the social implications of the 'future vision' of Smart Homes outlined in this section. What would be the advantages and disadvantages to a family living in this home? What are the implications to society as a whole? What implications are there for people who cannot afford to live in a home like this?

Task

11.10 The Impact of ICT on the Individual, the Organisation and Society

This part of the CCEA specification asks students to assess the impact ICT has had on society, organisations and individuals. Many aspects of these are addressed throughout this book and a few are presented here by way of a reminder.

The Impact of ICT on the Individual

ICT has made its way into most people's lives. Now, it is taken as much for granted as switching on a light or striking a match. Even the most basic and mundane functions are enhanced by ICT. Consider the following examples:

- There are now many different ways to communicate. Telephones, mobile phones, e-mail and chat rooms allow us to talk to one another verbally or textually in many more ways.

- Many banking tasks can now be carried out by telephone or over the Internet. Wages are automatically paid into a bank account, and bills are paid via direct debit. Purchases can be made online using a credit card. If cash is needed, a customer does not need to visit their bank, but simply visits an ATM.

- Many people now organise holidays over the Internet. Tasks such as booking flights, hotels and car hire no longer require a specialist travel agent.

- Information is available in more immediate and accessible forms. At one time, researchers would have needed to visit a library or contact an expert to find out about a specific subject. Today, we can carry out research via the Internet. However, while there are many online sites that provide useful resources, a number are edited by the public and therefore must be checked thoroughly for accuracy.

- Thanks to the changing nature of employment, nearly every individual has to be equipped with skills that enable him or her to use ICT in the work place.

The impact of ICT on the Organisation

Few organisations remain unaffected by the widespread impact of ICT in recent years. In a world driven by financial concerns, technology must offer a clear

Task

Figure 11.10: A classroom from 1911.

Study this picture. What aspects of this classroom are similar to today's classroom? What are the differences? Make a list of all the places you encountered ICT in your school in the past seven days. Using your list and figure 11.10, assess the impact of ICT in education.

Tower Bridge, London

Two-way bridge to Britain ...your telephone

Do you have family or friends overseas? Do you have business abroad which can best be settled in a friendly, personal discussion?

A telephone call is the fast, economical way to talk back and forth across the ocean

...make plans for a trip... close a sale. It's easy to do. Just tell the operator where you want to call.

P.S. If you're visiting Britain, remember that you can keep in regular touch with home and office by telephone.

You can cross the ocean for $12 by telephone

This is the daytime rate for the first three minutes from anywhere in the United States, not including the 10% federal excise tax. It applies not only to Great Britain, but to 27 countries in Europe. In most cases the rate is even lower at night and on Sunday.

BELL SYSTEM **OVERSEAS** TELEPHONE SERVICE

advantage if it will be purchased. ICT has been adopted by many organisations to increase efficiency and quality, automate laborious tasks, enable better communications and to share information.

Businesses have adopted ICT to gain a commercial advantage. This is achieved through the automation of manufacturing processes, using computer tools and through using generic computer applications in the day to day running of the business. The Internet dissolves national boundaries, and the consequences of not embracing the technological advances in communication and trade may be disastrous for a business. Resisting the tide of technological change is not possible for profit-making companies. It is possible to do business without a web site, e-mail address, mobile phone or fax machine. However, technology gives many businesses a series of advantages over their competitors which can make or break the company. As a simple example, any business that does not use Microsoft Office may find it difficult to transfer documents to and from partner firms.

Figure 11.11: Advert for a telephone. (from *National Geographic*, **September 1957)**

> **Task**
>
> Consider the advert in figure 11.11 which appeared in the American *National Geographic* magazine in 1957. At the time this would have been considered to be 'cutting edge' technology. What does this advert tell us about the way in which the use of technology and ICT has changed in businesses in the last fifty years?

Education has embraced ICT as a tool to enhance learning. Not only is it used to support the teaching process in the classroom, but it is also taught as an exam subject which will be needed in both personal and vocational arenas.

Governments use ICT to help run the country. Information about the inhabitants of a country is collected and used to make informed decisions about the running of that country. One example is the census, a collection of statistical information, which takes place every ten years. The census is now compiled almost entirely by a computer system. By looking at this information, the government can plan for the future. For example, by looking at the number of one-year-old children, they can estimate the number of places in secondary schools that will be needed in ten years.

> **Task**
>
> Discuss the effect of a twenty-four hour power cut on a modern company compared to a company operating forty years ago. What does this tell us about the impact of ICT in business? Do you think this is a fair way to judge the impact of ICT? Justify your answer.

The impact of ICT on Society

There is no doubt that technological change brings about social change. A key example from British history is the Industrial Revolution, which caused many people to leave their agricultural backgrounds to move to increasingly crowded cities to find work in factories. National economies grew and trade flourished, but cottage industries and agriculture suffered.

In a similar way, ICT has led to social change, for example:

+ Many jobs are less labour intensive with different degrees of automation;
+ People are better informed, as it is much easier to share information. In fact, it is so easy to share that many users suffer what they call 'information overload'.
+ ICT has 'collapsed' timescales as tasks can be completed much more quickly.
+ Geographical boundaries have been broken down as communication allows businesses, schools and other organisations to operate at a global level.
+ A 'digital divide' exists between those who have access to ICT and those who don't.
+ A person's use of ICT may be influenced by their background. Many young people today are described as 'digital natives', using ICT as a preferred tool for many tasks. Many older people may use ICT only when there is no feasible alternative (for example, to receive e-mailed pictures from relatives abroad, or preferring CDs to MP3 players). ICT is on the periphery of their culture.
+ Users of online services may interact with people they would not normally meet. It is possible for people who would ignore each other in daily life (due to distance, culture, age, disability, religion, race etc) to communicate on topics of interest and develop friendships that overcome traditional cultural barriers.

Task

Most of the discussion in this section relates to the experience of the western world, the wealthiest region of the planet. What would someone from a third-world nation think of the above assessment of the impact of ICT? Discuss the impact of ICT in the world taken as a whole.

Amoeba Antiques

Alison from Amoeba goes Christmas shopping

Alison recently bought a digital camera as a Christmas present. She used the Internet to access a few sites dedicated to digital cameras. These sites were arranged by brand name and also by megapixel rating and gave a detailed specification for each camera. She wanted a camera with at least 8.0 megapixel image resolution with movie capabilities and, after some research, she narrowed her selection down to a few different cameras. A different search on the Internet for independent reviews of each camera showed that one of the cameras seemed to be slightly better than the rest. Another search on a price comparison web site revealed a spread of prices for that model. She opted to use the company that provided the cheapest price for what she was looking for and purchased the product using her credit card. The company was based in Paris and delivery was with a major courier firm. She was given a tracking number and was able to track the package daily as it left the Paris depot and made its way to her house.

Task

Identify the ways in which ICT has been used by Alison and how this has had an impact on her as an individual and on the businesses involved. If Alison had wished to buy a film camera twenty years earlier, how would her experience have been different? Is the modern experience better or worse than this? Support your answers.

Questions

1. Describe how ICT has impacted on passports. (3)
2. Describe how ICT has impacted on advertising. (4)
3. Evaluate the positives and negatives of advertising in the current ICT-dominated environment. (6)
4. Discuss the impact of ICT with regard to entertainment. (6)
5. Describe the advantage of digital input when compared to analogue input. (2)
6. Describe the disadvantage of digital input compared to analogue input. (2)
7. Describe three changes that have occurred in shopping as a result of ICT. (6)
8. Identify the hardware required for virtual reality. (3)
9. Describe two benefits of using virtual reality. (4)
10. "The use of ICT in the home has made household management easier". Evaluate this statement. (6)
11. Evaluate whether virtual reality would be suitable for a doctor training to become a surgeon. (5)
12. Evaluate the impact of ICT on the Individual, the Organisation and Society. (10)
13. What is meant by CAD/CAM? Describe it and give an example of a scenario where it is used. (5)

CHAPTER 12
Health, Safety and Legal Issues

12.1 Introduction

The growth of ICT has resulted in both the creation of new laws and the updating of older ones to tackle the new types of crime that have come with it. It has also been amended to give protection to regular users of ICT, in order to reduce or prevent injuries that may result from their work.

12.2 Health and Safety

Although it might not appear that sitting at a computer can be dangerous, there are a number of serious health and safety issues associated with ICT. While most readers of this book will not suffer greatly from these, poor posture or poorly designed equipment can lead to severe problems in later life.

- **Repetitive strain injury (RSI)** is caused by repeated physical movement or overuse of a particular tool. It can result in damage to muscles, tendons and nerves in the arms, neck and upper back. RSI can also lead to a long-term loss of feeling or disability. For example, intensive typing at high speeds on a keyboard without a wrist rest or regular breaks, combined with the constant use of a pointing device such as a mouse, can contribute to RSI.

- **Back problems** often arise from poor posture while sitting at a computer. This can be reduced by using adjustable monitors and chairs along with footrests to ensure that a person is sitting correctly.

- **Eyestrain** is a common effect of ICT use, and can have several causes: working for long periods of time without interruption; not blinking frequently enough; flickering monitors; or reflections on the computer screen. Research has also suggested that the flashing or flickering of VDUs may increase the risk of seizure in epilepsy suffers.

- **Electromagnetic emissions** come from electronic equipment, including VDUs. Although research has not confirmed a link, there is still public concern that pregnant women who work with VDUs risk harming their unborn child. There is also public concern relating to WiFi in the workplace and evidence that some laser printers emit particles that may affect the lungs.

- **Stress** is a condition that can be caused by various problems in the workplace. Fatigue, worry, poor relationships and a heavy workload can all contribute to stress, but it can also be felt by some people when working with computers. This might be because they are not as ICT literate as their colleagues, or because the regular changes in technology requires constant staff training. Whatever the causes, workplace stress can be extremely debilitating. It can lead to ill health and long-term absence.

Task	What do experts currently recommend in order to sit 'correctly' at a computer?

By the way... This web page contains further reading on the topic of laser printers:

"Office printers are health risk", BBC News, 31 July 2007
http://tinyurl.com/2mp6wf

12.3 The Law and ICT

Any new technology can lead to fresh opportunities for crime. It is often the case that these are not adequately addressed by old laws. For example, in the early 1980s hacking was not illegal within the UK simply because existing legislation did not make provision for it. It had to be adapted to make provisions for this purpose.

There are four main laws governing the use of ICT:

+ The Data Protection Act 1998;
+ The Copyright Designs and Patents Act 1998;
+ Computer Misuse Act 1990;
+ Health and Safety (Display Screen Equipment) Regulations, 1992.

You should be able to describe these laws, together with their implications for individuals, organisations and society as a whole.

The Data Protection Act 1998

The Data Protection Act governs the use of personal data. It defines the:

+ Rights of **data subjects** (people whose data is stored);
+ Responsibilities of **data users** (people who store and use the data).

This is an updated version of the Data Protection Act of 1984 which was appropriate for the use of ICT at that time. The 1998 Act more accurately reflects the current use of ICT. Under the DPA, organisations using personal data are required to register with the Information Commissioner and state:

+ Who they are;
+ What data will be held and what it will be used for;
+ Where the personal data is obtained;
+ To whom the data will be disclosed;
+ A list of any countries outside the UK to which the data may be transferred.

There are a number of exceptions, including data held for personal, family or recreational purposes (such as an e-mail address book or a Christmas card list), for processing wages, and data relating to national security or crime prevention.

Personal data is defined to be any data from which a person can be identified and covers both facts and opinions about the individual.

Data users must adhere to eight principles of data protection to ensure that data is:

+ Fairly and lawfully obtained and processed.
+ Held only for the specified purposes and not used in a way that is incompatible with the purpose it was obtained for.
+ Adequate, relevant and not excessive.
+ Accurate and up-to-date: organisations should incorporate verification and validation procedures to maintain the correctness of personal data. Data should be obtained from direct sources where possible. Data subjects should be contacted regularly in order to verify that information held is accurate.
+ Not kept longer than necessary and deleted once it is no longer required;
+ Kept secure to prevent unlawful processing by unauthorised users, accidental loss or destruction of data. This can be achieved by password protection, limited access and regular backups.
+ Not transferred to countries outside the European Economic Area, unless that country ensures an adequate level of protection for the rights and freedoms of data subjects in relation to the processing of personal data;
+ Processed in accordance with the data subject's rights (see below).

A data subject has the right to:

+ Access data held about them (a small administration fee may be charged).
+ Have errors corrected, and to seek compensation for damages arising from such errors.
+ Ask a data controller not to process information for direct marketing purposes or information that causes substantial unwarranted damage or distress. The data controller will also be required to tell the data subject about the purposes to which the data will be put and also to give details of anyone else to whom the data will be disclosed. If the data is unintelligible to the data subject, the data controller has to explain what it means;
+ Compensation for the unauthorised disclosure of data.

The Copyright Designs and Patents Act 1998

Although it refers to a wide range of areas, in the context of a computer user this act identifies the following as offences:

+ Using software that has been illegally copied.
+ Copying or distributing software, or any manuals that come with it, without the permission or licence from the copyright owner.
+ Running purchased software covered by copyright on two or more machines at the same time, unless the licence specifically allows it.
+ Modifying software without the permission from the copyright owner.
+ Downloading or uploading software over a telecommunications line, thereby creating a copy without the permission of the copyright owner.

This means that any business must ensure that the software they use is properly licensed. For example, a multi-user or site user licence may be necessary. There should be one department or individual responsible for the maintenance and purchase of licences as this will make it easier to monitor copyright issues. Auditing software should be used to monitor network activity and so identify any illegal use of software. It will be advisable to train staff in compliance with the act and have an acceptable use policy. Disciplinary procedures should be in place and enforced for staff who fail to comply with the policy. For example, staff may be prohibited from installing software either downloaded from the Internet or from disk. This law also has effects on the individual. For a PC owner it may mean that some software they use, or some music they listen to, is being accessed illegally.

By the way...

Copyright theft: common excuses.

Everyone else does it. This is not a strong legal defence. Something does not become permissible in the eyes of the law just because lots of people do it.

CDs are overpriced. Most would agree that music CDs are too expensive, particularly when compared with their retail price in other parts of the world. However, both record labels and their artists will continue to suffer financially if people continue to acquire their music illegitimately, either through downloading files or copying CDs.

You can legally copy a CD for 'personal use'. While this is true, this rule only extends to the person who purchased the CD, not to their friends.

Bill Gates has more money than he can ever spend and I am a poor student. This is also true, but his software company and others still have programmers and hundreds of other staff members on their payroll. It is often suggested that the price of software would drop if more people paid for it legitimately. Many companies also offer reduced price software to students.

Computer Misuse Act 1990

Breaking into other peoples' computer systems became illegal after two men hacked into the Duke of Edinburgh's private electronic mailbox in 1986. They were convicted under the Forgery and Counterfeiting Act 1981. Their subsequent appeal was upheld by Lord Chief Justice Lord Lane, who pointed out that the earlier Act did not cover what these men did. Therefore, they did not actually break the law. Consequently, the **Computer Misuse Act 1990** was conceived. The following are classified as offences, which may lead to fines and/or imprisonment:

+ Intentionally gaining unauthorised access to programs or data, whether that material is held securely or not. For example guessing someone's username and password, then accessing their computer system or exceeding access levels, eg a pupil who gains access to another pupil's user area.

+ Gaining unauthorised access with the intent to commit or facilitate a crime. For example transferring money out of another person's online bank account or reading someone's e-mails for the purpose of blackmail.

+ Intentionally gaining access to programs or data and causing an unauthorised modification of the contents of any computer. For example deliberately altering

Task

The Fourth Annual BSA and IDC Global Software Piracy Study reveals that 35% of the software installed in 2006 on personal computers (PCs) worldwide was obtained illegally, amounting to nearly $40 billion in global losses due to software piracy. Progress was seen in a number of emerging markets, most notably in China, where the piracy rate dropped by 10% in three years, and in Russia, where piracy fell by 7% over three years. The data presented below is taken from the BSA/IDC Global Software Piracy Study (2006). The full study is available from the BSA web site, via http://tinyurl.com/24ro6v

Country	% of software that was pirated: 2006	2003	GDP per capita US$ (a measure of wealth)
Pakistan	86%	83%	$2,600
China	82%	92%	$5,300
Russia	80%	87%	$14,600
Poland	57%	58%	$16,200
Rep of Ireland	38%	41%	$45,600
UK	27%	29%	$35,300
USA	21%	22%	$46,000

What do these figures suggest about the motivation for software piracy? What other factors might influence differing rates of piracy around the world?

Task

Write a report on a recent incident of deliberate ICT misuse which was reported in the media (not one of those listed below). What damage was done? How many people did it affect? How could it have been prevented? What does it teach us about the impact of ICT?

or deleting computer material, or introducing viruses with the intent to impair the operation of a computer. It can also mean restricting the ability of other people to access computer systems to which they should have access.

The above apply whether a person commits the offence themselves, enables others to commit them or writes a program (eg a virus) that will have the same effect. This is regardless of whether any changes made are permanent or temporary.

As with other acts, staff should be trained as to what is and what is not acceptable. Audit trails could be used to identify unauthorised attempts to modify material. Only ICT administrators should not be allowed to install software. Appropriate security procedures should be implemented to prevent the misuse of:

+ Usernames and passwords.
+ Tiered levels of access.
+ Firewalls and antivirus software.

It is also important to ensure that no single employee is responsible for every step in a single transaction, or has the capability to do so. This measure can be achieved by implementing selective access rights. This is known as **separation of duties**. Therefore, any act of fraud or theft would require not one unscrupulous person, but a team working together.

The Health and Safety (Display Screen Equipment) Regulations 1992

A number of laws exist in the UK to ensure that employers provide a safe working environment for all staff who work with computers. As a result of an EC (now EU) Directive, UK regulations came into force directly relating to the use of display screen equipment. **The Health and Safety (Display Screen Equipment) Regulations, 1992**, apply to *'an employee who habitually uses display screen equipment as a significant part of their normal work'.*

The law states that an employer must:

+ Regularly assess the whole workstation. This includes equipment, furniture and the job being done, along with any special needs of individual staff. Where risks are identified, the employer must take the necessary steps to reduce them.

+ Ensure workstations meet minimum requirements for health and safety. These include adequate space, adjustable monitor screens and chairs, anti-glare screen filters, foot rests and suitable lighting. Faulty equipment should be replaced without delay.

+ Plan the working day to ensure there are regular breaks or changes of activity from working at a computer. As the need for breaks depends on the nature and intensity of the work, the regulations do not specify their timing or length.

+ Arrange eye tests, and provide spectacles if special ones are required. Employees covered by the regulations can ask their employer to provide and pay for an eyesight test. There is also an entitlement to further tests at regular intervals. Employers only have to pay for spectacles if special ones are needed and normal ones cannot be used.

+ Provide health and safety training and information. Employers must provide training, to make sure employees can use their VDU and workstation safely.

By the way...

These web pages contains further reading on the topic of ICT misuse:

"Credit card fraudster jailed", BBC News, 9 September 2003
via http://tinyurl.com/62sfky

"Hundreds disciplined in Revenue purge", The Daily Telegraph, 7 June 2003
via http://tinyurl.com/39lzde

"Bosses 'Ignore Toxic Data Risk'", BBC News, 29 October 2008
via http://tinyurl.com/55mexf

"Calls Grow to Save Autistic Scots Hacker from Threat of US Prison", The Scotsman, 30 October 2008, via http://tinyurl.com/5nnpx7

Piracy and the Business Software Alliance

The Business Software Alliance make recommendations in their *Guide for Software Management* for organisations wanting to avoid pirated software. The full report is obtainable from their web site as a PDF document, via http://tinyurl.com/2nu3so

Task

Summarise the main points of the Business Software Alliance's document *Guide for Software Management* in no more than 500 words (see "By the way..." above).

ICT, the law and Amoeba

An audit of ICT culture in Amoeba's offices has highlighted the following concerns.

+ Many employees regularly listen to downloaded MP3 music via their PC.

+ Several users have installed games that Amoeba did not authorise or pay for.

+ Many users have software at home which originated in Amoeba.

+ Although Amoeba employs several hundred people, some departments are using reduced price copies of Student Edition office software, whose licensing terms state that it is sold for non-profit use.

+ Several members of staff have been discovered accessing pornographic sites.

+ One employee was blocked from an web-based e-mail account after another changed his password as a prank.

+ Although employees are instructed to download updates for their PC's anti-virus software every Monday morning, most do not do this as they say it takes too long. As a result a series of viruses crippled several mail servers.

+ There was a recent exposure to hackers despite the use of a firewall. This resulted from a new member of ICT support reconfiguring the firewall so he could stream his favourite radio station, thus creating a security gap.

+ Many users sit on uncomfortable chairs, with VDUs placed at an awkward angle or with sunlight reflecting off them.

+ Many software developers work for several hours without a break, and are often forced to eat at their desks.

This audit was prompted after an employee who was sacked was given half an hour to say their goodbyes and clear their desk. During that time they downloaded confidential material from the Amoeba MIS and later sold it to a rival firm.

Task

Prepare the following for Amoeba's management.

+ A summary of the laws that govern ICT.

+ An outline of a security policy for Amoeba, addressing the issues they have uncovered and any other relevant issues.

Questions

1. Identify and describe three health and safety issues as a result of working with ICT. (6)
2. Describe two implications for an organisation as a result of the following legislation (a) Data Protection Act (b) Copyright and Patents Act (c) Computer Misuse Act. (4 each)
3. Describe two implications for an individual as a result of the following legislation (a) Data Protection Act (b) Copyright and Patents Act (c) Computer Misuse Act. (4 each)
4. What rights does a user have under the Health and Safety Act? (4)

CHAPTER 13
The Consequences of the Internet

13.1 Introduction

This section discusses the implications of the Internet for users and society at large. Although this section appears here in this book (due to its positioning within the CCEA specification) readers are advised to re-read chapters 7 and 10 to appreciate it within its proper context.

Originally a development of US Military systems, the Internet now spans the globe. In many countries there are few areas of life that the Internet has not affected. Conversely, in many countries, even in comparatively wealthy places such as the UK, there are areas in which Internet access is severely limited.

13.2 The Internet in Commerce

Many businesses offer online retail alongside their High Street stores. According to the Interactive Media in Retail Group (IMRG), Internet sales rose to £4.02 billion in July 2007. This was an increase from £2.34 billion in the same month a year earlier. This offers advantages to both the organisation and the customer. However, as with any element of ICT there are disadvantages as well as advantages.

Advantages of the Internet to business include:

+ The organisation can market goods and services to consumers across the world 24 hours a day, 7 days a week. Any consumer with a computer and access to the Internet can view their web site.

+ A virtual store allows the business to stock a greater range of items than a normal shop. This enables them to appeal to a wider customer base as well as reducing other costs. Rather than being restricted by the confines of one physical location, online retailers can present many goods on a single web page. In reality, these items may be stored miles apart. The only indication that goods may be sent from different warehouses is seen via the postmarks printed on particular parcels.

+ A company can save money through the reduced overheads offered by the flexibility of an online store. The costs of warehouse rental can be reduced by moving to a remote area, while the virtual store remains at the same URL. A prominent and expensive real world location is no longer an issue; rather, access to efficient transport and communication links are key.

+ The consumer can access a wider range of goods and services than are traditionally available, whether from firms based far from them or local firms that can offer a greater product range than a small shop can stock.

+ A web site can be updated immediately and with minimal effort, whereas printing leaflets and catalogues costs much more effort, time and money. In addition, automated stock-control allows a web site to be updated automatically with no human intervention.

Disadvantages of the Internet to business include:

+ While a business can benefit from a world-wide market, it also has added competition from many international firms. Some businesses may struggle to compete with foreign firms that have lower labour costs.
+ There is little interaction between customer and salesperson, thus reducing the prospect for repeat sales derived from this relationship.
+ Local retailers undoubtedly suffer as a result of this technological expansion. If lots of people shop online, what will happen to small independent outlets who cannot buy in the same volumes as mass-retailers or locate their premises in a remote place with low rental costs? In turn, what will happen to the customers who depend on these outlets?

Advantages of the Internet to customers include:

+ Because of their reduced overheads, businesses can reduce prices.
+ By using meta-search engines such as *Kelkoo*, consumers can easily find the lowest price for the item they wish to buy. A single query will reveal links to many shops and present the results in a single page.
+ The consumer can access a wider range of goods and services than are traditionally available. Firms can stock items that would not be available offline. This is of particular benefit to those who are housebound or live in rural areas.
+ Shopping is more convenient. It can be done at a time that suits the consumer and should take less time, especially as broadband connections are increasing in speed and no travelling is required. The product is delivered to the consumer's home.

Disadvantages of the Internet for customers include:

+ Not all consumers have the hardware and software needed to shop online.
+ Other customers will be hesitant to buy online because they are concerned about the risk of credit card fraud, identity theft and hoax web sites.
+ Arguably, online shopping lacks the social interaction of 'retail therapy'.
+ As with mail order, the customer has to wait for products to be delivered.

Discuss the advantages and disadvantages of the Internet for:
1. A schoolchild   2. A business person
3. A retired couple   4. A single mother
5. Government authorities.

Task

13.3 The Internet at Home

The Internet has brought many advantags to the home. Research, entertainment, shopping, contacting friends and many routine tasks have been greatly simplified through the widespread growth in use of the Internet at home. This growth was accelerated by the introduction of graphical web browsers in the 1990s and in more recent years through affordable high-bandwidth (broadband) access.

Advantages of the use of the Internet at home include:

- Users can access material on many topics that is not normally available outside university libraries or specialist publications.
- Access to entertainment, including streaming media from other countries and downloadable music.
- Online shopping offers a wide range of goods from remote places and immediate notification of availability.
- Users can access bank account details, transfer money and pay bills online. This benefits those who find it difficult to visit a local bank.
- Social networking, e-mail and and instant messaging make it easy to find old friends and stay in touch, especially for those who have moved away.
- Teachers can allow students to explore and research topics using a variety of sources that may not be available in printed form.
- Parents can offer their children a wide range of educational materials.

However, there are associated disadvantages of the use of the Internet at home:

- Students may rely on plagiarism. Online resources may not be as reliable as peer-reviewed publications.
- DRM may restrict the use of purchased files. Children may access unsuitable television programmes/films.
- Phishing web sites may impersonate genuine retailers. There is a loss of social interaction in online shopping.
- Financial services traditionally offered in rural post-offices have declined, and some have closed, with the result that the community has lost a social hub.
- Privacy can be compromised and bullying is a problem, particularly in teenage users. Paedophiles are known to impersonate children, to gain their prey's trust. Social interaction may be lost.
- Even innocent online searches can lead users to offensive material. In many schools, filtering is purposely over-strict to avoid exposing children to unsuitable images. Many parents are unaware of the need for filtering at home.
- Without strict supervision, children may view a computer as a toy for playing games and may access inappropriate web sites.

13.4 Security, Censorship and Plagiarism

Millions of people use the Internet on a daily basis to perform a wide variety of tasks. However, the opportunities and convenience offered must be balanced against the accompanying dangers. Due to the actions of unscrupulous persons, or even Governments, participating in online activities can potentially lead to many kinds of problems. Users should take these matters seriously, as will be seen in the following discussions.

Security

Contrary to what most people think, clearing your web browser's cache does not remove all traces of the sites you have accessed, and deleting files from your PC does not get rid of them entirely. With suitable tools, they can be recovered long afterwards. Many computer systems are designed to log users' activities. In most cases, this is to ensure that accidental mistakes, such as deleting important files, can be identified and corrected. These logs are maintained by ISPs and may also be used to identify criminals.

When a user visits a web site, the remote server records their IP address and their ISP records what they have been looking at. So-called 'anonymisers' are sometimes used to prevent the remote server knowing the IP address of the user by routing requests through a proxy server (so that the web-server only knows the IP address of the proxy server being used). With these the user's ISP still has a record of the data that went between the proxy server and the ISP. Anonymisers may offer a degree of security by blocking malware from being installed without the user's knowledge.

In addition, users of the Internet must be careful to avoid:

+ **Spyware**: Software that is designed to spy on a user's activities. This is often installed with illegitimate downloads or from unscrupulous web sites, but can equally be installed as part of an apparently legitimate program. Spyware remains hidden on a PC, where it logs personal details such as passwords or credit card details for the purposes of hacking or spamming.

+ **Spam**: Junk e-mail, often sent from virus-infected PCs. Spam continues to be a nuisance. When this book was first published in 2004, it accounted for 60% of the world's e-mail. By July 2008, that figure had risen to 94% (source: *Softscan*). Much of it is blocked by ISP filters, which costs them money and bandwidth, but much still gets through to users. Spammers can build lists of genuine e-mail contacts by harvesting them from discussion forums, generating random addresses and by buying them from unethical mailing list operators.

+ **Viruses**: Self-replicating programs that copy themselves from one computer to another. They may be designed as pranks (in which they put annoying messages on the screen and do little damage) but they are usually designed to be more malicious. This damage may include permanently altering data, stealing data (by transmitting it to another machine), or using the infected PC to transmit spam e-mail. While early viruses spread through infected media and some still do, most viruses today are Worms and Trojan Horses:

  + **Worms**: Similar to a virus, but can spread from computer to computer without the assistance of a user. By taking advantage of PCs that lack firewalls or other security measures, worms can travel unaided to other unprotected PCs, possibly causing damage, stealing data or sending spam. Unprotected operating systems interpret requests from worms on other machines as legitimate commands which they accept and process.

+ **Trojan Horses:** Programs that look attractive, but when installed can damage and delete data and files. Trojans do not self-replicate, but can create a backdoor on a computer that allows other users to access confidential information. They are typically spread as attachments to e-mails that the user opens, thinking they are legitimate.

+ **Pirated Software:** There is a reason that the seemingly legitimate version of Microsoft Office is free from a download site. It may well be designed to damage host PCs or spread various kinds of malware. If something seems too good to be true, it probably is.

+ **Filesharing:** While peer-to-peer sharing clients such as *BitTorrent* can be used legitimately, a number of such services can only be run fully by deactivating security, thus rendering the user's computer vulnerable to all forms of malware.

+ **Phishing:** A scam in which the user receives e-mail purporting to be from a bank, a trading site such as eBay or a wealthy tycoon who wants to share his fortune. These are actually from criminals intent on fraud or identity theft.

To reduce the likelihood of such problems, users should:

+ Ensure antivirus software is up-to-date.

+ Use spyware removal programs such as *Spybot - Search & Destroy* or *Ad-Aware*, both of which are available for free download.

+ Use legitimate software. If you are unwilling to pay the retail price of a package, enquire after a student discount or find an alternative. Don't download a copied version of Microsoft *Windows*, no matter how tempting it looks.

+ Regularly check for security updates for software. Much malware is designed to take advantage of vulnerabilities in common software such as *Internet Explorer*. As these become known, new updates and patches become available. Many users don't like the time that it takes for the latest updates to install, but doing so saves much more time and hassle later on.

+ Never share personal details with unknown web sites. Many users post private data in discussion forums or on weblog diaries (blogs), thinking that only their friends can read it. They do not realise that once data is on the Internet, potentially anybody can read it, and if it is posted to a public forum, there may be no way to delete it.

+ Never follow hyperlinks in an e-mail claiming to be from your bank. These are often easy to identify as they contain basic text without the bank's logo, or other pertinent details. Type the bank's URL into your web browser instead.

Censorship

Most readers of this book will have experienced the frustration of schools or educational authorities legitimately prohibiting access to specific sites. For example, many institutions within the United Kingdom block *Google Images* to prevent pupils from stumbling across harmful material. While the intentions behind this decision are laudable, it does cause problems for particular classes: for example, those studying Art can find it difficult to source useful material for research projects. However, such sites can sometimes be unblocked at the teacher's request.

Blocking can be achieved through routing a school's Internet traffic via a proxy server with inbuilt filters. Such systems look insignificant when compared to the **'Great Firewall of China'**, a proxy server that the entire nation's traffic must pass through, and which blocks material that authorities deem unsuitable. In the past, this has included BBC News, *Wikipedia* and many blogs.

By the way...

The Chinese Government's policy on censorship (and wider human rights) has led to criticism of some Western companies operating there. Some search engines only provide filtered results in China, while others pass details of users who are involved in 'unacceptable' blogging to the government. These news stories provide more information on this topic:

"The Great Firewall of China", BBC News, 6 January 2006
http://tinyurl.com/283znb

"Google censors itself for China", BBC News, 25 January 2006
http://tinyurl.com/tu6vg

While the actions of the Chinese government may seem unacceptable in the West, the idea of unrestricted Internet access is under threat within the United Kingdom. The principle of 'Net Neutrality', whereby all traffic is treated as equal, is under review in the USA. This would allow ISPs to give preference to certain traffic, such as allowing high bandwidth media downloads from some web sites but limiting bandwidth for others. A major objection to this is that ISPs are often part of the same firms as major media providers (such as AOL who are part of the Time Warner group). Such ISPs may allow data from partner firms through unhindered but limit other traffic. Therefore, media firms would control what people would be permitted to see as well as providing access. At present, ISPs in the EU charge users extra for using higher bandwidth services rather than restricting bandwidth for users of certain sites.

Task

Prepare a report / presentation outlining the arguments in favour of Internet censorship, researching where it is used and the rationale behind it. Then, prepare a report arguing against it.

Plagiarism

The Oxford English Dictionary defines 'plagiarism' as "*taking and passing off another's thoughts, writings, etc as one's own*". With the growth of the Internet, there has been an accompanying growth in plagiarism within schools and Universities. For various reasons, a number of students feel it is acceptable to hand in an article copied word-for-word from the Internet as their own work. A large number of web sites claim to sell 'original' essays to students 'for research purposes'. Plagiarism is often easy for teachers to recognise, as the tone of the article may be out of keeping with the student's usual writing style. Articles that are a mishmash of other sources can lack consistency of thought and may alternate between UK and US spelling. The difficulty for teachers may be in proving where the plagiarised work originated, though typing a few sentences into a search engine is often effective.

There are a number of solutions for examining boards. While changing coursework procedures are one, there are also plagiarism detection services (such as *turnitin.com*). Institutions using these services submit students' work to a massive database for checking against all work previously submitted to the database, plus web sites and periodicals that make their publications available for searching. After a piece of work is queried, it is given a 'score' indicating the probability that the work has been plagiarised. Sections of the work that appear to have been copied from elsewhere are also indicated. A common plagiarist's trick is to slightly re-word source material but linguistic analysis can also spot paraphrases that follow the ideas of the source.

While there is nothing wrong with using other sources in your work, these must be referenced correctly according to the guidelines of your specification. Students who are either interested in or concerned about this area should check the web site www.plagiarism.org for further information and advice.

13.5 Online Transactions

Figure 13.1: Example of a certificate being used. VeriSign (top) supplies a certificate which is indicated in the browser (middle). If anyone else copies the certificate and uses it on a different web site, the browser will warn the user (bottom).

Image ©VeriSign. Used with permission.

Many people use the Internet to buy and sell goods. While the experience is usually good, concerns such as hacking and credit card theft persist. Two technologies are relevant to this subject:

Encrypted Transmission. This uses **HyperText Transfer Protocol Secure (HTTPS)** to encrypt data sent between a client and server. By using an encryption 'key' known only to client and server, the data is put through a series of mathematical functions which are reversed at the receiving end. Any eavesdropping machine on the transmission route does not have the numeric key and therefore cannot decrypt data. HTTPS transmission is used on many commercial sites and is denoted by the presence of a Key or Padlock symbol on a web browser's toolbar.

An enhancement of HTTPS is the use of encryption keys that are issued by a central **Certificate Authority (CA)** along with **Digital Certificate**s, which certify that certificate holders are the entity they claim to be (and not, for example a phishing site designed to look legitimate). CAs such as *VeriSign* and *GoDaddy* provide encryption and authentication services alongside other products. Digital Certificates are downloaded by browsers as encrypted data and can only be decrypted if the decryption key for the site it was issued to is used. Certificates cannot easily be altered as the key used to encrypt them is known only to the CA and the certificate holder. See figure 13.1.

The server's name "amoeba.21000biz.net" does not match the certificate's name " *.amoebaantiques.com". Somebody may be trying to eavesdrop on you.

Intermediary financial services hold payment until a customer is satisfied with the goods, and may offer the ability to undo a payment if goods are not acceptable. The best known of these is *PayPal*, an e-commerce business which provides a companion service to the eBay auction site. The customer pays the seller through their *PayPal* account, which later transfers funds electronically to the seller's account. The main way in which it benefits the customer is that they do not have to give a complete stranger their bank or credit card details.

Chapter 13: The Consequences of the Internet

13.6 HyperText Markup Language (HTML)

HyperText Markup Language is used to create web sites. When a web browser requests a server for data, a file in HTML format is sent to the client, which in turn interprets and displays it. **Extensible Markup Language (XML)** is a derivative of HTML used with web sites in both the ISO **Open Document Format** and Microsoft's **OpenXML** formats for word processing. The HTML page you see is often stored remotely as a number of files. For example, graphics are separate images referred to in the HTML file. In order to recognise basic HTML tags, the exercise below which will take you through the creation of a basic web site. *This is by necessity a very quick, basic exercise and the student should use other tutorials to further understand these ideas. There are many HTML tutorials on the Internet.*

A Simple Web Site

Create a folder called *webdemo*. Open a new document in a text editor such as Notepad, and type the following precisely:

```
<HEAD>
<TITLE>Welcome to my web site</TITLE>
</HEAD>
<BODY BGCOLOR="00FF88">
<H1>This is my web site</H1>
<P>
<OL>
<LI>My page with a picture is <A HREF="picturepage.html">here</A>
<LI>My page with a background image is
<A HREF="bgimagepage.html">here</A>
<LI>My page with links is <A HREF="linkspage.html">here</A>
</OL>
</BODY>
```

Figure 13.2: How your first web page should look (background should be green).

Then save the file into your folder with the name *index.html* (you may need to choose *File Type -> all types* for this to work properly). Double-click the file to open it and see how it has been interpreted (figure 13.2). The angle brackets < > surround **tags** which carry instructions. Some tags such as <P> are used on their own, whereas others have a **start tag** and an **end tag**. The end tag is shown by the use of a forward slash / The tags used here are:

<HEAD>	begins the header of the web page.	</HEAD> ends it.
<TITLE>	begins the title to show in the browser window.	</TITLE> ends it.
<BODY>	identifies the main body (content) of the page.	</BODY> ends it.
<OL>	starts an ordered (numbered) list. Using <UL> instead would create a list with bullets.	</OL> ends it.
<LI>	starts an element of a list.	</LI> ends it.
<H1>	surrounds text that is to be displayed larger than normal.	</H1> ends it.
<P>	inserts a paragraph break. It has no end tag.	

Some tags contain additional information. The <BODY> tag contains the word BGCOLOR which defines the background colour for the page, by defining quantities of red, green and blue (in hexadecimal or base-16 values between 00 and FF). In this case 00 means no red, FF indicates full strength green, and 88 indicates some blue.

A **hyperlink** is defined using the <A> tag. The extra information in this tag, HREF, gives the location of the file to be linked to. Later you will prefix the file name with http:// for links to files stored on other web servers. However, for files in the same folder it is sufficient to just use the file name. Note that these links do not yet work.

Include an Image on the Web Page

Using a web browser, go to www.google.co.uk. Save the Google logo (on a PC this is achieved by right-clicking on the image and choosing *Save image as..*) into your folder and name it *googlelogo.gif*. (If your school computer does not have access to Google, find a different picture but make sure you save it into your folder with the same name.) Then create a second text file in the same folder called *picturepage.html*. Type the following into the second file:

```
<HEAD> <TITLE>Welcome to my page with an image</TITLE> </HEAD>
<BODY BGCOLOR="0088FF">
<H1>This page has an image</H1>
<P>Here is the Google logo:
<A HREF="http://www.google.co.uk">
<P><IMG SRC="googlelogo.gif" ALT="pic of Google logo">
</A>
<P>
<P><A HREF="index.html"><I>Back to Index</I>
</BODY>
```

Open your original page and click the first link. The second page should appear, with the Google logo visible with a line round it. Clicking on the logo will take you to the Google web site. The new tag here is <IMG SRC=...> which specifies an image within the same directory as the HTML page.

Task

The <IMG> tag is used to insert an image. But what is the purpose of the ALT element within the tag?

Giving the Web Page a Background Image

Using a web browser, go to the page www.openoffice.org. By the same method as before, save the OpenOffice.org logo into your folder. (Again, if you don't have access to this site, pick a different image). Name it *openofficelogo.png*. Then create a third text file, called *bgimagepage.html*, type the following and save it:

```
<HEAD>
<TITLE>Welcome to my page with a background</TITLE>
</HEAD>
<BODY BACKGROUND="openofficelogo.png" >
<FONT COLOR="#FF0000">
<H1>This page has a background</H1>
<FONT COLOR="#00FF00">
<P>It is the <B>OpenOffice.org</B> logo.
<P>
<P><A HREF="index.html"><I>Back to Index</I>
</BODY>
```

When you open this file in your web browser you should see a page with the OpenOffice.org logo in the background.

Task

Find out and write down the purpose and use of the <B>, <FONT> and <I> tags. Now modify your web page so that whenever the user clicks on the word *OpenOffice.org* it will take you to the OpenOffice.org web site. Hint: As this is on an external server, you will need to include the full URL including *http://*

Add Tables to the Web Page

HTML also allows you to create tables. Tables can be used in powerful ways that are beyond the scope of this exercise, but the basic tags are as follows:

Use	<TABLE>	to starts a new table.	</TABLE> ends it.
Use	<TR>	at the start of each row.	</TR> ends it.
Use	<TH>	at the start of each cell within a row that you want to display as a header.	</TH> ends it.
Use	<TD>	at the start of each cell within a row that you want to display as normal text.	</TD> ends it.

Within a table cell you can include anything, including formatted text, hyperlinks and images as will be demonstrated with this final example.

Open a new text file, called *linkspage.html*, type the following and save it:

```
<HEAD>
<TITLE>Welcome to my links page</TITLE>
</HEAD>
<BODY BGCOLOR="FF00DD">
<H1>This page links to sites I like</H1>
<TABLE border="1">
<TR><TH>TV</TH> <TD> Link to the BBC to go here</TD>
<TR><TH>More TV</TH> <TD>Link to ITV to go here</TD>
<TR><TH>Even more TV</TH><TD>Link to channel 4 going here</TD>
</BODY>
```

Figure 13.3: How your web page should look with tables (background should be pink).

There are no links as yet - just a table with text in it. When you open the file in a web browser, you should see something similar to figure 13.3. Change some of the <TH> to <TD> and vice-versa, and see what happens. Don't forget to change the closing tag as well as the opening tag in each case.

To create the links, reopen the document in your text editor and modify the contents of the table. The replacement text is shown below.

```
<TR><TH>TV</TH><TD>
<A HREF="http://www.bbc.co.uk">BBC</A></TD>
<TR><TH>More TV</TH><TD>
<A HREF="http://www.itv.com">ITV</A></TD>
<TR><TH>Even more TV</TH><TD>
<A HREF="http://www.channel4.com">Ch4</A></TD>
```

When you save the file and reopen it you should have links to three external web sites. You now have a small, but functioning, web site. The web site cannot be viewed from other computers unless you upload it to a web server.

Questions

1. Many businesses offer online retail alongside their High Street stores. Discuss the advantages and disadvantages to (a) an organisation (b) the consumer of the Internet as a business tool (5 each).
2. Evaluate the use of the Internet at home. (4)
3. Discuss security issues with regard to using the Internet. (8)
4. Suggest ways in which security issues with regard to the Internet can be avoided. (3)
5. Identify and describe two technologies used to make online transactions more secure (6)
6. What is HTML? (3)

CHAPTER 14
Factors Affecting ICT

14.1 Introduction

There are many factors that influence the uptake and use of ICT between cultures and nations. For example, there are people who primarily view ICT as: an entertainment device; an educational tool; a work tool or a tool for problem solving. There are people for whom using ICT is as normal as using a pen and there are those who are uncomfortable with ICT. A number of considerations that vendors and users face are introduced here and are returned to later.

This chapter also covers the threats that exist to the security of any organisation or person using ICT. We will also be looking at the various ways of addressing these security threats. As with the previous chapter, this one is in keeping with its place in the CCEA specification. However, it should also be understood in the wider context of Networks and the Internet.

Task

Imagine you are responsible for these projects. Research the challenges you would face:
+ Reaching children across the developing world with *One Laptop Per Child*.
+ Developing a long-term project to recruit more skilled graduates into software development.
+ Organising an ad-hoc party in a location where mobile phones and e-mail do not exist.
+ Introducing a group of novice computer users to e-mail, on-line banking and social networking.

14.2 Influences on ICT

Social Considerations

The Oxford English Dictionary (OED) defines society as *the aggregate of people living together in a more or less ordered community... a particular community of people.*

In affluent areas of the world, the growth of ICT in the areas of employment, education and how we socialise has made it inescapable. In developing countries the situation is different. Many people do not have access to the latest equipment, and where PCs are available, many applications rely on fast Internet connections that are not. In some situations it may not be possible to adequately configure a PC due to 'product activation', that requires communication with a vendor's server before an application is used.

The rate at which ICT has been accepted has transformed much of society. Customs and habits from as recently as the 1990s now seem old-fashioned (such as writing letters or coursework with a pen, using mail-order catalogues, meeting people face-to-face instead of using on- line communication). While the younger generation are used to the rapid changes in ICT, some older users struggle with the pace of change. Many users' limited understanding of how a computer works has increased opportunities for phishing and spyware (con-men aren't new, but their methods are). Another challenge is the emphasis in some areas of education on simply developing end-user skills rather than developing a technical understanding of computer science, with the result that some ICT companies have difficulties meeting recruitment targets.

Compare these two views of the social influences on ICT:

"'Technology 'baffles old and poor'", BBC News, 16 May 2005
http://tinyurl.com/5lj3qz

"Old people like the Internet", Silicon.com, 14 November 2003
http://tinyurl.com/6gemzg

By the way...

Cultural Considerations

Culture is *"the customs, institutions and achievements of a nation, people or group"* (OED). We all belong to several cultures, such as our nation, and sub-groups within society. These cultures may influence our use of ICT: some older people may feel they have got through most of life perfectly well without computers; people who travel or work far from home may use ICT to communicate with remote friends and colleagues; a person may strictly adhere to Copyright legislation or treat it with disdain, because of the attitudes of their peers. A person's culture may make them likely to quickly adopt new technology or may see little need for it and only adopt it when they perceive an associated advantage. For example, a person may only use *Facebook* and an *iPod* in order to create a certain impression and may soon move to the next 'cool' thing. Or, they may adopt them slowly because they eventually see a benefit in social networking and MP3 players and may gradually adapt their lifestyle to technology that they see as helpful, for example contacting long-lost friends and relatives through social networking and using podcasting or video-on-demand to change their radio and television habits.

Legal Considerations

Several laws influence ICT and are discussed in Chapter 12. The Data Protection and Computer Misuse Acts exist because of ICT, while current copyright and health and safely legislation have been influenced by how ICT is used. ICT may be used to break laws that were not written with ICT in mind, or it may be used to enforce laws in ways that were not considered when those laws were written. Therefore, the development of ICT may be affected by laws that were created in response to how it was used.

Technical Considerations

ICT is influenced by what is actually possible with current technology. Many tools we take for granted today exist because people were not satisfied with the technology they were using and sought ways to improve it, while at the same time pushing the boundaries of what hardware could do. While many people regard broadband Internet, *YouTube* or the interface of Microsoft *Windows* as recent innovations, they are not really: the ideas behind them had been around for decades though affordable hardware to facilitate them has not. Every ICT project must tackle the issue of technical feasibility.

By the way...

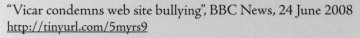

These news stories deal with the legal considerations of ICT:

"Vicar condemns web site bullying", BBC News, 24 June 2008
http://tinyurl.com/5myrs9

"Councils warned over spying laws", BBC News, 23 June 2008
http://tinyurl.com/5hlpau

"Who watches the watchers?", BBC News, 6 February 2008
http://tinyurl.com/6hvjwj

Ethical Considerations

A person's ethical views influence all aspects of their life. Because many people view ethics as relative to their current situation it cannot be assumed that everyone agrees on right and wrong – hence many ethical dilemmas are governed by employee codes of conduct or appropriate legislation. Major ethical issues relating to ICT include:

+ **Intimacy, friendship and bullying**: secrets can easily be distributed and distorted and momentary anger, expressed online, may be difficult to undo. Our view of friendship is affected – many people claim to be friends with, and share deep secrets with, people they have never met.

+ **Plagiarism**: Universities have reported a sharp increase of students copying work verbatim since the WWW became widely used. While Universities may not approve of such behaviour, their task is made more difficult by students who insist that because they were never formally told that "plagiarism is wrong", there should not be a problem.

+ **Intellectual property**: It is easy to copy books, CDs, software etc, that other people depend on selling to make a living.

+ **Privacy**: many people unintentionally leave personal details scattered all over the Internet on various forums and social networking sites. This data can be misused in many ways, whether by fraudsters or potential employers.

+ **Computer security**: many systems are not fully secure, although this does not constitute an invitation to access them.

ICT professionals must be aware of these issues and accept that just because something can be done, it is not always morally or ethically appropriate. Many ICT bodies have strict codes of conduct covering these areas.

Economic Considerations

Computer systems are not cheap to run. As well as hardware costs, there are the ongoing costs of software, consumables, maintenance and specialist staff. Even a perfectly tuned system will eventually need replaced so that new software can run. Many organisations accept that an ongoing cycle of upgrading and replacing functional equipment is inevitable and budget for this. With oil prices in 2008 at the highest they have ever been, many companies now have to budget far more for the energy of keeping all their computers running than before.

However, the growing use of ICT has meant that a number of countries have found lucrative markets for the raw materials used to make computers (such as copper, silicon and petro-chemicals) and many people now work in these sectors.

Environmental Considerations

As well as the cost of upgrading systems, there is the environmental impact of their disposal – whether through the energy and materials associated with recycling or with sending equipment to landfill sites. Also, the impact on the environment of mining, refining and manufacturing in many areas of the world has been significant. Many countries now have legislation designed to encourage more efficient electronics (hence, less pollution) and low-pollution disposal such as taxes on vendors, and legislation forcing manufacturers to pay the long-term disposal costs for whatever they make. Not all pollution related to ICT is due to design and manufacture – many devices waste electricity because they are left in a low-power 'standby' state for days when they could be turned off.

On a positive note, the use of ICT has led to more efficient fuel use (eg in cars and electricity generation), has driven the development of highly efficient rechargeable batteries and has improved our understanding of climate change through modelling the environment. Ironically, a tool that has led to much pollution could also help in its reduction.

Figure 14.1: The issue of what to do with functional, but obsolete, computer equipment raises legal, environmental and ethical questions.

14.3 The Consequences of Poor Security

Most modern companies are heavily reliant on ICT in their daily operation. ICT offers them many benefits, most notably the speed of data processing and transmission. However, heavy reliance on ICT also means that a failure in this area can be catastrophic.

The consequences of a failure in an organisation's ICT include:

- **Theft of hardware / software / data.** Money must be spent on re-collecting data or replacing equipment. In some cases, data such as customer orders may not be retrievable unless proper backups have been made.

- **Loss of business.** If customers are dissatisfied with the delays caused by the company having to acquire new hardware and restore files, they may take their business elsewhere. Customers will do the same if they are not confident that their personal details are secure during transactions. Significant cash flow problems will obviously have a hugely negative impact on the company.

- **Loss of reputation.** Similarly, if customers do not believe that they are valued, they are likely to tell their friends, neighbours and relatives. Such word of mouth, coupled with negative coverage in newspapers, will damage a business's reputation, often irreparably.

- **Legal action.** This can arise when an organisation fails to keep personal data private or correct. Under the UK's Data Protection Act, it is a crime not to properly secure customer's data. Other countries have comparable legislation.

How Security Can Be Breached

To minimise the chances of the physical security of any system being compromised, there must be many restrictions, all of which would have to fail together. These are known as **layers of security**. Data must be protected from:

- **Accidents caused by humans.** Examples include employees accidentally deleting or updating data incorrectly, sending confidential information to the wrong e-mail address, opening an attachment which contains a virus, printing out confidential information and neglecting to dispose of it correctly or neglecting to make backups and losing data through hardware failure or theft. These could be the result of human error, but the company can still be accused of not providing appropriate training. This in turn can cause an organisation to lose yet more money to pay for the resulting legal fees.

- **Theft of hardware or information.** Computers may be physically stolen, or the information stored on them stolen, by those gaining unauthorised access. Information is a valuable commodity and may be of use to competitors.

- **Man-made and natural hazards.** Fire, floods, earthquakes and hurricanes can all destroy buildings and therefore a company's databases. The likelihood of such a security breach will depend on the business's location.

- **Deliberate damage.** Individuals may physically vandalise computer equipment, or hackers may damage program files by planting viruses or deleting important records.

- **Failure of hardware / software.** Any ICT equipment is susceptible to not functioning properly, but older hardware is more likely to be unreliable. A read-write head may crash, making the contents of a hard disk unreadable. New software may contain undiscovered errors, resulting in the corruption or loss of data.

14.4 Hackers, Crackers and Viruses

While opinions on the morality of a **hacker** varies, FOLDOC (Free Online Dictionary Of Computing) offers this definition: *"One who enjoys the intellectual challenge of creatively overcoming or circumventing limitations."* Curious hackers like to understand the workings of a system and to identify any weaknesses in that system. Some consider it a personal challenge to break into supposedly secure networks, partly for the thrill of it, and partly for the recognition they receive from fellow hackers. Interestingly, some major corporations have employed convicted hackers to test their system's flaws.

In comparison, a **cracker** is more malicious. Such individuals are more intent on breaking into a system and doing damage, and have many means of doing so. Believing that they had been misrepresented by journalists, 'good' hackers coined the term circa 1985 to distinguish themselves from their less honest colleagues.

Hacking and cracking may originate from inside an establishment or it may be instigated from the outside. It has been estimated that 75% of hacking threats to a company are from within. This may be thanks to disenchanted employees or due to industrial espionage: spies within a firm acting for another company to gain access to valuable trade secrets. Steps taken to prevent hacking include:

* **Firewalls**. Prevent unauthorised access from outside an organisation.
* **Passwords**. Frequently changed and contain a mixture of numerals and letters.
* **Patches and updates**. Applied to operating systems and security software when available.

A **virus** is a self-replicating computer program. (The technical aspects of viruses were discussed in Chapter 13. This section discusses viruses from a user's perspective.) At best it causes minor inconvenience, but it can modify or destroy other files. At worst, it may render a PC inoperable. Many current viruses take advantage of security gaps in e-mail clients or any other operating systems that allow the sending of attachments. They generally fall into one of the following categories:

* **Logic bomb or time bomb**. Activates on a predefined date and usually destroys files that are necessary to a computer's operation.
* **Trojan horse**. Allows malicious intruders access to files by pretending to be something harmless such as a screensaver or a game. In Homer's *Iliad*, Greek soldiers pretend to make peace with their enemies, the Trojans, by presenting them with the gift of a large, wooden horse. The Trojans bring it inside their city gates, and at night a small band of Greek warriors leap out, open the gates, and let in the rest of the army to ransack the city.
* **Worm**. Replicates and spreads to other computers via e-mail or a LAN and has a negative effect on the host computer. The *ILOVEYOU* virus in 2000 is one of the most famous examples of a worm. Users received an e-mail, apparently from a colleague, with that romantic proposition in the subject line. It contained an attached file that, if opened, would damage files and send copies of itself to the people stored in the user's address book. Consequently, many businesses were forced to suspend their e-mail activity, which directly impacted

their productivity during that time. As more and more computers become permanently connected to networks, worms are becoming a growing threat.

+ **File virus.** Hidden inside an apparently useful program. Replaces a key system file with a bogus copy. When that program is run, the virus copies itself and inserts these copies into other programs. As it duplicates, the virus spreads into other programs. Once it is in the memory, it can spread further by writing itself to any disk inserted into the computer.

+ **Macro virus.** Infects user files created by applications. Written with a scripting language such as that used in Microsoft *Visual Basic For Applications*. When an infected file is opened, the macro executes and the virus does its damage. Some programs, such as Microsoft *Excel*, now have inbuilt facilities to guard against such macro viruses.

14.5 How to Protect Information Systems from Misuse

A number of measures can be taken to prevent accidental or deliberate misuse of data. Measures to prevent unintentional misuse include:

+ **Clerical procedures** can be used to reduce errors caused by staff. There should be a set of procedures for data entry to check accuracy of data. This might include verification and validation checks.

+ **Staff should receive training** on how to prevent misuse, for example by keeping passwords confidential, being vigilant for e-mails that may contain viruses, being able to spot scam web sites and being trained in how to comply with official ICT legislation.

Measures to prevent intentional misuse include the following:

+ **Unwanted visitors** can be prevented or deterred by methods such as bars on windows (especially at ground level), armed guards, electric fences, visible security cameras and walls topped with barbed wire. However, not all security has to be as intimidating as these examples.

+ **Employees and visitors** may be restricted as to the areas they are permitted to visit. Access to buildings or rooms may be controlled by using keypads on doors or by entering a PIN. Also, computers in those rooms could be controlled by requiring users to swipe an ID card (containing a bar code, magnetic strip or chip) through a reader before being permitted to log on. Visitors may be allowed entry, but only through a single door, which leads directly to an office where the visitors must wait for an escort. They are also issued with a security pass that has details of their visit written or printed upon it. **Biometric measures** check a physical characteristic which is unique to the user so that he / she can be distinguished from others. For example, fingerprint or iris recognition can be used to gain access either to a room or a particular terminal.

Security is also concerned with protecting data against threats to the physical building. A good policy should not only state what will be done to minimise the impact of damage to the building, but what will happen if a company can no longer operate in their current location. During the 'Troubles', for example, several firms in Belfast not only stored backup data in a bombproof safe, but had plans to relocate staff to sister firms if necessary, so they could continue work. A number of large firms in New York had to actually implement such plans after losing their offices in the terrorist attacks on 11 September 2001.

Measures to prevent unauthorised access and modifications to data include:

+ **User IDs.** Only authorised users should be able to log on to a computer system, and are uniquely identified by a username and password.

+ **Passwords.** An 'Achilles' Heel' for many organisations, simply because employees are prone either to forgetting them or making them easy to guess. For example, some workers will use their middle name, their birthday or the name of a pop group. Others will even write their password in their diary. Passwords should therefore:

    + Be changed regularly and kept confidential. Many companies force employees to change their password at set intervals.

    + Contain numbers as well as letters.

    + Be kept confidential and not written down in any form.

    + Be kept in an encrypted file which can only be decoded by network software.

+ **Limiting logins.** Security can be further tightened by controlling the number of logins. For example, after three failed attempts, the user account should be disabled, and the time and nature of the login recorded (figure 14.2). Some firms go even further by disabling an employee's account when that person is not supposed to be at work or forcing staff to log off during breaks. Others prevent employees from accessing more than one terminal at a time, or setting up password-protected screensavers to activate if an employee forgets to log off or is temporarily away from their desk. Many also disable the accounts of former employees.

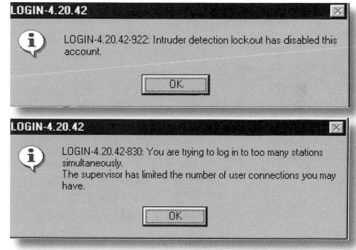

Figure 14.2: Novell Netware error messages resulting from (top) multiple failed logins and (bottom) an attempt to use more than one computer at once.

+ **Access rights.** These can be assigned to each user to ensure that they may only access particular files or records according to their information needs. Low level users within a database may have no access, while others may have the ability to view particular data (ie read access), modify it (edit access), create new files (write access) or run programs (execute access). For example, a school's junior secretary may have read access to most student records and edit access to their attendance whereas the senior secretary will have write access, allowing the creation of new records.

Other users have a combination of these access rights to files. They may have read-write access to their own files, meaning that they can read and create / modify them, but read only access to some other files, such as the company intranet. They may have execute access, but only on their own PC so that they can run programs.

14.6 Secure Communications

With increased use of telecommunications it is vital that communications links are secure. There are different techniques for ensuring security in this area, but the main method is encryption.

Data encryption is used to prevent unauthorised viewing of data during transmission. The sending device encodes data using an 'encryption key' (a mathematical algorithm). Any device intercepting the transmitted data cannot decode it, as it does not have the encryption key. The receiving device decrypts the message by applying the encryption algorithm in reverse. Because intercepted messages can eventually be decrypted by trying every possible encryption key in sequence, encryption keys must be complex enough to require months of computer time to decrypt them – modern encryption is often based around 1024-bit numbers ($2^{1024} \approx 1.8 \times 10^{308}$).

As some employees work from home and access a company database remotely, a **callback** system can be installed to prevent unauthorised remote access. Users must register a phone number, such as their home, from which they will connect. When they connect they enter a username and password and are immediately disconnected. Only if their details are correct will the server 'call back' their PC.

The use of a **firewall** can prevent unauthorised access to a network from outside. In the context of the Internet, a firewall is a hardware device that provides one access point to and from an organisation's network. It filters all data going out of and into the network, and restricts access by unauthorised users by making the organisation's network appear to be nonexistent while limiting the data that local users can transmit (by blocking streaming media, for example). The firewall analyses each packet of data and rejects it if it does not conform to predefined rules. It can act as a proxy for applications by performing all data exchanges with the remote server on their behalf, thus making devices inside the firewall invisible to outsiders.

Audit trails are used to **identify** misuse, although they do not prevent it. Audit software will automatically maintain a log of all computer activity, known as an **audit trail**. It can enable the security manager to see, either with or without the user's knowledge, everything being typed on any screen within the network. It will also record other information such as the times a system has been accessed, which terminal was used, by whom and for how long as well as any changes made to files.

Antivirus software. All PCs should have effective antivirus software installed and regularly updated. This software will scan files to detect and remove viruses. Because modern viruses are released all the time, out-of-date antivirus software is only slightly more useful than not having any antivirus software installed at all. Many viruses are targeted at security vulnerabilities in software, eg Microsoft *Outlook* and some versions of *Windows*. Most antivirus products will inform the user when updates are available, and it is important that they download and install these immediately.

Personnel security. Firms must be careful about who they employ, both to ensure that they do not have an interest in rival firms and that they are not potential hackers. Depending on the nature of the work, firms contracted to the UK government may ask employees to sign the **Official Secrets Act**.

Regular backups should be made so that lost data can be recovered easily. For many companies it is sufficient to make daily backups of all data files. Data is transferred to a backup tape or disk, which is then stored in a fireproof safe at a separate location.

Amoeba and modern communication

Amoeba's directors were sceptical about the use of the Internet in the early 1990s. Like many businesses they had survived using traditional (pen-and-paper) processing methods even after computers had become widespread. It was perfectly normal for a customer's enquiries to be dealt with a week or more after the query arrived in the post and this was rarely questioned. It had been this way for as long as anybody remembered.

For many years, suppliers would post invoices and cheques would be sent from Amoeba up to a month later. Some suppliers felt that technology offered ways to improve the efficiency of this area and moved to *Electronic Data Interchange*. On a weekly basis the suppliers expected Amoeba to 'dial in' to their computers to see how much was owed, and to authorise an *Electronic Funds Transfer* within 24 hours. This prompted Amoeba to start a process of overhauling their business methods. Many members of staff were fearful that their routine jobs would be taken over by computer and some opted for early retirement.

While Amoeba's more traditionally-minded directors deny it, others admit that it was the decision to commit fully to ICT in their business that made them into a much more efficient company. There was a painful time of change though, including early retirements and redundancies. The staff that remained were moved from routine tasks to new projects. Ultimately, this allowed Amoeba to become the market leader they are today.

"Looking back, we were crazy to hold onto traditional methods for so long", says Lynne, head of ICT at Amoeba. "I can see why many people stick with tried-and-tested methods – after all, there is an old saying 'If it ain't broke, don't fix it'. Our problem wasn't that our systems didn't work, but that they were too slow. Other companies had developed a far more efficient way of doing things and customers could see this. Fifteen years ago people understood if you had to spend a few hours looking for what they wanted in a warehouse but now, if you cannot tell by looking at a screen whether something is in stock or not, they will go elsewhere. I know it's difficult to change how you operate, but if we hadn't gone down that route I doubt if we would still be in business".

An ICT strategy was put in place that took Amoeba to the head of their market niche. All their shops and warehouses were connected to a central *Information Management System*. The effect was immediate – instead of phoning around various warehouses looking for an item, it was now possible to run a *query* which looked through the stock of all the stores and within seconds reported where the desired item was. Customers noticed the improvements and this gave management the courage to bring in more changes.

Connecting all operations to a central computer system meant that it was possible for an operator to take an order even though they were far away from the warehouse. This allowed Amoeba to develop a *call centre* in the west of Ireland, taking advantage of the cheaper wages brought about by the lower costs of living in these areas than in the city.

Lynne says that the Internet has made the largest impact of all their new technology. "Until the Internet came along, you could get away with barely having a computer in your company. Now, if a big company wants to be taken seriously they need to use the Internet in some form. In fact, a lot of small companies can pass themselves off as being big and important simply because they make good use of the Internet."

"In order to keep our data secure, a tight system of passwords and a firewall is used. The firewall blocks access from unauthorised sources. In case anyone inside the company decides to threaten us we have logs tracking all computer activity allowing us to repair damage quickly. There are some things that can be difficult to stop, however, such as a sensitive document being e-mailed out of the company. As a consequence we record all e-mail so that anyone doing this knows they will be found out."

"How we work has changed in so many ways. When I wanted a price list from our American supplier, I had to depend on it being posted out and it could take weeks to arrive. Now when it changes, the Americans can e-mail the hundred-page catalogue to me as a *PDF file*, without going near a printing firm and it arrives with me in seconds. Some other suppliers prefer to put their catalogues on the web, which is very useful, as we can see exactly what is in stock without phoning people on the other side of the world. Ten years ago, if you were in a hurry to check if an Asian supplier has something in stock you had to phone at four in the morning because of time differences. Now, you can check through their web site or send an e-mail and expect a reply that day."

"When I was preparing a joint report for the directors with a colleague in our Australian partner firm, we could work together even though we have never met – we never even spoke on the phone. We divided the report into sections. When I finished a section I would e-mail it to Australia and go home for the night. He would have sent any comments to me by the time I got into work the next morning."

"Our customers also benefit hugely. They can see what is in any one of our shops without having to leave their house. They can place orders over the Internet and let us take care of the delivery, instead of trying to get something large and breakable home in the back of their car.

"The Internet has changed our business for the better. I would encourage all businesses to use it."

Task

1. There is no doubt Lynne and Amoeba value the Internet. Summarise the main points of what Lynne said. You should find out the meaning of any terms you are not familiar with.

2. Compare how people of your age 30 years ago would have listened to music, read, or indeed done many things, with how you would do them today. Make a list of ways in which the Internet has changed how we do things on a day-to-day basis. List the type, with examples, of any software that can be used for each purpose you describe.

14.7 Disaster Recovery Plans

Disaster Recovery plans exist to ensure that if data security measures fail an organisation can continue to operate as normal. This is achieved through restoring data from backup media, replacing equipment or relocation. Even with the best security policy in the world, mistakes will be made, but the time and expense in making allowances for these eventualities is a worthwhile investment. If these preparations are not made, a significant lapse of security may do irreparable damage to a firm.

While it is possible to focus only on major threats, smaller problems such as a user accidentally deleting a file should not be neglected. A data backup and recovery policy, written in a self-contained section of a company's security policy, will ensure that all data can easily be recovered in the event of catastrophe.

A backup and recovery plan should:

- Ensure that all files are backed up. This should be done at specified, frequent intervals, using several generations of backup. This is traditionally known as the Grandfather-Father-Son method, though in practice many organisations use dozens of generations. As well as backing up all data, a transaction file should record all changes to data since the last backup was made.

- State how long backups are to be held. In addition to the Grandfather-Father-Son method, it is normal that backups for archive purposes will also be made. For example, a complete monthly backup, which may be held indefinitely.

- State how and where files will be backed up. To quicken the backup process, it is normal to only backup files that have changed since the last backup (known as incremental backups). These may be recorded on tape to be stored safely off site, or may be transmitted to another location.

- State how files will be restored. For example:

  - By restoring only selected files in the event of an individual user error;

  - By identifying and restoring affected files in the event of an electronic attack;

  - By relocating personnel and restoring all data to servers at the new premises in the event of catastrophe. These new premises (often called a cold standby site) replicate the company's usual equipment or provide a compatible alternative, and can be up and running quickly. There are a number of companies offering such facilities to firms who need them.

- Identify key personnel and clearly describe their roles. For example, who should liaise with partner firms and who should issue press releases? In the event of a disaster, affected workers should be able to use the Disaster Recovery Plan to identify who they should report to.

Disaster Recovery Plans are discussed in more detail in Chapter 19.

Task

US financial services company Cantor Fitzgerald lost many of its employees and its main offices in New York in the attacks of September 11, 2001. Using the Internet research how this company, or another company affected by the same events, used their disaster recovery plan to survive.

By the way...

These news stories deal with the issues of data security:

"Data loss prompts security move", BBC News, 9 April 2008
http://tinyurl.com/62elkr

"Honesty the best online policy", BBC News, 14 August 2007
http://tinyurl.com/3a4yuu

"Ameritrade lost 6.3 million names from database", DM News, 26 Sep 2007
http://tinyurl.com/43bnb4

Questions

1. The management of a multinational company is concerned about accidental and deliberate damage to their company's database.
   (a) Discuss the consequences of poor security for such a business. (6)
   (b) Suggest a way in which security could be breached **unintentionally** by an employee. (2)
   (c) Suggest ways in which security could be breached **intentionally** by an employee. (4)
2. What is the popular definition of hacking? (2)
3. What is a virus? (2)
4. Apart from hacking and viruses, there are many ways in which an organisation's data can be compromised. State and describe two of these. (4)
5. Describe three steps that can be taken to prevent unauthorised access and modification. (6)
6. Identify three items of information recorded by an audit trail. (3)
7. Describe the contents of a disaster recovery plan. (6)

CHAPTER 15
Developing ICT Applications

15.1 Introduction

Most people are 'end users' of ICT: they use a computer for some purpose and know or care little for how it operates. Their only concern is that it does work. As a student of ICT, you are more than an end user. You should not be content with just knowing how to use certain programs: you should have an interest in understanding their underlying technology. In previous sections you have looked at how various ICT systems are used. This section expands on that knowledge by discussing how and why an ICT system is brought into being.

All systems are created as a response to some need or problem. Therefore, long before a final working system is delivered, a detailed process must be undertaken to identify the actual problem:

1. Investigating the problem thoroughly, including documenting any existing system in order to establish the user requirements.
2. Designing a solution.
3. Building and implementing a working system based on that design.
4. Testing the working system against original objectives.
5. Later additions in functionality and corrections of errors ('bugs').

At each stage, a cross-check is made between what is being produced and what was originally requested, to ensure that errors and misunderstandings are uncovered before they lead to costly mistakes. Documentation is also generated as a written record of what has been proposed or done. This is vital, since understanding programs written in the past can be difficult even for the original programmer. Some may spend up to 80% of their time writing documentation.

15.2 The Main Stages of Developing an ICT System

As mentioned in the introduction to this chapter, successful problem solving involves following a series of logical steps. At first glance this may appear tedious or legalistic, because often a person's creative instinct wants to see immediate results. However abiding by the steps of this process forces the developer to think a problem through more fully and hence produce a more comprehensive and effective solution to the problem. Taken together the states of this process are known as the **systems lifecycle**. An overview of the stages involved will be considered first. The following sections in this chapter will look in more detail at each stage.

The seven main stages of the process of problem solving in ICT are:

+ **analysis:** precisely describing the problem in order to establish the user's requirements or needs, as well as suggesting solutions;
+ **design:** describing in detail how the chosen solution will function;
+ **software development**: turning the design into an actual, working system;

- **testing:** ensuring that the system works as expected and meets customer expectations;
- **installation** (or **implementation**): end users put the implemented system into use;
- **review** or **evaluation** of the system once customers have had a chance to use it;
- **maintenance.** After implementation, the system may continue to develop as new features are added (**adaptive** maintenance), bugs are corrected (**corrective** maintenance) or is made to work more efficiently (**perfective** maintenance).

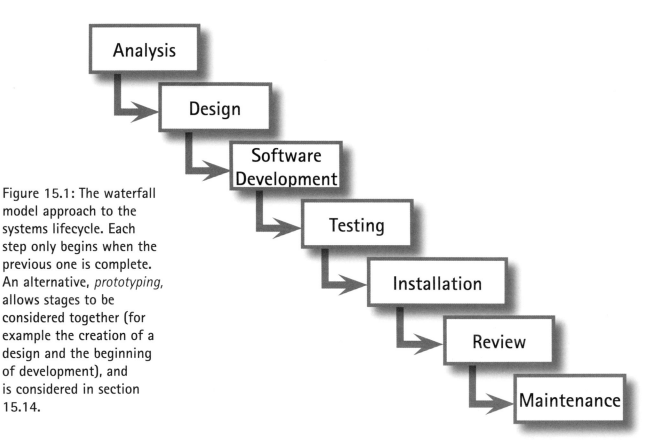

Figure 15.1: The waterfall model approach to the systems lifecycle. Each step only begins when the previous one is complete. An alternative, *prototyping*, allows stages to be considered together (for example the creation of a design and the beginning of development), and is considered in section 15.14.

By the way...

What about the Implementation?
Some books use 'Implementation' to refer to Software Development. Others use it to refer to Installation. Both of these are valid, depending on the context. If you are reading another textbook in conjunction with this one, make sure that you understand the context in which the word is used. Also ensure that you understand the context of examination questions.

15.3 Analysis

This phase involves a detailed examination of any current system in order to establish user requirements. It is possible that a system that was once perfectly adequate has become outdated due to changes in working practice, so no longer meets the customer's requirements. If this is the case, it is likely that the new one will be expected to do everything that its predecessor did as well as many new tasks. Any existing system may be paper-based or run on an obsolete platform.

This phase is carried out by a **Systems Analyst** who determines:

1. The user's requirements, ie what the customer / user needs their system to do.

2. Any failings of the current system.

3. Input data plus its source, and output data plus its destination.

4. The constraints on hardware, software, and development time.

5. Whether or not what the customer thinks they want is what they actually need.

6. Whether or not any proposed solution is feasible in reality.

The Systems Analyst investigates the customer's current system and their needs using a number of fact finding methods:

+ **Staff interviews**. Talking on a one to one basis with a broad spectrum of people within the organisation, from management to rank and file personnel, and seeking their opinions. Management's views are important as they ensure any solution will address company-wide issues. Other personnel may be expected to use a system daily, so failure to consider their concerns may lead to an inoperable system which in turn will create discontented staff and reduce productivity. They have the advantages of being flexible enough to be tailored for each person, of allowing follow-up questions to individuals and that facts are gathered from the system users, an example of a direct source. On the other hand, they take careful preparation (both open and closed questions are needed), they can be costly and time-consuming. Also, employees may feel uncomfortable or threatened about why they are being questioned about the system and fail to give full answers.

+ **Examining current business documentation**. For example, any paperwork entering or exiting the firm, and current management reports. They help the analyst identify data requirements and the current input and output for the existing system. This includes both internal data flows (within the system) and external data flows (outside the system). The main disadvantages are that studying documents is time consuming and tedious, and this approach does not give feedback or views from system users.

+ **Questionnaires**. Where it is impossible to interview every employee (eg in a large company) questionnaires may be used. They must be carefully written so that the answers given are relevant, clear and unambiguous. Consequently, multiple choice forms are often used. When used well they can gather information from a lot of people over a large area quickly and are relatively cheap to organise. As everyone is answering the same questions, the results can be input to a statistical software package (via OMR) and analysed. Graphs and statistics can be produced. On the other hand, they do not produce detailed answers, and it is common for users to misunderstand questions and therefore not answer as expected. This will affect the accuracy of results.

+ **Observation.** The analyst will spend time watching how users interact with the current system. This gives the analyst an opportunity to see where problems or bottlenecks exist in day to day practices. The analyst may notice problems both in the current ICT system and in current business practices, and can use the time to verify what has already been discovered in interviews / questionnaires. However, observation is time consuming, and people often behave differently when they know they are being observed. With this approach, the analyst cannot always obtain feedback from system users.

Once the analyst has completed their observations, interviews etc, they produce an **analysis document** which typically includes **Data Flow Diagrams (or DFDs)**. These illustrate how data moves within the organisation (see 15.11). DFDs are easier to follow than textual descriptions, but only show the movement of data. They do not specify how data is stored or the storage media used.

Contents of The Analysis Document

The analysis document represents the requirements specification for the new system and includes the following:

+ a description of the current system and any problems associated with it;
+ the information requirements of the user, including:
  + required outputs from the system;
  + inputs required (to allow the outputs to happen);
+ a feasibility study, which describes:
  + the technical feasibility of what is proposed – is the technology available for the suggested solution to be implemented?
  + the economic feasibility – are the development and running costs affordable?
  + the legal feasibility – for example, does it breach the Data Protection Act?
  + the operational feasibility - is the proposed system viable in daily use?
  + the social feasibility – for example, it might pose a health hazard, breach the ethics of the community or be hampered by a lack of available workers.
+ alternative solutions to the problem. For example, the analyst might give the alternatives as either updating only the out-dated parts of an old system or replacing the entire system.
+ costings, including hardware, software, and the cost of paying developers;
+ schedules. These may be negotiable, or may be in line with a fixed schedule.

The analyst presents their findings for discussion with the customer. To avoid expensive misunderstandings, it is important that the analyst is precise. There must be no ambiguity between what the customer thinks they have requested and what designers think has been requested. Once the customer has had time to study the proposals and ensure that they are correct, the requirements specification is finalised and passed on to designers.

New business at Amoeba – and a new system

Amoeba have recently bought over a smaller rival firm, *Mauvaise Antiquités*, a high-street vendor of reproduction furnishings based in Paris. Over the past number of years *Mauvaise* have developed an ICT system that links their offices, stores and warehouses. As part of the take-over, Amoeba's management want their two systems to be merged.

Lynne, Amoeba's head of IT, has met with her opposite number in *Mauvaise* and has found there is much work to do. Historically, *Mauvaise* have developed all their software internally. However in the past few years there was a high staff turnover in their IT department which has led to many problems.

In the 1990s their IT department consisted of one programmer (Jean) who did not see the need to document his work. This worked reasonably well while he remained. Even though the department expanded, Jean was still there and was available to answer any questions about how he did things. He has since left and, apart from a few brief notes, any analysis or design he may have carried out was never written down. He is no longer available.

The current head of IT at *Mauvaise* (Pierre) trained under Jean and still feels an amount of loyalty to him. Pierre is reluctant to state any problems with Jean's way of working. Since Jean left, Pierre took over much of his work and while Pierre does write slightly better documentation than before, much of the system remains undocumented.

This poses several problems for Lynne.

+ She would like to know why certain decisions were taken, but no analysis document exists.
+ The *design* document for the current system is brief and does not describe the entire system.
+ Since the design was written, changes were made that were not documented. As a result the system that exists today is not the system described in the old design.
+ She has asked Pierre to explain large aspects of the system but at times he cannot remember precisely what he did.

If Lynne is to allow the current system at *Mauvaise* to link into the Amoeba system, she must know how it operates. As Pierre cannot tell her, she decides to interview the people working at *Mauvaise*. This poses further problems as Pierre tells Lynne that everybody is on good terms at *Mauvaise* and insists on being present in many of her interviews with staff. Lynne feels his presence prevents many staff from being open with their views, as most of them tell her in interview that the current system works well, yet from observing them at work she can see this is not the case.

Although Amoeba was originally formed when two firms in Northern Ireland and Scotland merged, they have since expanded into other countries. Because

of differing work practices, differing business focuses and legislation in other countries, Amoeba's operations in those places generally have systems that were written specifically for them, but with the ability to *interface* with Amoeba's operations elsewhere. In some countries, however, the system used is just an adaptation of what is used elsewhere. For example, the system used in the Republic of Ireland is the same as the Northern Irish system with some amendments for local currency (the Euro) and laws.

One option Lynne is pondering is whether to take a copy of the Irish system and adapt it (choosing the Irish system because France uses the same currency). However, before she can recommend an option to management, she must do a full cost-benefit analysis. Her findings are summarised below. These findings come at the end of the analysis document which details current issues together with all requirements needed at *Mauvaise*.

Proposal 1: Keep the system currently used at *Mauvaise* in place and develop a new system to connect *Mauvaise* to Amoeba.

Advantages: Speed of implementation. No new hardware will be needed at *Mauvaise*. No need to re-train French employees.

Disadvantages: Because of uncertainty over the functionality of the *Mauvaise* system this may pose more long-term difficulties in sharing data. It does not address the issue of the current system which staff are clearly not happy with.

Proposal 2: Develop a brand new system for *Mauvaise*.

Advantages: This system will do exactly what is required of it. The old system will be gone. *Mauvaise* will have full access to the world-wide Amoeba operation.

Disadvantages: This will take between 12 and 18 months to implement fully, during which time *Mauvaise* will have difficulty accessing Amoeba's systems. Converting old data so that it can be accessed on the new system may be difficult. A lot of old hardware will have to be replaced.

Proposal 3 :Adapt the Irish system for use in France.

Advantages: This can be completed within 6-9 months. Because this system is known to have at least 80% of the functionality needed in France, development can be accelerated. Also, this system is tried-and-tested and known to be very reliable.

Disadvantages: Developers must be careful with what is removed, since if something is removed from the system 'because the French don't need it', other parts may stop working as a knock-on effect. Also, the current system may not do things exactly as the French require, due to legislation or work practises. The interface must also be translated from English to French. A lot of old hardware will have to be replaced.

Lynne is now ready to present her full analysis to the Amoeba's Board of Directors for discussion. Although she favours one particular solution, she cannot act without their approval, as any new system will force radical business changes at *Mauvaise*.

Task

Pretend you are Lynne from Amoeba Antiques. Prepare a brief written report for the Board of Directors recommending which of the three proposals *you* feel is most suitable. Your report should address the following issues:

+ length of time taken to implement the solution, and the impact this has on the business;

+ the benefits of any new system;

+ the costs of any new system.

15.4 Design

The design stage leads to a written description of how the requirements will be implemented. The analysis document must therefore be very precise, or designers could misinterpret it and a lot of money could be spent building something that the customer does not want. As the design is developed, each aspect of the analysis will be cross-referenced with the design document to ensure that all requirements have been included. A good design will read as a sequence of steps to be taken to build a working system. That is, the programmer(s) responsible should be able to start at page one and work through the design in sequence.

The design should address the following issues:

1. Selection of the most appropriate solution from the alternatives available.
2. Input data (where it is coming from, what format it is in, etc) and output data.
3. The functions of the modules of the system.
4. How data will be processed.
5. An outline of hardware and software needed to develop, test and implement the solution.
6. The user interface.
7. Security design.

Selecting the Most Appropriate Solution

During analysis, a number of different solutions are proposed but a single choice must be made at the design stage. There are a number of criteria for making the final decision:

+ **Usability**. Will the system make the user's job easier, or will it produce extra work with no obvious benefit?

+ **Suitability**. Will the system address current problems, or create new ones?

+ **Other software and hardware**. Any new system should be integrated with the systems that will be used alongside it.

+ **Maintainability**. Most systems need constant modification after they are 'complete'. This may be the addition of new features, or it may be the correction of errors that are only discovered after the system has been in use for some time. A system should be designed so it can be modified as easily as possible.

+ **Cost**. Sometimes the best possible solution is not chosen for financial reasons, such as development costs or the price of specialist hardware. This can lead to tradeoffs, ie sacrificing speed to facilitate less expensive hardware, or getting rid of rarely used features. Yet, it is important not to make so many compromises that the system is rendered useless.

Input Data and Output Data

Figure 15.2: An example design definition of the storage format for a table of input data.

It can be useful to delay consideration of input data and how it will be stored until output data has been planned, on the principle that the required output will determine what input data is required in order to make this possible. However, it is logical to place the description of how input data will be stored at the start of a design as it is the first step of development. It is only after data structures are in place that input/output interfaces and processing can be developed.

tbl_parishioners

Field name	Type	Comments / validation
ParishionerID*	Autonumber	Automatically generated
Forename	Text (20)	20 refers to how many characters can be stored.
Surname	Text (20)	
Addr1	Text (30)	
Addr2	Text (30)	
Town	Text (25)	
Pcode	Text (8)	In the form LL99 9LL
DOB	Date	In the form DD/MM/YYYY
Phone_no	Text (15)	In the form 028 9999 9999 or 07999 999 999

It is important that all structures used to store data, such as a database **table**, are thoroughly described together with any validation used, otherwise developers may be left guessing what to implement and may develop an unsuitable system. For example, in a parish administration system, if a table to hold a list of parishioners was being described, the format shown in Figure 15.2 may be used. Each parishioner is one record in this table and each element of data in a record is a **field**. An asterisk * denotes the primary key field, used to uniquely identify one parishioner.

Definitions of output data include:

+ What data is to be output and what layout is required;
+ Whether data is output as a hard copy or a soft copy;
+ Whether or not hard copies will look identical to soft copies;
+ If any output is generated automatically, and if so, with what frequency.

Functions of the Modules of the System

Figure 15.3: Example of a design definition of a query.

Once implemented, a complete system often appears to the user as a seamless whole. However, it is made up of many parts (or modules) which work together. The operation of each of these, both on their own and with each other, should be clearly and unambiguously defined. For example, in the parish administration system there may be queries (figure 15.3) which are designed to be displayed to the user as a formatted report (figures 15.4 and 15.5). Queries fetch data, and may manipulate or modify it.

Query:	*Qry_regularvisits*
Purpose:	to collate details of parishioners who are due a visit.
Fields called:	From *tbl_parishioners: parishioner_id, forename, surname, address1, town*
	From *tbl_visits:parishioner_id, visitdate*
Operation:	*Criteria* applied to certain fields are:
	For each parishioner, the date of their last visit, from tbl_visits. visitdate, is compared with current date. If the difference is more than 6 months they are listed as requiring a visit.

Report:	*Rpt_regularvisits*
Purpose:	to list people who are due a visit.
Operation:	formats the results of *qry_regularvisits*, sorting by surname and forename, showing date of last visit.

Figure 15.4: Example of a design definition of a report.

Parishioners due visits, w/b 6th June 2004

Brian Anderson, 852 Ballygawley Road, Dungannon
4 December 2003

John Quinn, 37 Brooke Street, Dungannon.
5 December 2003

Martha Williamson, 379 Scotch Street, Dungannon
2 December 2003

Peter Williamson, 108 Park Road, Dungannon
1 December 2003

Figure 15.5: Example output from a program module that implements the design represented by figures 15.3 and 15.4.

How Data Will be Processed

Before output data can be generated, some sort of processing must take place. How each element of output data is brought into being must be described in full detail. In the context of a data processing system, this includes a wide range of queries and reports (as discussed above).

Hardware and Software Required to Develop and Test the System

It is possible that the developers writing the system will use hardware that is quite different to the hardware owned by the end users. For example, in 2008 it may have been perfectly normal for a software developer to use a PC with a 4GHz processor running Microsoft *Windows Vista* and Microsoft *Office 2007*, with a colour laser printer for output. However, the target users of the system may only have had 800 MHz processors, *Windows 98*, *Office 2000* and a black and white inkjet printer. If developers do not account for these differences, it is entirely possible that the new system would not run at all on the target system.

Having said this, there may be good reasons for developing a system using software or hardware which is different from that of the end user. These include increased speed of development and the availability of development tools on some platforms that are not available on others. For example, a developer may use an MS-DOS emulator to develop an MS-DOS system, for the simple reason that their modern PC is very fast and MS-DOS is not available for it.

Once software is developed it must be tested. No matter what hardware or software was used to develop the system, it should not enter the customer's premises without having been tested on a similar or identical configuration. For example, if a mobile phone emulator was used to test a WAP system, the emulator may give the 'proper' results when tested. However, it is possible that the emulator used for development was flawed, so a 'real' phone must be used to confirm that everything functions correctly.

Other examples of development and user configurations not being the same include:

- Web-based services which have been developed for one particular browser yet should be accessible by all browsers;
- Terminal-based services which are developed to run on a Unix server yet are accessed via a remote Windows PC using a terminal emulator;
- A QWERTY keyboard used to mimic input from a concept keyboard (Q representing 'burger', W representing 'fries', etc.), before the 'real' concept keyboard is available.

The User Interface

In some ways, the user interface is the most important part of any system because it is the only component that the end user will see. If the interface is poorly constructed, users will not want to use the system, regardless of how many features it may offer. Therefore, the creation of the interface must be designed and documented rigorously just like other components of the system. The following aspects of the interface should be considered and, if necessary, sketched out:

- Menus and dialogue bars that allow the user to make choices;
- Forms (windows) used for input;
- Outputs (both hard and soft copy – see above);
- Help screens;
- Whether the interface will be designed to resemble any other package;
- Whether the interface will use third-party software, such as a web-browser.

Task

Choose a piece of software that you have used more than once. List some elements of the user interface that you think make it easier to use. List some elements that you think could be improved. Why have you made these choices? Why is it important that the user interface is well designed?

Security Design

This section of the design considers how the integrity of data will be maintained. Consideration is given to a range of security methods and how they will be used. Justification will be given for the decision on which security methods are to be used. Security methods under discussion here include:

- User identities and passwords;
- Levels of access and user privileges;
- Terminal security, such as restricting logins to particular terminals, or requiring that certain individuals insert an identity card into the keyboard;
- Firewalls and other network security;
- Backup procedures.

These concepts were discussed in more detail in Chapter 14.

Amoeba – the decision

After much consideration, Amoeba has decided to use the second option given in the analysis: writing a brand new system for *Mauvaise*. Their decision was not easy. Some people, including Lynne, felt that adapting the Irish system would be better. However, the overheads of translating the interface and thorough testing to make sure it worked exactly as the French expected convinced management that this option would actually take longer than was thought.

As an interim measure, a second system will be developed to allow the French stock database to be viewed via a HTML-based interface from other Amoeba offices, although ordering will be done by telephone or e-mail. Staff at *Mauvaise* will have full access to Amoeba's systems via Amoeba's existing HTML-based interface. However, this will be in English only. The main advantage of using a HTML-based interface is that once the system to allow access to the French database is developed, anybody can access it without the need to install special software. Proper security measures must be taken to prevent unauthorised access.

The new system, which will fully integrate both systems behind the HTML-based interface, will match the needs of both *Mauvaise* and Amoeba. As part of the design process for the new system, the list of requirements stated in the analysis document is carefully considered. Then a design is drawn up which states how each requirement will be met. It is very important that this document is made as clear and unambiguous as possible.

Once development and testing are complete (a process that is expected to take several months) Amoeba plan to use several experienced members of staff at *Mauvaise* for acceptance testing. They will use the new system for a period of time, but without removing the old system, so that any errors will not harm the business. After this, a period of **parallel conversion** will take place whereby both systems are used simultaneously and finally the new system takes over.

Amoeba Antiques

15.5 Software Development

This stage involves the development of programs and/or customisation of software packages to translate the design specification into a fully working system. If a design is easy to follow and covers all aspects of the system, development should be straightforward. If the design is difficult to follow, development will be difficult with greater potential for errors. Within the **waterfall model** the design is completely implemented. Only minor changes can be made, especially if a large team is working on the project.

At this stage, developers may notice flaws in the design or feel the need to make small changes. It is absolutely vital that they inform each other about this and amend the design document accordingly. This will benefit anyone who works on the system at a later date. The need for good documentation is discussed below, as part of maintenance (section 15.7). It is good practice for developers to keep a logbook where such changes and observations are recorded before being formally written up. In any case, changes should not be made without referring to project managers. This prevents causing other parts of the system to malfunction.

See section 15.14 on **prototyping**, an alternative to the waterfall approach.

15.6 Testing

There are different ways of testing a system, and each one is applicable to different stages of development. To ensure effective testing takes place a **test plan**, created as part of the design process, will be followed. The plan will identify the purpose of each test, the method of testing, the data to input and the expected outcome.

+ During development, **unit testing** ensures each component functions properly when completed. This leads to **integration testing**, carried out when components are brought together, once they are known to function independently.

+ **System testing** (or **application testing**) is carried out to verify that the complete system works according to the specification. Data from the current system is duplicated and inputted to the new system to mimic realistic demands and to highlight any serious flaws without corrupting user data. Application testing ensures that all modules work together.

+ **Acceptance testing** is carried out next. The system is given to end users to operate in its final environment. The system is tested with real data and normal daily workloads and users can realistically assess whether it meets their expectations. Minor modifications to the system may result, and testing continues until there is agreement between the user and the developer that the system meets the user's requirements.

Testing should seek to ensure that (a) the data the system was built to operate on is processed normally and (b) unexpected inputs do not crash the system. To cover both of these scenarios, three types of input data are used:

+ **Reasonable, correct data**. Normal data which the system was built to process.

+ **Extreme, correct data**. Data that is correct, but is unlikely to be encountered every day. For example, a library system may accept books with titles 40 characters long, but what happens if a much longer title is published? Or, what if a school administration system accepts classes of up to 25 students but an unusually large class has to be entered?

+ **Incorrect data**. Data that is erroneous and which should not be accepted. For example, what happens if a program that computes a square root is given a negative number? Or what if a pupil is entered into a school system with a birth date that is in the future?

15.7 Changeover / Installation

Once the system is fully developed, it is put into use on the customer premises. This may lead to a number of problems that have to be overcome.

+ New hardware may have to be purchased, installed and tested. Technical staff may have to be hired and paid to install the new system.

+ Training will have to be provided to all staff, which can be costly. Training must suit the needs of all the staff intending to use the system. It is also time sensitive: staff must be ready for the implementation of the new system.

+ Data held on the old system must be imported to the new system with complete accuracy. As part of the development process, data conversion tools may have been created to automate the process of converting data.

- Employees may not want to change from systems they are used to. Redundancy payments may be offered to employees who cannot adapt to the new system.

- The changeover method must be considered carefully. There are four methods:

  - **Parallel changeover**. All users duplicate all work on old and new systems for a certain period. When the new system is deemed to meet all requirements, the old system can be dropped. This process may take a number of months. The main benefit is that the accuracy of the new system can be tested by comparing its output against that of the old system. If difficulties occur, operations can continue under the old system while these problems are amended. The major drawback is that all users must duplicate their efforts which may put an extra strain on staff, and can be costly because of the employment of extra staff or overtime working for existing staff. In 'mission critical' applications where faulty software can result in catastrophe (such as financial management or industrial control and safety systems) this approach is often the only option.

  - **Direct changeover**. An organisation stops using the old system one day and starts using the new one the next. The advantage of this method is that only one system is operational at any time, so no time is wasted running two systems. It is also inexpensive if it works seamlessly, as extra staff are not required to operate both the old and new systems. However, this is impractical for many organisations , as normal business could be seriously disrupted if the new system is later discovered to have serious bugs or does not work as expected (eg it has not properly imported data from the old system). At this stage it may be impossible to revert to the old system.

  - **Pilot changeover.** A select group of end users access the new system first and any errors can be dealt with before the system is made available to all users. Training can also be modified in the light of experiences during the pilot changeover. For example, a new school attendance system may be used by a few teachers for a number of weeks before it is made available to all teachers.

  - **Phased changeover.** Occurs in stages that can be implemented separately at different times. It is vital that the old and new systems can share data as both will be used together for some time. In this scenario, a large firm may move half of a department each week onto the new system, thus allowing problems to be tackled at a manageable rate. Once a significant number of people have moved, most serious problems will have been discovered and will have been fixed or the users will have been told how to overcome them. This makes the changeover process easier for subsequent groups. Phased changeover is only suitable for systems that operate as clearly distinct modules.

What do you think would be the best way to change over to a new system for:

Task

- an insurance company with 1000 staff using a computer system for quotations;
- a small business with one employee who wants to change to a new e-mail system;
- an air-traffic control system in a UK airport;
- a school that uses a computer system to keep track of pupils and exam results;
- a taxi firm that uses paper and is introducing an ICT system to track cars.

Support your answers with reasons.

15.8 Review

Once the new system has been in use for an agreed period of time, the developers seek feedback from the client and end users to assess how well the system is performing. The system is compared to the original user requirements, as well as user expectations regarding ease of use and functionality. It often happens that, despite accepting a clear analysis or design document, users expect more functionality than was agreed. It is normal that shortcomings of the system may only be discovered when it is put into use. This may be because of flaws in the design or because of new functionality that was identified only after the original analysis was complete. Changes may be identified and as a consequence the review leads into systems maintenance. In some ways, the systems lifecycle starts again.

Amoeba
Antiques

Eventually the new Amoeba / *Mauvaise* system was completed and declared a success. While the interim solution of giving limited access to the two companies' systems was in use, it gave the two firms a better understanding of each other's existing business practices. This has led to suggestions for a number of improvements in functionality in both the new *Mauvaise* system and the existing Amoeba system. Transition was not perfectly smooth as there was a lot of difficulty transferring data from the old system into the new system: a vital task since this old data relates to current customers. The workaround of entering all new data into the new system, while keeping the old system in operation for a short time, was used. This provided time to improve the program that would import the old data.

In general, staff at *Mauvaise* find the new system more reliable and easier to use than the system it replaced. Some members of staff initially expressed reservations about the new web-based system, which they were not used to.

These findings will be used by Amoeba's project team to produce a detailed review. Moreover, they will form the basis of the maintenance phase of continued software improvement which involves correcting bugs and adding functionality.

Task

Do some research on the Internet to find out what happened when the "London Ambulance Service Computer Aided Dispatch System" was installed in October 1992. What does this episode teach us about the importance of the testing, implementation and review phases of the systems lifecycle?

15.9 Maintenance

This process ensures that the system continues to run as required, by being adapted to new requirements. Many systems actually spend more time in the maintenance phase than in the original development. For example, a product may take two years to build but may have a life span of twenty years or more with maintenance throughout this period.

There are three main types of maintenance.

+ **Corrective** maintenance corrects bugs or remedies aspects of the system that do not properly meet requirements.

+ **Perfective** maintenance makes the system work more reliably by removing inefficiencies and improving performance.

+ **Adaptive** maintenance adds new functionality to the system as a result of changing business needs or factors outside the business's control. Adaptive maintenance could be required to take advantage of new hardware or to respond to changes in a system's environment, such as new tax legislation or competitors' products.

15.10 Documentation

Accompanying documentation must be produced at each stage of development. This is vital as there is no guarantee that the same people will be with the project from start to finish. People with key knowledge may leave the firm or may simply forget how they did certain things months or years before. There are two types of documentation: **technical** and **user**.

Technical documentation is written solely for the benefit of those involved in developing the software and is not released to the public. The analysis and design documents can be used during the development stage to ensure all developers are working to the same specification. This must be documented as it is important to keep a record of work performed and yet to be performed. Various components of technical documentation will be used at the maintenance stage. Before any work can take place to add features it is vital that programmers understand what previous developers did. When fixing bugs, documentation can be used to identify possible sources of errors and the original test plans can be used to re-test the system. Any maintenance carried out must be incorporated into the technical documentation. This documentation includes:

+ The system requirements / aims;
+ The data dictionary (a 'database about the database') which defines the purpose and use of all fields, tables and queries;
+ Data Flow Diagrams;
+ A description of how each developed section works, including one or several of:
    + A verbal description of the components;
    + 'Pseudocode', a detailed, very precise step-by-step textual description;
    + A flowchart;
+ Any amendments to the design;
+ All testing strategies, plans and results;
+ Full program listings.

User documentation is written as a reference guide for the end user on how to use the software in normal operations. It does not go into detail on how the system operates (this is not its purpose and is not of interest to the reader). It describes:

+ The purpose of the system;
+ How to install the system;
+ The minimum hardware requirements and software needed to use the system;
+ A user guide or reference section explaining how to use each feature and enter

data. This should include step by step instructions on performing all tasks along with appropriate sample of input/output screens. This may be written from several perspectives, such as:

+ A quick reference for users;
+ Simple guides for non-technical users;
+ Detailed material for systems administrators.
+ An online help facility including an index of useful topics as well as a search facility for the user to browse for the appropriate help. A list of FAQs (Frequently Asked Questions) or a troubleshooting section could also be incorporated to provide examples of common problems or error messages along with the steps to resolve the problem.
+ The user may be directed to additional Internet support by the inclusion of the web site's URL, which may link to software patches, forums, FAQs etc.

User documentation can be distributed in several ways, for example:

+ As printed manuals. For large systems these can be quite bulky and will run to thousands of pages and several volumes;
+ As online documents, often using Adobe's *Portable Document Format* (PDF) which allows an electronic book to be viewed and searched using Adobe *Acrobat Reader*. These are electronic versions of the printed text;
+ As 'help' files built into the system. The manual is presented in the form of an indexed database.

For very popular systems a number of 'third party' user guides are often available. These are usually aimed at specific user groups, such as novice or specialist users. For example, there are approximately 1,500 books available for Adobe *Photoshop*, the vast majority of which are not published by Adobe. There include texts for new users of graphics software, art students and users of other packages such as *Paint Shop Pro* who want to quickly adjust to *Photoshop*.

15.11 The Suitability, Effectiveness and Usability of an ICT Solution

At the outset of a project, a number of alternative solutions will be considered and the most suitable one chosen. This will be determined by factors such as compatibility with existing systems, costs of hardware, maintainability and training costs. What appears to be the cheapest or best solution may be rejected because of ongoing support costs or the fact that other hardware/software is nearing obsolescence and will soon be replaced.

Many different solutions to a particular problem will have been examined before a particular solution is chosen. The criteria on which the final choice is based will include:

+ **Usability.** The interface must be easy to use, suitable for the task and appropriate to the skill level of the user. Windows, icons and menus should be included for novice users while shortcuts should be available for experienced users. The interface should be consistent across application packages so that the user can transfer learning skills from one package to another. Adequate and context sensitive help should be included. Consideration will be given to the need for additional training for staff to use the system. For the system to be useable the processing speed of the system must be acceptable even when large volumes of data is being stored.

+ **Performance**. For the system to perform well it must meet the system specification. It should not suffer from bugs, or slow access times when retrieving data from a database. Screens should not take minutes to change after a command is typed. Hardware must be reliable and not crash easily.

+ **Suitability**. Will the system provide a solution to the problem and meet its specification? Will it integrate with existing software? Can current manual methods be adapted for the new system?

+ **Maintainability**. Software that is difficult to modify leads to excessive costs in software maintenance. For a system to be maintainable it must be easy to add new functionality or make modifications and corrections when required.

15.12 Custom Built versus Off-the-Shelf Packages

The term **off-the-shelf** refers to commercially available software that has been developed for the mass market. It usually addresses a general need and has a fixed set of features, although users may have limited options for customising it. It is sold as a package, often on a CD containing the software and manuals. Common applications such as word processing, spreadsheets and accounting programs fall into this category. Off-the-shelf solutions are suitable for home PC users and small firms who do not have the resources to commission or develop their own software. For common needs, all firms will benefit because the problem is one that has been given much thought over several years.

The advantages of off-the-shelf software are:

+ Software is immediately available for use and can be implemented quickly.

+ The software tends to be relatively cheap as the cost of development can be spread over a large number of customers.

+ The software will be of a reasonable quality with few problems, as most bugs are addressed by the time it is bought,

+ The software can be highly complex and therefore may have useful features that the customer did not realise they could use.

+ As it is a commercial package, training and technical support may already be available from a wide variety of sources. Other users may be able to assist with training. As one small voice amongst many others a single customer's maintenance requests may not carry much weight.

The disadvantages of off-the-shelf software are:

+ The software may not meet the users' exact requirements: there may be operations that users require but the software does not support.

+ The customer will pay for functionality they may never use.

+ The customer does not 'own' the software, merely the right to use it. This may involve annual licence fees, calculated on a per-PC basis. Reduced fees may be available if large quantities are licensed.

+ The customer may have to alter the way they work in order to fit in with the way the software has been designed.

Bespoke software solutions are designed to address needs and problems unique to one customer. This can be developed in-house, ie within the company by an IT department, or it can be out-sourced, which involves the hiring of an outside organisation to provide and implement a software solution. A firm whose scenario is unusual or whose needs often change may choose this route as they recognise that an off-the-shelf solution may not evolve with their requirements. Significant advantages are that the system will do precisely what is required and that maintenance can be addressed much more quickly than with off-the-shelf systems.

The decision over developing a system internally or externally depends on a number of factors:

+ Does the company have the required expertise available internally?
+ If the expertise is available internally, can the company afford to divert these people from other work for a long period?
+ Does the company want to risk outsiders having access to commercially sensitive data?

An organisation that uses a third party to develop software will have the option of bringing maintenance in-house, or paying annual maintenance fees to developers. It is possible that the customer may not wish to pay for an extended support contract, so they will ask developers to train their own staff. In many cases, the customer wants to hire the expertise and manpower needed to develop the system but does not need this manpower on an ongoing basis.

The advantages of bespoke software are:

+ It meets the customer's precise needs as a result of customer involvement and so unnecessary features are removed.
+ The system should match the previous expertise of users. Aspects of the new system may seem familiar therefore reducing change and the need for training.
+ Support is more comprehensive than with an off-the-shelf package. In many cases it is possible to talk directly to the developers. Support and training will have been included as part of the original contract and specification.
+ It is more flexible than packaged software and can be modified and changed over time as requirements and business practices change.
+ It can be designed to interface with the customer's existing hardware and software systems.
+ Depending on the nature of the system, some of the development cost may be recovered through licensing the system to other customers.
+ There are normally no licensing fees with custom solutions. Once the customer has paid for the product, they can make as many copies as are needed.

The disadvantages of bespoke software are:

+ The purchase cost of the software will be high as the customer must pay all development costs. In large systems, this may be millions of pounds.
+ The system is not tried and tested. As a result, if problems manifest, the users

must wait for developers to address them. Users of off-the-shelf solutions can expect problems to have been discovered by a wide user base and to have been addressed.

+ Software is not available immediately and development may take months or even years. If development takes too long then the requirements may be obsolete by the time development is complete.

15.13 Diagrams for Representing a Problem

When a problem is broken down it is often represented as one or more diagrams. Two types of diagram you should know are **Data Flow Diagrams (DFDs)**, which represent a process of **stepwise refinement** (breaking a problem into progressively smaller and more manageable parts) and **Entity-Relationship Diagrams (ERDs)**, that show the relationship between the tables within a database.

Data Flow Diagrams

DFDs help system analysts and aid design by showing the flow of data through a system by defining data sources, data inputs, data processing, data stores and data outputs. DFDs will include a top level diagram showing the complete system (Level 0) which is subsequently split up into lower, more detailed level diagrams (Level 1, Level 2...) which represent different processes or aspects of the system. DFDs provide a number of advantages over a textual narrative:

1. The systems analyst is free to describe the system at a conceptual level, without committing to technical specifications for any new system. For example, DFDs do not specify exactly how or on what media data is stored.

2. The process of drawing up DFDs develops a deeper understanding of how the system will operate and how its different parts will interrelate. They will show in great detail how the data input can be processed to produce an output.

3. Both developers and the client often find diagrams easier to understand than a long narrative.

All DFDs are made up of just four key symbols, a notation which allows the system to be represented in enough detail to convey its meaning, but without adding unnecessary information about hardware etc. The four symbols are given below. If a series of DFDs are properly constructed, they will provide solid documentation of a system.

Symbol	Example

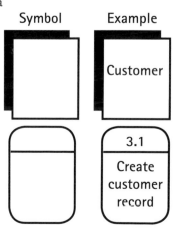

External Entity – any data source or data destination. An external entity is not part of the system being described, but interacts with it.

Process – signifies that some transformation of data takes place. The number in the space at the top is used in multi-level DFDs (see below).

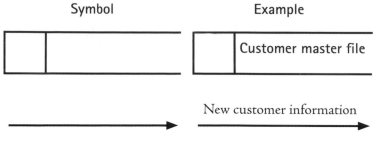

Symbol	Example
	Customer master file

New customer information

Data Store – shows that data is stored in some way. However the physical media used (eg hard disk or magnetic tape) is not specified.

Data Flow – this shows the flow of data between an entity and/or a process and/or a data store. A Data Flow arrow should be labelled with a description of the data.

Developing DFDs

DFDs are developed in stages, with the analyst adding more detail in each diagram than in the one before. The first diagram produced is called the **context diagram** (or 'top level diagram'). It has four main features: (a) the whole system is shown as a single process; (b) no data stores are shown; (c) inputs to the overall system are shown, together with data sources (as external entities); and (d) outputs from the overall system are shown, together with their destinations (as external entities) Figure 15.6 shows an example of a context diagram, using generic names for the entities and the processes involved. A real world example is discussed later.

Figure 15.6: A generic DFD context diagram.

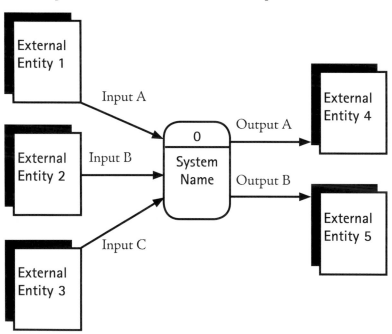

Next, a **Level 0** diagram is developed (figure 15.7). This focuses on the single process that was drawn in the context diagram by 'zooming in' on its contents and illustrating what it does in more detail. Because we have simply expanded the single process, the same external entities remain. Each new process is given a number, the importance of which will become clear later, when we 'zoom in' on these processes.

The next step in developing the DFD is to show more details for any process above that requires further explanation. The numbers previously assigned to processes are used to tie them to their corresponding, more detailed, diagrams. These are called Level 1 diagrams, with the '1' referring to how far into the system we have 'zoomed'. This process of refinement is repeated until all details of the system are properly described.

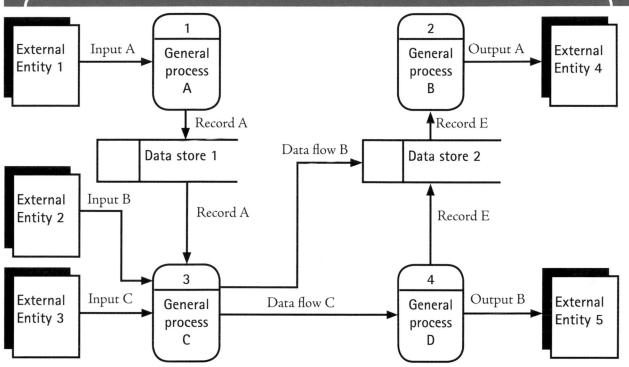

For example, *General process C* from figure 15.7 can be shown as in figure 15.8. Note that the inputs from the parent and the outputs from the parent match those found in the Level 1 diagram shown here. The dotted line is used in this example to show the boundaries of the original Level 0 process. Although this is not a necessary requirement of a DFD it can be useful to aid readability.

Figure 15.7: A generic DFD Level 0 diagram.

Figure 15.8: A generic DFD Level 1 diagram.

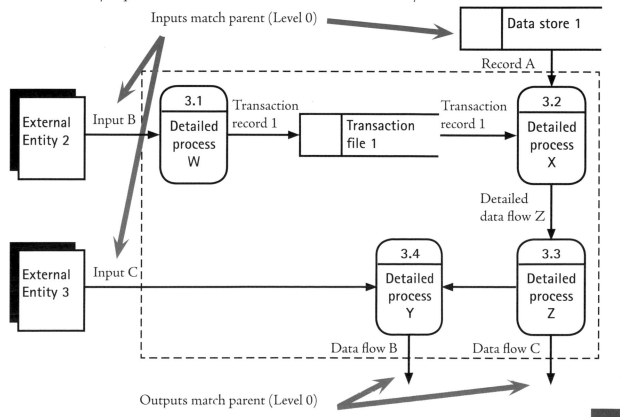

An example of an actual system

Consider a simple parish administration system, used to produce the following information:

- For the minister / parish priest:
  - A summary of households who are due a pastoral visit;
  - A list of households who are due a visit outside their regular time, such as those with a recent bereavement or birth;
- For the treasurer:
  - A weekly summary of parish offerings;
  - An annual summary of offerings for the purpose of gift aid (a scheme where charities can reclaim income tax from the government).

To produce a DFD for this system we first produce a context diagram. At this stage we must think about the inputs to the system. These are the parishioners' name and address details, details of visitations and details of gifts to the church. A context-level diagram of this is shown in figure 15.9.

Figure 15.9: A context diagram for the parish administration system.

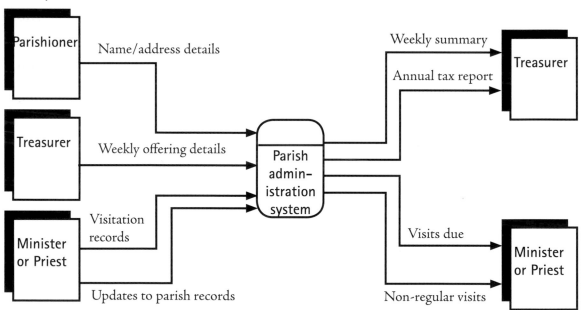

This system is then refined (shown in more detail) as a Level 0 diagram as shown in figure 15.10 (right, top). Note that the external entities and the data flows to/from them remain the same, but more detail is given to the original process.

The systems analyst then repeats this process of refinement. For example, Process 5 ('list parishioners due a visit') is developed in the Level 1 diagram in figure 15.11 (right, bottom) as a series of sub-processes. If necessary, the sub-processes themselves can be further developed. By carefully following this procedure, a complete set of data flow diagrams can be produced to accurately model a system.

Task

Discuss the relative strengths and weaknesses of data flow diagrams. What are they useful for? What are they not useful for?

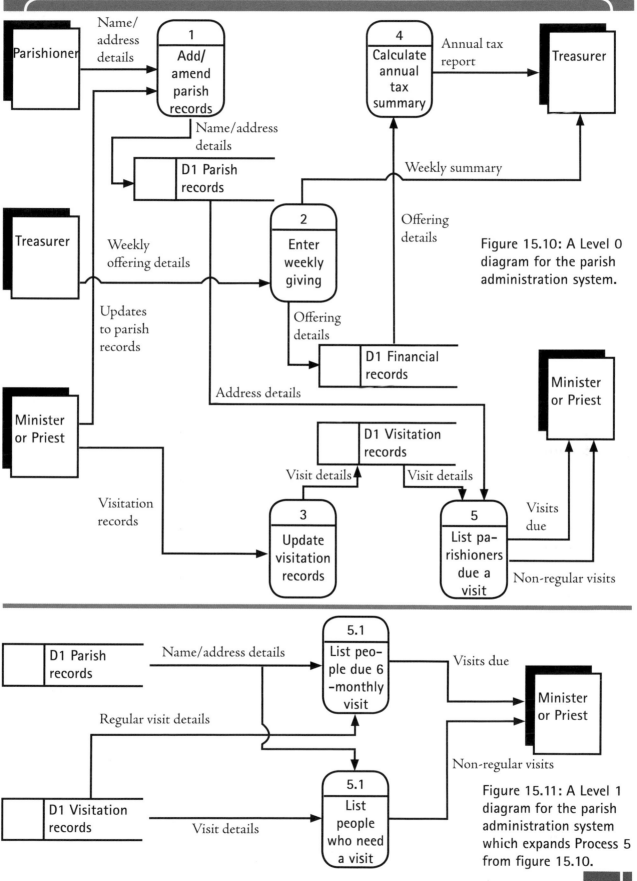

Figure 15.10: A Level 0 diagram for the parish administration system.

Figure 15.11: A Level 1 diagram for the parish administration system which expands Process 5 from figure 15.10.

Entity–Relationship Diagrams

A database represents some part of the real world by modelling the world as a number of **entities** (real-world 'things' about which certain **attributes**, or facts, are known). From a design perspective, **tables** store information about several entities that have common attributes. For example, a system in a school may use a single table to hold teachers' details because they share common attributes (forename, surname, address and so on). A different table holds details of courses, because courses have different attributes to people.

Entities can be **related** to each other in a number of ways, and these are explained through the examples below. Suppose in a particular school, the following facts hold true.

1. Each teacher has a single room, in which all their classes are taught.

2. A single teacher teaches each course.

3. If two teachers share an A Level class, it is considered as two separate courses (eg module 1 and module 2).

In this example, the entities are related in three different ways:

+ **One-to-one (1:1) relationship.** Each teacher teaches in one classroom. Each classroom has one teacher. Therefore, there is one teacher for one room.

+ **One-to-many (1:M) relationship.** A teacher can teach many courses, but only one teacher will teach each course. Therefore, there may be one teacher for many courses.

+ **Many-to-many (M:N) relationship.** A teacher can teach many students. Many teachers can teach each student. Therefore, there are many teachers to many students. (Note that it is written M:N, not M:M).

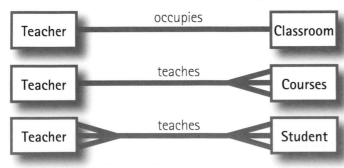

Figure 15.12: Different types of relationship expressed as an entity–relationship (ER) diagram.

These are represented through **Entity-Relationship diagrams (ERDs)** as shown in figure 15.12. Notice how the 'one' side of a relationship is connected with a single line, while the 'many' side uses a forked line. The purpose of an ERD is to identify what data is to be stored and processed by the system to ensure that data needs to have been thoroughly investigated, to identify what files will be linked or related in the system and to identify how data should be organised to ensure that it is held in a structured way which will allow for efficient retrieval and future extensions.

The advantages of ERDs are:

+ An ERD can be used to directly implement a database system;

+ Like DFDs, both the developers and the client will find diagrams easier to understand than a long narrative;

+ ERDs provide a method for ensuring that the database is structured in an efficient manner.

Entity-Relationship Diagrams are sometimes called **ER diagrams**.

15.14 Prototyping

One common problem encountered by software developers is that customers may not know all their requirements at the beginning of a project. They might know high level requirements, but cannot specify them in the detail required to make a successful system. They are often unaware of the technical capabilities of a hardware/software system and needlessly sacrifice functionality as a result. The **prototype model** provides an alternative to the waterfall model of the systems lifecycle that still produces a quality system without having to identify all requirements in advance (these themes are returned to in Chapter 23).

A **prototype** is a working model of a new system used to identify/refine the user requirements to ensure that the system meets their needs. The prototype gives the user a useful insight into what is being developed. The user repeatedly evaluates the prototype providing feedback to the systems analyst so that it can be improved and a system which meets requirements can be produced.

Evolutionary prototyping is the building of a working model of a new system which is repeatedly refined in light of the user's feedback until an acceptable system (which meets user's requirements) has been developed. The objective of evolutionary prototyping is to deliver a fully working system to the customer.

Throwaway prototyping is the building of a working model which is repeatedly refined until the customer is satisfied that requirements have been met. The prototype is then discarded, ie it does not become the final system. Only knowledge gained about user requirements and how the system should work is used as the basis for completing the design and developing it from scratch. The purpose of throwaway prototyping is to confirm or clarify system requirements.

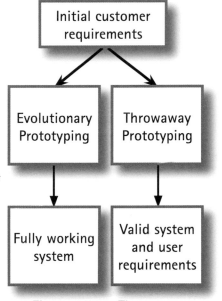

Figure 15.13: The intended outcomes of the two main uses of the prototype model.

The advantages of prototyping are:

+ The model accommodates requirement uncertainty very well.
+ The customer will see a partially working version of the system early on.
+ A system can be developed which meets the exact needs of the user because of the user's direct involvement.
+ Prototyping may reduce development time as inconsistent user requirements will be detected early and resolved. This may lead to reduced costs because changes cost more to implement the later they are detected in development.

The disadvantages of prototyping are:

+ If the analyst or customer is impatient, design may take place when all the requirements are not clearly known.
+ Prototyping often creates a situation whereby the customer mistakenly believes that the system is finished (via a good, late-stage prototype) when in fact only the interface has been developed and the coding has not yet started.
+ Time scale and budgeting may be difficult to manage and control, especially if the user continually changes their requirements.
+ Less comprehensive documentation is produced and this makes maintenance more difficult.

15.15 Roles of ICT Professionals

Any one ICT professional may fulfil a number of roles at one time or another during the course of their career: a software developer, a programmer, a database administrator, a PC salesman etc. In this section, some of the main types of IT professional are described, but a glance at the Jobs section in a newspaper will show this list could be greatly expanded.

A **project manager** is responsible for overseeing a project and will coordinate the work of several programmers and designers. At the outset of a project, they may divide a large piece of work between many **team leaders**, who in turn will divide that work between many **programmers**. It is the project manager's responsibility to ensure that the entire project has been accounted for and a reasonable development and testing schedule has been drawn up, although they may also be leader of a small team of programmers and may have their own programming responsibilities. This role is comparable to that of a building site foreman: in a large site, they have extensive supervisory roles but do little hands-on work.

Before a project is assigned to a project manager, there will be contributions from other people such as a **systems analyst** (who investigates the original problem) or a **systems architect** (responsible for an overall design). These people and their teams will not have written a detailed specification for each module, but will have refined the project into small parts so that individual teams or programmers may refine it further. Clear paperwork is needed to reduce the need for clarification. Each document is **peer reviewed** thoroughly to ensure that there are no unclear areas.

Once a project has been broken into large sections, team leaders further subdivide a project into modules. Each programmer is assigned a number of modules to design, develop and test. In conjunction with the team leader and other programmers, modules undergo integration testing when they are ready to be integrated. A project manager has a high-level design relating to overall functionality. As a project is broken into modules, team leaders draw up a design for their aspect. This is further refined by programmers responsible for each module. Each programmer's design undergoes a lengthy peer review process and the team leader ensures all the designs can interoperate. The project manager then reviews work to ensure the work of all teams can interface together. If any changes are required, the programmer responsible will often be required to refer them to the team leader (or project manager) to ensure there are no undesirable knock-on changes.

A small project may have one or two teams, while large-scale commercial applications, such as Microsoft *Office*, are developed by dozens of teams. In such large projects, the project manager's role in coordinating work is vital. In very large projects, the role may be handled by several people, with one overall chairperson.

It is estimated that a **programmer** spends between 70 and 80% of their time writing documentation, either for the benefit of others in their team or those who will be involved in later maintenance. Such people are often referred to as **software engineers**, a term which more accurately reflects the true nature of their job. Once work has been allocated by a team leader, programmers firstly produce a detailed design for the modules they will write before going on to develop and test it. They will thoroughly document all decisions to aid those who are involved in subsequent maintenance and testing. Each programmer will draw up their design in conjunction with other members of the team whose work will interface together. They review each other's work before presenting it to the team leader.

Once a team's work is completed, they may carry out full integration testing themselves or may pass their work onto specialist test engineers. These are experienced people with a background in programming, whose daily job is to rigorously ensure a system can handle the necessary amount of expected input and output. They will also attempt to break the system with unexpected data. After testing, results are presented to the team who developed the system for them to investigate and correct any problems. In some cases, this is to advise the users to avoid certain scenarios that are known to cause problems, eg uploading a large amount of data or simultaneously running a large number of queries. These 'known issues' are not forgotten, but are usually further investigated and addressed during maintenance. Once a system is complete, technical writers develop user manuals that should list all aspects of the user requirements. While many technical writers have worked as programmers, their writing is aimed at non-programmers, including technicians and end users. Many programmers study Computing at university and graduate as 'general purpose' programmers. However as their career develops, they may specialise in certain fields, eg firmware, Visual Basic or SQL.

Technicians, in a variety of guises, are responsible for the installation of systems and for user support. A technician's job depends on programmers doing their job of development according to the design and of technical writers writing manuals fully. If programmers deviate from the design, the end product may not work as indicated in the manual, which creates difficulties for technicians. If manuals are incomplete, problems may arise as technicians need to follow a lengthy diagnostic process instead of a documented procedure.

In many schools there is more than one type of technician, such as a network manager (to install and maintain hardware and software, to provide technical support, and liaise with external ICT suppliers) or a C2K engineer (when problems arise within the C2K managed system, they are often off limits to a school's ICT staff and the school's technicians must contact C2K, who can remotely access the schools systems or send an engineer).

If bugs or other inadequacies are found in a system, technicians must document these as clearly as possible: a description of the error message, what other software or hardware was being used at the time etc. These reports feed back to suppliers and form the basis of software maintenance.

Finally, **end users** are the people who use computer systems on a daily basis. The majority are not extensively trained in any aspect of ICT, but it is vital that they are fully aware of how to use these systems. In many organisations, this takes the form of the **European Computer Driving License** (ECDL), a comprehensive course that can only be completed by demonstrating competence in a wide range of applications (**Advanced ECDL** offers further training). In other organisations, especially those using niche market or bespoke software, training courses may be specific to the software they are using. If users are properly trained, they will at least have basic fault-finding skills and will be able to address many problems themselves without troubling support staff with trivial matters.

The above list is far from complete. Examples of the numerous other ICT roles that exist include support desk operatives, database administrators, IT trainers, web developers and network managers/engineers.

Questions

1. State and briefly describe the main stages of problem solving. (21)
2. Describe four methods used in fact finding. (8)
3. Evaluate each method of fact finding. (8)
4. Discuss three areas of a feasibility study. (6)
5. Outline the main components of a design, briefly describing their functions. (8)
6. Explain the difference between application testing and acceptance testing. (4)
7. Describe three types of test data. (6)
8. State three types of changeover methods. Describe each one, with any associated advantages and disadvantages. (12)
9. Identify three of the contents in (a) user documentation (b) technical documentation. (6)
10. Give two reasons as to why maintenance is necessary. (4)
11. Explain what is meant by suitable, effective and usable. (6)
12. Describe three reasons for using a custom built package as a solution to a data processing problem. (6)
13. Describe three reasons for using an off-the shelf package as a solution to a data processing problem. (6)
14. Describe the purpose of DFDs, along with the symbols used. (6)
15. Describe the purpose of an ER diagram. (2)
16. Describe two types of prototyping. (6)
17. Describe two benefits of prototyping. (4)
18. Describe the role of the following (a) project manager (b) programmer (c) technician and (d) end user. (12)
19. Give examples of other professional roles found within IT. (3)

A2 Module 1: *Information Systems*

A2 Module 1

Module 1 of the course introduced the main areas in which ICT has affected society. As was seen, ICT has affected almost every aspect of human life and new uses for it continue to be developed.

In Module 3, a number of these topics are explored in more depth (particularly networks and databases). Also explored are the construction of effective ICT systems: from the perspective of the systems lifecycle, the development of an effective user interface and training users to use the system. This module concludes by returning to the legal and ethical issues surrounding ICT.

Within this section, the main topics are:

+ Databases, their design, and their myriad uses in the modern world;
+ Management Information Systems, the specialised databases and analysis tools used in modern business to make informed decisions;
+ Data Security: avoiding and recovering from threats to data;
+ Computer Networks, used to share data in many ways that are now taken for granted;
+ Software Development: the processes followed to design and develop software that, in engineering terms, is as complex as the largest feats of civil engineering;
+ The User Interface: the ways in which human and computers interact and how poor interfaces can render systems useless;
+ User Support and Training: equipping users to be as effective as possible in using ICT solutions;
+ Legal and Professional Issues: the legal and ethical issues surrounding ICT;
+ Implications of Information Systems: how ICT has affected, and continues to affect, every aspect of society.

A2 MODULE 1 SPECIFICATION MAP
How this book relates to the CCEA specification

Content....	...is covered in Real World ICT 2nd Edition by:
3.1 Database systems Relational databases Database Management Systems (DBMS)	Chapter 16: Relational Databases
Management Information Systems (MIS)	Chapter 17: Management Information Systems and Chapter 18: Decision Support Systems and Expert Systems
Data security	Chapter 19: Data Security
3.2 Networked systems Types of network	Chapter 20: Types of Network
Communication Error detection	Chapter 21: Network Communication
Security issues	Chapter 22: Network Security
3.3 Software development The software development process	Chapter 23: Approaches to Software Development and Chapter 24: The Software Development Process
Software Quality	Chapter 25: Software Quality
3.4 The User Interface	Chapter 26: The User Interface
3.5 User support and training	Chapter 27: User Support and Training
3.6 Legal and professional issues Legislaton	Chapter 28: Legislation
Professional issues	Chapter 29: Professional Issues
3.7 Implications of ICT	Chapter 30: Implications of ICT and Chapter 31: Managing Change

CHAPTER 16
Relational Databases

16.1 Introduction

Definition	A database is an organised, structured collection of related data, designed to allow access by a number of different applications. It holds information about **entities** in a series of related **tables**.

A database is used to store information about a group of related entities, for example:

+ Information about students in a college;

+ Information about cars in a showroom;

+ Information about compact discs in a record collection.

However, it is not enough for a database to contain data without also giving it a context. For example, if it contained the three entries 'Lower Sixth', 'Alloy Wheels' and 'Simply Red', this might refer to a student in a particular class who has a car of a particular colour with alloy wheels. Yet, it could equally refer to a student who has placed an order for new wheels and who owns a CD by Simply Red. For data to be meaningful it must be given a context. What gives it a context and makes it useful is the way in which data is **organised** and **related**.

16.2 The Purpose of a Database

In order to understand what a database offers it is useful to look at how they have evolved over time. Consider, for example, the workings of a school filing system before computers were in common use.

When a new student joined a school their details were written on a paper form which was then duplicated and given to the appropriate people: the principal's secretary, general office, form teacher etc. Under this scheme, the period at the end of August was chaotic as dozens or even hundreds of paper records were created, each of which was copied multiple times and passed to many people.

A paper-based filing system is incredibly inefficient. Consider these examples of how it can fail:

+ A parent phones to tell the school they have moved house and their daughter will go elsewhere. The secretary notes this on her form but forgets to pass the information on to those who hold copies. A few days later, a form teacher tries to get in touch with the parent to ask why the child is absent because his list clearly states that she is enrolled in 8B. Her father is confused when told his daughter is absent as he drove her to school that morning.

♦ A student is moved from 10C to 10B by a form teacher. However, the information is lost among all the pieces of paper in the office and not passed on to other staff members. Panic occurs when the student's mother phones the school to say she will collect her son at lunchtime, yet the child is not in class and was marked absent on the 10C roll that morning.

Early computerised systems relied on each department having their own independent system, but this did not solve the problem as data could not be easily shared between systems. This led to a number of problems. Data was often printed out and re-entered and was therefore prone to typographical errors. Utility programs were developed to convert data between formats, but this was not always 100% reliable and data integrity was still affected.

For example, a **source** file may have held addresses as 20 characters while the **destination** may have used only 15 characters. Hence the address "45 Clonagaskin Drive" is truncated to "45 Clonagaskin". You can see how this would lead to confusion when the addresses "45 Clonagaskin Street" and "45 Clonagaskin Terrace" both appear the same.

As computerised record keeping improved, designers developed better ways of storing data. The two main types are **flat files** and **databases**.

Data integrity refers to the completeness and accuracy of data. Data duplication and redundancy can also compromise data integrity since several contradictory versions of data exist at once.

Definition

16.3 Flat Files

A flat file is a single **table** often stored as a plain ASCII text file. When viewed on screen it looks similar to a spreadsheet. Compared to a **relational database**, flat files are not very versatile, but simple operations such as sorting and filtering can be performed. The first table of figure 16.1 shows a flat file being used to store details of teachers in a school. The second table shows this flat file sorted by surname, while the third table shows it filtered to show only English teachers.

Teacher_id	Forename	Surname	Subject	Room
1	John	Smith	English	12
2	Peter	Jones	French	13
3	Sarah	Donovan	RE	23
3	Sarah	Donovan	English	23
4	Ronan	O'Neill	Science	4

Figure 16.1: A flat file table of data with the same data sorted (overleaf top) and filtered (overleaf bottom).

Figure 16.1 continued.

Sorted

Teacher_id	Forename	Surname	Subject	Room
3	Sarah	Donovan	RE	23
3	Sarah	Donovan	English	23
2	Peter	Jones	French	13
4	Ronan	O'Neill	Science	4
1	John	Smith	English	12

Filtered

Teacher_id	Forename	Surname	Subject	Room
3	Sarah	Donovan	English	23
1	John	Smith	English	12

It can be seen in figure 16.1 that Sarah Donovan's details are duplicated because she teaches both English and RE. This **data redundancy** is a feature of flat files and can lead to problems when data is updated. Suppose she marries and changes her name to Sarah Kelly. If the person updating the file does not realise she has two entries, **inconsistencies** (contradictions) may arise within the file, as shown in figure 16.2, where now it seems that two teachers share a room. Data redundancy and inconsistency is eliminated through normalisation (section 16.7).

Figure 16.2: Data redundancy leading to an inconsistency in a flat file.

Teacher_id	Forename	Surname	Subject	Room
3	Sarah	Kelly	RE	23
3	Sarah	Donovan	English	23

16.4 Databases

Like a flat file, a database consists of many rows or **records**. Each row in a table relates to a single **entity**, or item in the table. Each column relates to a specific **field**. A field holds data of a certain **type** (eg text or number), specified when the database is created. If the table shown in figure 6.1 were in a database, each of the column headings would be a field, and each row below that would be a record.

Related Tables and Key Fields

Unlike a flat file, the inconsistencies highlighted above can be avoided in a database through the use of **related tables** and **primary key** fields. A **primary key** is a field, or combination of fields, that uniquely identify any row of a table. Examples include *person number* in an employee database and the combination of *date*, *time* and *doctor* that uniquely identifies a particular appointment in a surgery. It is not necessary to include *patient* in the latter example, since a doctor could be only seeing one patient at a particular date and time. A primary key should consist of as few fields as is necessary to identify a row uniquely. A primary key that includes more than one field is called a **composite key**. A **secondary key** refers to one or more fields that identify a small group of records, but does not necessarily identify them uniquely. For example *form class* can be used as a secondary key in a school database or *model* in a car database.

To continue the example of the list of teachers in the school, we can eliminate the redundancy by identifying any **repeating groups**. In this case, a repeating group is any field that may create multiple records for a single entity (teacher). Hence, *subject* forms a repeating group in this case.

We store all the information about teachers in one table, except for the repeating group which is removed to a table of its own, along with a duplicate of the primary key field from the original table. It is necessary to store the primary key of the teachers' table in each table so that the database can relate the two tables to each other. The two resultant tables are shown in figure 6.3.

Table_teachers

Teacher_id*	Forename	Surname	Room
1	John	Smith	12
2	Peter	Jones	13
3	Sarah	Donovan	23
4	Ronan	O'Neill	4

Table_teachers_subject

Teacher_id*	Subject*
1	English
2	French
3	English
3	RE
4	Science

Figure 16.3: The related tables designed to eliminate redundancy. An * indicates a field that forms part of the key for that table.

The redundancy is now gone, because changing a teacher's name results in just one change to the *table_teachers*, and changing a teacher's subject results in just one change (at a time) to the *table_teachers_subject*. There is now no possibility of the same teacher appearing twice with two surnames.

Normalisation is a process of simplifying complex tables by dividing them into separate, related, tables. This leads to an efficient database design that avoids duplication and redundancy. A flat file table is said to be **un-normalised**, hence it contains redundancies, as described above, which in turn lead to inconsistencies. The steps involved in normalising data are described in section 16.7.

Task

Identify suitable *primary* and *secondary* key fields to store the data in the following scenarios.

1. A mail-order firm wishing to store customer details.
2. A library wishing to store details of the books on its shelves.
3. A school former pupils association that stores details of students to organise reunions every ten years after they leave.
4. A home-heating oil delivery firm that delivers to several people in each street of a large town.

16.5 Querying a Database

To extract data from a database involves the use of a **query**. The two most common forms of query are **Query By Example** and **Structured Query Language**.

Query By Example (QBE) is a query-forming method that relies on the database program displaying a blank record into which the user then types the criteria they are seeking. For example, figure 16.4 shows a QBE form in *Microsoft Access* being used to select all teachers called "Smith". In this case, the person chooses which fields they want in the results and types "Smith" under *surname*.

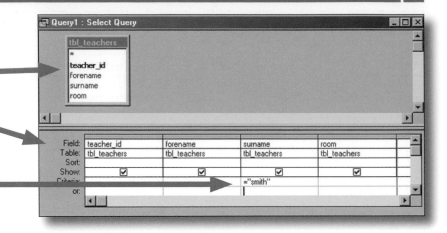

The tables to be queried are shown at the top.

Fields are selected.

Criteria to select fields are entered. In this case ="smith" is used to find records based on the *surname* field.

Figure 16.4: A Query By Example shown in Microsoft Access.

Structured Query Language (SQL) is a method of forming queries that relies upon the user typing in a textual command, generally in the form:

Select <fields> From <tables> Where <some condition is met>.

For example the QBE query above could be performed in SQL by typing the command:

SELECT teacher_id, forename, surname, room
FROM tbl_teachers
WHERE (tbl_teachers.surname="smith");

Figure 16.5: Results of the query shown in figure 16.4.

In either case, the result is the same, as shown in figure 16.5.

Many novice database users prefer QBE over SQL because of QBE's visual layout. Many experienced users may choose QBE for the same reason, although once a person is used to SQL they may find it quicker and more precise to use. In most, but not all, instances a query can be expressed in both SQL and QBE and many database applications allow users to build queries by either SQL or QBE.

Once a query has been written and executed the results can be presented as a **report**. A report is an organised and formatted presentation of data in a form suitable for printing. It may involve sorting and summarising the data, applying font and style information, adding headers and footers and other formatting.

For example, a query to determine loans within a DVD club may produce the data shown in figure 16.6. However, this could then be used to generate either of the two reports shown in figure 16.7.

Member_ID	Forename	Surname	DVD_title	Date Borrowed
1245	Peter	Petersen	Ocean's Twelve	09/09/04
1587	Andrew	Andrews	The Bourne Supremacy	09/09/04
4817	William	Williamson	The Stepford Wives	10/09/04
1245	Peter	Petersen	The Bourne Supremacy	11/09/04
7889	John	Johnston	The Stepford Wives	11/09/04
7415	Richard	Richardson	Ocean's Twelve	11/09/04
4817	William	Williamson	The Bourne Supremacy	12/09/04

Figure 16.6: Raw query results for loans from a DVD club.

Figure 16.7: Two reports each based on the results shown in figure 16.6.

DVD Loans (by date)

09/09/04
1245 Peter Petersen Ocean's Twelve
1587 Andrew Andrews The Bourne Supremacy

10/09/04
4817 William Williamson The Stepford Wives

11/09/04
7415 Richard Richardson Ocean's Twelve
1245 Peter Petersen The Bourne Supremacy
7889 John Johnston The Stepford Wives

12/09/04
4817 William Williamson The Bourne Supremacy

DVD Loans (by title)

Ocean's Twelve
1245 Peter Petersen 09/09/04
7415 Richard Richardson 11/09/04

The Bourne Supremacy
1587 Andrew Andrews 09/09/04
1245 Peter Petersen 11/09/04
4817 William Williamson 12/09/04

The Stepford Wives
4817 William Williamson 10/09/04
7889 John Johnston 11/09/04

One of the advantages of queries and reports is that they can be tailored for different target audiences. For example, if the managing director of a chain of video stores wants to know how the *Lord of the Rings* trilogy is performing in rentals, he or she does not need a listing for every single copy of the movie hired as shown in figure 16.8 (left). Rather, a query can be created to summarise the data, and then display it in a report as shown in figure 16.8 (right).

Figure 16.8: Ineffective presentation of data (left), compared to an effective summary of the same data (right).

Rental Analysis: Lord of the Rings
Pg 1/24

12/04/03, 1000: LOTR: Fellowship OTR (Armagh)
12/04/03, 1001: LOTR: Return of the King (Lurgan)
12/04/03, 1005: LOTR: The Two Towers (Enniskillen)
12/04/03, 1009: LOTR: Fellowship OTR (Coleraine)
12/04/03, 1012: LOTR: Fellowship OTR (Armagh)
12/04/03, 1016: LOTR: The Two Towers (Moira)
12/04/03, 1016: LOTR: Return of the King (Moira)
12/04/03, 1016: LOTR: Fellowship OTR (Moira)
12/04/03, 1032: LOTR: Fellowship OTR (Larne)
12/04/03, 1033: LOTR: The Two Towers (Antrim)

Rental Analysis: Lord of the Rings

Week beginning 11th April

- Fellowship OTR: 2932
- Return of the King: 3123
- The Two Towers: 3211

People hiring all three at one time: 236

People hiring all three in past 2 weeks: 1025

Task

A DVD club system is discussed above. Design tables for this system, based on the following pieces of information:

1. Details of members and DVDs must be stored.
2. Each title may exist on several DVDs.
3. Each DVD has a unique reference number.
4. There is no limit to how many DVDs a customer may borrow.
5. The dates a customer borrows and returns each DVD must be stored.
6. Details of what a customer borrows are kept for an indefinite period.

The more detailed example of a school database system given on the Real World ICT section of the Colourpoint web site (see preface) should be referred to by those students not already familiar with the process. While the example is not exhaustive, it does provide a useful introduction to skills that can be used in coursework.

16.6 Parts of a Database

A database represents some part of the real world by modelling the world as a number of things (**entities**) about which certain facts (**attributes**) can be known. Databases are designed using **entity-relationship (ER) diagrams**, where tables store details of entities that share attributes, while one-to-one, one-to-many or many-to-many relationships describe how they inter-relate. ER diagrams are described in more detail in section 15.13, and it is important that the student re-reads that section before proceeding to the task below.

Task

1. Describe and draw an ER diagram for the following situations.

a) Plane	and	Holiday Maker
b) Person	and	Car
c) Actor	and	Film
d) Person	and	Passport
e) Vet	and	Appointment
f) Job	and	Candidate

2. Draw a fully labelled ER diagram for this situation:

   A tile company stock various types of tiles each of which originate from a particular supplier. The company orders from a range of suppliers each specialising in a unique product. When a customer comes into the showroom to make an order a bill is produced listing the various items to be ordered. The tile company prides itself on its good customer service with customers making more than one purchase in the showroom.

3. A veterinary surgery's database includes the following three entities

Owner Entity	OwnerID	Name	Address	Postcode	PhoneNo	
Pet Entity	PetID	Name	AnimalType	Breed	Gender	OwnerID
Appointment Entity	PetID	Date	Time	Treatment Performed		

i. Identify suitable examples of primary, composite and foreign keys
ii. Draw a fully labelled entity relationship (ER) diagram for this database.

16.7 Normalisation

Non-normalised databases suffer from a number of problems that make them very difficult to use and unreliable as sources of data. Normalisation removes the problems of **data redundancy** and **data inconsistency**, leading to a system that is more flexible and easier to maintain.

Normalisation follows a series of set steps to remove data redundancy and inconsistency. This process was developed by Edgar F Codd in the 1960s and 70s and has become a fundamental concept in modern database design. The rules of database normalisation may appear complex at first. However, with a little practice they can be understood and applied.

The steps involve analysing the relationships between known attributes (facts) of different entities within the database. A key term is **functional dependency**, ie, the idea that knowing one fact about an entity can allow others facts to be worked out.

For example:

+ If a civil servant has access to a person's National Insurance Number, this is enough to find their name, address and date of birth. Hence name, address and date of birth are functionally dependent on the National Insurance Number. However, a person's date of birth is not enough to determine their name, so there is no functional dependence in that case.

+ If a book's ISBN is known, this is enough to find the book's title and author. Hence title and author are functionally dependent on the ISBN.

Functional dependence

For the relation between any two entities,

attribute x is functionally dependent on attribute y,

if for every record in a table,

   knowing x leads to y being determined.

Definition

We consider three **normal forms** known, unsurprisingly, as **first normal form (1NF)**, **second normal form (2NF)** and **third normal form (3NF)**. They will be explained below through the example of a video club lending system. The purpose of the system is to record:

+ details of customers;
+ details of material hired by customers, including title, media, due date, price;
+ details of suppliers of each video.

Diligent students may encounter BCNF, 4NF and 5NF if they search the Internet for database normalisation. These additional forms are usually not considered at A Level. In practice, the first three normal forms are considered sufficient to produce a functional database design.

By the way...

Non-Normalised Data

At the start of the normalisation process, data is considered to be in a single **non-normalised** table. Figure 16.9 shows a non-normalised table, including a **repeating group** (a set of attributes that could repeat many times).

Repeating group

custno	custfname	custsname	...	vidstockid	vidcatno	vidname	vidrating	...	vidstockid	vidcatno	vidname	...
1	John	Woods	...	211	CC 7524	The Shawshank Redemption	15	...	858	053 9063	Notting Hill	...
2	Peter	Smith	...	232	VHR 4915	The Italian Job	PG	...				...
3	Kevin	Davis	...	635	37115 05523	The Shawshank Redemption	15	...	489	RCC 3064	Brief Encounter	...
4	Debbie	O'Neill	...	489	RCC 3064	Brief Encounter	PG	...				...
5	Jack	McReynolds	...	858	053 9063	Notting Hill	15	...				...
6	Megan	O'Sullivan	...	634	9028522	The Bourne Identity	15	...	635	CC 7524	The Shawshank Redemption	...
7	Clare	Johns	...	576	D888888	Pirates of the Caribbean	12	...	232	VHR 4915	The Italian Job	...
8	Kate	Dewar	...	878	UDR 90098	Gladiator	15	...				...
9	Annie	Orbison	...	193	053 9063	Notting Hill	15	...				...

Figure 16.9: A non-normalised table. For reasons of space, only some fields are shown. The repeating group could carry on through unlimited repetitions, allowing each person to hire a vast number of videos.

The conventions used in describing attributes and entities are as follows:

1. Fields that could occur many times are known as a **repeating group** and are indicated with a line above them, eg, vidname, vidrating.

2. **Primary key** fields are indicated by underlining, eg, custno.

3. When writing down a description of the **table**, the table name is written first, with field names enclosed in brackets, eg, Customer (custno, custfname, custsname…)

Thus the entire table in our video club is:

Customer (custno, custfname, custsname, custaddr, custtown, custphone, vidstockid, vidcatno, vidname, vidrating, vidmedium, dueback, vidprice, suppid, suppname, suppaddr1, suppaddr2, suppcode, supptown, suppphone)

First Normal Form (1NF)

Definition A table is said to be in **first normal form** if it contains no repeating groups.

1NF is achieved by creating a new entity based around the repeating group. The **primary key** of the original table remains part of both tables, to facilitate a relationship between them. Without the primary key, there would be no way to tell which lines in one table related to which lines in the other.

In our example, the primary key of the Customer table remains unchanged, while the new Video table has a composite key (made up of more than one field): *vidstockid* identifies each video; *custno* retains the relationship with the customer. The set of tables in 1NF is thus:

Customer-1 (<u>custno</u>, custfname, custsname, custaddr, custtown, custphone)

Video-1 (<u>custno</u>, <u>vidstockid</u>, vidcatno, vidname, vidrating, vidmedium, dueback, vidprice, supplierid, suppname, suppaddr1, suppaddr2, supptown, suppcode, suppphone)

This structure simplifies storage of customer details, although details of videos still require duplication. This will be addressed in **second normal form**. The new structure of the video loans system is shown in figure 16.10.

Customer-1

custno	custfname	custsname	custaddr	custtown	custphone
1	John	Woods	15 Brooke St	Portrush	8200 0111
2	Peter	Smith	23 Mark St	Coleraine	7031 1458
3	Kevin	Davis	10 Ashbeg Grove	Portstewart	8399 9753
4	Debbie	O'Neill	3 Empire Avenue	Castlerock	8600 1741
5	Jack	McReynolds	1 Fairfield	Portrush	8282 2288
6	Megan	O'Sullivan	9 Park Road	Coleraine	7038 1100
...	...	...	...	...	...

Figure 16.10: Set of two tables from figure 16.9 in first normal form.

Video-1

custno	vidstockid	vidcatno	vidname	vidrating	vidmedium	dueback	vidprice	suppid	suppname	suppaddr1	suppaddr2	...
1	211	37115 05523	The Shawshank Redemption	15	DVD	17/12/03	£2.00	AMS	Alpha Movie Supplies	108 Botanic Gardens	Botanic Avenue	...
2	232	RCC 3064	Brief Encounter	15	VHS	19/12/03	£3.00	AMS	Alpha Movie Supplies	108 Botanic Gardens	Botanic Avenue	...
3	635	053 9063	Notting Hill	15	VHS	19/12/03	£2.50	AMS	Alpha Movie Supplies	108 Botanic Gardens	Botanic Avenue	...
...	...	...	...	...	...	...	...	...	...	...	...	...
7	576	CC 7524	The Shawshank Redemption	15	VHS	15/12/03	£3.00	AMS	Alpha Movie Supplies	108 Botanic Gardens	Botanic Avenue	...
8	878	XRP 90098	Gladiator	15	DVD	22/12/03	£3.00	PTN	Pro Tanto	1 Daisy Gardens	Edinburgh Rd	...
9	103	053 9063	Notting Hill	15	VHS	19/12/03	£3.00	AMS	Alpha Movie Supplies	108 Botanic Gardens	Botanic Avenue	...
10	858	053 9063	Notting Hill	15	VHS	21/12/03	£3.00	AMS	Alpha Movie Supplies	108 Botanic Gardens	Botanic Avenue	...
...	...	...	...	...	...	...	...	...	...	...	...	...

Second Normal Form (2NF)

Definition | A table is in **second normal form** if every non-key attribute is functionally dependent on all parts of the primary key. An alternative definition is that a table is said to be in second normal form if it contains no **partial key dependencies**.

Any 1NF table with a single key field is considered to be already in 2NF. But if a table has a **composite key field**, each field in the table must be functionally dependent on each part of the composite key for the table to be in 2NF. If any fields are functionally dependent on only part of the key, the table is split into two or more tables in order to have no partial key dependencies.

To return to our video club example, we can see that Customer-1 is in 2NF already, as it has a single primary key. However, Video-1 is not in 2NF, as some fields (such as *vidname*) are functionally dependent on only *vidstockid* and not *custno*. The only field that is functionally dependent on both the *custno* and the *vidstockid* is *dueback*. Hence, Video-1 is split into two tables. One table contains all primary key fields plus any other fields that are functionally dependent on all parts of the primary key. A second table contains the fields that were functionally dependent on only part of the primary key, together with the part of the primary key they were functionally dependent upon.

The set of tables in 2NF is thus:

Customer-2 (<u>custno</u>, custfname, custsname, custaddr, custtown, custphone)

Videoloan-2 (<u>custno</u>, <u>vidstockid</u>, dueback)

Video-2 (<u>vidstockid</u>, vidcatno, vidname, vidrating, vidmedium, vidprice, suppid, suppname, suppaddr1, suppaddr2, suppliertown, supplierpcode, supplierphone)

Examples of these three tables are shown in figure 16.11.

Figure 16.11: Set of tables from figure 16.10 in second normal form.

Customer-2

custno	custfname	custsname	custaddr	custtown	custphone
1	John	Woods	15 Brooke St	Portrush	8200 0111
2	Peter	Smith	23 Mark St	Coleraine	7031 1458
3	Kevin	Davis	10 Ashbeg Grove	Portstewart	8399 9753
4	Debbie	O'Neill	3 Empire Avenue	Castlerock	8600 1741
...	...	...	...	...	...

Videoloan-2

custno	vidstockid	dueback
1	211	17/12/03
2	232	19/12/03
3	635	19/12/03
...	...	...
9	193	19/12/03
1	858	21/12/03
3	489	22/12/03
...	...	...

Video-2

Figure 16.11 continued

vidstockid	vidcatno	vidname	vidrating	vidmedium	dueback	vidprice	suppid	suppname	suppaddr1	suppaddr2	...
211	37115 05523	The Shawshank Redemption	15	DVD	17/12/03	£2.00	AMS	Alpha Movie Supplies	108 Botanic Gardens	Botanic Avenue	...
232	RCC 3064	Brief Encounter	PG	VHS	18/12/03	£2.00	XEN	Xenith Entertainment	23 Evergreen Estate	Antrim Road	...
635	053 9063	Notting Hill	15	VHS	19/12/03	£2.50	AMS	Alpha Movie Supplies	108 Botanic Gardens	Botanic Avenue	...
489	VHR 4915	The Italian Job	PG	VHS	19/12/03	£2.50	XEN	Xenith Entertainment	23 Evergreen Estate	Antrim Road	...
...	...	...	...	...	...	...	...	...	...	...	...

Third Normal Form (3NF)

> A table is in **third normal form** if it is in 2NF and if no functional dependencies exist between non-key attributes. An alternative definition is that a table is said to be in third normal form if it contains no **non-key dependencies**.
>
> **Definition**

3NF means that no field should be functionally dependent on a non-key field within a table instead of being functionally dependent upon the table's primary key. For example, looking at the 2NF tables above, it can be seen that *suppname*, *suppaddr1*, *suppaddr2*, *supptown*, *suppcode* and *suppphone* within *Video-2* are functionally dependent on *suppid*, rather than *vidstockid*.

These fields are therefore moved to a new table to fulfil the 3NF requirements. If they remained, the duplication of each supplier's details would lead to data redundancy and inconsistencies. For example, if *Xenith Entertainment* changed their address, the user would have to alter every single instance of *Xenith Entertainment* if the table remained in 2NF.

The table to be modified is split into two new tables. One table contains fields that were not functionally dependent on the primary key while in 2NF while another table contains the key field from the first new table, plus the rest of the former 2NF table.

Hence, in 3NF there are four tables in total:

Customer-3 (custno, custfname, custsname, custaddr, custtown, custphone)

Videoloan-3 (custno, vidstockid, dueback)

Video-3 (vidstockid, vidcatno, vidname, vidrating, vidmedium, vidprice, suppid)

Supplier-3 (suppid, suppname, suppaddr1, suppaddr2, supptown, suppcode, suppphone)

Examples of these four tables are shown in figure 16.12.

Figure 16.12:
Set of tables
from figure
16.11 in third
normal form.

Customer-3

custno	custfname	custsname	custaddr	custtown	custphone
1	John	Woods	15 Brooke St	Portrush	8200 0111
2	Peter	Smith	23 Mark St	Coleraine	7031 1458
3	Kevin	Davis	10 Ashbeg Grove	Portstewart	8399 9753
4	Debbie	O'Neill	3 Empire Avenue	Castlerock	8600 1741
...	...	...	...	...	...

Video-3

vidstockid	vidcatno	vidname	vidrating	vidmedium	dueback	vidprice	suppid
211	37115 05523	The Shawshank Redemption	15	DVD	17/12/03	£2.00	AMS
232	RCC 3064	Brief Encounter	PG	VHS	18/12/03	£2.00	XEN
635	053 9063	Notting Hill	15	VHS	19/12/03	£2.50	AMS
489	VHR 4915	The Italian Job	PG	VHS	19/12/03	£2.50	XEN
...	...	...	...	...	...	...	...

Supplier-3

suppid	suppname	suppaddr1	suppaddr2	supptown	suppcode	suppphone
AMS	Alpha Movie Supplies	108 Botanic Gardens	Botanic Avenue	Belfast	BT7 1JN	028 90147585
XEN	Xenith Entertainment	23 Evergreen Estate	Antrim Road	Belfast	BT2 2WQ	028 90199871
PTN	Pro Tanto	1 Daisy Gardens	Edinburgh Rd	Glasgow	G1 2RQ	0141 223 6677

Videoloan-3

custno	vidstockid	dueback
1	211	17/12/03
2	232	19/12/03
3	635	19/12/03
...	...	...

A Fully Normalised Database

Our example database has now been fully normalised and could be used to construct a functioning database. Three **normal forms** have been considered:

First normal form (1NF): a table is said to be in first normal form if it contains no repeating groups.

Second normal form (2NF): a table is said to be in second normal form if every non-key attribute is functionally dependent on all parts of the primary key.

Third normal form (3NF): a table is said to be in third normal form if it is in 2NF and no functional dependencies exist between non-key attributes.

Improving the example database

In the example used above, each customer can hire a single video only once. This is restricted through Videoloan-3, uses *custno* and *videostockid* as a composite key field. Hence, a particular combination of *custno* and *videostockid* can be entered only once. Also, there is no record of whether or not videos that were borrowed were returned.

Suggest a way to improve our example so that:

1. a customer may borrow a particular item many times;
2. the date a customer returns an item is recorded.

16.8 Database Locking

A key problem in databases is the possibility of several users trying to change the same piece of data at once and consequently over-writing each other's changes. This can be avoided through the use of **locks**.

When records are opened, they are **locked**, and are then **unlocked** when editing is complete. There are five ways to undertake locking.

1. **Open entire database in exclusive mode.** Only one user/process will have access to anything in the database. This is impractical in daily use but is desirable in the context of overnight batch processing or creating backups.

2. **Lock all records being modified in the table.** This is effective but if several users/processes need access to a locked table it may be very restrictive. Many users will be unable to access locked data, or only be able to view a read-only copy of that data.

3. **Lock only the record being edited.** Once a user/process locks a record, any other users/processes trying to access it will receive a suitable error message, or view the table in 'read only' mode.

4. **No locks at all.** While this avoids the problem of restricting users it also relies on users communicating to avoid problems. This can work in an environment where a handful of people are in close contact. In any other situation it is impractical and will almost certainly lead to problems.

5. **Open tables in read-only mode by default.** Users/processes can access any data at any time, but only as a non-editable copy. If changes are to be made, editing rights are requested from the database management system (or DBMS, see section 16.9. This avoids the problem of users receiving many messages saying, "You cannot access this record because another user has it open".

Deadlock (also called 'Deadly Embrace') occurs when several processes are waiting for resources held by each other before they can complete. For example, process A cannot continue until B acts but B is waiting for A to act. Suppose there are two processes, A and B, with the algorithms shown:

Process A:	Process B:
Open Record 1 for editing	Open Record 2 for editing
Open Record 2 for editing	Open Record 1 for editing
Process records	Process records

If both processes are initiated at the same time then deadlock will occur: **A** could wait forever for **B** to release Record 2 and **B** could wait forever for **A** to release Record 1. While this example shows two processes, it is possible that a chain of many processes could all wait for each other. A DBMS will detect this and will either terminate the processes and re-start them separately, or alert database managers to the problem.

16.9 Database Management Systems (DBMS)

While a database is a structured collection of related data, a Database Management System (DBMS) is the software used to manage the operation of databases. It performs a number of useful functions, including presenting data to the user and managing security. Many people are unaware of using a DBMS in their daily life, but any system used for searching data, such as online directories, is probably managed by a DBMS. Common DBMS software includes *MySQL* (which powers well-known web sites including the social networking site *Facebook*), *Oracle* (which powers *Bebo*), and Microsoft *Access*.

Modern databases are the product of considered evolution, as discussed in the previous sections. The development of Database Management Systems solved many of the problems of earlier systems. While older systems required programs to manipulate data directly, the DBMS acts as intermediary between programs and data. For example:

- Program-data dependence is removed because the DBMS ensures that existing programs are not rendered inoperable by changes to the structure of data.
- Security is easier to enforce under a DBMS. The DBMS is told about access rights for different users or programs and enforces this.
- A DBMS adopts a normalised data design, leading to an efficient storage of data without redundancy.

A **Relational Database Management System** (**RDBMS**) is a particular type of DBMS designed for the construction and use of relational databases. Relational databases are those which conform to the rules of normalisation (see section 16.7). Figure 16.13 shows how a DBMS operates between data and programs.

Figure 16.13: Each department uses programs tailored to their precise needs. All those programs send requests for data via the DBMS which ensures that the data is passed back in a way acceptable to clients. If clients request data they are not authorised to access, the DBMS denies the request and may alert the database manager.

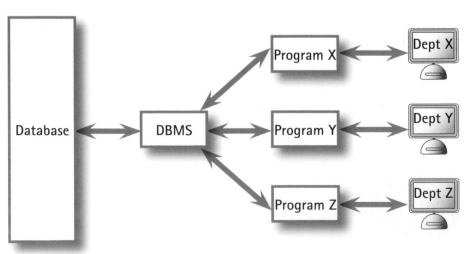

The Components of a DBMS

A DBMS is a collection of programs used to create and maintain a database and:

- Facilitate the **definition, construction, update, manipulation** and **sharing** of data among users and applications. When the database is shared the DBMS must ensure that problems do not occur when two people simultaneously access a record and try to update it;

- Provide an **interface** between the programs that access the database and the database itself. It makes itself as **invisible** as possible to the user. As a result, programs are independent from the data that is stored;

- **Enable protection** of data by way of password allocation and levels of access. Each user will be allocated a password and will have their own 'view' of the database with a suitable level of access, eg some users may have read / write access, read only access or no access;

- Facilitate **maintenance** of the data **dictionary**. This is a stored record of all the elements of the database, ie names of entities, attributes, validation checks etc;

- Facilitate **backup and recovery** of data in the event of system failure.

The software that makes up the DBMS consists of two parts:

- The Data Description Language (DDL). This is a programming language used by the **Database Administrator** that defines the logical structure of the files within the database. Attributes, primary keys and validation rules are defined using DDL.

- The Data Manipulation Language (DML). Provides a comprehensive set of commands to allow the Database Administrator to access and modify the required data. Data is usually accessed using a series of statements in a query language (such as Structured Query Language or Query By Example - see section 16.5). Both are available within standalone database systems such as Microsoft *Access*. Query output is normally formatted by some sort of reporting tool, to present data to the end user.

The Users of a DBMS

A DBMS has a wide variety of users, ranging from the people who construct the database to the end users who may have little idea of how it works. A DBMS provides an interface that caters for all abilities or requirements, usually categorised according to these three levels:

- **Database designers**, who design and construct new systems;
- **Database Administrators (DBAs)**, who run the database day-to-day;
- **End users**, ranging from the casual user to the advanced user.

Users' differing needs are met through **access rights**, which define what particular users can and cannot access; and by good **interface design**, which means hiding irrelevant detail from users. For example, a receptionist should not be able to execute data operations that are performed by the accounting department. Good design ensures that the receptionist has no knowledge of this extra, inaccessible material and therefore cannot use it in error.

Different views of the system (known as **Database Schemas**) are offered to each type of user, depending on their job or role. Each schema separates users from the physical computer system by providing a level of abstraction. This transforms what actually happens inside a computer to something more meaningful to humans, without the user being aware of it: the less advanced the user is, the more abstract their view. The three database schemas are:

+ **Internal** (Physical). How data is internally organised in a storage medium;
+ **Conceptual** (Logical). How DBAs and designers view the database, including tables and query design;
+ **External** (User). How end users view the system. End users should never have to be concerned with the details of how tables, queries, etc are designed.

Database Designer

Like any other software system, the design will only be successful if there has been a proper understanding of users needs. The database designer is responsible for:

+ Deciding how data is stored and organised;
+ Ensuring data will be held securely;
+ Providing means of accessing data that meets the needs of each type of user;
+ Creating access levels, ensuring users cannot access unauthorised data;
+ Fully documenting the design of the database, including the data dictionary, to facilitate later maintenance.

Once the database is initially created, the Database Designer may take on the role of Database Administrator (DBA) or this role may be taken by another person.

By the way...

Data Dictionary

The data dictionary defines the type and format of the data and the relationships between data. This is initially created at the analysis and design stages to provide a record of the data requirements. Once the database is operational, it can act as a useful reference point for the DBA.

It will contain information such as:
+ Entities and attribute names;
+ The properties of each attribute, such as its field length, data type and formatting information;
+ Attribute **validation** rules;
+ Existing **relationships** between the entities;
+ **Levels of access** such as who is allowed what access to particular entities or attributes;
+ Which programs access which items of data, and whether they merely read the data or change it;
+ Statistical information showing how often the database is accessed.

Database Administrators

Database Administrators (DBAs) are responsible for the day-to-day maintenance of databases. However, it is normal for a DBA's job to occasionally include database design. Like any other system, databases spend only a small portion of their life in their initial design and development, and the vast majority in maintenance. In a large organisation, the role of database administration may be undertaken by a team of people, while in smaller companies the DBA may be a person who is part of the main ICT department.

A Database Administrator will:

+ Decide how data is stored and organised (within the context of maintenance);
+ Ensure data continues to be held securely;
+ Ensure new users are given access to the appropriate data and ensure they continue to have the appropriate access rights if their job role changes;
+ Create and modify data structures in response to new requirements;
+ Create and modify queries and reports in response to user need;
+ Continue to maintain the data dictionary.

Each of these tasks is aided by dedicated software within the DBMS.

End Users

Regardless of their 'rank', the DBMS offers a range of features to users. In the case of Database Administrators, it is possible that they will have several user accounts. In case of abuse or accident, they may have an ordinary administrator's account for day-to-day use, and a separate 'super user' account with unlimited power that is only ever accessed when particular administrative functions are necessary.

A DBMS must allow users to:

+ **Maintain** or **update** tables in a database by adding, deleting or amending existing records. A shared database will use locking for this task. End users manipulate data via special-purpose forms, within parameters set by DBAs. The DBAs will have the facility to bypass locks and other security, though will not do this normally because of the consequences of an accident;
+ **Search** the data using a query language, and save their query for re-use;
+ Run **macros**. Macros automate important actions, by running several commands in sequence after the user has issued a single command. DBAs may create a macro to simplify some task for users, such as running several queries or reports in sequence;
+ Allow users to **print** information. Both tables and the results of queries can be printed. A **reporting tool** is often used to format the results of a query or contents of a table before printing;
+ Allow users to change their password (and DBAs to reset end user passwords when they forget them);

16.10 Summary of Main Terms

Data redundancy: storing data multiple times in multiple locations. This leads to unproductive maintenance and may compromise data consistency and data integrity.

Data inconsistency: contradictory data about an entity being held in different locations. This arises from data redundancy. In such a system, an update to one file may not be automatically reflected in other related files – thus, inconsistency arises. Data consistency is achieved when each attribute of each entity is recorded only once within a normalised database.

Data integrity: the accuracy and correctness of data. Data changed in processing retains its integrity as long as the act of processing does not lead to incorrect output. The integrity of data can be compromised by accident, negligence or wilful intent – either on the part of the user or the programmer.

Program-data independence: designing data in a way that allows its structure to change without preventing programs that access that data from operating. This is achieved through the use of a DBMS. Program-data dependence is a situation whereby a change in the structure of data will prevent client programs from working.

Data modelling: a process of identifying and organising the data that must be stored. A data model describes what data will be contained in a database, how the data will be used, and how the items in the database will be related to each other. A database design can be difficult to change once constructed and populated. Hence, a data model should be well thought through or it will be difficult to amend later without damaging data and may suffer from data redundancy, data inconsistency and a lack of data integrity.

Entity: a real-world object or thing. For example, a car or a person.

Attribute: a property, or known fact, relating to an entity. For example, a car's registration number or the colour of a person's eyes.

Entity-relationship model: a diagrammatic representation of the relationship between entities. ER models define the structure around which a database is built.

Database normalisation: steps followed to obtain a database design that allows for efficient access and storage of data in a relational database. These steps reduce data redundancy and data inconsistency.

Deadlock: A situation where two or more processes are unable to proceed because each is waiting for one of the others to do something.

Database Management System (DBMS): the software used to manage the operation of databases. It performs a number of useful functions, including presenting data to the user and managing security.

Questions

1. Describe the main features of a database. (4)
2. Compare a relational database and a flat file system using the headings below
   i. Data consistency (4)
   ii. Data redundancy (4)
   iii. Data integrity (4)
   iv. Data independence. (4)
3. Explain what is meant by:
   (a) entity (b) record (c) attribute (d) primary key (e) foreign key. (5)
4. Describe the purpose of data modelling. (3)

Questions

5. Identify the relationships that can occur between entities. (3)

6. A library is developing a new system to catalogue its books. The following facts are known about all books within the library (note: the term 'book' refers to a single physical book and not multiple copies of a single title). Represent these facts through a fully labelled ER diagram.
   + Each book has one main author.
   + Each author can be responsible for several books.
   + Each book is published by a single publishing company.
   + Each publishing company is responsible for several books. (5)

7. A life assurance insurance company is developing a new database system for maintaining private individual's details. The following facts are known, or have been agreed by the company.
   + Each policy can relate to only one person.
   + Each person's life can be assured by several policies (for example, a wife may take out a policy on her husband, as may their children).
   + Each policy will be paid monthly by direct debit from a single nominated bank account, though several policies may be serviced through the one bank account.

   Represent the above through a fully labelled ER diagram. (5)

8. Describe deadlock and two ways of avoiding or resolving it. (7)

9. Explain why the data in a database is normalised. (2)

10. Describe the steps in normalisation. (6)

11. Within a college administration system, the following data will be stored:

    For each student:
    + student ID number
    + forename
    + surname
    + DOB (date of birth)
    + course(s) studied

    For each course:
    + course ID number
    + course title
    + course tutor's *tutor id, forename, surname*

    Represent the above as a single, non-normalised table. (2)
    Develop your single table into 1NF. (2)
    Develop your 1NF tables into 2NF. (3)
    Develop your 2NF tables into 3NF. (3)
    At each stage, show all working together with all tables. If a table is the same in any normal form as it was in the previous normal form, this should be made clear.

12. State the meaning of QBE and describe its use. (3)

13. State the meaning of SQL and describe its use. (3)

14. What are reports used for? (2)

15. Describe the purpose of a Database Management System. (3)

16. Describe the main components of a Database Management System. (6)

17. State four functions performed by a DBA. (4)

18. Explain the purpose of a data dictionary. (2)

19. Describe three types of database user. (6)

20. State, and describe, three database schemas. (6)

CHAPTER 17
Management Information Systems

17.1 Introduction

Information is a valuable commodity for any organisation. In any part of a company, people need information that is specific to their job. For example, factory managers and production line supervisors require different information. Depending on their role, someone may be concerned with information from within the company (**internal sources**) or outside the company (**external sources**). They may also prepare data to be used within the company or to go to some external body.

Different employees will have different uses for data. Firstly, there are senior managers, who make decisions concerning the company's overall direction, and who depend on relevant information coming from the lower levels. Middle managers also rely on data from lower levels to make day-to-day decisions. Lastly, the people working at these lower levels also have information needs. For example, the person at a cash register needs the price of items to be displayed whenever they scan a bar code. Most people are only concerned about information that is relevant to their role, rather than the minute detail of everything the company does.

Just as there is a hierarchy of personnel, so there is a hierarchy of systems:

+ **Transaction Processing Systems** (or **Data Processing Systems**). Used with an organisation to process day-to-day events such as logging sales or the movement of products within a warehouse. This data is entered into an information system. Some Transaction Processing Systems process in **real time** (as soon as it is entered), eg the TPS that produces the running total of a bill in a supermarket. **Batch Systems** are another type of TPS that process data at set intervals, such as those that process electricity bills or bank statements.

+ **Management Information Systems (MIS).** Monitor and control an organisation's internal operations. An MIS gathers data from a TPS and often aggregates or summarises it in some way to give it meaning or a context for management. This allows management to see past huge amounts of detail to the 'big picture'. Without an MIS, many companies could not do business in today's world.

17.2 Information Systems versus Transaction Processing Systems

Transaction Processing Systems are used within an organisation to process day-to-day events. These systems perform many useful functions on which an organisation depends such as logging sales or the movement of products within a warehouse. Such a system passes data into an information system.

Definition

A Transaction Processing System (also called a **Data Processing System**) gathers data for use within an **information system**. It handles routine events which prompt some form of input into a system thus enabling the master files of the organisation to be kept up-to-date. Examples of these include the systems that process data from a supermarket checkout, or process data relating to stock movements within a warehouse. Therefore, it is the people at the lowest levels of an organisation's structure who generally use these systems.

An Information System gathers data from Transaction Processing Systems and often aggregates or summarises it in some way to give it meaning or a context. For example, a supermarket manager will not be concerned about every single can upon the shelves but will be concerned with the overall view of stock. The sales data is gathered by a Transaction Processing System but the summary is produced by an information system. Systems used by progressively higher levels of management, such as **Management Information Systems** (see below) will aggregate more and more information, but present it in an increasingly summarised form.

17.3 Decision Making and Strategic Planning in a Typical Organisation

Only very small businesses survive with a 'flat' management structure, ie no overall leader. Usually, somebody is in overall charge. They delegate day-to-day decisions to a layer of middle management. These managers in turn run their own departments. Employees report to their middle managers, and generally have little to do with senior management.

This hierarchical structure is mirrored in the way that people access data. At the lowest level, employees access data that is relevant and useful to them. For example, a packer in a warehouse only needs to know which items to pack. Likewise, an accounts clerk is not concerned with the firm's overall financial situation. Middle managers access information that gives them a broad picture of their department, while senior management may only want a broad picture of the whole company.

A person who is highly placed within an organisation has a view of the company similar to the view from the top of a mountain: they see everything, but without detail. As you move down the mountain, fewer things become visible, but those that are can be studied in more detail.

Within an organisation information can be used for decision making at three different levels:

+ **Strategic Level:** The view from the top, for example senior management and company directors, or the principal and board of governors in a school. The information at this level allows overall company objectives to be identified and evaluated. Decisions taken can impact even those at lower levels after only a few weeks, or over a few years. Strategic decisions relate to the development of new products or services, the purchase of new premises etc. These decisions will affect the whole organisation, or large sections of it. Senior management in a supermarket chain may use such information to identify notable trends, such as the sudden decline in performance of certain stores or a sudden surge in sales of particular brands. Information at this level will be summarised if an overview of the whole organisation is needed. For example, a senior manager responsible for all of a chain's supermarkets in Northern Ireland has no interest in precisely how many boxes of fish fingers are selling in Dungannon, but rather in how well all their stores are doing. Therefore, a manager will want a summary of each store with particular trends highlighted. In addition, the information required will relate to an extended period and may come from both internal and external sources.

+ **Tactical Level:** Here, information is used by middle management such as department heads or regional managers who are responsible for implementing the objectives set at the strategic level. Information can be used to make decisions relating to the management of operations, budgets and allocation of staff to resources. Decisions taken in relation to the running of a department will be felt that day, or may involve planning ahead into the next few months, ie the short to medium term. These decisions will affect large groups of people within an organisation, such as a factory or store. Tactical information will be more detailed than at a strategic level, but it will still be summarised: for example a report showing the performance of sales in a particular department to identify popular or unpopular products. It will be received on a weekly or monthly basis and can be in tabular, graphical or pictorial form.

+ **Operational Level:** The view from the lowest level, including production operatives, heads of minor departments or groups of people with a specific, small area of responsibility. Such people will often work face-to-face with the public. This information relates to the short term such as day-to-day operations. Decisions taken will be felt immediately and only impact upon a few people. For example, a shop floor employee should be able to tell a customer if a product is in stock. Information for operational decisions will be detailed and will be received regularly.

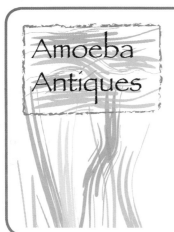

The hierarchy of Amoeba

Already in this book you have met a number of Amoeba's employees, at various levels within the firm. They form only a small part of Amoeba's operations. We will now look at how Amoeba is organised. The structure described here is summarised in figure 17.1.

Amoeba's board of directors are at the top of the structure. The directors assume overall responsibility for different areas of the company such as manufacturing and retail. They make few day-to-day decisions, but rather plan overall strategy. High-ranking managers report directly to the directors and implement these decisions further down the command structure. It is not practical for a senior director to have a detailed knowledge of each factory or store, so instead he or she trusts their senior managers to organise these areas effectively and only relate the most relevant information to a higher level. While Amoeba has international operations, the directors have little hands-on experience with this, depending instead on other managers.

Alison and Lynne, who control retail and ICT, are high-ranking managers. They control their areas of responsibility and exercise a large influence in the company without having to refer to anyone else, since the directors trust them to do their job. However, very important decisions concerning the directions of retail or ICT strategy are first discussed with the directors.

Alison and Lynne have people who report directly to them. Alison gives a lot of autonomy to various buyers because their judgement can be trusted. However, 'big' decisions, such as whether to end one product line or whether to invest in a completely new type of product are referred to her. She may use an **expert system** or a **decision support system** to aid her.

At a level below are people such as Martin, who runs ICT in the main warehouse. On a day-to-day basis he is in charge, although big decisions, such as the recent replacement of ageing *Unix* fileservers with *Linux* systems, are first discussed with Lynne to map out a strategy for achieving this. Martin has, in turn, people who report to him. While Martin has a more detailed knowledge of the warehouse system than even Lynne, he has little experience of other areas of the company.

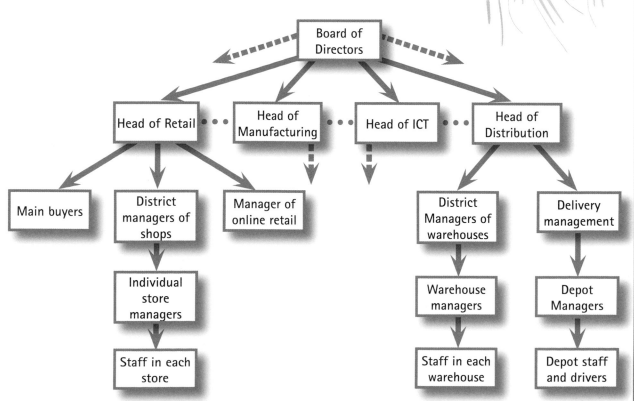

Figure 17.1: The management structure of Amoeba Antiques. Dotted lines indicate the most common lines of communication between managers, while dashed lines indicate further parts of the structure that have been omitted.

At the lowest level of the company are those on the 'factory floor', sometimes called 'production operatives'. They know a lot about their role but know little of overall company strategy. This term includes all those who have nobody reporting directly to them, whether they be cleaners or people working on an IT support line. They report to their line managers who in turn report to their seniors, and so on. It is worth noting that while the people at the lowest levels seem less important in the hierarchy, they are just as important to the running of the company as those at higher levels.

As can be seen in figure 17.1, Amoeba have a large and complex structure that depends on each person playing their part. Information needs are different at each level of this structure. At the very bottom, data processing systems gather transaction data and staff at this level access reports based on this. At each level further up the hierarchy, the information a person has access to is drawn from the level below, so by the time data is received by **Management Information Systems** at higher levels, many of the day-to-day details will have been amalgamated into an abstract view.

Task

Identify the people involved and the decisions that could be made at operational, tactical and strategic levels in the following scenarios:
1. A school.
2. A bank.
3. A car manufacturer.

17.4 Factors Affecting Quality of Information

The factors which affect the quality of information

As information is vital for each daily task and for guiding business decisions, using low quality information inevitably leads to mistakes. As discussed in section 1.4, there are five main factors that affect the quality of data. It should be:

+ Accurate;
+ Up-to-date;
+ Complete;
+ Relevant;
+ Presented effectively.

It is important to note that quality is not static. As information moves within an organisation, its quality may change. For example, if management receives poorly presented production figures from the factory floor, they may be given many irrelevant details. Therefore, data that is considered 'high quality' in one place might be considered 'low quality' in another due to a lack of relevance.

Data quality can also be affected by the way an information system is actually constructed. If it is the result of a well-considered analysis and design, it should present high quality information, but a poor system can lead to problems:

+ It may address the wrong problem, and therefore be of no help to users. This may happen if analysts have misunderstood the main problem;
+ It ignores the structure of the organisation. That is, analysts or designers have

tried to impose an unrealistic vision of how the company should operate and it has not been accepted;

- The above two examples assume the analysis was reasonable, but slightly flawed. There is also the possibility that the analysis was totally wrong but this was not realised until an ineffective system was up-and-running;

- The system was developed for the wrong reasons, for example a new manager wanting to make a mark or because the ICT department have bought unnecessary new technology. Users may resent this approach because they believe the old system worked fine and all they feel they have gained is a lot of unwanted hassle.

Consider the example of a vegetable processing plant. Each day, reports are produced by different departments for internal use, eg which farmers have supplied vegetables and the weight and type of those vegetables. These reports are given to the accounts department so that the farmers can be paid. These documents are long and detailed: if one hundred farmers bring in vegetables then one hundred sets of data must be recorded. Also, the individual weights of vegetables are needed by each supermarket. This data is given to production managers so that the production lines can be told what to pack. At the start of the day, packing room supervisors are told what they need to pack that day for collection that night. Each supermarket must receive what they have requested.

Each week, the directors need a report detailing the previous week's production. At this stage, a summary of the aforementioned reports must be produced. It would be possible to give management exact copies of the other reports, but this method, while accurate, lacks quality at this level because of superfluous detail. Management do not need to know the details of every single carrot.

On the other hand, the summary could be oversimplified by stating the gross weight of all vegetables going in and the gross weight of all processed vegetables going out. In this case the information has also lost quality, because it is now incomplete and lacks sufficient detail for directors to make informed decisions. A good quality report treads a fine line between providing either too much or too little detail.

17.5 Internal and External Sources of Information

External data is data entering an organisation from outside (from an external source), or data created within an organisation and then outputted to an external destination.

Internal data is data whose source and destination are within a single organisation.

Transaction data is generated internally by routine events and is gathered at the lowest level of a data processing system. This data may be further processed and aggregated and used internally (within a Management Information System, see section 17.6) or be sent to another organisation as external data.

Definition

The distinction between external and internal data is best illustrated with an example. Consider the information required by the different people in the example of the vegetable canning firm described above:

- The person in charge of packing needs to know how much of each product is to be packed. They give appropriate information to production line supervisors;

- The supervisor of a particular production line needs to know how much of each product must be packed in a day;

- Company managers need to monitor production trends. At this level, the manager is not concerned about what is produced on each production line, but the overall volume of each product. This allows them to make decisions about purchasing vegetables from farms;

- People working in the human resources department (ie those responsible for hiring people) also need to know of changes in production. This is so that they can hire new people with appropriate skills or arrange for the retraining of existing staff.

Figure 17.2 illustrates some of the typical data flows in company such as this.

Figure 17.2: Data flows for a typical company.

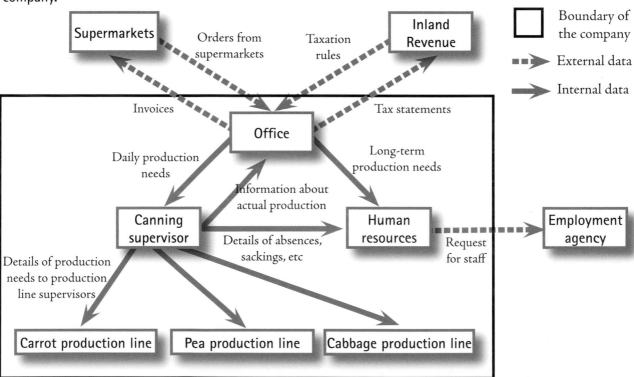

In addition to this internal information, there is a need for external information. This relates to the environment an organisation is part of, and can be either an input to or output from the overall system. This includes the following:

- Data entering the firm for business purposes, such as customer details, customer surveys in order to ascertain preferences and order details and information relating to deliveries from suppliers.

- Information generated by the firm to be presented to others, such as receipts for customers and statements for the Inland Revenue.

- Information relating to outside forces on a firm, for example:

  - Information about population changes, which may affect worker availability or help identify new markets.

- Legislation to ensure a firm complies with all laws and directives. For example, a change in the law on the correct disposal of waste material may increase production costs; or a change to the number of hours that employees are permitted to work may force a firm to recruit more staff.
- Information to enable a firm to compete effectively, such as the price of a competitor's products, sales performance or a rival firm's plans to compete for another organisation's market share.
- Economic considerations, such as changes in the minimum wage, interest rates or in trends and fashions, which may make products less saleable and open up opportunities for new products.

Because of the sheer volume of data being collected, there must be a formal method of recording and storing it for future access. This data is vital to a company's future, so organisations will go to great lengths to protect it and ensure it is up-to-date:

External information can be gathered and used in many ways:

- Data needed for day-to-day operations. This is the most obvious flow of input/output data and includes details of customer orders and the arrival of new stock.
- Data relating to influences outside a company's control, such as new legislation and taxation.
- Data gathered over time to build up a picture of competitors' activities. For example, some organisations employ people to read newspapers and trade journals to gather information about other organisations. Managers often meet competitors at trade fairs and conferences or over-hear conversations with employees that can yield much useful information. Some companies may even resort to spying on competitors. For example, company X may have one of their people apply for a job in company Y to gain access to sensitive data.

Amoeba, newspapers and rival firms

Alison is the head of retail operations at Amoeba. As part of their business it is vital to keep track of what competitors are doing. One of her employees, Aaron, has the task of scouring each national newspaper and other journals, including web sites, for information and presenting a daily summary to Alison. This leads to criticism from others that he has no work to do if he can spend most of the day reading newspapers. Aaron's critics fail to realise the importance of his job as this is often the only way to find out what other firms are doing.

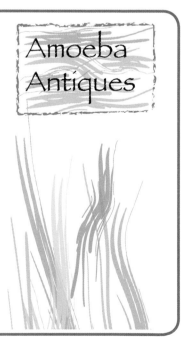

Each piece of information is entered into a database with a record of its origin. In other countries where Amoeba have operations the same database is accessed and updated. On a daily basis management are given summaries of what is happening in their business sector. The database software is also designed to produce a report on any business that appears to be doing a lot of new business in competition to Amoeba.

For example, it was recently reported that a rival firm (*Olde Worlde Furniture*) had agreed a contract to supply *Freddo's Furnishings*, a small chain of furniture

stores, with reproduction Victorian furnishings. In the next few months and in different publications there was more information in the press about *Olde Worlde*, including several new contracts with clients and manufacturers and rumours of a bid to buy *Freddo's Furnishings*.

None of these stories may have been very important on their own and could easily be overlooked. However, when put together it became apparent that *Olde Worlde* were attempting to become a rival of Amoeba. Because of the volume of information in the database it is important that the system automatically produces a report about this in case the people in charge have not realised what is happening. That is, when a significant amount of related data accumulates it should be reported automatically.

This was major news for Amoeba as this is an area of the market they have been dominant in for a long time. Being able to determine what rival firms are doing allows Amoeba to react before their market share is damaged.

By the way...

Spying! I thought that was only in James Bond movies?

While spying between nations does happen, spying also takes place between companies. Consider the following cases of 'industrial espionage':

"Microsoft software 'stolen'... Steve Ballmer [Microsoft President and CEO]... "It is clear that hackers did see some of our source code ... [but] we know there has been no compromise of the integrity of the source code; that it has not been modified or tampered with in any way."... While the firm's reluctance to say much is understandable, more details of the attack have been reported in New York's *Wall Street Journal*. It says the security breach was discovered by staff on Wednesday. They detected internal passwords being sent remotely to an e-mail account in St Petersburg in Russia... Computer security experts say the hackers appear to have used a virus called *Qaz* to break into Microsoft's network... Once installed, the *Qaz* program allows hackers unauthorised access to the network by, for example, relaying back to them passwords and other secret information. *BBC News Online*, October 27th, 2000, via http://tinyurl.com/ysy77

"South Korea's Samsung Electronics has banned the use of camera phones in some of its factories for fear they could be used for industrial espionage... 'Use of camera phones will be restricted in our most sensitive plants...' said Samsung." *BBC News Online*, July 7th 2003, via http://tinyurl.com/yvo8bw

"The US Air Force has punished Boeing for resorting to industrial espionage in order to better its defence rival Lockheed Martin... Lockheed Martin sued Boeing for acquiring about 25,000 confidential documents during a 1998 contract competition." *BBC News Online*, July 24th 2003, via http://tinyurl.com/2b3omd

17.6 Features of a Management Information System (MIS)

In its simplest form a **MIS** is:

Definition

- A system to convert data from internal and external sources into information. This system is a combination of computers and human users that manage data collection, storage and the transformation of data into useful information.

- The MIS must then make sure that information is communicated in an appropriate form to managers at different levels to enable them to make effective decisions for planning, directing and controlling the activities for which they are responsible An MIS could, for example, generate sales data and show trends to help managers plan a marketing campaign or to assist them when deciding to adjust prices or production.

- If the MIS works effectively it enables the computer system to work together with the business organisation to achieve the business goals.

- The MIS will provide routine summary reports on the firm's performance.

- The MIS is used to monitor and control the business and predict future performance ie provides information to address recurring managerial issues, such as "Which salesperson sold the most units?"

An MIS should allow management to:

- Achieve the organisation's goals;
- Help establish objectives and monitor the performance of those objectives;
- Access data that is accurate, up-to-date and relevant and presented in an effective way;
- Access data from within the company in real time, not just data that is processed at set periods of time (as batches).

As previously discussed, as an employee progresses up a company hierarchy so their information needs change. An effective MIS aggregates information together, presenting pertinent data whilst hiding trivial details. The ability to aggregate is an important feature of any MIS, as it saves those accessing it a great deal of time and effort on repetitive analytical work.

The needs of users are paramount in the design of an MIS. Those who are not experienced in using ICT do not have time to waste on an incomprehensible interface. Therefore, a typical MIS must be user friendly, and must present information in a manner that helps rather than hinders.

Because of the importance of ICT to an organisation, the management of ICT will be represented at Board level. While ICT staff may operate as a department in its own right, ICT is an integral part of every part of an organisation. That is, the ICT management have their own plans and schedule but provide a service throughout a company. Often the structure and maintenance of the MIS will be the responsibility of the ICT department, though in larger firms the MIS may be managed by a self-contained team of people.

Therefore, a carefully considered MIS policy within an organisation will not consider MIS as solely the responsibility of the ICT department, but recognises that the MIS is something which everybody interacts with at some level.

Executive Support Systems are specialist MIS used at the highest levels of an organisation. They draw on transaction data and external data (see section 17.5). A middle management MIS is usually only concerned with transaction (and hence internal) data.

The output of a MIS is in the form of reports that present information in an accessible format to management. Two types of report are produced:

+ **Summary report**. Presents aggregate data from several transactions, for example a summary of a day's sales within a supermarket;

+ **Exception report**. Outlines deviations from the expected output to draw attention to any unusual performance patterns, for example a report of any product that is selling less than 50 units per day, or that is selling out before new stock arrives.

In all cases, reports should be (a) succinct (b) accurate (c) timely (d) reliable (e) verifiable (ie the data it is based upon should be easy to check) and (f) readily useable.

17.7 Factors Leading to the Failure of a MIS

There are many reasons why an MIS is not guaranteed to succeed:

+ **Failure to meet user requirements**. The problems, exact needs and constraints of the users must be fully investigated, understood and documented before the design or selection of a new system. Errors made at these early stages will lead to incorrect output from the MIS.

+ **The system may not be delivered on time**. Development time should not exceed the completion time agreed with the user and specified in the contract. Delays in development may drive away the customer and cause the system to fail especially as user's requirements may have changed.

+ **The system may exceed the original budget.** If costs exceed the budget agreed at the time of signing the contract the MIS may fail due to a lack of funds.

+ **The information output may be incorrect.** The TPS used by the MIS may not include all the required data or it may record data incorrectly. The MIS must also summarise data correctly and present information appropriately to management at all levels. It should be able to link to both internal and external sources. It is essential that those needing the new system are involved in its design.

+ **The information output must be in an appropriate format** and suitable for its purpose. If the information has no meaning it cannot be used effectively and therefore is of no value.

+ **The user interface should be easy to use** and take account of the requirements of users. The user should find it easy to manipulate the data in order to obtain suitable information. Prototyping (see Chaper 15.14) could be used by the developers to gain feedback from the users of the system.

This list draws on many aspects of ICT and the human factors that influence it. Expand each reason in detail, suggesting why user needs may not be met, or why different departments' systems may not be easily made compatible.

17.8 Advantages and Disadvantages of a MIS

The advantages of a MIS are:

+ An MIS is very effective in its presentation of data. It can be used to aid effective decision making at all levels, which will in turn allow the organisation to realise its goals. For example, a company's strategic decisions relating to increasing their market share and outperforming the competition.

+ The facility of an MIS to summarise information is crucial. It reduces the time taken to sift through irrelevant detail. The system allows users the flexibility to manipulate data in a way that shows them the information they need, eg which department is making the most sales this quarter.

The disadvantages of a MIS are:

+ Errors in analysis or design will lead to incorrect output from the MIS. This can lead to poor decision making.

+ There can be too much dependency on the system which can cause critical losses if the system goes down, rendering output unavailable. By being overly reliant on the MIS management may lose their intuition and their ability to respond to the unexpected.

+ The MIS may not be able to easily accommodate unexpected events.

For any of these reasons, it is vital that management are fully trained in their area of responsibility and are not blindly making decisions because their computer instructs them to do so. Management should have a depth of experience that allows them to cope when the MIS fails, and to recognise when output data is incorrect or unreliable.

1. Explain the differences between a data processing system and an information system. (4)
2. There are three 'views' of a firm's operation. Name and describe each. (6)
3. State, with explanations, two types of people within a school who would fit into each level of management. (12)
4. Describe three factors which affect the quality of information. (6)
5. Distinguish between internal and external sources of information. (4)
6. Describe the purpose of a typical MIS. (4)
7. Describe the main features of a typical MIS. (4)
8. What is an Executive Support System? (2)
9. Outline three criteria that lead to the success or failure of a MIS. (6)
10. Name and describe two types of report produced by a MIS. (4)
11. Describe one advantage and one disadvantage of using an MIS. (4)

CHAPTER 18
Decision Support Systems and Expert Systems

18.1 Introduction

Human abilities have been enhanced by machines for centuries. This was once restricted to simple devices such as pulleys and engines, which were designed to make physical labour less strenuous. However, the development of early computers and counting machines had other applications. Once programmed, they could perform repetitive calculations faster than any mathematician. As technology has advanced, it has been integrated into most modern workplaces: offices, hospitals, schools, factories, garages and farms all rely upon machinery and computers for the smooth running of their daily operations. Until fairly recently, the area of human intelligence has remained off limits, due to both hardware restrictions and limitations in our understanding of how intelligence operates. A computer could be programmed with instructions to do something, but it could not 'think' its way through a new or even slightly altered situation.

There are two classes of systems that now pose a challenge to human intelligence:

+ **Decision Support Systems (DSS):** still based around programmed rules, but designed to examine a particular course of action by considering factors that humans may ignore. A DSS does not make decisions itself; rather, it analyses decisions made by the user.

+ **Expert Systems (ES):** designed to mimic the decision-making of a human expert in some domain. They learn from experience in the same way as a human expert. While there are a number of ways of programming systems to learn, their benchmark is whether they can successfully mimic a human's output when given the same input.

18.2 Decision Support Systems

A **decision support system** (DSS) is a set of integrated tools designed to help in problem solving, such as scheduling work activities, allocating resources and forecasting future trends. It can operate as a standalone tool, though it is more often integrated with existing transaction processing systems and/or management information systems. Basically, a DSS analyses data gathered by other systems, and combines this data with decision making models. This produces information to help the user solve problems. A DSS has a number of distinct features that make it much more than a 'powerful MIS':

+ It brings together data and mathematical models to support human judgement;
+ It supports several interdependent decisions by modelling the impact that differing problems have on each other;
+ It supports a wide variety of decision making processes and styles;
+ It assists decision making within dynamic business conditions;
+ It supports ad hoc queries.

A DSS can assist with several different types of problem:

+ **Independent Problems.** Problems that are completely separate from each other. In this case, the goal is to find the best solution to a single problem;

+ **Interrelated problems.** Problems that affect each other. The goal is to find the best overall set of solutions, not just the solution to independent problems;

+ **Organisational problems.** Problems that span a number of departments within an organisation and may affect the organisation as a whole.

A DSS has three main components:

+ The **database management system** (DBMS) stores internal and external data that are analysed by the DSS. The MIS accesses the same DBMS;

+ **Model Management Systems** take input data, perform some sort of computation on it and deliver output that is often in the form of a forecast. There are many different kinds of model. **Statistical models** are used to analyse statistics, such as production rates or sales figures. **Accounting models** assess the financial implications of different courses of action including 'optimistic', 'pessimistic' and 'realistic' scenarios. For example, in an optimistic scenario, sales may be 30% above the expected rate whereas in a pessimistic scenario sales may be 60% less than expected. **Production models** perform functions such as calculating the number and type of machines needed, amount of raw materials required and their rates of consumption. **Marketing models** are used to aid decisions such as locating new stores, pricing products and forecasting sales. Finally, **human resource models** help managers to make decisions that involve personnel, including planning numbers of workers needed, assessing training needs, maintaining a skills inventory and assessing implementation of government rules and regulations.

+ **Support tools** allow a user to interact with the system. They include the user interface, tools for graphical analysis and online help;

Although we have seen how a DSS is composed and the types of problem it can deal with, the underlying function of a DSS is fivefold:

+ **Model building.** Identifying appropriate models for solving a given problem. This involves analysing input variables, relationships between the variables, assumptions made about the problem and constraints on the problem.

+ **'What-if' analysis.** Used to assess the effect a changing variable will have on operations, for example "What if interest rates rise?", "What effect will rising oil prices have on manufacturing costs?" or "How much will demand increase if we reduce prices?"

+ **Goal seeking.** Works in the opposite way: a desired goal is entered and analysed, allowing decision makers to input the values needed to achieve this. For example, a company may want to increase profits by 10% but seek to do so without forced redundancies or hefty price rises.

+ **Risk analysis.** Assesses the uncertainties of different courses of action. Probability statistics are used to evaluate these risks.

+ **Graphical analysis.** Allows data and information to be viewed as graphs and charts.

18.3 Expert Systems

An **expert system** (ES) is an application that carries out a task otherwise performed by a human expert, at or near the skill level of the expert. Such a system is given the knowledge an expert would have in a specialist field, and it makes recommendations based on that knowledge. While a DSS makes recommendations that humans are expected to discuss, evaluate and query further, an expert system is expected to give the correct answer without the need for discussion. This means that it is suitable only for certain applications where rules can be clearly defined.

Some human experts may use an expert system to give them a 'second opinion'. For example, a doctor may use one to analyse X-ray images. Alternatively, a human who is not an expert may use one to make decisions. An expert system could carry out fault diagnosis in a machine before repair details are passed on to the human expert. This approach is efficient because the human expert does not have to waste time making a diagnosis when the computer can do so. Expert systems have been developed in many fields, including medicine and law.

Many expert systems rely on an amount of **Artificial Intelligence** (AI), and seek to model some aspect of human reasoning. An expert system must be capable of taking the same inputs as a human expert, and must be correct in its output at least as often. Therefore, the ability to learn from experience is very useful.

Figure 18.1: Alan Turing, pictured in 1946.

The Turing Test

Alan Turing (1912–1954), considered by many to be the father of modern computer science, proposed what is now called **The Turing Test** as a means of determining whether a machine was successful in mimicking human intelligence. In the test, a human 'talks' via a text messaging system with unseen humans and AI programs. The user is not told in advance who they are talking to. At the end of each conversation, the user is asked to assess whether the unseen person was human or otherwise. Turing suggested that a program can be considered intelligent if, following such a series of conversations, the user cannot tell which conversations were with computers. Although no system has comprehensively passed the Turing Test, some, such as specialist legal or game playing systems are considered to have met its standards in limited areas because they consistently give the same output as a human would.

By the way...

Learning Systems

A key feature of expert systems is the ability to analyse the effectiveness of their output and learn from experience. Unlike human beings, such systems are often restricted to a single domain and their ability relies on rules defined by their programmers. When world chess champion Gary Kasparov played IBM's

Deep Thought in 1989 he gained an understanding of the machine's style of play, much as he would analyse a human opponent's play and adapted his own play where appropriate. *Deep Thought* also analysed Kasparov's play, in accordance with programming that it could not deviate from. *Deep Blue*, as it was renamed, lost a 1992 rematch 4-2: significant because no computer had ever won a single game against a human champion before. After further improvements, *Deep Blue* won their 1997 match. Kasparov commented that *Deep Blue* (of 1997) played a different game from what he expected and that he sometimes saw deep intelligence and creativity in the machine's moves – albeit by following rules that told it how to be creative.

By the way...

Chinook, a draughts playing program, follows similar principles to *Deep Blue*. Having first written chess programs, Jonathan Schaeffer moved to draughts as he initially considered it a simpler game. Schaeffer, and his team, found the problem more difficult than they first thought: while the rules were simple, mastering the game was very difficult indeed. Their ultimate goal was to play against the world champion.

In 1992, a world championship match took place which Marion Tinsley narrowly won. Tinsley was considered the best player of all time, unbeaten in competition since 1952. A rematch in 1994 was considered a draw, after Tinsley withdrew on health grounds. Through years of research, *Chinook* had reached a point where it was comparable to the best human player and it went on to beat Tinsley's human successor, Don Lafferty. Like *Deep Blue*, *Chinook* was created with knowledge of the general rules and principles of play. A deeper understanding followed analysis of leading players' matches to develop knowledge of effective play. This analysis used rules that were programmed into the system. Both *Deep Blue* and *Chinook* passed limited versions of the Turing Test by passing themselves off as human within a limited domain.

Such programs us a **minimax** algorithm to look several moves ahead in a game. By determining all possible moves from the current position (and all possible replies by the opponent, and all possible responses, etc) they determine which courses of action yield the minimum losses and the maximum gain. A significant flaw in a basic minimax search is that to effectively evaluate a position, the algorithm must consider all possible board positions that follow it. For example, at the start of a game of draughts:

+ After each player has moved once, there are 48 possible board positions;
+ After four moves, there are approximately 2500 board positions;
+ After eight moves, there are several million possible board positions, some offering an advantage to player 1, some offering an advantage to player 2 and some offering neither player an advantage.

(In chess, each player has 20 possible opening moves, leading to 400 possible board positions after 2 moves have been played and several billion board positions after 8 moves!)

The basic minimax algorithm is therefore impractical, as it could take years to properly consider positions 10 or 20 moves ahead of the current position, which

By the way...

is regularly done by top human players. Humans have an advantage, in that they know from experience that many moves are a waste of time. For example an experienced player knows that of all the moves they could make, several will hand the opponent an immediate advantage so they are ignored (and all positions that follow).

A refinement of minimax, known as **alpha-beta** searching is used to eliminate redundant lines of play. In draughts, a minimax algorithm that may consider a million positions can be drastically reduced through alpha-beta searching and possibly only a thousand worthwhile positions are evaluated. This 'brute force' approach, while effective in mimicking the results a human would give, is restricted to rule-based games and cannot independently solve new problems. However, this research set significant milestones and has set the target for future AI systems, as 'general purpose' learners and possibly machines that can mimic human creativity in artistic fields. Research from current systems has found its way into many fields, such as the work of Jonathan Schaeffer that has been incorporated into fields as diverse as biomedical research, poker and EA Sports' FIFA Soccer.

An expert system has the following features:

+ It is limited to a certain area of knowledge, or **domain**;
+ It is based around rules, facts and principles;
+ It can deal with **fuzzy logic.** Instead of answers of **yes** or **no**, it can process a third value: **don't know** or **maybe**;
+ The system's reasoning can be explained to the user;
+ It is capable of learning from experience.

An expert system has three main components:

+ A **knowledge base** which is a store of facts, rules and principles from a given field. **Knowledge representation** is the process of translating knowledge into a form that can be programmed into the expert system;
+ The **inference engine** solves a problem by applying the rules and knowledge already in the system to the facts that are entered concerning the problem;
+ The **user interface** which includes menus, graphics and facilities for explaining the system's reasoning.

18.4 Examples of Expert Systems

There are many scenarios where expert systems are used to provide a response to a query within some limited domain. Some examples are considered below.

Language Translation

Language translation is a far more difficult problem than it may first appear: there is much more involved in translation than simply replacing a word in one language with its counterpart in another. Most languages have different sentence structures (eg French verbs follow nouns and German verbs come at the end of the sentence).

In addition, our understanding of a sentence is often derived from context.

Consider the phrase: *"The teacher ran through the door. 'Sorry folks, I had to talk to the head. Time flies!'"* We understand this to mean that the teacher entered a room in a hurry and apologised for a longer-than-expected conversation with the Principal. However, without a knowledge of English phrases, our culture and so on, this could be misunderstood to mean that the teacher smashed through the door after talking to a disembodied head somewhere and asked the class to conduct an experiment with stopwatches and insects. Add to this the complexity of slang and specialist terminology, and the difficulty for effective translation systems can be seen. Comparing results from programs such as *Babelfish* or Google *Translate* illustrate the difficulty of producing effective translation:

Original: taken from *LeMonde.fr*, on 21st February 2008

Ligue des champions : Lyon laisse échapper la victoire contre Manchester United (1-1). Opposé à un Manchester United au meilleur de sa forme, l'OL a livré un match sérieux, illuminé par un but de Karim Benzema, mais la force offensive des Red Devils a fini par payer, grâce à Tevez en fin de match (1-1). Le Milan AC a tenu Arsenal en échec (0-0), Barcelone a gagné à Glasgow contre le Celtic (2-3), et le FC Séville s'est incliné à Istanbul contre le Fenerbahce (3-2).

Translation by *Babelfish*, 21st February 2008:

League champions: Lyon lets escape the victory against Manchester United (1-1) Opposé to Manchester United from best from its form, the OL delivered a serious match, illuminated by a goal of Karim Benzema, but the offensive force of Red Devils ended up paying, thanks to Tevez at the end of the match (1-1). Milan AC held Arsenal in failure (0-0), Barcelona gained in Glasgow against Celtic (2-3), and the FC Seville was inclined in Istanbul against Fenerbahce (3-2).

Translation by Google *Translate*, 21st February 2008:

Champions League: Lyon leaves escape victory against Manchester United (1-1) Opposed to a Manchester United at its best, OL delivered a serious match, illuminated by a goal from Karim Benzema, but the strength of the Red Devils offensive has paid off, thanks to Tevez in the final match (1-1). The AC Milan held Arsenal defeat (0-0), Barcelona won against Glasgow Celtic (2-3), and FC Seville bowed in Istanbul against Fenerbahce (3-2).

While both of these produce a translation that can be 'figured out', neither is suitable for publication without human proof-reading and editing.

Medicine

Expert Systems are useful in medicine because of specialisms in which few human doctors have expertise, and in the developing world a doctor may be unavailable. In addition, GPs may often benefit from a ready 'second opinion', without taking up another doctor's time. In a locality where few doctors are available, treatment centres can be set up where nurses interview patients. Nurses already have a good amount of medical expertise but may not be trained to recognise unusual conditions. Nurses use the expert system as a diagnostic tool, following the same questions as a doctor might ask:

+ Which part of your body hurts? - My head

+ Whereabouts is your head sore? - At the front

+ Have you had a good night's sleep? - No

+ Do you work long hours? - Yes...... etc

Using the ES, the nurse follows the same procedures as a doctor, such as asking questions and physically examining the patent. In the case above, the ES's knowledge base will be interrogated and a possible diagnosis may be that the patient is over-working and needs proper rest. Because the ES can learn from experience, it will notice certain trends (much as a GP would). For example, if a child has a red spotty rash, and the ES has seen a hundred such children in the past month who have measles, it will diagnose measles as the likely condition. If the patient with measles-like symptoms has had the MMR vaccination and there are no recent occurrences of measles in that area, the ES may ask further questions (as a GP would), such as "Have you recently travelled outside the EU?". In this case, the patient may have a tropical disease, which untrained personnel may have mis-diagnosed as measles.

The systems described above can be used at out-of-hours treatment centres, with many nurses dealing with routine conditions and prescribing medication. A single doctor may be on-site, so that anything beyond the nurse's ability to treat or to prescribe for is dealt with. This also gives the nurse a second-opinion if their experience leads her to disagree with the ES.

Such Expert Systems also have use in remote areas, where it is not feasible to provide continual medical care, such as tribal settlements. A trusted person with suitable training (such as a medical or educational worker) can have a supply of medication for conditions that are likely to be seen in that area. In the event of a serious illness, patients are more likely to be diagnosed before their life is in peril, giving them time to get to a distant hospital.

The Law

The Law is not contained in a single reference book that all lawyers are taught. Rather, it is a steadily developing body of work that has evolved over centuries. It is not unknown for a new Law to be passed by Parliament that is later discovered to contradict some ancient piece of legislation that had been forgotten, or for EU legislation to contradict UK legislation. In this event, competing Barristers will argue in court in a **Test Case** to decide the interpretation which is to be applied. The losing side may appeal against the decision and the case will be argued over again, possibly in various levels of courts. Lawyers and judges involved in any subsequent case will have to be aware of the original legislation, plus the rulings of various courts on how contradictory laws are resolved.

Because of the complexity of many cases, and the expense of hiring lawyers, incorrect outcomes may be reached because:

+ A lawyer and court are unaware of a forgotten piece of legislation that may affect the decision;

- A lawyer and the court are unaware of a decision reached in another court in a similar case, that has set a precedent;
- A company with lots of money keeps raising seemingly petty issues in appeal courts, until the other side of the argument runs out of money and concedes defeat;
- A person who cannot afford specialist legal advice may not use the legal system, and hence be denied justice.

In many of these circumstances an Expert System can be of benefit. If its knowledge base was constantly updated with landmark decisions made in Test Cases and new legislation, it could provide a useful reference tool for the many solicitors whose daily work is largely property transactions, divorce, wills and petty crime. People without the money to take proper legal advice could consult an ES to see if they had a case that could stand in court or not, before hiring a lawyer.

Legal Expert Systems are not without controversy: in 2007, *Wired* reported how an online ES that specialised in bankruptcy law was closed down, after it was deemed to be so good that it was effectively practising law, like a lawyer, but without a proper licence (see http://tinyurl.com/2kwgnr). Such objections, though, indicate that it may have met Turing's standard of passing itself off as a human, at least within this narrow domain.

Gaming

As already described above, Expert Systems have been pioneered in many areas of gaming. While draughts may seem trivial game, it was actually very difficult to construct a system that could consistently play well. The research from such systems has led to systems that specialise in providing human-like opponents in online poker, soccer games and 'first person shoot-em-up' games (such as *Halo 3*). A related system is the *Smarterchild* project that talks with humans in on-line chat systems and learns from their responses. These systems can learn from the human player's response to them, and modify themselves to be more human-like in the future. From these systems, a lot of understanding is being gained about how good our AI systems really are, compared to a human, and the research from them will lead to further improvements and new uses.

Online Help

Many on-line help systems restrict the user to searching for a few key words. If the user is unaware of the proper term, they may find the help feature less than helpful. One response allows the user to type a query in **Natural Language**, such as "How do I use bullet points". If the user's query is vague, such as "How do I put dots at the start of a list", the help tool can contact an Internet-based Expert System, that based on previous queries, will deduce that the user probably wants to know about bullet points. Some applications have the ES built into the help feature, allowing it to be used without an Internet connection (although it may update itself from a remote server when possible). Such Natural Language Processing is used in some Internet search engines.

Questions

1. Describe the purpose of an expert system, stating clearly what it does. (3)
2. Compare **decision support systems** with **expert systems**, stating their similarities and differences. (4)
3. State and describe three types of problems that a DSS is applied to. (6)
4. State and describe three components of a DSS. (6)
5. State and describe the functions of a DSS. (10)
6. List and describe three components of an expert system. (6)
7. Describe the operation of an expert system. (6)
8. Give two advantages and two disadvantages of an expert system. (4)
9. List five features of an expert system. (10)

CHAPTER 19
Data Security

19.1 Introduction

All organisations exist within a surrounding environment that presents many threats to data, for example:

- Events outside an organisation's control, such as natural disaster, fire or civil disturbance.

- Events which will happen, but whose frequency can be controlled, such as operator error, faulty software or hardware failure.

- Threats from the Internet, such as hackers, viruses and 'trojan horses'.

- Insecure communications, such as intercepted phone calls or e-mails. Related to this is the threat of employees removing secure data on portable media.

- Unauthorised access to premises, including break-ins or impostors, for example thieves posing as workmen and stealing property or data.

- Disgruntled ex-employees who access company systems from the outside world to cause damage.

All organisations must seriously evaluate these threats. While serious, the impact of many of these threats can be minimised if managed properly. It is normal for a senior member of an organisation to have the responsibility of managing threats. This is not a cosmetic exercise: if systems fail and a company cannot fulfil orders, they will lose business, and if private data from customers is stolen the firm may face legal action. The cost of properly managing threats is cost effective when compared to the serious implications of not doing so.

19.2 Managing Security in a Database Management System

There is a need to ensure the security and privacy of data in any system. The main methods of achieving this with a DBMS are:

- **User IDs/passwords**
- **Limiting logins**
- **Access rights and locking**
- **Audit trails**

The first three of these are discussed in more detail in section 14.5 (and there is a degree of overlap between these ideas and general network security in Chapter 22).

Auditing and accounting software automatically maintains a log of all database activity. In the event of data being corrupted, either by accident or on purpose, the changes made can be undone to restore the original data. Rather than storing the data that users see on screen, systems that use auditing record the steps that were taken to create that data (see figure 19.1). Auditing software records information such as:

- the time a system was accessed, on what terminal, by whom and for how long;
- changes to files, ie records of access and inserting, deleting, updating of records or files;
- the number of times the database was accessed;

Auditing cannot prevent misuse or guarantee security, but it does allow an organization to recover data if data is corrupted. For example, the web site *Wikipedia*, and many other wikis, include auditing software to allow erroneous or malicious edits to be reverted easily.

Figure 19.1: Example of how data in a DBMS becomes damaged, and how one employee works late to fix it, despite the fact that the accounting software could have fixed the errors much more quickly.

Steps taken	What user sees	What is stored by the accounting software
John creates a file	The file created by John	The original file
John inserts new data	Modified file	(Original file) + (details of John's changes)
Mark adds a new paragraph	Mark's modified file	(Original file) + (details of John's changes) + (details of Mark's changes)
While editing the file, Paul accidentally overwrites large chunks of it	The now-damaged file	(Original file) + (details of changes) + (details of Mark's changes) + (details of Paul's changes)
John works late to correct what Paul did	Corrected file	(Original file) + (details of John's changes) + (details of Mark's changes) + (details of Paul's changes) + (details of John's further changes)

19.3 Disaster Recovery Planning

A 'backup and recovery policy' is a self-contained section of a security policy that describes how all data can be recovered in the event of a natural or man-made catastrophe. A company cannot focus on 'routine' threats, such as viruses and hackers but must plan for the worst-case scenario of a total loss of data, software or hardware. A company that has planned in advance for these will be in a far better position to recover from such an incident than a company that has not. A company that has not made plans may face a number of consequences:

- Time and money wasted re-collecting and re-inputting data all over again. There is no guarantee that this data will still be available.
- Suitable replacement equipment or premises may not be easily available;
- Loss of reputation and credibility for failing to keep data safe;
- Loss of business as the organisation may be unable to function normally. A loss of data may lead to orders not being fulfilled (as there is no record of them): as a result, customers go elsewhere.
- Directors may have a legal liability, under the Data Protection Act, if data has been accessed by third-parties.

Companies must maintain a full **backup** of all data in a secure off-site location. They should also have plans in place that allow the company to **recover** if some disaster occurs, so that each person in the firm has a clear understanding of their responsibilities. From a customer's perspective, there should be a perception of business-as-usual.

By the way...

It's not just private sector firms who lose data.

Exam candidates are expected to demonstrate an understanding of how data loss can cripple businesses. While both private and public-sector organisations take many precautions in this area, it is the public sector who are under the most scrutiny at the time of writing, due to a number of high-profile mishaps.

On 5th December 2007, a £20,000 reward was offered for the return of two data disks lost by HM Revenue and Customs (see BBC News article via, http://tinyurl.com/35tgdj). Following the well-publicised loss of HMRC data, a number of private-sector firms confessed lesser losses of data (see BBC News article, via http://tinyurl.com/3dlwty).

The data-loss scandal came to Northern Ireland on 11th December 2007 when DVLNI reported that thousands of drivers' details had been compromised (see BBC News article, via http://tinyurl.com/2fdhjb). The public outrage that followed indicated a growing distrust for the organisations involved holding data and, at a wider level for Government IT usage in general (see Daily Telegraph, via http://tinyurl.com/2s2r26).

19.4 Backup Strategies

In general a backup strategy should:

- ensure all files are backed up at specified, frequent, intervals and held securely;
- state how long backups are to be held;
- state how and where files will be backed up;
- state the media used to perform the backups

Because it can be extremely time-consuming to perform a full backup, a number of alternative backup strategies may be used in addition, to focus only on files that have changed since the last full backup. These backup strategies are:

1. Full, Periodic Backup

A full backup involves all data files being copied to a separate portable storage device (typically, magnetic tape) which is stored off-site in a waterproof and fireproof safe. A full backup is carried out at regular intervals, usually automatically every evening when computers are not being used. The results of the backup are automatically printed so that the network manager can easily check that the backup has been successful. The full backup method has some disadvantages

- Data files that change after a backup cannot be recovered (as they have not been backed up). Hence this method is often used in conjunction with the **Grandfather/Father/Son cycle.**
- A full backup can take a long time and for this reason it is usually done at night, when users are not logged-on.
- Recovery from the backup can be time consuming (as every single file must be copied from tape to the server's hard disk).

2. Transaction Logging and the Grandfather–Father–Son Cycle

One common procedure is to use three **generations** of backup tapes, which are continuously recycled (in practice, many companies prefer to have more than three generations, but we will use three here to illustrate the point.) For example, suppose there are three tapes labelled 1, 2 and 3. On Monday, the entire database is copied onto tape 1, on Tuesday, the entire database is copied onto tape 2 and on Wednesday the entire database is copied onto tape 3. This results in three generations of tape. Monday's tape (the oldest) is known as the **Grandfather** and the youngest is the **Son**. Then, on Thursday, tape 1 is reused and becomes the **Son** (youngest generation) while tape 2 is now the **Grandfather** (oldest generation) etc. This process is shown in figure 19.2.

Figure 19.2: The operation of a Grandfather–Father–Son backup system on three consecutive days. Each day, the oldest generation is replaced by a new generation.

	Wednesday	Thursday	Friday
Tape 1	Monday backup (Grandfather)	Thursday backup (Son)	Thursday backup (Father)
Tape 2	Tuesday backup (Father)	Tuesday backup (Grandfather)	Friday backup (Son)
Tape 3	Wednesday backup (Son)	Wednesday backup (Father)	Wednesday backup (Grandfather)

In addition to the backup tapes, a series of **transaction files** are kept. A transaction file is a continuous record of all **transactions** (alterations to the database) made on a particular day. Further sets of tapes are used to store the transaction file. Transactions are useful because they allow changes to a database to be 'undone' one at a time, they allow the impact of errors to be traced and they can even be used to reconstruct destroyed backups. For example, if Wednesday's backup was destroyed, it could be re-created by taking Tuesday's backup and then applying Tuesday's transactions to it. If both Wednesday and Tuesday's backups were destroyed, they could be re-created with Monday's backup and then applying both Tuesday and Wednesday's transactions to it (in that order).

Figure 19.3: Example backup and transaction recording regime for a company.

Figure 19.3 shows a typical backup and transaction file log book for a company using three backup tapes (1, 2 and 3) and three transaction tapes (A, B and C).

Day / Time	Backup	Transaction files
Monday, midnight	Tape 1 is used for backup	Tape A starts recording every transaction
Tuesday, midnight	Tape 2 is used for backup	Tape A stops, Tape B is started
Wednesday, midnight	Tape 3 is used for backup	Tape B stops, Tape C is started
Thursday, midnight	Tape 1 is used for backup	Tape C stops, Tape A is started
Friday, midnight	Tape 2 is used for backup	Tape A stops, Tape B is started
Saturday, midnight	Tape 3 is used for backup	Tape B stops, Tape C is started
Sunday, midnight	Tape 1 is used for backup	Tape C stops, Tape A is started

While this may seem like a lot of over-complicated use of tapes, it has the effect of making it very unlikely that lots of work will be destroyed by accident. Because it can be extremely time-consuming to perform a full backup, a number of backup strategies focus only on files that have changed since the last full backup:

3. Incremental Backup

An incremental backup involves backing up all files that have changed since the last full backup. This is done at set intervals (such as, nightly, or every few hours). To recover data from this method the last full backup will have to be restored first, followed by each of the subsequent incremental backups in the correct order, otherwise recovery could be incomplete.

4. On-line Backup (Redundant Array of Inexpensive Disks or RAID)

In addition to saving work on the primary server, a second 'mirror' server (often at a remote location) is used to provide duplicate storage. Each transaction is written simultaneously to primary and mirror servers. In the event of the primary server failing, the mirror server becomes available immediately and users may not notice this taking place. The main disadvantage is that on-line backup cannot recover data when it has been lost as a result of accidental deletion or incorrect processing. Note that this is just one way of using a RAID data storage system. Other uses include real-time backups of a PC's hard disk.

To effectively protect against data loss, a company will typically use a combination of these methods, for example:

+ A full backup is scheduled for 00.00 hrs on Saturday;
+ Transaction files record each day's events (from 00.00 to 23.59);
+ Incremental backups take place each weekday at 00.00.
+ On-line backups are used continually.

Amoeba and the use of backups

Amoeba have a strict policy regarding backups that states the following:

+ All data is held on servers that are backed up on a daily basis.
+ Sales are logged in transaction records in case of disaster during the day.
+ Transaction records form a transaction tape kept in each store and are also transmitted via the company WAN to head-office.
+ Employees are not permitted to store work on the hard disk of their PC, in case something important is lost. Rather, all work is stored within user accounts on WAN servers which can be backed up automatically.
+ Data on any server is copied to tape each day to be held on-site, in a safe. The same data is transmitted to another Amoeba location for backup there. For example, data from Belfast is backed up to Edinburgh. Data from Edinburgh is backed up to France.

* Safes must be able to withstand bombs, fires, floods and any other conceivable disaster.

The following are examples of cases where Amoeba has had cause to use their backups.

1. A software developer accidentally deleted an important file. The use of the previous day's locally-held backup allowed the deleted material to be restored.

2. In the early 1990s, Amoeba's software development centre was destroyed by fire. Because backup data was held in a fire-proof safe on-site, and also copied to another office, the software development centre was able to re-locate to temporary premises and continue work.

3. A power-cut at 3.30pm led to a failure within the server of a busy store. The previous day's backup tape was combined with the transaction tape (which held every transaction until 3.30pm), and the server restored to how it was just before the power cut.

4. An over-enthusiastic new employee accidentally deleted several personnel records but did not realise his mistake. This was discovered two weeks later when their pay was not processed. Because Amoeba's grandfather-father-son system extends to several weeks' of data, the records in question could be restored from tape.

19.5 Recovery Strategies

While a backup strategy describes how and where data will be duplicated, a recovery strategy describes how data will be re-loaded onto the hardware it came from, or onto alternative hardware, in the event of disaster. Recovery strategies should allow for fairly small events, such as a virus, through to larger events (such as premises being destroyed).

In general a disaster recovery strategy should:

* state the key business functions that must be recovered, and in what order
* state the contact details such as telephone numbers of technical experts or emergency services appointed to help in the immediate aftermath of a disaster
* state the hardware, software, communications, data, personnel and facilities that are essential for the business to resume and return to normal operations. This list must be kept up to date (it would be pointless to try to recover daily operation with a 5-year old list of hardware, for example);
* state the procedures to be followed before, during, and after a disaster.
* state how parts of the network and files will be restored, for example:
    * in the event of an individual user error, by restoring only selected files;
    * in the event of electronic attack, by identifying and restoring affected files;
    * in the event of catastrophe, by restoring data from off-site servers and relocating personnel to an alternative site.

It is essential that training exercises take place in a simulated environment to test the plan to ensure that it functions and that staff know what to do. The plan must be regularly reviewed and updated to ensure that it is applicable to current business circumstances.

Companies will often make provision for **different facilities** in the event of a disaster, for example:

+ Redundant hardware at an alternative location owned by the company which is located off-site. The ongoing cost of such a site may be expensive but it will be built to meet the company's requirements. While the authors of this book worked at a particular software firm in Belfast, during the 1990s, disaster recovery plans included relocating personnel to other business sites in GB in the event of terrorism making the Belfast premises unusable.

+ Large businesses often outsource their disaster recovery requirements to specialist disaster recovery firms. Such firms provide a range of services, including off-site storage of backups to a complete facility where a business can work in the event of a catastrophe. In the case of the 2001 attacks on the World Trade Center, a number of firms moved to such **cold standby sites** that were provided by third party firms. Such sites are effectively a large office-site with a computer network standing by and PCs and servers that can be configured to a company's requirements at short notice.

+ Reciprocal arrangement with another company whereby they agree to assist each other should one be affected by a catastrophe by providing facilities to relocate to. In 2007 a serious malfunction affected one of the main Belfast newspaper's printing facilities. However, long-standing agreements between rival papers allowed for electronic copies of papers to be transmitted to the rival for printing and distribution. While it may seem strange for rivals to help each other, it is in their mutual interest to have such arrangements, especially when they are the only companies in their locality with similar equipment.

Questions

1. Outline five threats that could realistically affect a company in Northern Ireland, and the steps that could be taken to minimise their impact. (15)
2. Describe three methods of managing and restricting access in a DBMS. (9)
3. Describe an audit trail. (3)
4. Give three reasons as to the need for disaster recovery planning. (6)
5. What is the purpose of a backup? (2)
6. Outline the contents of a Disaster Recovery Strategy. (8)
7. Describe the Grandfather-Father-Son process. (3)
8. Describe a suitable backup strategy for a (a) college (b) bank branch (4 each).
9. Describe a recovery strategy. (3)

CHAPTER 20
Types of Network

20.1 Introduction

Computer networks are important in almost all aspects of daily life, yet we often take them for granted and do not pause to consider how they function. By this stage in the course, you should be familiar with the main types: **Local Area Networks** and **Wide Area Networks**. In this section, the various physical topologies are not of primary concern. Rather, the aim is to examine the status, or importance of machines within various types of network in relation to each other.

20.2 Client–Server Networks

A **client** is a program or a hardware device that requests a service from a **server**. Communication between the two follows a set protocol such as HTTP or FTP. A client-server methodology can be followed on either LAN or WAN, provided terminals are equipped with appropriate software. Common examples of a **client-server** network include:

+ A LAN using a **file server**. PCs are equipped with client software to allow them to communicate with the file server, which manages shared network storage for all users. In this case, communication is normally to request files or to send data to be saved. Within the same network a print-server may be a machine dedicated to managing printers, at the request of client PCs. Network Servers may manage traffic flow on the network and communication with any WANs or LAN they are connected to. The file server, print-server and network-servers may be separate hardware devices or may be separate programs that run concurrently on the same computer (this machine being generally referred to as the 'Server').

+ **E-mail**, in which a remote e-mail client communicates with a server to upload (via SMTP) or download (via POP) a user's messages.

+ The **World Wide Web**, in which remote HTML client programs (ie web browsers) make requests for data from web servers, via HTTP. Clients may also transmit data to servers.

Thin and Fat Clients

Modern PCs store and run most applications locally, making use of client software to access data held on a server, for example private data on a file server or public data on a web-server. However, it has not always been this way. Until the 1980s, many network clients were **dumb terminals** with no processing power of their own. They had to rely on mainframe computers to do all the processing (plus storage of data and applications). Network administrators may have benefited from having full control over the environment within which software would run, unlike the situation today where many users within a network may have unusual configurations due to the wide range of hardware from many vendors used in modern networks.

During the 1980s, it became common for a network to have PCs with their own processing capabilities, but due to the cost of hard disks they would store little or no software locally. A PC without a hard disk would download everything including the operating system to RAM from a network server when needed. If the network was busy, this could result in a tedious wait for applications to load. However, it made network management straightforward as any change of applications could be carried out with a single server installation.

This **thin client** approach is still used in large networks where a standardised set of applications are needed and where funds are not available to buy modern hardware. One common use is in education, as schools can reuse old PCs as thin clients that run Linux. Here, a high specification server is bought and all applications are downloaded to the PCs as needed. As these are downloaded from the server, security issues associated with installing software on individual PCs are avoided. It is possible that a high specification server might do all or most of the processing for a number of lower specification clients that may only run a GUI client or even a web browser that acts in a similar way to a dumb terminal (see "*Linux thin clients revitalize student desktops*" at DesktopLinux.com via http://tinyurl.com/2u2akr).

Other examples, such as the C2K network in Northern Irish schools, use a **fat client** model. In these networks, as much software as possible is held on client PCs, and the central server is primarily concerned with managing data storage and Internet traffic. If a standardised set of applications is used, it is possible that installations can be managed centrally: a network administrator chooses a group of PCs (eg from the Art department) and has the same set of applications (for example Microsoft *Office* and Adobe *Photoshop*) installed on them all.

Identical specifications of hardware and software makes overall management and identifying faults within a network much easier than it would be if there were many specifications. It is for this reason that many large organisations using **fat clients** have been reluctant to move from *Windows XP* to *Windows Vista*. Managing a standard configuration of *XP* and *Office 2003* is easier than a combination of *XP* / *Office 2003*, *Vista* / *Office 2003*, *XP* / *Office 2007* and *Vista* / *Office 2007*, plus dealing with older unsupported applications and hardware. In the **thin client** model, the installation of *Office 2007* for all users would be a one-off event done at the server.

Task

Write a report outlining the advantages and disadvantages of fat and thin clients within a small company (5 to 10 employees) and a large company (1000 + employees). Your report should consider both network administrators and users.

Characteristics of Clients and Servers

A client:

+ Initiates requests for data from a server. This may be at the user's request (such as fetching data from a web server) or may be done at set intervals (such as an e-mail client connecting periodically to a POP3 server to download new mail);
+ Waits for the server's response and acts upon it, for example by downloading and displaying data;
+ May connect to several servers simultaneously, for example a web browser communicating with several web servers at once;
+ Hides complexity of data requests from users, by only presenting received data and no details of communication with the server.

A server:

+ Waits for clients to request data;
+ Processes clients' requests for data and serves a reply, either the data or a message explaining why it is not available;
+ May accept connections from many clients simultaneously, for example a web server presenting data to thousands of remote users at once;
+ Does not interact with end users; rather, the client acts as an intermediary.

A typical client-server interaction might take place as follows. A user types a URL into their web browser (client), which communicates with a remote server. The client and server have a brief dialogue, in which the client identifies itself (for example as Mozilla *Firefox*) and states the URL of the data it wants.

If the request is successful, HTML data plus linked images are sent to the client. The images may be on a different server (which the client must communicate with separately). In most cases, the user is only aware of the data they requested being displayed. If however the request is not successful, the server may simply send back a coded message, such as **403** (access forbidden) or **404** (file not found). The client may present the user with a more meaningful message than simply '403', or the server administrator may have set up their own message instead of the default.

20.3 Peer to Peer (P2P) Networks

These networks are made up of nodes that are considered to have equal status, with no central server. Ian Foster and Carl Kesselman describe P2Ps as:

"Internet applications that harness the resources of a large number of autonomous participants. In many cases, these peers form self-organising networks that are layered on top of conventional Internet protocols and have no centralised structure. Inspired by the successes of early P2P systems such as Napster, Gnutella, and SETI@Home, a large and active research community continues to explore the principles, technologies and applications of such applications." (Taken from *The Grid 2: Blueprint for a New Computing Infrastructure*).

Notable applications in the history of the development of P2P include:

Usenet (1980)

A predecessor to web-based Internet forums. Usenet 'groups' were hosted on dedicated servers maintained by ISPs. Users' postings were replicated from their ISP's server to other Usenet servers. Through this global mesh, postings were quickly copied around the world. If a user's local Usenet server became unavailable they could access data via another, ie if a web server fails, that site becomes unavailable to the entire world. While users required a client program to access servers, there was no central server as such. Instead, servers communicated on a peer-to-peer basis. A full P2P system would not have been practical as most users had limited hardware or limited access to hardware resources.

Napster (1999)

Napster is primarily known for being a source of illegal downloads. Originally designed by university student Shawn Fanning for sharing music files, Napster used a central database to record details of MP3 files stored on the PCs of its users. Anyone looking for a particular file could search the database and select which remote user's PC they wanted it from. However, the use of a central server proved to be Napster's undoing, as it provided the US Authorities with a single place through which they could shut down the network. Later file sharing networks, such as Gnutella (2000), are truly peer-to-peer in that they have no central directory but rely on nodes with permanent Internet connections to communicate constantly with each other, to maintain a directory of where files can be found. Users who have a temporary Internet connection make initial contact with one of these 'primary' nodes to access directories. The development of a full P2P approach prevents a closure in the same way as Napster was closed. Importantly, this full P2P approach also prevents any one company from controlling the network or the data on it: while the original Gnutella software is no longer available, the Gnutella protocol has been adopted by a wide number of inter-operable applications, such as *LimeWire* and *iMesh*. In modern file-sharing programs, users' PCs may be connected to a number of remote hosts to download segments of a particular file from each. Although file-sharing is often associated with illegal music distribution, such services do have legitimate purposes, such as the use of *Bit Torrent* as a distribution method for some open source software.

Freenet (1999)

Freenet is a current system which stores multiple copies of content on users' PCs. Users access data via special purpose client software which hides the complexity of the network from them. If any one user goes offline, the data they were hosting is still available via other users. As with the original Napster, Freenet is without censorship and hence users may ignore the laws of the state they live in. However, unlike Napster, Freenet has no central point from which it can be de-activated. *Freenet China* is an adapted version of this open-source project designed to challenge state-censorship in China. See www.freenet.org.

This news story gives more information on using P2P to combat censorship: **By the way...**

"Guerilla Warfare Waged With Code", New York Times, 10 October 2002, http://tinyurl.com/26x8nz

Figure 20.1: A Peer to Peer system in use. *(Adapted from The Grid 2, page 600).*

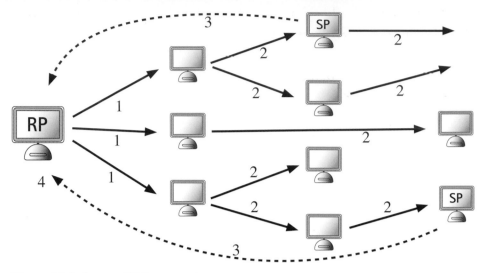

Figure 20.1 shows a P2P system in use:

1. The **Requesting Peer (RP)** sends a request for data to its neighbours.

2. The request for data is flooded through the network and information about suitable peers is returned to the RP.

3. The RP initiates transfer directly from selected peers. The **Serving Peers (SP)** may provide several files. In addition, each SP may provide all of a file, or only part of it. If a file is available from several locations, the RP can choose which to download from.

4. Downloaded files are held on the RP, which can now itself act as a SP of these files for others.

Task

Compare the use of centralised and P2P systems in the following applications:
1. Downloading applications software (from a user's perspective);
2. Legitimately distributing software (from a software developer's perspective);
3. The distribution of illegal material;
4. The distribution of 'free speech' material that may oppose governing authorities.

20.4 Centralised and Distributed Databases

A centralised database is useful to firms based on only one site. A single server holds all data and is accessed via a LAN: as the data is held centrally it is easier to control access to it. A centralised database is also easier to maintain as only one version of the database is kept so the data remains consistent without redundancies. Such a system is less complicated than a distributed database and is less expensive to install.

However, there are a several associated disadvantages of centralised databases:

+ If a single central database fails or is corrupted, data may become inaccessible;

+ Other branches of the firm may connect via a WAN, but if communication lines fail, remote sites will have no access to data;

+ If someone gains unauthorised access to a central server, they will have access to the entire database;

+ Data access may be slow if many users attempt to gain access simultaneously.

Companies operating from several sites may prefer to **replicate** a single database in several sites or to only hold data relevant to a particular site at that location.

Replicating a Master Database

In this scenario, a master database is held in one site and periodically copied to remote sites to be used as a duplicate. Duplicates are **read-only** to ensure that changes made by remote users are enacted on the master database, via communications links. If this was not the case it would be possible for remote users in various sites to make contradictory changes and inconsistencies would arise.

Any changes must be transmitted to the copies in real-time, otherwise the copies will quickly become out of sync with the master. If this method is used in a system with a high volume of transactions, remote systems can become out of sync simply because processing cannot keep pace with the amount of data being transmitted. Inconsistencies are avoided because permission is sought from the master database before a remote site changes data. The remote system locks the record it wishes to change. Hence two sites cannot write to the same record simultaneously.

The advantage of this type of system is that it allows users in remote sites who rarely update data to access it quickly, while still allowing them to make changes if necessary. Any delay required in updating data is transparent (they enter new details, press 'OK' and leave the system to look after itself). A key disadvantage is that in systems that update large volumes of data, a large amount of network traffic is generated and this may lead to delays.

Peer-to-Peer Replication

In this scenario, a complete database is replicated at several sites. As the name suggests, all replicas are considered equals and hold identical data, ie there is no 'master' copy. Changes can be made at any site and changes in one database are transmitted to others. Transmission may be at intervals (called **store and forward**) or in real-time. Store-and-forward can be useful in high-volume applications where several sites do not alter the same records. For example, a supermarket that updates internal stock details with transaction data from cash registers may transmit details of stock to a warehouse each hour. In this case, there is no possibility of another supermarket changing the first supermarket's stock levels at the remote site so inconsistencies are avoided.

The main disadvantage of replication is that data inconsistencies may arise if the same record is modified at the same time at two sites. For this reason record locking (see section 4.1) must be well thought through by designers. Also, replication relies heavily upon external communications links being available: if they are disrupted, work may be halted or the integrity of data compromised. The DBMS must address potential conflicts between sites, specifically:

+ one site accessing and changing a record, while another attempts to delete it;
+ two sites simultaneously making contradictory alterations to a single record;
+ if automatically generated primary keys are used, records created on different sites at the same time may allocate the same primary key to different records.

Distributed Databases

A **distributed** database is split up into two or more files and stored at different locations where they are managed by a local server. Data files are held on the site where they are most relevant and frequently accessed. Processing is carried out locally and so there is no dependence on a single central database. As the data is physically stored close to the anticipated point of use access to the local database is faster, thus the system is more responsive to the needs of local users. All the servers are interconnected making it possible to request data from other locations. In such systems, the distribution of the database is transparent to users who will not be aware that data comes from different places.

For example, a mail order firm may hold stock details in a warehouse and customer details in a call centre. In this example, call centre workers may view customer and stock details simultaneously while confirming an order. It is possible that the user will make a change that affects both sites, such as updating a customer address and also taking an order.

While data redundancy is avoided, users may notice a fractional delay in accessing some data. In the above example, customer details may appear for call-centre operatives as soon as they request them whereas details of products will take slightly longer to appear as the tables holding this information are in a warehouse 500 miles away (though the user may not know this). From the user's perspective, a delay that is present at some times and absent at others, may become confusing and frustrating. Such a dependence on communication lines can be expensive and their failure may prevent access to data at other servers.

Summary

A centralised database is held one site.

+ Data duplication is avoided;
+ Most users access this system via a LAN;
+ Access via a WAN may be slow; hence some distribution may be preferred.

Databases may be replicated via:

+ a replicated master database;
+ a peer-to-peer system;

However, data consistency may be difficult to maintain.

Distributed databases are a single database, held in geographically remote sections.

+ Several sites are linked;
+ Sites are co-dependent on each other;
+ Data is only held once, so conflicts can be avoided.

In any system that relies on a WAN, robust communications links are vital and are usually the responsibility of a telecommunications vendor. Because any distributed database maintains permanently open communications lines, security procedures must be stringent. Even if good auditing practice is employed a large volume of transactions may make tracing and/or repairing unauthorised access difficult and time consuming and it is therefore preferable not to have to do this.

Questions

1. State three features of a client-server network (3)
2. Describe a peer to peer network. (3)
3. Describe the main features of a centralised database. (3)
4. Describe the main features of a distributed database. (4)
5. A database may be held on a single site or on different sites. Describe:
   (a) a method of holding all data in a central location. (3)
   (b) a method of replicating data at several locations. (3)
   (c) a method of holding data at several locations, without replications. (3)

CHAPTER 21
Network Communication

21.1 Introduction

Networked devices have been transforming human communications for over a hundred years. Our world has been transformed by a successive generations of technology: from the telegram to the telephone; from radio to television; early computer networks to the Internet; Personal Computers and laptops equipped with WiFi capability; mobile telephones; the WWW; modern mobile devices. Each of these advancements have transformed the way in which we communicate.

The success of any new device is influenced by existing devices. For example, mobile telephones built on the success of fixed line phones and mobile Internet devices rely on existing wired connections between devices. In some instances, this reliance proves to be a limitation: for example, until fairly recently the maximum speed with which PCs connected to the Internet (56kbaud) was dictated by design decisions made when telephone networks were established a hundred years previously. Even with broadband, many rural areas are affected by decisions made when their area was first reached by telephone services many decades before.

As any new technology must integrate with existing devices, it must often follow existing protocols. For example, the PC used by the author employs a wireless LAN connection. However, this connection relies on TCP/IP, a protocol developed long before the widespread use of wireless technologies. To be successful, wireless LAN had to use TCP/IP – part of a wider family of standards, the **OSI 7–layer model**. When this protocol was defined, it had to be broad enough to cope with likely new requirements. In the same way, HTTP, HTML, POP, ODF, PDF and others represent standards that were written with the need to adapt in mind. With time, these have been broadened to cope with new requirements.

21.2 Bandwidth

Bandwidth is a measurement of the maximum amount of data that can travel along a communication channel in a given time. It is usually measured in bits per second. It is determined by the transmission medium being used and the need to prevent electrical interference. Most homes in the UK have a telephone link that allows access to the Internet. This link has a flexible bandwidth from 56kbits per second through to broadband connections up to several megabits per second.

Figure 21.1 illustrates the difference. High bandwidth lines usually cost more than low bandwidth lines, although the price of domestic broadband is dropping rapidly. Ethernet LANs used in business and education usually have a rate of either 10 or 100Mbits per second. The speeds quoted here are not measurements of the transfer of data alone, as error handling information etc. must also be transmitted.

The table below shows common bandwidth rates.

Name	Bandwidth in bits per second	Typical users
Basic telephone system	56,000	Home Internet
ISDN	128,000	Home Internet, Small business Internet
Broadband	560,000	Home Internet, Small business Internet
E1	2,048,000	Large business Internet
Ethernet	10,000,000	Home LAN, Business LAN
Fast Ethernet	100,000,000	Home LAN, Business LAN
STM1	155,000,000	Communication vendor
STM4	620,000,000	Communication vendor

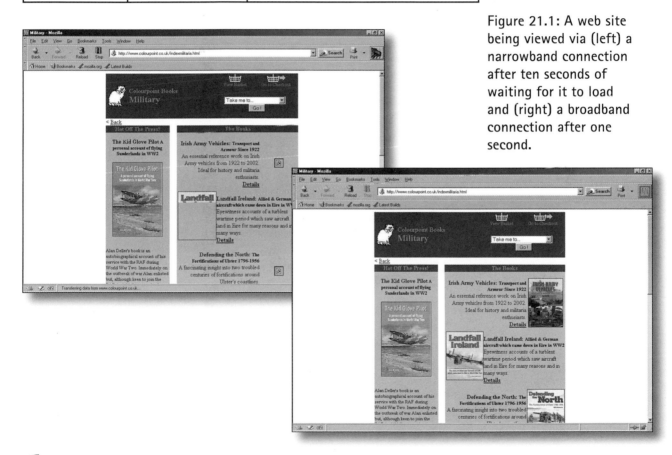

Figure 21.1: A web site being viewed via (left) a narrowband connection after ten seconds of waiting for it to load and (right) a broadband connection after one second.

21.3 Mobile and Wireless Communication

Wireless data transmission has had a major impact on the use of ICT to share data. In particular, the technologies discussed in section 10.10 (Bluetooth, Zigbee, WiFi etc.) have increased the use of portable devices in powerful ways. This was simply not possible ten to fifteen years go.

All of these devices build on technologies that already existed. For example, WiFi networks use a derivative of the Ethernet protocol that was used for wired LANs.

There is no doubt that portability is a huge advantage, but the main disadvantage of any of these transmission methods is that extra steps must be taken to ensure that data remains secure. There is the possibility that any device within range of a radio transmission can intercept it. Also, to run a mobile device requires long life batteries. During the past decade, many advances have been made in this field, but the need for regular recharging has not been removed altogether.

To appreciate the impact of modern wireless technologies, it is worth comparing typical mobile devices over the past few decades:

+ **1980s**: Battery powered transistor radio; portable audio cassette player; carphones with large batteries; mobile televisions with limited battery life.
+ **1990s**: Small FM radios; portable CD players; mobile telephones that clipped to the user's belt; mobile televisions with limited battery life; laptop PCs that can connect to the Internet via a telephone line.
+ **Early 2000s**: Pocket–sized mobile phones with FM radios; portable DVD players; laptop PCs that can connect to the Internet via an inbuilt mobile phone transmitter; MP3 players are commonplace.
+ **Late 2000**s: A single device combining radio, camera, video player, telephone, Internet access and MP3 player. Laptop PCs can be connected to the Internet via WiFi or 3G mobile phone networks by using a USB dongle.

In the above examples, a series of interconnected developments can be observed:

+ The widespread growth of mobile telephone networks, and the new possibilities they offer;
+ The rapid miniaturisation of technology, accompanied by a drop in manufacturing costs;
+ An increased user expectation of what the latest device can offer.

In 1965, Intel founder Gordon Moore predicted that processor speed would double roughly every two years: a statement that has become known as **Moore's Law**. It has held true so far. As such trends continue, it is likely that the possibilities offered by wireless technology will continue to develop.

21.4 The Impact of Modern Network Technologies on Communication

Modern technologies transformed communication in the past century, and have done so again in the past few decades. Compare the world of past eras with the world of today:

Early 19th Century

It was possible to access newspapers, such as London's The Times within major cities, but news could be days old before it was printed as reports depended on traditional postal services. Outside cities, important news may eventually be reported in local weekly papers or by word of mouth. Communication between businesses depended on sending messages by foot or traditional post (which depended on horses and, later, trains). Most people knew little of events outside their locality.

Late 19th Century

The development of the electric telegraph allowed information to be transmitted much more rapidly than previously, and newspapers were thus able to report events more quickly than before. Businesses and private citizens could pay to use this service at a local post office. Telegraph messages were transmitted to a distant post office and were then delivered by local post. The telephone was just becoming available, for those who could afford it.

Early 20th Century

By 1939, radio transmissions by the BBC allowed listeners to hear about events in other parts of the UK and the world on the day they took place. Automated telephone exchanges made it possible to call a person directly by dialing their number, rather than depending on a human operator to connect the call, although operators were still required for international calls. A dependence on copper-based Circuit Switching restricted bandwidth for these services. The forerunners of modern programmable computers were developed in the 1930s/40s.

Mid 20th Century

The 1960's 'space race' and Apollo missions led to many advances in small-scale electronics, which in turn lead to mini- and micro-computers. Millions of people watched live pictures of Neil Armstrong's "one small step". *ARPAnet*, a military research project became the world's first large network based on packet switching. Packet switching (the principle of dividing large pieces of data into small packets that are independently routed around a network) prevents any two devices from requiring exclusive use of a communications channel and is vital to modern communications. Also, serious research into glass fibre as a transmission medium was gathering pace.

Late 20th Century

Launched in 1974, BBC's *Ceefax* allowed people to read news stories on their televisions within minutes of being written. Home computers, such as the *ZX Spectrum* were popular from the 1980s and Computer Studies became a separate subject in schools. Until the 1990s, storms in the Irish Sea routinely prevented newspapers from reaching Northern Ireland from Great Britain during the winter, but from the 1990s modern network communication allowed electronic copies of papers to be transmitted to Belfast for printing. This idea also allows national papers, such as *The Sun*, to have regionalised news and advertising. The 1980's saw the launch of twenty-four hour news channels such as CNN and Sky News, and a growing number of people watched news events live, instead of depending on evening news bulletins or the next morning's newspaper.

Educational research depended on printed books and students were often restricted to what their local library had access to, although widespread use of the WWW started to change this by the late 1990s. Internet access was slow compared to today, relying on fixed-line analogue telephone services offering a speed of 14.4 kbit/s in the late 80s, and 56 kbit/s a decade later. Fibre-optic cables were steadily replacing the core of the telephone network at this stage, in anticipation of widespread demand for high-bandwidth services.

Communication was nevertheless still largely dependant on traditional post and land-line telephones. Many people used payphones on street corners. The first 'mobile' phones became commercially available in the UK in the 1980s and by the late 1990s most people had at least one telephone in their home and a large number had pocket-sized mobile phones that supported voice calls and SMS.

Early 21st Century

Sales of paper newspapers are in decline as more people access news online, including web sites operated by newspapers themselves. Printed newspapers rely more on providing comment and analysis on the basic facts that may be 24 hours old by the time they are printed. Newspapers and web sites compete with a plethora of digital television channels that broadcast throughout the world.

Internet access is now taken for granted in schools, with many in Northern Ireland having a 2 Mbit/s ADSL connection shared among their students. Home users who live close to their exchange may have access to ADSL bandwidth in excess of 5 Mbit/s, and may have a wireless router in their house that allows them to access the Internet from a laptop anywhere in the house. Third-generation mobile phones also support WWW access and are often used as an alternative to fixed-line ADSL. The Internet is also used to access radio and television services. It is taken for granted that most people in the UK have a mobile phone, though many will use it for services other than telephone calls. E-mail has replaced written letters in many instances, due to the speed and reliability of this service. Instant messaging and social networking are also popular communication tools. Traditional telephony remains expensive for international calls and is under threat from Internet-based voice calls (such as *Skype*).

Many office workers now use the Internet to work away from a traditional office environment. For example, employees can carry out administrative work from home while sales representatives can access orders via their company's network without ever going to the office.

21.5 The Open Systems Interconnection (OSI) Seven-Layer Model

The **OSI seven-layer model** provides a solution to the problem of connecting different networks with different protocols. The OSI seven-layer model is important because it provides a framework that all other network protocols must work within. The model was discussed in detail in section 10.7, but a summary is provided here for reference.

The model is based on the concept of **packet switching**, in which large pieces of data are divided into small **packets** for transmission. These packets are then sent separately across the network, being directed on their journey by routers, which determine the optimum path to their destination where they are reassembled into the correct order.

Within the OSI model seven **layers** of header information are added to each packet of data to be transmitted. The sending device adds this information in a particular order and transmits the data. The receiver removes this header information in the reverse order, leaving the original data. As well as the data itself, the seven layers are:

Layer	Description
Application	Represents the services that directly support applications such as software for file transfers, database access, and electronic mail.
Presentation	Manages security by providing services such as encryption, and compresses data so that fewer bits need to be transferred on the network.
Session	Establishes dialogue control between the two computers in a session, regulating which side transmits, when and how long it transmits for.
Transport	Handles error recognition and recovery. It also repackages long messages when necessary into small packets for transmission and, at the receiving end, rebuilds packets into the original message. The receiving Transport layer also sends receipt acknowledgements.
Network	Addresses messages and translates logical addresses and names into physical addresses. It also determines the route from the source to the destination computer and manages traffic problems.
Data Link	Packages raw bits from the Physical layer into frames (logical, structured packets for data). This layer is responsible for transferring frames from one computer to another, without errors. After sending a frame, it waits for an acknowledgement from the receiving computer.
Physical	The actual stream of bits along some physical medium. This layer defines how the cable is attached to the network adapter and what transmission technique is used to send data over the cable.

James Bond meets the OSI 7 layer model [1]

By the way...

Another way of understanding the OSI seven layer model is given in this extract, which describes the encoding and decoding of data.

The OSI model describes the flow of data in a network, from the lowest layer (the physical connections) up to the layer containing the user's applications. Data going to and from the network is passed layer to layer. When a layer receives a packet of information, it checks the destination address, and if its own address is not there, it passes the packet to the next layer.

When two computers communicate on a network, the software at each layer on one computer assumes it is communicating with the same layer on the other computer. For example, the Transport layer of one computer communicates with the Transport layer on the other computer. The Transport layer on the first computer has no regard for how the communication actually passes through the lower layers of the first computer, across the physical media, and then up through the lower layers of the second computer.

James Bond meets Number One on the 7th floor of the spy headquarters building. Number One gives Bond a secret message that must get through to the US Embassy across town.

+ Bond proceeds to the 6th floor where the message is translated into an intermediary language, encrypted and miniaturised.

+ Bond takes the elevator to the 5th floor where Security checks the message to be sure it is all there and puts some checkpoints in the message so his

By the way...

counterpart at the US end can be sure he's got the whole message.

+ On the 4th floor the message is analysed to see if it can be combined with some other small messages that need to go to the US end. Also if the message was very large it might be broken into several small packages so other spies can take it and have it reassembled on the other end.

+ The 3rd floor personnel check the address on the message and determine who the addressee is and advise Bond of the fastest route to the Embassy.

+ On the 2nd floor the message is put into a special courier pouch (packet). It contains the message, the sender and destination ID. It also warns the recipient if other pieces are still coming.

+ Bond proceeds to the 1st floor where Q has prepared the Aston Martin for the trip to the Embassy. Bond departs for the US Embassy with the secret packet in hand.

At the other end the process is reversed. Bond proceeds from floor to floor where the message is decoded. The US Ambassador is very grateful the message got through safely. "Bond, please tell Number One I'll be glad to meet him for dinner tonight".

[1] Reproduced with permission from the original by Dick Lewis
See http://www.lewistech.com/rlewis/Resources/JamesBondOSI2.aspx

21.6 Detecting and Correcting Errors in Transmission

Errors in transmission are normal. They typically happen because of some sort of interference, for example loose or damaged connectors, damaged cables, or electrical 'noise' from other devices. Other transmission problems can occur due to a connection or a transmission node being disabled. Often, hundreds of errors occur invisibly when a user transmits data, but the network protocols can normally correct them without user intervention, unless the error is very severe.

Careful management of transmission media is needed to prevent transmission errors. Special ducting is built into office space to protect cabling from damage. Shielded cables can be used to prevent interference from other devices.

By the way...

Electrical noise – interference from other electrical devices

While it may appear unlikely that two separate devices can interfere with each other, this can actually be a serious problem. Electromagnetic interference can be caused by a number of devices, such as fluorescent lights, motors or even placing a LAN cable too close to a high-voltage power line. If you are not convinced, tune a radio to an AM station and turn on/off the lights – you should hear a 'thumping' noise while the lights are coming on. As an alternative, tune a radio to an AM station and bring it close to a PC.

It is important that computers can easily detect, and if possible correct, errors should they occur. Two strategies can be applied:

+ **Error detecting coding** includes a small amount of redundant data that allows the receiver to deduce if an error has occurred. The receiver will request a re-transmission if this happens.

- **Error correcting coding** involves sending each block of data with a large amount of redundant data that allows the receiver to detect an error and also to deduce what the transmitted data must have been.

The amount of redundant information needed for error correction is significant when compared to the data sent. As it is usually quite easy to re-transmit data, error **detecting** codes are generally used in preference. Error detection uses **parity checking, echoing** and **cyclic redundancy checks**, while error correction uses **block code parity** and **forward error correction**. These are explained below.

Parity Checking

Parity checking is one of the most common methods of checking errors. In each byte, seven bits represent data. The eighth bit (usually the **most significant bit**) becomes the **parity bit**. Once the parity bit is set to odd or even, the data is transmitted. At the receiving end, a check on each byte is performed and if the parity has changed then the receiver knows that an error has occurred.

In **even parity**, the parity bit is set to 1 or 0 in a way that makes the total number of ones per byte even. In the byte 111 0011, the parity bit must be set as 1 to make the number of 1s even. Hence this byte is transmitted as 1111 0011. Therefore in an even parity system, receiving an odd number of 1s in a byte indicates an error. Re-transmission is requested. **Odd parity** follows the same principle, but the byte is set to contain an odd number of ones.

The weakness of this form of parity checking is that two errors in a byte can make it appear uncorrupted. For example, if 1111 0011 is transmitted and 1011 1011 received, the received signal is accepted because it passes a parity check. As an improvement, parity can be applied to several bytes together as a two dimensional array. Consider the following seven bytes (before parity has been applied):

```
110 0111
110 1100
011 1110
101 1001
011 1001
100 1011
100 1001
```

Parity can be applied both horizontally (as before) and vertically, to make a new byte that only contains parity bits. This is known as **block code parity**. In this example an error has occurred, but the erroneous byte can be identified.

Horizontal Parity	Original seven bits	
1	110 0111	
0	110 1000	
1	011 1110	
0	101 1001	
0	011 1001	
0	100 1011	
1	100 1001	
0	101 0111	< Vertical Parity

Parity and block code parity checking are best suited to transmission in which random single bit errors are present. When large bursts of errors are present a more rigorous method of checking must be used.

Echoing

The received data is transmitted back to the sender where it is checked against the original data transmitted. This method is slow and crude. A byte could have been received correctly by the receiver but an error could corrupt it on the way back. The user has no way of knowing how and at what point an error occurred.

Cyclic Redundancy Checks

Cyclic redundancy checks (CRC), or **checksums**, are a more accurate alternative to parity. Transmissions are divided into packets of predetermined length. Each packet has a mathematical calculation applied using an appropriate algorithm. The remainder of this calculation is sent with the data as part of its header information. The receiver recalculates the remainder using the same calculation and compares it to the transmitted remainder. If the numbers do not match, an error is detected and re-transmission requested.

Simple CRC checks are similar to hashing algorithms used in data validation (such as **Modulus 11** check digits - see section 1.6). CRC checks with more complex calculations have been developed to ensure error detection exceeds 99.99999%. This is required because errors that occur when simple CRC methods are used can occasionally appear 'correct' by fluke – as with simple parity checks.

Forward Error Checking

Forward Error Checking (FEC) puts data through a predetermined mathematical algorithm (not unlike CRC). However, FEC also adds extra data to the end of each character or block of code to enable data to be corrected if errors occur in transmission. If an error occurs, this allows the receiving device to (a) detect the error and (b) look at the extra material to see where the error arose. FEC is important in applications where the re-transmission of data is not practical, such as mobile telephony and broadcasting.

Questions

1. Define bandwidth. (2)
2. Describe one benefit of wireless communication. (2)
3. Describe two drawbacks of wireless communication. (4)
4. What is the OSI 7-layer model? (3)
5. State and describe by way of example **two** causes of an error in data transmission. (4)
6. Describe the difference between **error detecting coding** and **error correcting coding**. (2)
7. Describe how parity can be used to detect an error. (4)
8. Identify and describe two further methods of detecting errors. (6)
9. Identify and describe a method of error correction. (4)

CHAPTER 22
Network Security

22.1 Introduction

Organisations and individuals alike rely on computer networks in their daily lives. However, just as there are people who use networks for good purposes, so there are those who misuse technology for their own gain. In this section, you will learn about the various measures employed to ensure that data is only accessible by people who should have access. You will also see how security provides protection against accidental disasters due to human error.

22.2 Network Security Systems

Large companies spend thousands of pounds each year trying to keep data secure. Security can be considered as two broad issues:

+ Preventing unauthorised people from accessing data.
+ Making sure that data is not damaged, either accidentally or deliberately.

No security system is impervious to all attempts to breach it. It is therefore good practice to have many **layers of security**. That is, several security measures which all have to fail simultaneously for data to be compromised. The more layers there are, the less chance there is of them all failing at once. The insurance provided by such a set-up is invaluable.

Examples of the elements that might be included in a layered security system are:

+ User authentication to prevent unauthorised access to data;
+ Network security to protect against hacking and malicious programs, for example worms;
+ Backing up data to provide security in the case of files being damaged.

Access to Data

There are many reasons why users should not have access to all data:

+ Some files should be viewable only by people who require access to them. For example, certain financial data should only be seen by management or by the accounts department, while employees' health records should only be available to their senior manager.
+ Data may not be vital to a person's job. For example, a junior secretary does not normally need the facility to alter files on a company web server.
+ While some data may not be sensitive, it may only be the immediate concern of those people using it. For example, files related to product development may be of interest to many people in a company, but is only the immediate concern of people specifically involved in product development.

- Some employees may not be trusted. New recruits should not have access to high security areas of a network for a considerable time after starting employment. Temporary employees will often not have access to this at all.

Within a file structure, users normally have access to files as a combination of **read, write** and **execute**. Users automatically have **read–write** access to their own files (meaning they can read files and create or modify them), **read only** access to some other files, such as the company intranet, and **execute** access to program files on their PC. They generally have no access to other files. Restrictions placed on users form part of a system known as **AAA**, which stands for Authentication, Authorisation and Accounting:

- **Authentication.** Identifying an individual through information unique to them, such as a username and password, or biometrics.
- **Authorisation.** Granting or denying access to network resources once a user is authenticated. The data and services which a user can access will depend on their authorisation level.
- **Accounting.** Tracking a user's activity while accessing network resources.

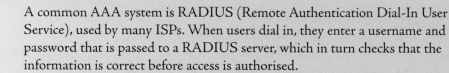

By the way... AAA in practice

A common AAA system is RADIUS (Remote Authentication Dial-In User Service), used by many ISPs. When users dial in, they enter a username and password that is passed to a RADIUS server, which in turn checks that the information is correct before access is authorised.

As part of AAA procedures, the following tools may be employed (as you read this list, ask yourself which 'A' they relate to).

- **Access rights** prevent users from accessing data they do not need to access.
- **Usernames and passwords** form the most visible part of many systems' security.
- **Terminal security** restricts where users can log on. For example, allowing users to log on only within their department's office or even the PC on their desk.
- **Log on restrictions**, such as restricting logons to within working hours only.
- **Terminal locking** and **password-protected screensavers**. If an employee views sensitive data and has to leave their desk, it is desirable that the terminal can be 'locked'. Additionally, should the user forget to do this, a **password-protected screensaver** should activate within a few minutes of inactivity.
- **Firewalls** make a PC or a network appear not to exist to unauthorised users trying to gain access via the Internet. This makes hacking such a system difficult.
- **Encryption** is used to store data as 'cipher text' instead of 'plain text' that cannot be decoded without a password.

Many more means of authenticating and authorising users exist, such as biometric measures, including retina scanning. As can be seen from the stories in the box below, a small fortune spent on high-tech security can be in vain if staff are not trained to spot intruders, secure equipment properly or close windows.

By the way...

The TV show *The Real Hustle* is not completely unrealistic...
Criminal gangs often spend a lot of time researching their target and security weaknesses that surround it. Hence all people within an organisation must be vigilant.

"**Airport theft shocks Australia:** Australian authorities have ordered an urgent review of security at Sydney's international airport after the theft of two mainframe computers from a restricted customs area. It is believed they were taken by two men posing as technicians... The two suspected thieves told guards they were employees of the airport's computer department. They were allowed to enter the customs division mainframe room, which is a high-security zone. The men spent two hours disconnecting the computers, before calmly walking out, pushing the machines on trolleys... The government has insisted that no sensitive information was kept on the computers." BBC News Online, 5 September 2003, via http://tinyurl.com/3v59rq

"**Burglary Leaves Bust Firm in Trouble:** Computers have been stolen from a company which went bust amid a dispute over work carried out on a new £200 million power plant in Northern Ireland, it emerged yesterday. Five hard-drives and back-up files were taken during a break-in at Steamplant's offices at Ballylumford Station near Larne, Co Antrim. Blood stains found at the scene have been examined by police forensics experts in an attempt to identify the thieves..." Belfast News Letter, 23 April 2003.

Task

Discuss what the firms above could have done to avoid data loss, even if a break-in did occur.

Secure Data Transmission in Networked Systems

With increased use of telecommunications it is vital that communications links are secure, and there are a number of techniques for ensuring that data transmissions are secure. (This topic was introduced in Chapter 14, and the reader should refer to section 14.6 for further details on the bullet points below.)

The main techniques are:

+ **Data encryption:** before transmission, data is encoded using an **encryption key** to follow a mathematical algorithm. The receiver uses the same key to decrypt the data. Data is therefore incomprehensible to any device or person who intercepts it.

+ **Callback systems:** users access a company network from home and are automatically called back on their registered phone number before accessing secure data. Calls from anywhere else are therefore unsuccessful.

+ **Firewalls:** filters traffic going into and out of a network to prevent unauthorised inbound or outbound data due to hackers, viruses or other breaches in security.

+ **Restricting the programs** that users can run on their computers to reduce the opportunities for viruses, trojan horses and worms to harm data security.

Another way in which businesses can maximise the security of their transmissions is to use a **secure / dedicated communication line.** This is a permanent telephone connection between two geographically separated points. It is supplied by a telecommunications provider. A business will pay a fixed monthly fee for the service. As the connection does not carry any other communications, the business can assume a level of quality and security.

22.3 Accounting and Auditing

As it is impossible to remove security threats completely, it is good practice to record all transactions within a system so that security breaches can be clearly analysed. The record that develops can be used to investigate a single incident, such as reversing a user's mistake. Accounting software (see section 19.2) records each event within a system and can also be used for auditing purposes. Do not confuse it with financial software, which is entirely different.

When a user accesses or transmits data, the accounting software logs this. It is also possible to log everything users do in terms of files accessed or created, or even their keystrokes. Indeed, some systems not only save the data the user sees on-screen, but also the steps used to create that file. This means that if somebody creates a file, and then a second person edits it in a poor manner, it is a simple matter to restore the file to its original form by 'rewinding' the changes as recorded by the accounting software.

This example may seem trivial, because it is possible (although time-consuming) to repair the file by hand. However accounting software has many useful applications in areas where this would be simply impossible:

+ If a hacker enters a system, everything they do, including their IP address, is logged. As well as locating the hacker, everything the hacker did can also be reversed;

+ If an unscrupulous person damages data, they can be apprehended since the log files show what they did and when it was done. By reversing the changes, the original data is retrieved;

+ If an employee surfs the web or accesses Internet chat during working hours, a record of their activities makes it difficult for them to say they were working at that time. This also acts as a deterrent against time wasting;

+ If errors lead to data inconsistencies (for example, if record locking fails), it is possible to see what changes were made, when they were made and who made them. Administrators can take the system offline and correct the data.

Audit Trails

Auditing is the process of monitoring usage statistics and user habits. It may be done for performance reasons (for example a group of files that are found to be accessed frequently may be moved to a dedicated server or applications seen to be unused can be removed), or it may be done to monitor undesirable practices.

> An **audit trail** is a record of events carried out by a computer system and is generated by accounting software. It allows an action to be traced through all stages of processing beginning when data is input to information is output.
>
> **Definition**

Within an ICT system, five types of information are stored in an audit trail:

+ The **software that was used**. This will allow usage of the software to be monitored, enabling network managers to assess the popularity of software and to ensure licence agreements are being obeyed;

+ The **time** when a user has logged on and logged off, and on **what** terminal, along with unsuccessful logons. This will alert the manager to attempts by hackers to gain unauthorised access while allowing the activities of authorised users to be monitored;

+ **Files that have been opened**. This will help detect unauthorised access to data files on the network;

+ **How many read-write operations** were performed, whether by a user or on a particular file. This will help detect unauthorised access to a file;

+ **How often a server is accessed**, whether by a user or a group of users. This will allow usage of the server to be monitored.

An audit trail is needed:

+ **To meet formal or legal audit requirements**. An external audit may be performed to assess whether or not an organisation's systems are maintaining the accuracy of records and complying with legislation. Public companies have to be able to give account of all money and business carried out in order to prevent fraud. As part of this, all business documents, including e-mail, must be recorded for six years.

+ **For billing purposes**. In commercial systems that calculate charges based on the resources customers use, such as the number of files accessed or quantity of data downloaded, accounting and auditing are used within the billing process. In a business audit trails could be used to bill departments for the number of pages printed or time spent on the Internet.

+ **For maintenance reasons** so that network's resources and performance can be monitored. For example, Database Managers may notice that a system slows considerably at certain times and an audit trail allows this to be investigated: perhaps many departments all access the same area of the system at the same time. Informed decisions can be taken concerning equipment upgrades or asking some departments to change their schedule.

+ **For security reasons**. As an audit trail will produce an automatic record of any transactions it is possible to trace and recover deleted data. Making employees aware of auditing can both deter malpractice and allow administrators to trace when something does go wrong.

Amoeba Antiques

Paranoia or genuine problems?

Some users and businesses consider security and auditing to be paranoia, or that security firms are 'hyping up' threats to make money. Consider the experience of Billy, Amoeba's recently re-located security manager and his assistant, Linda.

Billy: "A team is responsible for creating and implementing a company-wide security policy that must evolve over time. The threats we face change rapidly – for example a few years ago we were rarely threatened by hackers but now, through worms that spread automatically, any server connected to the Internet is under threat 24 hours a day. These worms are often used by spammers, so a LAN can be turned into a little factory constantly spewing out adverts for all sorts of bizarre products if security is not taken seriously.

"Recently, I alerted a local firm to the fact that every day at 9.25am I received an e-mail-borne virus that traced to one of their IP addresses. The virus randomly sent out customer data. Another recent experience involved a local garage that could not give me a receipt for a tyre because their servers were off-line due to infection. In many such cases, a little training could sort these problems out.

"We record everything our employees do. While this might sound like snooping, we haven't time to actually read the log files. Logging all keystrokes within databases, recording Internet traffic and backing up PC data has benefits – employees gain confidence through knowing that if they do mess up they can be bailed out. Also, knowing that logging exists means employees try to avoid the easy trap of spending all day web-surfing. Of course we don't get annoyed if someone sells some old CDs on eBay or takes a few minutes to check the news – as long as they don't get carried away. Some companies have recently disciplined workers for accessing 'adult' material – we don't want to have to do that, but we can take action if necessary. Also, many porn sites are known to install spyware and hence compromise security. If any employee is looking at unsuitable material their line-manager can be asked to talk sensitively to them and the problem usually goes away. We prefer employees to be educated and sensible, rather than seeing their colleagues sacked, which can damage morale."

Linda: "The use of auditing has other important cost-saving benefits. There are four types of audit trail. In the past few months we have found each to be useful. For example:

+ **An audit of software used**, and the frequency of its use told us we were paying for site-wide licenses for software only a few people regularly use (though a lot of people complain it is 'important' any time we suggested getting rid of it). We have since reduced the scope of the license, and saved money.

+ **A record of files that are often accessed** is important in several ways. If a file changes regularly through the day we have to ensure it is included in transaction logs, just in case of disaster between nightly backups. Also, if a file is accessed too much it may be that some software is not behaving properly, and should be investigated. Within one area of the company it became apparent that a certain group of files were regularly accessed by the same people. In this case we moved those files to a dedicated server, to improve performance for all concerned.

+ **A record of read-write operations** allows hardware performance to be evaluated. If a database creates several records per minute, as in the case of on-line sales, customers may notice delays if hardware is not good enough. In this case hardware can be upgraded to avoid delays.

+ **A record of the number of times a server has been accessed** has implications for hardware and software. If a particular group make heavy use of a server, they may require a server dedicated to their project. On the other hand, if a user appears to access a server too much, their PC may be malfunctioning. This is how we discovered that a particular user's PC was infected with spyware – because it was in constant contact with our mail server, attempting to send data out of the company.

"Backups are also vital. During the 'Troubles' we lost access to one building. Data was safe, as backup tapes were in a bomb-proof safe as well as being copied to our Scottish offices. Business re-commenced in rented accommodation and customers were not affected.

"Most weeks, at least one user realises that they need access to an old version of a file, such as a programmer who notices problems and wants to reverse some work. In this case, a back-up can be used to **restore** their file. Having such a backup encourages people to work with confidence and risk mistakes, safe in the knowledge that mistakes can be undone.

While a lot of back-up procedures may seem like wasted effort for 99% of their existence, it is the 1% that justifies their entire use. A single unfortunate event could cripple this business, so investing heavily 'just in case' is well worth the money and effort."

Questions

1. Describe the meaning of "layers of security". (3)
2. State three ways in which a user may have access to a file. (3)
3. What is AAA? (6)
4. Describe 'encryption'. (3)
5. Apart from encryption, describe two methods for ensuring that data transmission over a wide area network is secure. (6)
6. State four types of auditing. (4)
7. Describe three reasons for making use of audit trails. (6)

CHAPTER 23
Approaches to Software Development

23.1 Introduction

Chapter 15 introduced the idea of a step-by-step approach to software development. This section builds on that material by looking in more detail at the two main models of software development.

A **system** is any set of items joined together to carry out a specific task, such as the respiratory system in biology. In a similar way, every ICT system has a number of components that work together to perform a task or series of tasks. ICT systems usually have a mixture of hardware, software and human elements. These ICT systems are the result of a logical and well thought-through development process. This process must be fully understood as much of it directly relates to A-level coursework.

There are many approaches to software development, and each has its own strengths and weaknesses. The traditional **waterfall model** approach has its roots in industrial engineering and heavily emphasises clarifying requirements precisely before any development is undertaken. Once development starts, it is carried through to the end, and the only indication a customer may have that their requirements have been misunderstood is when they see the final system.

However, this can be impractical because customers may not always know what they want. While the waterfall model is now well established, alternatives such as **prototyping** and **Rapid Application Development (RAD)** place greater emphasis on ongoing communication with the end user through quickly building working models of the system that may be discarded. These have only become available recently because the hardware and software needed to quickly build systems did not exist.

23.2 The Waterfall Model

The waterfall model (introduced in Chapter 15) exists because, until fairly recently, the tools that allow for the rapid development of software were not available. Thanks to time and budget constraints, it was not practical to develop a partial system that would later be discarded. Instead, the analysis and design had to be correct before any software development could commence.

The waterfall model defines seven stages in software development. Each stage must be completed before the next step is considered:

1. Analysis
2. Design
3. Software development
4. Testing
5. Implementation

6. Review

7. Maintenance

At the end of each stage, an item called a **deliverable** is produced, for example the specification requirements, design documents, program code or finished database application and test plan. This deliverable must be reviewed and **signed off** by all concerned parties before approval can be given to proceed to the next stage. The arrows in figure 23.1 show the flow of development; when one stage is finished the next is commenced. A previous step may be revisited or restarted if serious weaknesses or problems are discovered. The objectives of each stage are shown. The concerned parties usually include the end users, management and developers, as well as other experts such as database administration personnel. This sequence continues until the review stage has been completed and the finished system is delivered to the end users.

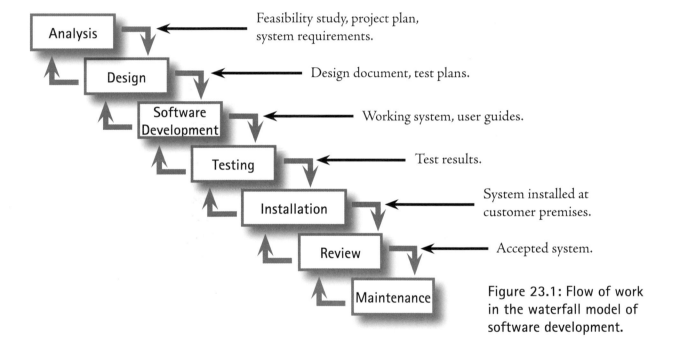

Figure 23.1: Flow of work in the waterfall model of software development.

In the waterfall model, the **end user** has very little say in the critical development (or coding) process. This is carried out by technical specialists such as systems analysts and programmers. The end user is involved:

+ **In the analysis stage**. Through fact-finding, they can establish the requirements specification. For example the end user could be interviewed, observed or fill out a questionnaire;
+ **In acceptance testing**. They will have the opportunity to test the completed system and provide feedback to the analyst;
+ **In the review stage**. They are presented with the finished system at the end of the development cycle. At this stage it is generally too late or costly to make changes if the system is not quite what was originally requested.

Therefore, it is extremely important that the system requirements are very clearly specified and understood by all parties before being signed off. This is very difficult at such an early stage as users often do not know exactly what they want. Consequently, this is one of the drawbacks of the waterfall model. This model only performs well for projects with system requirements that are clearly understood prior to development, or where an existing system is to be developed for some reason such as migration to new hardware or a new operating system.

The waterfall model is suited to projects which have a high risk in terms of budget and schedule over runs, as the project can be controlled and monitored using the staged approach of the waterfall model. This is because the waterfall model does not allow for an exponentially expanding feature set because the customer keeps thinking of features they want: rather, the feature set is established early on in the process and cannot be drastically changed.

Although it has been used extensively over the years in the production of many quality systems, the waterfall model is not without its problems.

Advantages of the waterfall model include:

+ It is universally understood within the ICT industry because it is still taught as the standard model of software development.
+ It ensures that the system requirements are in place before design begins.
+ It discourages developers from prematurely jumping ahead in a project, as each stage must be signed off by management before the next is undertaken.

Disadvantages of the waterfall model include:

+ End users must be able to describe their requirements clearly, completely and correctly. Likewise, the systems analyst and developer must interpret these requirements correctly. However, users frequently have difficulty in explaining their objectives at the start of the proposed system since they do not know what is possible and cannot visualise how the final system will work. This can result in a system which does not match their requirements. The splitting of the project into distinct stages makes it difficult to respond to changing end user requirements.
+ The role of the end user is limited. They cannot see a working version of the system until late in the process. As a result, valuable user feedback is concentrated at the end when the application is tested and delivered.
+ The lifecycle can take so long that the original requirements may no longer be valid by the time the system is implemented. Too much emphasis can be placed on producing documentation for each stage and delays can occur in the design, coding and testing.
+ Developers using this model may not always go back to a previous stage and address weaknesses. This may result in a specification that does not include new requirements uncovered at the design stage, or a design document that does not describe all of the developed system because the need for new features was determined at the development stage.

23.3 The Prototype Model

Drawing up analysis and design documentation is very time consuming. Time can be saved with the development of tools that can be used to quickly create a prototype or even build a system from the requirements specification. It is possible for development to follow a more exploratory route where potential solutions are quickly built and evaluated. The **prototype model** (introduced in section 15.14) addresses the common problem of customers not knowing all requirements at the beginning of a project. They often know high level requirements, but cannot specify them in the detail required to make a successful system. They are often unaware of the technical capabilities of a hardware/software system and needlessly sacrifice functionality as a result. The prototype model provides a development approach that produces a quality system without having to identify all requirements in advance.

An important reason for undertaking any software project is that the current situation is not acceptable. However, it may not be easy to determine what is wanted instead. Prototypes can be developed quickly using special purpose development tools. These working models may be inefficient or incomplete for a variety of reasons, for example lacking certain functionality, speed or robustness. These inefficiencies are acceptable at this stage, as a prototype exists to give users an impression of what the future system will offer, before large investments of time and money are made. Depending on the scale of the project, a prototype may evolve into the final system (**evolutionary prototyping**) or may exist purely to help determine the requirements, before a more formal approach like the waterfall model is used to develop a working system (**throwaway prototyping**).

Figure 23.2 (overleaf) shows a diagram of the processes involved in the prototype model. Each of the phases is briefly described below:

A **prototype** is a working model that serves as a basis for future development. It allows the customer to determine if their requirements have been fully understood and the proposed system serves their needs.

Definition

Requirements Capture

As with the waterfall model, the analyst and customer meet to discuss the system's requirements. The end user will identify the requirements which will lead to the production of a specification by the systems analyst. This stage is very similar to the analysis phase of the waterfall model, with the notable exception that a less detailed statement of requirements is produced. The customer considers this analysis and a decision is made to either proceed with the creation of a prototype, scale down the project or abandon it altogether.

Figure 23.2: Flow of work
in the prototype model of
software development.

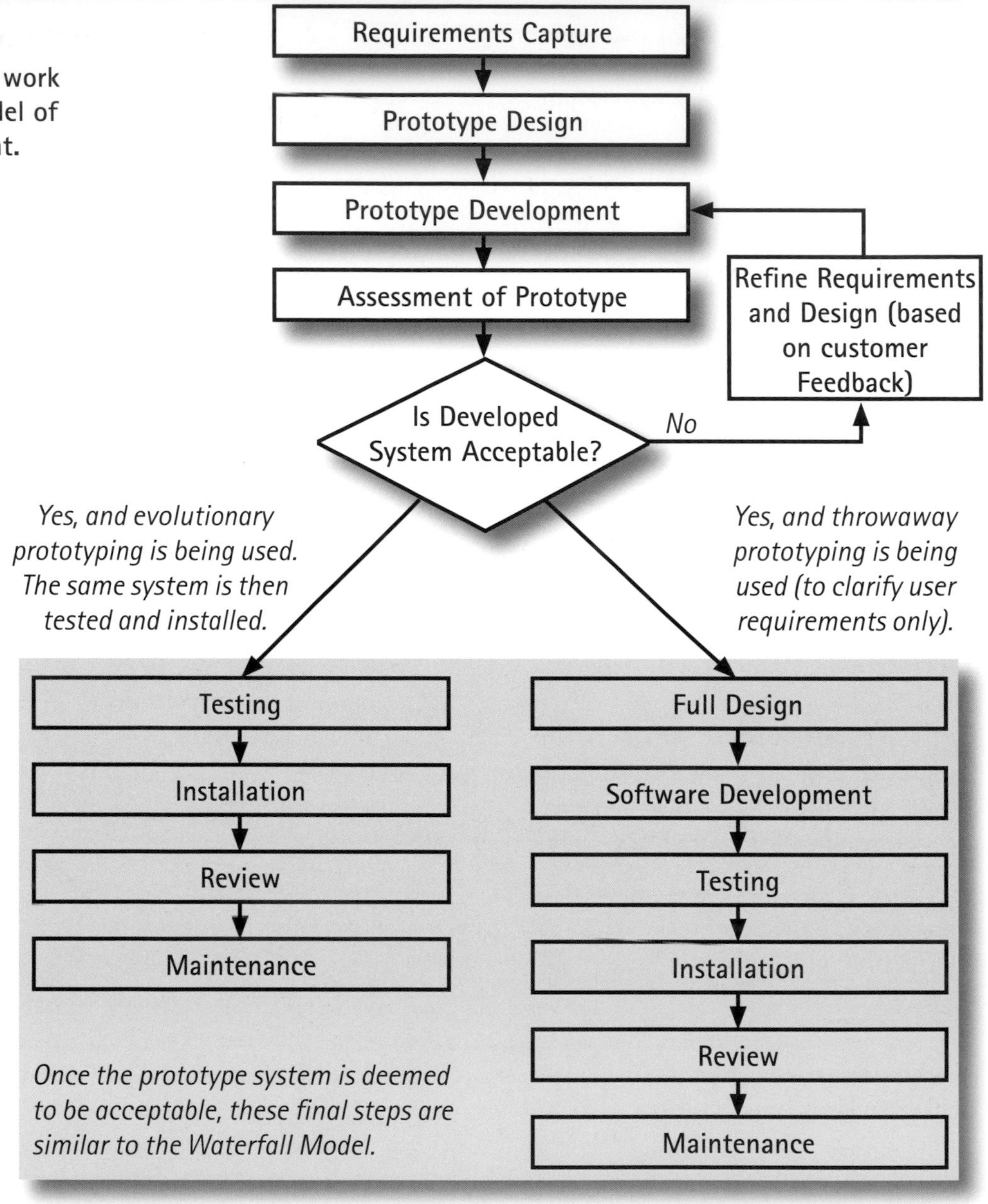

```
Requirements Capture
        ↓
Prototype Design
        ↓
Prototype Development  ←────────────┐
        ↓                            │
Assessment of Prototype    Refine Requirements
        ↓                   and Design (based
                              on customer
                               Feedback)
   Is Developed      No
  System Acceptable? ──────────┘
```

Yes, and evolutionary prototyping is being used. The same system is then tested and installed.

Yes, and throwaway prototyping is being used (to clarify user requirements only).

Testing	Full Design
Installation	Software Development
Review	Testing
Maintenance	Installation
	Review
	Maintenance

Once the prototype system is deemed to be acceptable, these final steps are similar to the Waterfall Model.

Prototype Design

The analyst uses these high level requirements to design a prototype. If several solutions have been suggested within the analysis stage, a prototype of each may be developed and the best solution chosen. This decision may depend upon:

+ Usability;
+ Suitability;
+ Presence of any existing systems;
+ Maintainability of the solution and cost.

The design commences once a way forward has been decided. Often, the user interface is developed as fully as possible with the internal workings only partially designed because the designer is still not entirely certain what form these will take. The interface may have menus that simply state their purpose instead of having live features (figure 23.3). This allows the depth of understanding of the problem to be gauged.

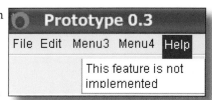

Figure 23.3: An incomplete interface.

The design document must be structured, detailed and meet all **known** requirements. No formal testing plans are created, as the prototype is used only to demonstrate an understanding of requirements. The outcome of this stage is a document that details how the prototype will work.

Prototype Development

The system analyst is responsible for working with the development team to build a prototype as specified by the design. This may take the form of paper representations (such as screen layouts) or the creation of a working model of the system that is focused on defining what interfaces will look like, and has little or no internal processing. CASE (computer-aided software engineering) tools are available for building such prototypes quickly.

Assessment / Further Requirements Capture

The systems analyst presents the prototype to the customer for consideration. With this tangible prototype, a meaningful demonstration of requirements can be shown and the customer can get a feel for how the system will operate. Feedback in the form of comments and suggestions are collected from the customer in order to further develop or refine the system requirements.

Prototype Refinement

The analyst digests the feedback and extra requirements from the customer, and the prototype design is modified to take these into account. The developer revises the prototype to reflect these suggestions. With prototyping, the user is continually involved so that changes can be made at every stage of development. The result is a better product which meets the end user's needs.

Full Design

The customer assessment and prototype refinement stages are repeated until the analyst and customer are sure that all system requirements have been accounted for. The final system is then designed. Formal testing and implementation strategies are also considered.

Development

In many scenarios, completely redeveloping the system is preferred over evolving the prototype. This is because a prototype is, by its very nature, a more makeshift product, and may be unstable in a high demand environment. Therefore, a new system is built from a complete design in a manner similar to the waterfall model.

Summary of the Prototype Model

Once a design is established, the prototype model proceeds in a fashion similar to the waterfall model. Therefore, the key difference is how the design is produced. The prototype model addresses a potential weakness in how the waterfall model gathers requirements by acknowledging that the customer may not know from the outset what they want. However, the prototype model also has disadvantages, especially if it is used without reference to traditional development methods.

The advantages of prototyping are:

+ A system can be refined to meet the user's exact needs because of their direct involvement. Misunderstandings between developers and the customer can be identified and solved.

+ No formal specification is required as the system can be built from very general user needs. The prototyping model addresses the common problem of end users not knowing all requirements at the beginning of the project.

+ It can reduce development time and cost. Misunderstandings, incomplete or inconsistent user requirements will be detected early on through end user feedback and can be completed or corrected. Changes cost more to implement if they are detected later in development.

+ A prototype version will be available quickly to demonstrate the feasibility and usefulness of the proposed system to management.

+ The prototype can sometimes be used for user training before the final version is delivered.

The disadvantages of prototyping are:

Note: these primarily apply to **evolutionary** prototypes, where the initial prototype has been gradually modified until the user is satisfied their requirements have been met. There are few significant disadvantages of using a prototype as an enhanced version of the waterfall model, when compared to the traditional waterfall model.

+ The performance of the resulting system is worse, because it has been modified many times and may retain redundant components.

+ The design is of less quality, because it may include hastily conceived 'workarounds' to problems that existed in old versions of the system which are no longer present.

+ The resulting system is harder to maintain because of the above inefficiencies.

+ The prototyping approach requires more experienced team members, to avoid a final system that contains many inefficiencies.

23.4 Rapid Application Development (RAD)

One major drawback with both the waterfall and the prototype model is the length of time it takes to move from initial consultation to finished product. It is normal for many commercial projects to overrun their anticipated time scale considerably. However, rather than deciding on requirements and worrying about deadlines later, Rapid Application Development (RAD) enforces a strict time scale that cannot be overrun. Requirements are prioritised so that some are simply not implemented if time runs out. Therefore, customers must determine which requirements are vital, and which are desirable add-ons that can be sacrificed if necessary. For this to happen, customers are heavily involved in the early stages of RAD.

There are four phases in RAD:

+ Requirements planning;
+ User design;

- Construction;
- Cutover.

Requirements planning takes place in a **Joint Requirements Planning** (**JRP**) workshop. Analysts and end users work together to prioritise requirements. A triage process is followed to establish a list of priorities. It is not unlike the **triage** process in a hospital emergency unit, where patients requiring immediate treatment and those who are able to wait are identified. The design is then considered in advance of the **user design** stage.

User design involves two **Joint Application Design** (**JAD**) workshops, with developers and users working together. After the first workshop a prototype is developed for use in the second workshop. In the second workshop, users experiment with the prototype and give feedback. It is here that the design is finalised.

Construction is carried out by a **Skilled With Advanced Tools** (SWAT) team, which comprises around four highly skilled developers. As time is crucial, they reuse previously developed software components wherever possible. A SWAT team works closely with end users in developing a series of evolutionary prototypes within a fixed time scale they have decided upon. This is unlike other software development models, where the time scale is imposed by somebody else. CASE tools may also be used (see section 24.7) to quickly generate software from stated requirements.

Cutover encompasses final testing, user training and installation. This may follow a similar routine as the waterfall model, of systematically testing every component and requirement.

The continual dialogue with the user makes RAD suitable for small bespoke projects. However, it may be unsuitable for large projects such as developing office applications or operating systems. In traditional software development models, time scales are imposed on developers by outside agencies, eg salesmen making promises without understanding the pressures and market forces that affect developers. Allowing SWAT developers and end users to decide the time scale together gives both parties an understanding of how the other works. Developers will appreciate that a firm deadline is an important motivator, while users will

By the way...

FOLDOC ("free online dictionary of computing") states: RAD

"A loose term for any software lifecycle designed to give faster development and better results and to take maximum advantage of recent advances in development software.

RAD is associated with a wide range of approaches to software development: from hacking away in a GUI builder with little in the way of analysis and design to complete methodologies expanding on an information engineering framework.

Some of the current RAD techniques are: CASE tools, iterative lifecycles, prototyping, workshops, SWAT teams, timebox development, and re-use of applications, templates and code."

appreciate that it takes time to develop quality software. Also, the high degree of communication with the end user ensures misunderstandings are identified quickly and time is not wasted on developing unnecessary functionality.

Traditional software development models suffer from a weakness in estimating time scales. The time consuming process of establishing requirements and a design can mean that by the time that development begins in earnest, a significant overrun is inevitable. Also, both the waterfall and prototype models are orientated towards **Third Generation Languages** (3GL) such as C or Java, which require developers to spend lots of time typing commands. RAD tools, such as *Visual Basic* or *Delphi*, have many inbuilt 'building blocks' that allow users to quickly construct standard components, eg an interface generator. A major benefit of this is that the commands to make a button that could take an hour to type can be generated in a few minutes through **dragging-and-dropping**, and setting some values to indicate the button's function.

As standard building blocks are already tried and tested, many issues of prototyping are avoided. Also, if a pre-existing component (X) has a similar functionality to one that is desired (Y), X can be easily adapted, rather than writing Y from scratch. However, in some instances it may be desirable to rebuild the system via a 3GL route, for example to improve speed of response.

By the way...

3GL vs RAD

Third Generation Languages are used extensively in the software industry and are studied on university computing courses. They are similar to **Structured Query Language (SQL)**, as used in database packages, as one option for developing queries. **Query By Example (QBE)**, also used in databases, is much quicker to use and allows rapid development. From the developer's perspective, everything done in QBE is invisibly translated to SQL, but is much quicker to use. Syntax errors associated with 3GL, such as putting a comma in the wrong place, are avoided. There is very little that SQL can do that QBE cannot, hence the development of RAD environments has had a transforming effect on large parts of the software development industry.

3GLs are still taught, as there are a number of specialist applications for which RAD is unsuitable. Also, 3GLs give a good background to understanding how RAD works.

Below: SQL commands for a typical database query and the QBE interface for the same query (known as **Design View** in Microsoft *Access*). Most developers would likely find the latter quicker to use. Millions of lines of text commands, with a similar appearance to SQL, form most modern applications, hence the need for thorough testing, as errors can easily creep in. The use of RAD reduces the likelihood of typographical errors or carelessness affecting performance.

```
SELECT Tbl_Contacts.ContactNo, Tbl_Contacts.ContactName,
Tbl_Contacts.TotalPaid, Tbl_students.sname FROM Tbl_Contacts
INNER JOIN Tbl_students ON Tbl_Contacts.ContactNo =
Tbl_students.[Pupil No] WHERE (((Tbl_Contacts.TotalPaid)<375));
```

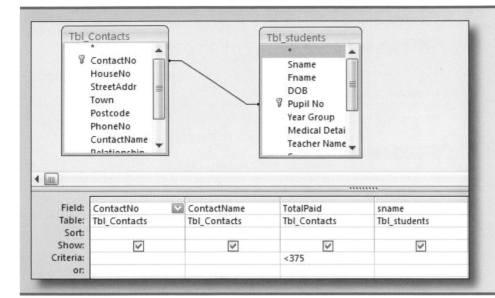

Field:	ContactNo	ContactName	TotalPaid	sname
Table:	Tbl_Contacts	Tbl_Contacts	Tbl_Contacts	Tbl_students
Sort:				
Show:	☑	☑	☑	☑
Criteria:			<375	
or:				

Time scales: a real life example

By the way...

Within the ICT industry it is perfectly normal for companies to contract several providers to develop hardware when they outsource development. For example, a telecommunications company that needs to develop new exchange equipment might approach two or three firms (such as *Nortel*, *Alcatel* or *Fujitsu*) to provide for those needs. In such a race, the competing firms are guaranteed a portion of the UK market, with the larger portion going to whoever is first to deliver reliable equipment that meets requirements. They have an incentive to work quickly and to meet deadlines. This also gives the customer protection from the drawbacks of outsourcing that are often associated with public sector contracts which rely on a single contractor, namely delays and spiralling costs. But note that this approach is not suitable for all ICT projects.

Questions

1. What is a system? (2)
2. State four main stages of the waterfall model. (4)
3. Describe the waterfall model approach to the software lifecycle. (4)
4. Describe the prototyping approach to the software lifecycle. (4)
5. Describe why prototyping may be chosen over the waterfall model. (3)
6. Compare the role of each of the following in the waterfall model, prototyping and rapid application development:
   i.   The end user (3)
   ii. The client (3)
   iii. The ICT specialist. (3)

CHAPTER 24
The Software Development Process

24.1 Introduction

In the previous chapter, three different methodologies for software development were considered: the **waterfall model**, **prototyping** and **Rapid Application Development**. In this chapter, the features common to all are discussed. Regardless of the development method used, some sort of analysis is needed so that the customer's requirements can be established. Regardless of the methodology, some sort of design is also needed so that programmers know what they are to do. Likewise, programmers must always document the processes that they have followed so that maintenance can be undertaken by others at a later stage.

Any large project is carried out by a team of people working together. It is the role of project managers to ensure that different areas of the problem are matched to the team members with the skills best suited to those areas. Project managers must also ensure that team members communicate effectively and develop software components that will work together. In many cases, **Computer Aided Software Engineering (CASE)** tools are used to partially automate this process.

Before software can run it must first be **installed**, ie copied to a PC's hard disk and prepared for use by setting various options such as locality and user preferences. For ICT administrators, installation can present a challenging task as a typical company may have several hundred PCs, most of which have to be set up identically and upgraded in a controlled fashion despite many different hardware configurations.

When any software package is introduced to replace something else, a number of **changeover methods** must be considered. The old package may be discontinued on one day and the new package brought in on the next, or there may be a gradual phasing in. Ongoing maintenance is not the only consideration of ICT management in protecting an effective system. There are the costs of acquiring software and ensuring technical support is available from vendors, but there are also ongoing costs related to maintaining hardware and training personnel.

24.2 The Purpose of Analysis and Design

After reading the previous chapter, you may be asking what the purpose of analysis and design is. While the waterfall model presents a formal, methodical approach to development, you may have the impression that prototyping and RAD allow developers to immediately start building a system which can be tinkered with until the customer is happy. The reality, however, is very far from this.

Early in the development of computer systems, problems were often simple enough for engineers to 'hack together' a solution. Only very small problems may be solved in that way today. As soon as computers started to be applied to increasingly large and difficult problems, 'hacking together' a solution became infeasible. As you may have already discovered in your coursework, once a database contains more than a few tables it is easy to forget where data is stored. Things get even more confusing once a few complex queries exist. Therefore, any development process is simplified if those involved take time to properly document their work. Although A-Level coursework is designed to give individual students experience of all parts of the development process, most projects are carried out by a team who must communicate effectively.

Here is an analogy: in a simple DIY project, such as putting up shelves or even building a small wall, very little is needed in terms of a formal design. However, nobody would dream of building a house without architectural plans, a timetable, details of building contractors etc. Some modern software projects have been compared to civil engineering projects on the same scale as the Channel Tunnel, in terms of their technical complexity and the large number of people who must be co-ordinated. In these circumstances, 'hacking together' a solution is not viable.

24.3 Analysis

Whether it is the waterfall model's approach of interviews, surveys etc, or the RAD approach of a more open dialogue, it is vital at some point to find out exactly what the customer wants. In any approach, an experienced **systems analyst** must talk openly and honestly to the prospective customer about that they want and what can actually be achieved. A systems analyst should have experience of the entire software development process, so that they do not make promises that developers will be unable to keep. While it may be tempting to convince customers to agree to things they don't need, systems analysts have an ethical duty to honestly report their findings, even if this means that the customer invests in a less expensive product.

Based on their experience, a systems analyst may quickly develop a feel for a new customer's situation, avoiding the temptation to cut corners by treating a project as if it were identical to a previous one. Regardless of the method used, the analysis must clearly establish what the user wants and needs. Whether this results in nothing but a written statement of requirements or a model of a system, the need to carefully consider the customer's current position is still present.

As analysts may not always be responsible for creating the design, it is vital that their work must cover **all** of the customer's requirements. Otherwise, the final system will not be what the customer wants.

The Requirements Specification

This is a clear listing of everything the customer wants in the final system. Typically, requirements will be numbered to form a 'check list' to be used in future testing and to aid traceability in the development process. The requirements specification is produced during the **analysis** stage and should include:

+ All aspects of the customer's current system;
+ All proposed functionality in the customer's new system;
+ What functionality is being carried over from the old system and what is new;
+ What functionality is vital, and what functionality can be deferred in the event of time or financial constraints;
+ Any processes that will be needed to import data from the old system.

As the requirements specification forms the starting point for the next phase in development (the **design**), it must be very precise. It must also be clearly understandable and presented in a way that is appropriate for its readers. For this reason, it may be necessary to present the requirements in several formats, for example a highly descriptive technical document for designers and a higher level, non-technical format for management.

Requirements should be:

+ **Correct**, ie thoroughly verified against the customer's actual requirements.
+ **Unambiguous**, to both its authors and its readers. Confusing language, slang or wording that is difficult to translate into other languages should be avoided. Terms should also be used consistently; for example if the term 'implementation' is first used in reference to the process of developing software, the same term should not be later used to refer to installation.
+ **Complete**. All matters relating to functionality, performance, constraints etc should be clearly documented. If any matters are unclear, the point in time at which they will be clarified should be stated.
+ **Consistent**. Requirements should not conflict with each other.
+ **Ranked**. Developers should know if requirements are 'essential', 'worthwhile' or 'optional'. In the event of conflicting requirements, unforeseen delays or financial constraints, it may be necessary to sacrifice optional components or omit them until the maintenance phase.
+ **Verifiable**. It should be possible to determine whether or not all requirements have been met, for example the requirement *"The output of queries X, Y and Z should be less than two seconds in 90% of cases"* has a clear yes/no answer. However, *"The system should be user friendly"* or *"There should be few delays"* are vague and open to subjective interpretation.
+ **Modifiable**. Software projects mirror real life, where people change their minds for many reasons. The requirements specification should allow for this, so documentation should avoid duplication as a change in one area may be missed in another, resulting in inconsistencies.
+ **Traceable**. All requirements should be uniquely numbered, allowing for cross-referencing.

Amoeba: a Real World Requirements Specification

The excerpt below is taken from a real world document to illustrate traceability. The same project will be illustrated later in the section on Design. In this example, the personnel database is being redeveloped following a change of server hardware, which in turn has forced a change of server software. The database is used by Amoeba's administrative department, who have decided that this presents a good opportunity to overhaul the system.

The real world project from which this is derived was designed for administration within a large company that was organised in many departments across several buildings. In this example, several pages have already been spent summarising interviews before presenting the requirements. The reasoning for any of these decisions should be included with those interviews. **Req-nn** indicates non-negotiable requirements, while **FR-nn** indicates future requirements. There are many reasons why requirements may be identified but not implemented immediately. In this case, 'future requirements' were those that were not required to meet a non-negotiable deadline for the switch over of server platforms.

...Output lists (for the Clerical Department) - summary

The old system generates personnel lists for circular, mail and e-mail distribution. These are:

+ circulation lists for departments, as hard-copy for circular lists [Req-15], label lists for mailings [Req-16] and as an e-mail distribution list [Req-17];
+ circulation lists for each building, as hard-copy [Req-18] and as an e-mail distribution list [Req-19];
+ an e-mail distribution list for the entire company [Req-20];
+ circulation lists for each project-group, as hard-copy [Req-21] and as an e-mail distribution list [Req-22];
+ circulation lists for each building, as an e-mail distribution list [Req-23];

It is vital that these lists are retained for the use of the Clerical department.

Also, it is required that a new list is defined: by Post-Point. At present, mails are often circulated round a group. It is desirable that in the case of a group being split between floors (as often occurs), mails are sent to a "Postpoint" ie an area within a floor. However, the post-point identifier should not be tied to the floor identifier, in case a person's post-point differs from their normal place of work for some reason, such as a temporary move to another department. [Req-24]

Entering updates

It is necessary that personnel should be able to update their entries as they change location, project-group or married name [Req-25]. It is also required that a person's entry should be able to be changed by their group leader or by administrative staff [Req-26].

Data to be held

All data items which are held at present should be retained [Req-27], these are:

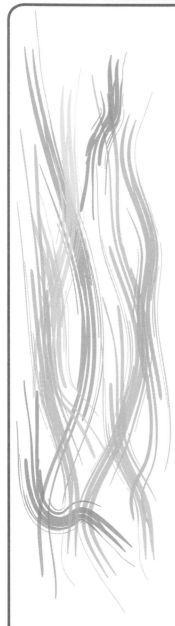

Field Name	Additional Details
Personnel No.	A person's unique identifier within the company; this field should be unchangeable once it is assigned. A former employee who returns should be re-assigned their former Personnel No. It is in the format AA-9999, assigned by the personnel dept. as defined in internal documentation. New personnel will initially be identified as "ZZ-nnnn", where "nnnn" is a random 4-digit integer, if the Personnel Dept. have not yet assigned a number
Forename	
Surname	
E-mail address	Assigned by network admin, in the format forename.initial.surname@amoebaantiques.com, for example Jake.q.smith@amoebaantiques.com
Grade	A 4 letter code, such as, 'STUD' (Student), 'MGR1' (Manager, level1), as defined in the company's internal documentation.
Department	A code, as described below
Location	The building and floor they work upon: in the case of Ashton House, this is ASH1, ASH2 or ASH3. In the case of Lincoln house, this is LIN2, LIN3, LIN4.
Phone number	4 digit extension, in the format 3xxx
Project Description	A (maximum 20 character) summary of the project, for example "Network Admin", chosen from a list of options that are maintained by administrative staff.
Project Details	A fuller description of the project and their role within it, for example "Network Admin: Unix accounts, NT servers, backups", keyed in by individual personnel.

In addition, several additional fields have been identified as necessary:

Post-Point	[Req-24, see above] A field splitting a floor into areas, for distribution purposes, normally adding a single character to their location (for example "ASH1-C").
Machine name	[Req-28] The network name given to their PC or Unix workstation, max. 15 characters.
Status	[Req-29] "enabled" or "disabled." Details of everyone who has ever worked in the company are held perpetually, for auditing purposes. Those who have left are flagged as 'disabled' and are normally unseen by all but system administrators. Those who return are "re-enabled."

Departments will be stored as 4-letter codes, using the current system [Req-30]:
+ ACCN (Accounts)
+ CLER (Clerical)
+ NETW (Network Admin)
+ SFTW (Software Development)
etc

(several pages, not needed for this example, have been omitted at this point)

Security Constraints

There are no security requirements other than date must only be visible to internal users [Req-86]. Data will be backed up on a daily basis as part of the normal back-up routine and all changes to the database are logged [Req-87]. While not considered a vital requirement, there is a future requirement to add password security for updating records [FR-8].

24.4 The Design Specification

Whether it is written before any development takes place, or is the product of feedback from a prototype, a clear design is needed. However, you may have felt from your coursework that the design stage feels unproductive while actually starting to develop a system gives the feeling of achieving something.

However, the design will save much time and effort in the long term. In conventional engineering, such as house construction, nobody would start building without careful planning. The analogy holds true for software engineering. Rushing into development, for example to save time or quickly create a product to show customers, leads to a messy, difficult system with many long-term costs. A clearly written design is needed to aid communication within a team. Even on solo projects, this is still needed for the sake of later maintenance.

Each identified requirement should be clearly met within the design. It may be helpful to provide an index to facilitate cross-checking. This is especially useful if requirements are not designed in the order they were identified.

Amoeba: A Real World Design

The previous section on 'Amoeba' showed a real world requirements specification that Amoeba Antiques might face. The real world companion document (the design) opens with an overview of the document and its purpose, and then lists all requirements in order together with a reference to where they are designed (to aid traceability and find it easier to locate features):

Requirement	Overview	Place in design
Req-15	Hard-copy circulation list per department	Page 13
Req-16	Hard-copy mailing labels	Page 14
Req-17	E-mail circulation list per department	Page 27
Req-18	Hard-copy circulation list per building	Page 14
... ...		
FR-8	Password security for updating records	Page 58

Within the body of the design document, each requirement is clearly described so that any programmer can implement it. For example:

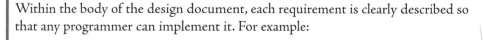

Circulation Lists by Department [Req-15]

These will be printed out in the format shown below, with the Department leader's name at top and the rest of the names in no particular order. Clerical members should be able to enter a department's short-code or access a list of departments, via a screen similar to the once below, with a text-input box or a drop-down menu.

Enter group code: [_____] (this is from tbl_personnel.groupid)

Alternatively, select a group from the list below. For multiple groups, hold CTRL while clicking on each one.

ACCN – Accounts Dept
CLER – Clerical
CUST – Customer Relations
...

This table will list all options in tbl_groups.groupname, linked to tbl_personnel.groupid, via tbl_groups.groupid. The user will also be prompted to enter a return address for slips, which is sometimes required to ensure all members of a department have indicated they have read a circular. The fields that appear here are tbl_personnel.fname, tbl_personnel.sname and tbl_groups.groupname and a response to a question asked of the user: "Do you wish to specify a return-to person?" Circulations slips appear as thus:

Circulation Slip for ACCN

Bronagh McNicholl	[space for signature and date]	__/__/__
Conor O'Kane	[ ]	__/__/__
Shane Rainey	[ ]	__/__/__
Colin Quigg	[ ]	__/__/__
etc.		

Circulated on [date automatically inserted]
Please Return to _____* [name can be specified before printing]
* Confidential Waste, if not specified

24.5 Documentation

Any project generates a large amount of documentation, and the writers have a duty to ensure their readers will be able to understand them. For example, developers need clear and complete descriptions of all parts of the system they will be working on, while they only need a high level understanding of other parts. Suppose, for instance, Bronagh designs queries and Colin designs reports. Colin needs to know what fields Bronagh's query will give his report but he does not need to know the details of how the query extracts this data. Likewise, Bronagh doesn't need to know how Colin will build the report; she just has to be sure she gives him the right fields. Hence, Bronagh and Colin are interested in a detailed design for their own work, but only need a high level view of each other's work. In some projects, the developer of a particular module will be responsible for the detailed design of that particular module: the inputs, output and storage methods have been clarified by high level designers and the Team Leader, and it is the programmer's responsibility to decide how they will progress from one to the other.

The documentation surrounding any project will therefore exist as:

+ A summary, to give readers a rough idea of the work;
+ An overview of each area, so that people involved in one area can easily see how a related area will operate;
+ A detailed breakdown on how each piece of the project will work, that will only be read by a handful of people.

In the case of an analysis, summaries and overviews will be read by developers and customers; the latter may not be technically minded. In the case of the design, all readers will be developers, though what they read will depend on their role within the project.

Before any document is approved, it must be thoroughly reviewed to ensure that it is consistent with other parts of the project, and that it is clear and unambiguous. Documents will be reviewed by people not directly involved to ensure they are easy to understand. For example, if Bronagh writes the design for her query, she may ask a selection of people to review it:

+ Colin, as it impacts on his work;
+ Other developers who are not directly involved;
+ A Team Leader with suitable experience to weigh up potential problems.

Technical Versus Non-Technical Documentation

Depending on its audience, documentation may be **technical** or **non-technical**. That is, aimed at those who need a detailed understanding of how a system functions, or non-specialist readers who are involved either at the project's outset or as end users. Documentation that is aimed at developers will make use of specialist terms that are only used within the software development industry, or possibly only within the context of that project. Non-technical documentation will be aimed at non-ICT specialists, and its language should reflect this. The term **non-technical documentation** is often used to refer to documentation at the end of the project (the user guide), thought it may also refer to any project document that is aimed at non-ICT experts, for example questionnaires.

Technical documentation will rarely leave the developers unless it is being distributed to a partner firm who may be responsible for a companion product. Non-technical documentation will be widely distributed in the form of user guides (both printed and copied to CD) and may also exist as interactive help features in a program or available on the Internet. In addition to this, popular commercial software will have many reference guides written by third parties who have no connection with the developers.

A process of review must be undertaken for non-technical documentation, just as it takes place with technical documentation. In this case, a document is reviewed by non-ICT specialists to ensure that it is free of industry jargon. To avoid this, documents such as user guides may be written by specialist writers instead of software developers. They may use notes made by developers or may write the document fresh, based on their own experiences. As they use the system, they might have a similar perspective to the end users they are writing for. To guarantee that the meaning of a document is clear and unambiguous, the writer should strive to avoid:

- Dated terms;
- Overly technical jargon;
- Slang;
- Local dialect, such as American or British terminology that is not widely used outside that country;
- Anything that will confuse those whose first language is not the one in which the document is written.

24.6 Project Management

A software project involves many people throughout its lifecycle. It is important that people are assigned to the project as part of a development schedule that takes into account the skills of the people involved and the other work they are doing.

For example, if Conor is a C++ expert and is involved in a particular project for the next six months, there is little point assigning him to a month's worth of SQL for another project. It would make more sense for the project managers to choose Shane, a database programmer. An integrated project management tool within a company will take into account that Shane may currently be busy elsewhere, so he should only be scheduled on the new project once his other work is complete. In addition, he cannot be scheduled to do this before certain preceding tasks are complete (for example, the design), nor can interface programmers do their job until Shane is finished.

A project management tool will be used to systematically schedule and assign jobs to people. It will also take into account the other projects the people are working on, so each person will be aware of their deadlines. Project management tools also allow the evaluation of risks associated with a project, budgets to be controlled and problems to be identified.

A project manager is the person who has overall responsibility for a project. They will use specialised software to enable them to do their job, which typically involves:

- **Project planning.** At the outset, a project must be planned and broken into small work tasks with estimates for how long each will take to complete. Additional resources such as staff, money, hardware and software will be allocated to each task. The scheduling of tasks must be done carefully as it is common for some tasks in a project to run over time, which will affect those which follow. Graphical aids such as charts, which show the project broken down into its constituent parts, help managers plan the project effectively.
- **Risk analysis.** The project manager must outline the risks: scenarios or issues that could lead to the project failing or being delivered late or over budget:

- **Staff availability.** Will the right people be available to carry out the tasks. What if certain people leave the company?

- Availability of the system hardware and other software. If special hardware or different software components are being developed, then there will be a point at which all the various parts of the project must be integrated together. If any part of project cannot be delivered on time this has an impact on the overall delivery of the project.

- **Progress monitoring.** Few projects follow their original plan exactly, as it is continually being reviewed. It is important that the project manager takes immediate corrective action when a task begins to deviate from the plan. It may change when progress in a task moves more quickly or slowly than expected, or when staff become unavailable or money runs out.

- **Reporting project status.** Periodic reports need to be compiled to show progress and highlight issues or concerns. Managers within the development firm use these to keep people informed of progress and to adjust activities if some areas fall behind. The customer may also have access to this information.

- **Budget control.** The project must be profitable, therefore all spending must be justified and development costs (salaries, equipment etc) kept under control.

- **People management.** Team members must remain motivated and focused on the objective. Identifying the strengths and weaknesses of individuals allows project managers to plan training and to match skills to tasks.

24.7 Computer–Aided Software Engineering (CASE)

With the growth of programming as a discipline, software and hardware projects have become more complex. As a result, it is no longer possible for a single programmer to hack together a quick fix to many of today's problems. Consequently, the ICT industry has matured in its approach to problem solving and has borrowed many practices from engineering. Programmers are often referred to as **Software Engineers**, and senior, very experienced developers with a high level design role may be referred to as **Systems Architects**.

Although many modern software engineering projects are as complex as building a large bridge, many customers still complain about the cost as they simply see a DVD and complain that it costs too much ("£100 for a bit of plastic?!"). Being able to put such a large system into such a small space hides its complexity. If software is well designed the interface will also hide much complexity from users.

A number of tools have been developed to make the management and design of complex projects easier. **CASE tools** are programs used to automate, manage and simplify the development process and provide a development environment for teams of programmers working together.

Definition

CASE packages normally contain components for:

- **Modelling a system.** A graphics (modelling) tool can be used to construct DFDs, ER diagrams and system flow charts using standard templates or shapes. Diagrams can be saved, reused or modified without the need for starting again. The graphics tool will also validate diagrams automatically: for example, the CASE tool will check that the DFD is reasonable and correct, and it will ensure that inputs/outputs from a level 1 process are maintained when that process is expanded at level 2.

+ **Data dictionary development and control.** The data dictionary is a file containing a description of the structure of data together with other information about the database. It is hidden from database users but is essential for software developers. A data dictionary tool is present in many modern database packages and most will automatically create and validate a dictionary from entities and attributes. Its purpose is to ensure that no action can be taken which leads to inconsistencies with what is already stored.

+ **Source code generation.** Based on a specification of inputs, outputs and processes, a source code generator produces the necessary procedures in a programming language. This code should be without errors, in order to reduce the time spent testing it. Programmers may wish to tweak the generated code to improve performance. The feature is included in many modern applications in the form of a code-generation 'wizard'.

+ **Interface generator.** This allows the automatic creation of a user interface such as a menu, dialogue box and report. The user employs the toolbox to select, place and modify different components such as labels, text boxes, buttons etc. The source code needed to produce the interface is automatically generated. Such a tool enables prototypes to be created quickly for customers to evaluate.

+ **Project management.** These tools allow the creation of a schedule and the allocation of resources, from analysis to installation, to ensure software is developed on time and as efficiently as possible. A **Gantt** chart will allow the progress of a project to be monitored by showing the order in which tasks have to be completed and the relationships between each task. Time sheet tracking can be used to record the time spent on each task by project team members. The software may also allow the critical path to be calculated, allowing tasks to be implemented in the most efficient order. This will identify the shortest time possible to complete the project.

The advantages of CASE tools are:

+ **Reduced time** to complete many tasks, since the graphics tool speeds up the production of diagrams, while the source code generation automatically generates code for applications. If software development time is shortened then costs can be reduced.

+ **Improve the quality of software** by performing error checking. The automatic creation of source code and interfaces also reduces the opportunities for human error. Fewer errors can lead to less time taken during testing, which in turn reduces development time and corrective maintenance once the system is in use.

+ **Will automatically produce documentation**, which may make maintenance easier to carry out.

+ **Allow for better planning** and monitoring of a project using the project management tool, including functions to track people or budgets and generate reports in order to identify any problems or tasks that are behind schedule. This allows the project manager to react as needed.

+ **Provide collaborative software** to enable many users to communicate requirements and progress. This may be via e-mail or discussion forums, or it may provide access to an intranet to update the sections of the project plan that they are working on.

+ **Assist in meeting the user's needs fully**. CASE tools such as the interface generator can be used to generate prototypes. This gives the user a working model to evaluate and comment upon. Developers will use this feedback to adapt the system and ensure that the software solution will meet user requirements fully.

24.8 Software Installation

Whether software is acquired as a bespoke or off-the-shelf solution, it must be installed before use: copied from **source media** (such as a CD) to the **backing store** (usually a hard disk) and prepared for execution. This preparation includes:

+ The setting of file associations, such as:
    + A word processor telling the operating system to associate it with **.doc** and **.odt** files;
    + A media player being associated with **.mp3** and **.avi** files.
+ Setting user preferences, such as:
    + A word processor giving the user an option to install file convertors for rival products;
    + A media player giving the user an option to install sample MP3 files.
+ Setting local options, such as:
    + A word processor installing a UK English dictionary;
    + A spreadsheet setting the default currency as Pounds Sterling.

Most readers of this book will have experienced software installation involving some version of Microsoft *Windows*. For the user of a standalone PC, installation is often simplified through good design through the use of prompted dialogue and help wizards. Special purpose installation software, such as Microsoft's *Windows Installer* or Macrovision's *InstallShield* hide much complexity from the user.

This complexity includes:

+ Copying compressed files from distribution media to a temporary location on the local hard disk;
+ Validating a checksum, to ensure the installation files were not corrupted during transfer or already corrupt on the distribution media;
+ Removing any old version of the software that the new one is replacing. This may be moving it to a temporary location, rather than deleting it, to allow for a **rollback**, ie undoing what was done in the event that the installation fails;
+ Uncompressing the temporary files and copying them to their permanent home, eg a subfolder within C:\Program Files\... on a Microsoft Windows PC;
+ Presenting the user with installation options. For example, if an office suite is

installed the user may decide to install only the spreadsheet manager and word processor but leave out the presentation graphics package;

♦ Making changes to the Windows **Registry** (or equivalent on other operating systems) that tell the operating system what file types are associated with the software and where that software is stored. Rollback information will also be provided to the registry so that the previous version of the software can be recovered in the event of the installation having failed for some reason.

When the user first runs a piece of software, they may have some choices to make, such as a layout of the interface, local settings (for example which dictionary a spell checker will use) and what file types are to be associated with the application. Figure 24.1 shows the installation of Mozilla *Firefox*, seen from a user's perspective, which illustrates the steps that users must follow and some of the choices they can make during the process.

Figure 24.1: The installation of Mozilla Firefox from a user's perspective (left to right, top to bottom): files are decompressed; the user is welcomed; the user agrees to the license; the user chooses some options; the software is copied to backing store; the software is ready for use.

While 'advanced' users have the option of customising the installation in some way, non-experts may view the process as a simple matter of clicking 'next' several times while ignoring the detail of the on-screen messages. However, this approach causes problems of its own. The typical 'next, next, next' user will probably experience some of the following unresolved issues:

+ A word processor that is permanently stuck with a US English dictionary;
+ A spreadsheet that thinks US Dollars are the appropriate currency for the UK;
+ A third party media player that has taken control of all file types, leaving the user with no idea how to reassociate .wmp files with *Windows Media Player*;
+ An office suite that has not installed clipart graphics from the CD.

The issue of user training , which can remedy some of these issues, is dealt with elsewhere in this book. However, administrators may prefer not to take chances on whether users are trained or not. Rather, some sort of package management system may be preferable, to ensure that all PCs are set up in the same, standardised manner.

Consider the following problems faced by schools in Northern Ireland:

+ Most schools do not have full-time trained technical support staff;
+ Most schools cannot afford staff the time to install software for themselves;
+ Most teachers are not ICT experts, and could inadvertently install software incorrectly.

The solution to this problem was the **C2K** system which specifies a standardised set of hardware and software for most schools in Northern Ireland. Currently, special purpose **package management software** ensures that all PCs are configured in the same way. All schools have the same basic programs, though there is software specific to the Primary, Secondary and Special Needs sectors. If a school requests extra programs, this is done for all selected PCs within that school in a controlled fashion, for example adding Adobe *Photoshop* to machines within the Art department or *Sibelius* to those within the Music department.

Figure 24.2: Google *Pack*, a free online suite of applications.

Home PC users may have encountered such package management systems, for example Google *Pack* (shown in figure 24.2) which is a free online suite of applications including software from Google and third party firms. A single installation delivers popular software: Google *Earth*, *Skype*, Adobe *Acrobat Reader*, *Picasa* and *SunStarOffice*. Google *Pack* monitors for available upgrades to all installed packages. Such tools are more effective for inexperienced users who are unwilling or unable to search for and install upgrades manually.

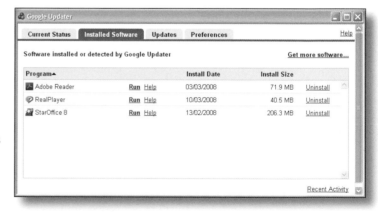

Admittedly, this solution may feel restrictive to expert users. In schools, for example, ICT teachers may want the freedom to install whatever they like. However, a central support system will need to restrict some users' freedoms in order to provide a manageable, functioning service for everyone. The alternative scenario (of users installing, copying and downloading whatever they like) is discussed in the context of Amoeba Antiques.

Amoeba
Antiques

Amoeba: The PC Support Nightmare

Simon once worked within Amoeba's technical support department. He was responsible for a standardised installation on all their networked computers. If a new PC was being configured, it was connected to the network, had a package management client installed, and was left to look after itself. Following a preset script, the package management software:

+ Downloaded appropriate applications from Amoeba's server and configured them with UK local options;
+ Installed Amoeba standard templates for document layout and fonts;
+ Installed and configured a standardised web browser and e-mail client;
+ Installed all necessary software over night, via half a dozen reboots, and was ready for use in the morning.

Simon recently moved to the **University of Hibernia (UH)**, where he manages their computing infrastructure. When he first arrived UH's setup was very different to Amoeba's. Although most office PCs were identically configured with the same software, they were all managed separately. This involved walking round many offices, asking people to log off, then logging on under his own username and installing the software from files held on a central server. When he had to perform the same job on a pair of 150 seat computing suites, he found the most effective option was to log on to 20 PCs at a time and run the installation from a number of pre-prepared CDs because the server could not cope with sending the same large files to so many computers simultaneously. In this situation, Simon:

+ Walked between the 20 machines, logging on and inserting CDs;
+ Walked between them again to start the installation program;
+ Walked between the next 20 machines, logging on and inserting CDs;
+ Waited for the first group of PCs to complete installation so he could retrieve the CDs.

However, this process was extremely disruptive to student access. Simon comments: "*A much more effective way to manage this would be to install a package management system on all the PCs. This would check the server for updates. I could put the update files on the server and the next time any PC rebooted, the software management package would check with the server to install any available updates. To avoid disruption, I could send an e-mail round the campus asking staff to reboot their PCs during lunch. PCs in the computer suites could be sent a signal to reboot at a time when they were free of students, such as 11pm on a Saturday. If problems arose, PCs could be updated in groups over successive nights, so that only a small number of machines would be out of use at one time.*"

Often, when people become used to an inefficient way of working, they treat it as 'normal'. When Simon first arrived at UH, his colleagues thought that his suggestions were too good to be true. However, this is now the standard way of managing software within UH's campus. A key benefit for technicians is that software can be installed on many machines without spending hours walking around the building.

This approach did not go down well with everyone. Simon continues:

"There were some people who resented the fact that we had taken away their ability to add or modify software on their system. Those users who insisted on using their own favourite software were not only exploiting a hole in our procedures, but also leaving us vulnerable to malware. They might also have installed unlicensed products. Most of the people affected by this lost the opportunity to have instant messaging facilities, but this is not vital to their working routines. We also got rid of any liability UH might have had for paying for unapproved applications. Some employees had installed file–sharing software, which we were glad to remove because it was illegal and prone to viruses and other security risks."

"Having a standard configuration for each PC reduces our overhead for software management. When new software is installed, ICT technicians can check it on their own PC. With a few mouse clicks, it is ready for the whole campus the next time they reboot. New PCs we order are equipped with the ability to be booted up during the night, by sending a 'wake up' signal from the server. Therefore, large upgrades can be managed without forcing people to stop work for an hour – when they return to work the next morning, they are probably unaware that anything has changed. While there are still a few PCs that need to be manually configured due to special purpose software used within some faculties, the vast majority of PCs can be centrally managed."

The next step in UH's development was to standardise all new PC hardware. Doing this meant that updates to drivers became predictable and more easily managed. Also, this allowed a 'clone' image of a 'standard' PC's hard disk to be made (sometimes called '**ghosting**'). When a new PC is configured, it is connected to the server and the contents of the hard disk are overwritten with a duplicate of a standard hard disk image. This greatly simplifies the installation of standard applications, as the install-reboot-install-reboot process for a dozen programs is replaced with a single, quicker, process of copying files and then rebooting from the newly copied operating system. The part of the installation that involves configuring the OS registry and options within applications is removed as the entire hard disk, including the OS and registry are copied. In the event that a user accidentally damages the contents of the hard disk, a PC can be completely reconfigured inside an hour. Of course, this is only feasible on machines with identical hardware to the 'standard' PC because of the settings within the OS that are particular to certain types of hardware.

Changeover Methods

A number of potential problems can arise when migrating a large group of users, along with their data, to a new system, for example:

- Employees may not want to change from the current system;
- Data held on the old system may be important, so must be imported to the new system with complete accuracy;
- The system may be used in some 'mission critical' application and as a result, failure is not an option.

There are four main methods of carrying out a changeover. These methods were discussed in detail in section 15.7, but can be summarised as:

- **Direct changeover**: everybody switches over at once. This is easy, but can cause problems if the new system is found to have major problems.
- **Phased implementation**: users switch to the new system in groups, with any problems resolved during each phase. This can be a more time consuming but safer approach.
- **Parallel implementation**: users use both systems at once until the new system has been shown to work. Ideal for mission-critical applications, such as a power station, but causes users to duplicate their efforts.
- **Pilot conversion**: a selected group of users try out the new system to discover and eradicate errors, before everybody later switches over.

24.9 Ongoing Running Costs

The installation of any ICT system has many associated costs that may not always be considered at the time of purchase. On a simple level, a less expensive PC, eg one that is bought for a teenager's Christmas present, has the ongoing costs of ink cartridges, broadband fees and new software. Any company has similar ongoing costs that must be considered before a system is installed. Failure to consider all costs, including those for development, training and running, may lead to a system that is poorly resourced and ineffective. Cutting hardware costs may lead to a system that feels slow and temperamental.

The following hardware costs must be considered:

- **Servers** that seem perfectly fine today may need to be upgraded in the future. They may be unable to cope with future processing or storage demands, for example if the company expands. If PCs are improved, or the network bandwidth is increased, an old and relatively slow server may become a 'bottleneck' that causes delays. Companies may have to choose between buying extra processing and storage capacity today as a safeguard, or waiting until it is definitely needed. The latter will be much cheaper, but a company will have to put up with the down-time caused by the upgrade process.
- **Network infrastructure and communications links** may need to be upgraded to cope with future network use. For example, a 1990s LAN could not cope with either the expectations of today's Internet users or the demands of Web 2.0 applications. Likewise, it is probable that today's LANs will seem dated in due course. Similarly, a company's external WAN connections that seem fast today will eventually appear slow due to a growth in use that places more traffic on the line.
- **PCs** have a usable life of only a few years. Software developers often have access to state of the art hardware, hence applications software developed today does not always take account for hardware more than a few years old. If users are to run such software effectively, their hardware must be upgraded. Also, users often expect to be able to run several applications simultaneously, but this might not be possible on an older, slower machine. The growth of new technologies such as LCD displays has brought an unexpected cost to many businesses as users shun functional CRT displays that can easily be used with a new PC.

There are numerous ongoing software costs associated with off-the-shelf software:

+ **Software licences** are often for a set period of time. If a company wishes to continue using the package, regular fees must be paid. These may be on a fixed per-PC basis for an entire LAN, without consideration of how often the package is used on each machine. In some cases, software may cease to function properly once its licence expires.

+ **Upgrade costs** may be unavoidable. For many firms, an office applications package would be perfectly fine. However, new versions of such a package may produce files that are not fully compatible with older software. A firm may feel they have to upgrade in order to continue sharing data with other firms. This has a knock-on effect on training costs.

+ **Server software upgrades** may be required to permit the full functionality of modern applications for effective data sharing via a network.

There are also ongoing costs associated with bespoke software:

+ **Support contracts** are for a limited time after installation and must be renegotiated. Although this allows for a rapid response to maintenance requests, it should nonetheless be remembered that bespoke solutions do not entail a one-off cost.

+ **Hardware upgrades** to allow the software to run. As with off-the-shelf products, a package developed today may not run effectively on older hardware. Even if compatibility with older platforms is mandated in the requirements, it may transpire that running on older platforms (such as a Pentium II PC running *Windows 98*) is a less satisfying experience than a modern platform, and the firm is forced into an upgrade.

Once hardware and software costs have been considered, the implications of any new system for staff must be considered:

+ **Training** is a significant ongoing commitment for any firm. New members of staff may not be familiar with the off-the-shelf packages used by the company, and definitely will not be familiar with any bespoke solutions. Even though it can be assumed that younger staff are ICT literate, they will not be familiar with company policies such as where to store data, the correct layout of document templates, how to e-mail data outside the firm etc.

+ **Staff turnover** may result in money being spent on more training. Indeed, there are those firms that offer such effective training programmes that some graduates join simply to benefit from training then move on after a few years. In this case, it is up to management to provide incentives for staff to remain. Not training short-term staff may damage morale, recruitment and productivity.

+ **Staff time wasting** may also be an issue. In the early 1990s, many people played *Solitaire* or *Minesweeper* instead of working. Nowadays, high bandwidth technology has opened up further possibilities of online gaming and social networking, further damaging productivity. Management have to consider whether such activities can benefit morale, and whether blocking them will damage morale too much.

Questions

1. Describe the purpose of the analysis stage. (2)
2. Describe the purpose of the design stage. (2)
3. Identify information that should be expected in analysis and design documentation. (6)
4. Describe two reasons as to why technical documentation is required. (4)
5. Describe two reasons as to why non-technical documentation is required. (4)
6. Describe four tasks performed by a project management tool. (4)
7. Outline the main tasks performed by a project manager. (5)
8. What is a CASE tool? (2)
9. Name and describe three different CASE tools. (6)
10. Describe two reasons for using CASE tools. (4)
11. What is meant by the term software installation? (2)
12. Outline the steps involved in installing software. (5)
13. What is a Package Management System? (3)
14. Describe three methods of changeover. (6)
15. Describe the costs of developing, implementing and using an ICT system: in terms of hardware, software and personnel costs. (6)

CHAPTER 25
Software Quality

25.1 Introduction

Quality: The standard of something as measured against other things of a similar kind... general excellence. (*Concise Oxford Dictionary*)

Quality assurance: a system of procedures undertaken to guarantee that a product or system adheres or conforms to established standards. (*The Complete A-Z ICT and Computing Handbook*)

Definition

Like any other product, software is evaluated against people's predetermined standards, for example:

+ **By customers**, who decide if software meets their objectives or not;
+ **By end users**, who may decide that software is unusable;
+ **By developers**, who decide if a design will lead to a good or bad product;
+ **By senior developers**, who monitor development and can recognise and correct problems in their early stages;
+ **By developers in the maintenance phase**, who expect a system to be maintainable and well documented.

The criteria people use to make judgements on a system are relevant to their particular needs. Users might decide that a system that does what they want with no fuss is 'good', but programmers might consider the same system 'bad' if it is poorly documented and full of redundant data. People measure the quality of software according to how successfully it fits their **own** purpose.

This section examines the impact of software that is not suitable for its intended purpose, along with the procedures developers can follow to avoid producing this kind of software. These procedures include software testing. However, it is essential that rigorous quality assurance procedures are in place so that good quality is not ensured by the testing process alone, but is built into the development process.

25.2 Software Testing

The testing stage involves ensuring a system meets its requirements and that the software is of sufficient quality. The test plan is used to evaluate the actual system. If tests fail, the designer is informed and sets about fixing the problems. A corrected design is then used to correct the system, which is re-tested. Test results are presented in a formal document with any tests that did not pass highlighted and any other weaknesses also documented.

There are four main types of testing that take place during development. These were introduced in section 15.6 and are elaborated below.

+ **Unit testing** (or module testing). As programmers complete each section, they test it to ensure that it works. Doing this helps to isolate problems, and they are easier to detect now than if testing was left until the end of development. For example, each query within a database system is tested once it is written.

+ **Integration testing**. When components that are to work together are completed, they are tested together. Again, this approach avoids the issue of finding a large number of problems in a completed system and having no idea which components are responsible. Within a database it is possible that a series of queries run in sequence to supply data to a report. These are tested together once they are written, rather than waiting to test all queries plus the report plus the aspects of menus, and finding problems that are difficult to isolate.

+ **System testing** (application testing). The completed system is examined, including an evaluation from an end user's perspective. Most serious problems should have been found and corrected by this stage. The purpose of application testing is to verify that the complete system works correctly, according to the requirements from the analysis. As part of system testing:

  + **Alpha testing**: the system is tested in-house by the developer when it is almost complete to ensure that it meets the specification. At this stage, most features are functional though some areas will need further development, for example the interface may not be complete, or help screens may be missing. Alpha testing allows a product to be used in a realistic environment and will lead to a beta test.

  + **Beta testing** is the final stage of testing, when a complete product is made available to chosen users to evaluate and provide feedback. This is vital for commercial software as it exposes the system to real use. There is no other way to evaluate a system with a large number of users. Such testing may detect problems which were not expected by the developers. A beta version of software must already be rigorously tested before being made available to the testers so their daily work is not damaged. Some organisations have long standing agreements with commercial software firms to act as beta testers, giving them a chance to influence the future of a project and to obtain completed software at reduced prices.

  + **Acceptance testing**. This is often done later, at the review stage. Once testing and implementation are complete, the customer compares the final system with what they were expecting. This involves acceptance testing, ie determining whether users accept the system or not. As well as considering functionality the customer will evaluate training methods and user documentation for correctness and ease of use.

For each of the testing types mentioned above, a **black box** or **white box** approach can be taken. Unit testing often takes a white box approach, whereas system testing often takes a black box approach:

+ **Black box** testing (or **functional testing**) does not consider the detail of what happens within program modules, but only considers inputs and outputs. As long as the system reacts properly to various inputs, the test has been passed.

+ **White box** testing (or **structural testing**) is not only concerned with end results, but also with how a program behaves internally.

By the way...

Getting it right – multiple beta tests

In many commercial systems there may be several Beta releases, each one designed to canvas a wider range of opinions than previous tests. For example, **Beta 1** is released to a select group of users for evaluation. Their feedback allows for corrections and the release of **Beta 2** which may be released to a few more people, but still a select group. This phase will continue until all obvious 'rough edges' are removed, leading to **Public Beta 1**. At this stage there should be few surprises, and most problems found by users should be trivial issues that have been left for the maintenance phase. There may be several public betas. Eventually a **release candidate** is made available. This software is now considered fit for release but developers want to be absolutely sure there are no serious problems awaiting paying customers. There may be several 'release candidates' with the last one becoming the commercially available program.

Many companies allow users to download late-stage betas. To ensure that these people buy the software, betas are often designed to cease functioning after a certain date or purposely have some key features disabled.

Beta versions of two popular applications in use during 2008 (Mozilla *Firefox 3* and *OpenOffice.org 3*) are shown below. Students would benefit from reading the material available on the web sites of large projects such as these in order to see how a large team and major development project is organised.

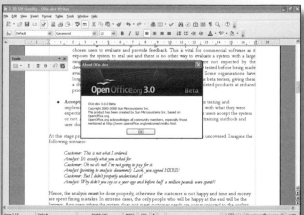

It is during the acceptance testing stage that problems in the customer's understanding of the analysis may be uncovered. The worst case scenario is that a customer may not be happy because the system that is delivered is not what they were expecting to get. For this reason, the analysis **must** be done properly, otherwise more time and money will be spent rectifying mistakes. Any areas where the system does not meet customer needs will be communicated to the analyst. This forms the start of the **maintenance** phase (see section 25.3).

25.3 Review and Maintenance

It is rare for a computer system's lifecycle to come to an end once it has been put in place. Rather, a period of formal review compares the system to its original requirements while it is in the working environment. It is normal that a number of issues will be found:

+ Misunderstandings in minor requirements;
+ Certain parts of the system not working as efficiently as users would like;
+ The new system not being compatible with third party products and causing instabilities;
+ The customer identifying new requirements that have arisen since the original project was commissioned or that have become apparent once the system is in place.

Over time, a system that has generally been accepted will likewise develop operational issues:

+ New requirements;
+ Old features that are no longer needed;
+ The need to run on a hardware platform or operating system other than those for which it was originally designed.

Various surveys have suggested that a software development firm can spend up to 70% of its budget on maintenance. As the number of ongoing projects developed by the firm increases, so a larger and larger proportion of their revenue is dedicated to maintaining them. A well-known example is Microsoft, who derive around 90% of their income from the ongoing maintenance and support of two large projects that date from the 1980s: Microsoft *Windows* and Microsoft *Office*. A similar situation will exist in any large development firm.

Maintenance is only effective if senior analysts and developers are involved in a process of review:

+ Listening to users as they did at the original analysis;
+ Deciding which requirements are vital and which can be 'put off' for a while;
+ Deciding how to incorporate new requirements into an existing system.

Four categories of maintenance can be undertaken:

+ **Corrective maintenance**: Essentially, fixing bugs;
+ **Perfective maintenance**: Improving the system by removing inefficiencies;
+ **Adaptive maintenance**: Adding new functionality to a successful product so

that it continues to meet customer demands;

+ **Preventative maintenance**: Modifying a functioning system to make it easier to maintain in the future.

In the case of Microsoft *Windows*, the current product (*Vista*) is the fifth generation of a product (*Windows NT*) that was originally designed as a more stable replacement for another Microsoft product (simply called **Windows**). During its lifetime, the operating system has changed in various ways:

+ Bugs have been corrected;

+ Certain elements have been perfected;

+ It runs more efficiently and appears faster to users;

+ It has adapted to new requirements, eg different CPU designs, and multimedia;

+ It has been modified with no obvious change in functionality, thereby preventing features intended for obsolete hardware or that were never properly documented from causing future maintenance problems.

As time progresses and a system becomes increasingly complex and difficult for programmers who were not present for much of its life, this increases the risk of introducing changes that may have undesired knock-on effects. In such cases, a system that has worked well for years may have to be rewritten to introduce new functionality because of the complexity of interlinked modules in the original, and the desire to avoid destabilising the whole lot. In particular, old systems may have been created using development methods or programming environments that modern programmers are not familiar with, making redevelopment the only option. In these instances, **reverse engineering** a system to convert it into a modern programming language such as C++ or Java may reduce the workload involved. Such old systems are still used by many companies to handle their bill processing, but there are few active software developers who are familiar with 1960s development environments, such as *Fortran* or *Cobol*.

In the case of any modifications, a project must return to the analysis phase because changes to a program may affect other aspects of the system. Any change has the potential to cause confusion amongst engineers, who may find the design specification they have been using is suddenly obsolete, or realise that it is 99% correct and 1% incorrect, with no way of knowing which part has been changed. Any confusion is compounded if the changes are made without reporting them to the rest of a project team. Therefore, any requests for changes are usually referred to a senior developer who has a more detailed understanding of the whole system than a programmer who works on only one part. Updated analysis and design documents are produced as a result. Any documentation relating to development is also updated. Minor changes may be implemented through patches or service packs, which replace faulty components, while significant changes involve the installation of a completely new version.

Maintenance requests derived from a review process may not be implemented immediately, due to the timescale in designing new program components and ensuring that implementing them will not introduce unforeseen issues. For example, Microsoft *Office 2007* includes the ability to export files in PDF format. This may seem like a simple feature, but it involves a careful consideration:

- How an *Office* document will output to a PDF file;
- How fonts will be encoded;
- Whether features such as hyperlinks will be retained;
- Whether the output document will open with all versions of Adobe *Acrobat Reader* or only the most recent;
- How to convert non-Microsoft file formats that have been opened in *Office*;
- How to handle new Office *Open XML* file formats (denoted by the **docx** extension, in *Word*) as well as old formats still in use.

By the way...

These news stories provide examples of the issues raised by maintenance:

"Native PDF Support in Office 12", via http://tinyurl.com/74vem

"Martian Headsets", via http://tinyurl.com/2ra6w2

"Microsoft to support PDF in Office 12", via http://tinyurl.com/2svrda

Maintenance is by far the largest cost in system development, so it is prudent to put effort into making a system as maintainable as possible. Factors affecting maintenance include:

- **Good system design**. Involving functional decomposition to the lowest level of detail with clearly defined inputs, processing and outputs at each level. Each aspect of the design must be clearly developed.
- **Good technical documentation**. Effort made in this area pays off in the long term, as all aspects of development need to be communicated to people involved in maintenance. All documentation from the analysis, design, software development, testing and implementation stages must be kept up to date in order to reflect the final system.
- **Quality assurance processes**. Set in place in order to create a system with as few problems as possible. At each stage of software development, suitably competent people review the work done at that stage to ensure that it is correct and complete.

Questions

1. Testing approaches must be planned at the design stage. Describe three different testing approaches. (6)
2. What is the difference between black and white box testing? (2)
3. Describe the difference between alpha and beta testing. (4)
4. Identify and describe three types of maintenance. (6)
5. Suggest how each type of maintenance can be reduced. (3)

CHAPTER 26
The User Interface

26.1 Introduction

Since an **interface** is the place where any two systems meet, the **user interface** is therefore the place where the user and the computer system meet. In this section, we will look at five main types of interface:

+ **Command line;**
+ **Graphical user interface (GUI);**
+ **Natural language;**
+ **Prompted dialogue** (wizards and forms);
+ **Menus.**

Some systems use more than one of these types of interface. For example, modern applications normally use menus and a GUI, but employ prompted dialogue to guide the user through installation. Command line interfaces were once common, but are now used only by advanced users. Most GUI operating systems, such as *Windows* and *MacOS*, allow access to a command line if desired.

Human computer interaction (HCI) covers many fields including computer science, engineering and psychology. Based on studies of how people interact with existing interfaces, HCI is used to design user-friendly systems. Effective use of HCI techniques can create a system that can be used by non IT specialists and experts alike. HCI plays a part in the design of all interfaces between people and computers, whether that interface is to a PC, VCR, power plant safety system or even a digital watch.

26.2 The Importance of Human Computer Interaction

HCI is important to ensure that a user can use a computer:

+ **Without injury.** A poorly designed workspace which does not consider psychological and ergonomic factors can lead to injury, such as the development of Repetitive Strain Injury.
+ **Effectively.** The computer should meet the exact needs of the user. It should increase productivity and reduce the time taken to perform tasks. In critical applications it is essential that the system is effective, so as to avoid loss of life.
+ **Without confusion or stress.** The interface should be operated with ease thus increasing job satisfaction, motivation and reducing stress.

To understand the importance of HCI, it is useful to consider some examples of man-machine interfaces developed both before and after HCI was widely researched. In the 1980s, the term **user friendly** came into use to describe a new generation of non-threatening interfaces designed with non-experts in mind.

The Personal Computer

In contrast to today's 'point and click' WIMP interface, the command line interface from early PCs often required users to remember difficult commands. Many commentators credit Apple's GUI-based *Macintosh* and, later, Microsoft *Windows* 95 as important milestones in bringing the PC to the mass market. In early applications, what was seen on the screen often did not resemble what was printed (see figure 26.1). This problem led to the development of 'What You See Is What You Get' interfaces (or **WYSIWYG**, pronounced 'Wizzy Wig').

```
#STARTBOLD##SIZE=LARGE#Human Computer
Interaction#ENDBOLD#

#SIZE=NORMAL#There is no real purpose to
this paragraph apart from showing the
difference in old and new interfaces. Old
interfaces were #STARTBOLD#not#ENDBOLD#
very #STARTITAL#user-friendly#ENDITAL#
as you can see.

#SIZE=NORMAL##In fact if you even wanted
to change the font you had to type in
all sorts of strange commands that were
#STARTBOLD#hopefully#ENDBOLD# understood
when you printed the document.

#SIZE=NORMAL##Thank heaven for WYSIWYG
and WIMP
```

Human Computer Interaction

There is no real purpose to this paragraph apart from showing the difference in old and new interfaces. Old interfaces were **not** very *user-friendly* as you can see.

In fact if you even wanted to change the font you had to type in all sorts of strange commands that were **hopefully** understood when you printed the document.

Thank heaven for WYSIWYG and WIMP

Figure 26.1: A simulation of what users would see on their screen in early 1980s word processors and the same document using a modern WYSIWYG system. The document on the left is formatted only when printed, so if the formatting is incorrect the user might not realise until they have wasted paper finding out.

By the late 1980s, PC applications began to resemble the ones we are used to today, although it took time for WYSIWYG to be fully available (see figure 26.2). While the interface in figure 26.3 may appear quite simple by today's standards, readers should remember that modern interfaces result from many years' research and often depend on graphics hardware that was not available in the 1980s. By the early 1990s, WYSIWYG interfaces had been fully developed, as show in figure 26.4. Applications with good, usable interfaces will generally succeed over applications which may have many features, but have poor interfaces. Companies who have succeeded in the PC application market, notably Microsoft, re-used and developed successful ideas from elsewhere. They kept in mind what customers were used to and made every effort to make new users feel at home, for example, the "Help for WordPerfect Users" feature in Microsoft *Word* (figure 26.5).

Figure 26.2: Microsoft *Works* (1988). This is not yet WYSIWYG. The first line of text prints in bold and the second in italics. Font settings are chosen from menu bars: a new feature that was being included in many applications.

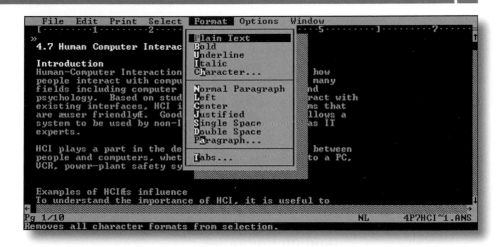

Figure 26.3: (Above) Microsoft *Word* for DOS version 5 (1989) with commands along the bottom.

Figure 26.4: (Right) Microsoft *Word* for Windows version 1 (1990) with a new WYSIWYG interface and menu system.

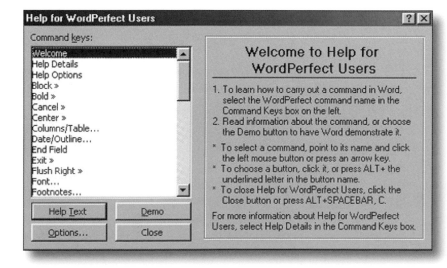

Figure 26.5: The "Help for WordPerfect Users" in Microsoft *Word* helps to explain the package in terms that users already understand.

The Video Recorder (VCR)

Early video recorders (VCRs) had simple interfaces: buttons to control the tape (**rewind, fast forward, play, record, pause** and **stop**) and for changing TV channels. As later models added more features, so the front panel of buttons grew increasingly complex. Often, these VCRs used a small LCD or LED display that was difficult to read. For many people, these devices brought more complexity than they felt was worthwhile: a generation of adults depended on their children to operate them.

Good HCI practice means that most modern VCRs have reverted to a simple design with four or five buttons on the front panel and more complex options available on the TV screen via a menu-driven interface. This allows most users to get on with the business of watching movies without being confused by features they may rarely, if ever, use. Lessons learnt here have influenced the design of DVD players and recorders.

Figure 26.6: Lots and lots of features, but all the user wants to do is keep heating last night's leftovers at 30 second intervals until they are ready.

Microwave Ovens

As with VCRs, the interface on microwave ovens became very complicated as an increasing number of features were added (see figure 26.6). Most modern microwave ovens have a more user-friendly interface.

Watches

In addition to telling the time, the 1980s saw a series of watches made available with a myriad of features, for example the ability to see the time in any city in the world, a calculator with minuscule buttons, or a built-in game. However, many users found the interface difficult to use and, for the most part, pointless. During recent years, many watches have returned to a simple design.

26.3 Types of User Interface

There are many different types of user interface available. The interface chosen in any particular application depends on a number of factors:

+ The end user's expertise;
+ Hardware to be used;
+ The purpose of the software.

The main types of user interface you should be aware of are as follows (Note that it is normal for an application to use two or more of these. For example, many office application use both a graphical user interface and a forms-driven interface):

+ Command Line Interface
+ Graphical User Interface
+ Natural Language Interface
+ Prompted Dialogue
+ Forms-Driven Interface
+ Menu-Driven Interface

Command Line Interfaces

A command line interface displays a **command prompt** (which looks like **'C:\>'** when accessed in *DOS*), which gives the user a means of typing commands directly to the computer along with any **required parameters** or **switches**. Once the user presses 'Enter' the command is interpreted by the computer and, if valid, carried out. The computer responds by displaying text on the computer screen. The user can make use of a predetermined number of commands, which can range from single characters and abbreviations to whole-word commands.

Command line interfaces were once used almost universally by general users on PCs (such as *DOS*) but today remain popular only with computer professionals such as systems managers who use Unix. They may also be used in applications where a user's typing skills are limited and only a small number of commands have to be inputted, for example operating a robot on an assembly line. The main drawback is that few clues are given to inexperienced users as to what they are supposed to type, so they can easily become confused and frustrated. However, experienced users who know exactly what they are doing may prefer the command line option because it allows commands to be entered quickly, thus avoiding the need to navigate through a sequence of menus or dialogues. In addition, command line interfaces do not demand huge processing power and require little computer memory, due to the lack of use of graphics for the interface. This can make command line interfaces cost-effective in particular situations.

Figure 26.7 shows a command line interface being used to launch Microsoft *Word*. The "C:\>" is the command prompt and is displayed by the system when the computer stars up. In the second image, the user types "cd ms", a command to navigate into a folder called "ms". This is reflected in the next command prompt (third image), displayed under the previous command. Finally the user types "word" to launch *Word* (last image).

Figure 26.7: Example of a command line interface in use.

Most modern PCs give users the option of using a **command prompt** (*Windows NT/XP/Vista*), **DOS prompt** (*Windows 95/98/ME*) or **terminal** (*MacOS X*) to give the user access to a command-line interface. Figure 26.8 shows a DOS prompt running in *Windows 98*. Some applications, such as schedulers, also allow the user to type long commands in order to make a program do something in particular when it opens, as part of a **wizard** or **form** dialogue. In figure 26.8, a single command is being used to both open *Excel* and force it to open a particular spreadsheet as soon as it is launched.

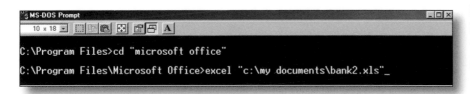

Figure 26.8: DOS prompt in Windows 98 being used to launch Excel and open a file at the same time.

Graphical User Interfaces (GUIs)

GUIs are the most popular interfaces for PCs today and have a number of features, often known as **WIMP**:

+ **Windows.** The computer screen is organised into windows. A window will usually display one program or file. Multitasking is possible because several programs can appear on the screen at once, in different windows. Windows have a standard layout, generally including a scroll bar and minimise, maximise and close buttons. Windows can be moved, resized, opened, closed and stacked on top of one another.

+ **Icons.** An icon is a small picture representing an item such as a piece of software, a file, storage medium (such as disk or tape) or command. A user selects icons to run a program by clicking or double-clicking on the icon.

+ **Menus.** These allow an option to be chosen from a pre-defined list, hence eliminating the need to learn a list of typed commands. Users are only presented with options that are valid at that particular time, so are not confused by error messages resulting from mistyped commands.

+ **Pointers.** A mouse pointer is used to navigate around the screen and select icons or menu options.

Over and above the traditional WIMP elements, GUI's often have additional features which include:

+ **Context sensitive help.** This provides help based on the task that the user is working on within a particular applications package. For example, if a user repeatedly clicks in a blank area of the document, the help system may appear (figure 26.9) and offer suggestions on how to create a new text box. It may offer to guide the user through the steps needed to solve the particular problem. Additional help can be accessed via the Internet.

+ **Wizards** and d**ialogue boxes** - these are discussed in more detail under "Prompted Dialogue Interfaces" below.

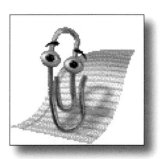

Figure 26.9: The animated paperclip, well known to a generation of Microsoft *Office* users for appearing and offering help and advice.

GUIs rely on some sort of pointing device (discussed in Chapter 2) which is usually, but not always, a mouse. Figure 26.10 shows three screenshots of a computer using a GUI. Many people prefer GUIs for the simple reason that they are easier for non-expert users to understand. Even advanced users of ICT will often prefer a GUI interface to a program that they are not used to. A GUI is likely to have shortcut operations, such as **hot keys**, for the experienced user. A hot key is a special combination of key presses that executes one of the menu commands (for example Control-S to save a document). The menus present all options available within a program, although the downside to this is that in large programs, menus can become cluttered. Some operating systems, such as *Windows Vista*, hide menu commands that the user has not recently accessed to reduce the clutter effect.

Task

Find the hardware requirements of:

1. Microsoft *DOS*.
2. Microsoft *Windows 98*.
3. Microsoft *Vista*.
4. A typical Linux distribution.

What trends do you notice and what conclusion can you draw?

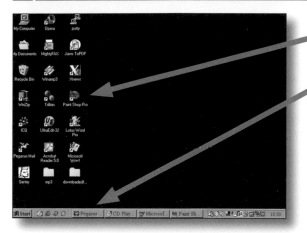

Icons representing often-used applications and some folders. The user can customise these.

Icons representing currently running (and **minimised**) applications.

Programs that are running as *background processes*, such as virus checkers. These can be accessed by the user but will often perform their tasks independently.

Using the mouse or keyboard, the user can navigate through a series of folders to find the program they want.

Options which lead to an arrow represent sub-folders, containing more options.

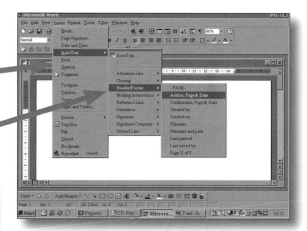

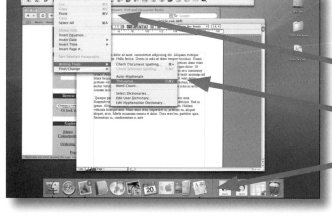

Keyboard shortcuts are a legacy of the period before GUIs.

Hierarchical menu system navigated by the mouse.

Common programs are displayed as icons in the **dock**.

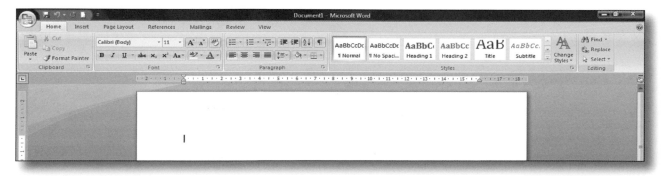

Figure 26.10: Four screenshots showing typical GUI interface elements. The first two are Windows 98 and the third is MacOS X 10.3. The last image shows the new 'Ribbon' menu-driven interface of Microsoft Office 2007, an overhaul given to the interface that had been in use with Office for many years. Compare it to the interface used on the earlier versions of Office shown above.

The advantages of a graphical user interface are:

+ The user does not need to learn a complex computer language to communicate with the computer. Commands are replaced by icons and menus, which can be selected by a pointer.

+ There is a reduction in the use of irrelevant instructions as only valid options are made available to the user by way of icons and menus.

+ The layout of each package is consistent, which enables users to transfer skills.

+ The availability of online help, especially if it is context sensitive, makes it possible for users of all skill levels to find out how to use new features without the need for extensive training.

+ More than one program can be run at the same time.

The disadvantages of GUIs are:

+ They require extra main memory (RAM) and backing store as a result of the software being graphics-intensive.

+ They require a more powerful processor and a better graphics display.

+ They can take more time to load or execute a command because more stages of interpretation are required to comprehend the command.

+ They may be irritating for some experienced users because a number of operations are required to perform a single task. For example, copying a file may require opening two windows and then dragging an icon from one to the other. A command line interface could achieve this with one line of text.

Natural Language Interfaces

Natural language interfaces recognise queries and commands written in standard language, such as English. This benefits users who cannot remember precise commands or navigate menus. Natural language input may use a keyboard, or be coupled with speech recognition software in applications where a keyboard or mouse are unsuitable.

Natural language input is particularly suitable for database querying, especially where users do not have the expertise to construct complex SQL or QBE queries. An example of this is seen in some search engines and telephone-based ordering and enquiry services. One difficulty in natural language input is the ambiguous nature of grammar. For example, does "The pretty girls' school" refer to a pretty school for girls or a school for pretty girls? These issues are discussed under Language Translation in section 18.4.

The advantages of a natural language interface are:

+ Users do not have to remember special commands in order to use the interface. Consequently, novice users may find operating a computer easier and less intimidating than conventional input.

+ Natural language input is similar to normal thought processes, which is easier for the user than having to mentally translate between English and a more restricted command language.

The disadvantages of a natural language interface are:

+ Systems may not cope with non-standard or ambiguous grammar.

+ Systems that successfully interpret the full range of human language are much more complex to program than a conventional interface with one button or word per action and no ambiguity.

+ It may be less efficient than an 'artificial' command language with concise input as it may take longer to describe commands in 'normal' English.

Prompted-Dialogue Interfaces

Prompted-dialogue interfaces use a window to guide the user through a series of steps. In order to complete a task, the user is offered a series of options and text boxes to fill in. Options will be allocated default values and will be clearly labelled for the user to understand. By clearly prompting for all necessary data and assuming little expertise from the user, the probability of unacceptable input is greatly reduced. As well as being of benefit to novices, experienced users can find prompted dialogue useful when inputting a sequence of complex commands, for example when configuring new software or hardware.

There are two basic types of prompted dialogue:

+ **Wizards** are interactive utilities that automatically guide the user through the process of performing particular tasks. A wizard consists of a number of dialogue boxes that the user moves through one at a time, filling in details as required. Examples of wizards include:

  + In a desktop publishing program, to guide the user through the steps of preparing a greeting card;

  + In a database, to assist the user in preparing a query;

  + In a word processor, to assist the user in tasks that they may be doing at that time. Figure 26.11 shows a wizard that appeared in some versions of Microsoft *Office*, with help based on what the user was doing at that time.

  + In an e-mail client, to guide the user through setting up their account. Figure 26.12 shows part of the set-up wizard in *Pegasus Mail*.

Figure 26.11: Wizard from Microsoft Office.

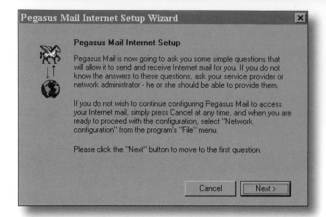
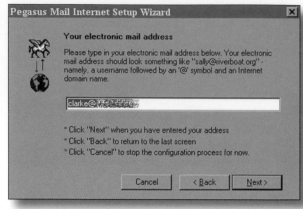

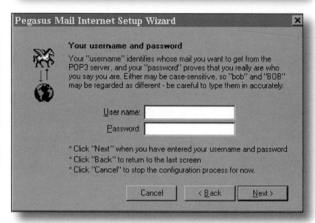

Figure 26.12: A wizard in Pegasus Mail is used to guide the user in setting up an account.

+ **Forms** are formatted dialogue screens containing a number of blank response fields and corresponding prompts or labels. The form interface is similar in appearance to a printed data collection form. However, drop down menus, check boxes and radio buttons may be used to limit the options available to a user. Each field on the form will often relate to a data field in a database. The user types and corrects their input on the form until they are satisfied, before choosing an execution button. Figure 26.13 shows an example of a form.

A benefit of the form interface is that it allows data which has been captured on a data collection form to be entered into a database in a step by step, straightforward way. The screen layout will match the layout of the filled data collection form.

Menu-Driven Interfaces

A menu-driven system presents the user with a number of options. These may lead to programs or to another menu. Figure 26.14 shows two examples of menu systems. On the top left, a simple menu-based program presenting the user with some options; on the top right, an ATM machine's screen asks the user to select the amount of money they would like to withdraw. Systems such as this eventually evolved into WIMP-based GUI systems, as shown in the bottom of figure 26.14. However, many entirely menu-driven systems remain in use.

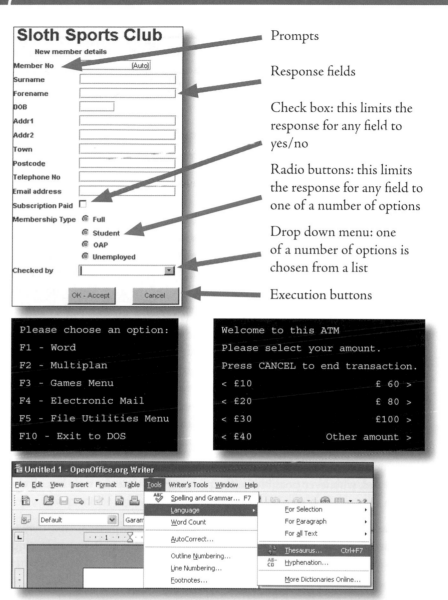

Figure 26.13: A form being used to acquire data from the user.

Figure 26.14: Two examples of a menu system in use. Left: an ATM machine at a bank. Below: Cascading menus in a modern WIMP interface, where one menu leads to another.

It is common for an operating system or an application to use a variety of interface styles. Good designers realise that no single interface is perfect, so they use different interfaces for different tasks depending on which is most appropriate:

+ The *DOS* version of many older programs used a series of keyboard shortcuts. While these could have largely been replaced in more recent programs with the menu aspect of GUIs, shortcuts are retained because many users prefer them.

+ While many *Windows* users only ever use the GUI, the *DOS*-based command line interface has been retained because others prefer it, and also because some older programs need this option to function properly.

+ *MacOS X* added a powerful command line interface to the traditional Mac GUI because systems administrators found it much more convenient.

+ It is common for both command line and GUI programs to use wizards or forms for some tasks, often when it is desirable to restrict user options, or to simplify a difficult task.

How Users Receive, Store and Process Information

An understanding of how users receive, store and process information can be used to design efficient and user-friendly systems. Consideration should be given to the importance of human senses in this process, such as sight, sound and touch. Factors to consider in how we receive, store and process information include the following:

- **Sight** is usually the first method of communicating information to users. Colour must be chosen carefully: the colour scheme should relax rather than irritate the user. Therefore the number of colours per screen should be limited, typically to four. Also, as some users are colour blind, the programs operation should not depend on everyone being able to discriminate between colours. Many find it easier to work with white text on a dark blue background than black on white. Careful consideration must be given to brightness, levels of contrast, use of blinking icons etc.

- **Use of text.** A GUI is more visually appealing than a command line interface but since icons cannot express all concepts, textual menus are sometimes needed. Although upper case text is best for attracting a user's attention, humans find it easier to read lower case text. Therefore, a combination of upper and lower case is a good approach. An experienced user may find it more efficient to input textual commands rather than to navigate through menus or dialogue boxes. Sometimes text and icons are combined (figure 26.17).

Figure 26.17: Text and icons are combined in the Mail Merge toolbar in Microsoft *Word 97*.

- **Hearing**. Humans respond more quickly to sound than to visual stimuli. By using speakers, the computer is able to provide audible feedback or warnings to the user. Specific sound cues activate to indicate that a desired action has either been successful or has failed. For example, some e-mail programs play a particular sound to indicate than an e-mail has been sent or received. However, an overuse of sound effects can become irritating.

- **Touch**. Multimedia applications make use of our sense of touch via the keyboard, mouse, joystick, touchscreens etc. Such devices must be ergonomically designed and comfortable to operate. On-screen options must also be of a suitable size to select. For example, users find it frustrating to try to click on buttons that are too small for convenient use.

26.5 Ergonomic Factors Affecting HCI

The term 'ergonomic factors' covers the user's workplace, including their physical environment and the people they work with. Good ergonomic design leads to a feeling of comfort and satisfaction in the workplace, as well as increased safety. This leads to increased productivity.

Examples of ergonomic factors with an impact on HCI are as follows:

- **Lighting**, which should be carefully chosen to avoid eyestrain and headaches. It should not flicker or be sited in a place that causes reflections off monitors. Fluorescent tubes with frosted covers are helpful, although they can generate irritating noise. Reflections can be reduced by avoiding brightly painted or shiny, white walls. It is advisable to fit adjustable blinds to windows.

+ **The VDU** should be stable and allow its height and tilt to be adjusted. It should also present a flicker-free image that is large enough to be clearly read. There should be easily-adjustable controls for brightness and contrast, and a swivel base as well as being free from reflective glare. It should have an anti-glare panel fitted, although many users wear glasses with an anti-glare coating. LCD screens on laptops can only be used with ease at a certain angles otherwise they appear blurred. Frequent breaks should be taken (every hour) to reduce eyestrain. Finally, it is essential that computer users have regular eye tests.

+ **Furniture** must be comfortable and adjustable. **Repetitive Strain Injury** (RSI) can be caused by poorly designed furniture, poor posture or repeating similar movements such as clicking buttons or typing. If a user has to turn or crouch to reach disk drives or printers, or has to sit at a strange angle to see the monitor, serious physical injuries can develop over time. Symptoms include aching, weakness, swelling, tenderness, numbness or pins-and-needles in the arms, hands, shoulders and neck.

The chair should be chosen carefully. If it is poorly designed, it can be responsible for back pain. The seat must be adjustable in height, or it can contribute to the onset of RSI, and the back rest must be adjustable in all directions so the user's eyes are level with the screen. The chair must be stable and capable of swivelling. Feet must rest flat on the floor, so employees are now legally entitled to ask for a footrest.

+ **Keyboards** should be moveable and separated from the screen. There should also be sufficient room for users to rest their hands to minimise strain on joints, and a wrist rest may also be used. **Alternative keyboards** have been ergonomically designed to alleviate muscle strain. Alternative keyboards are discussed in more detail in section 2.2.

+ **The office space must be suitable**. Users need sufficient space around them to work comfortably. Desks should have plenty of room for the keyboard, mouse, other equipment and any documents. If paper documents are being transcribed, or read in tandem with on-screen material, a document holder should be available, which will minimise head movement. Peripherals should be located for easy access. Users should not have to continually turn or crouch as this places unnatural strain on the joints.

+ **Noise level**. A noisy environment could prevent people from concentrating, leading to headaches and increase stress levels. Noisy peripherals such as printers should be placed in a separate room from those people who are using computers. Earphones could also be provided so that users can hear any sounds associated with the task in hand without disturbing other users in the room.

+ **Environment.** The temperature and humidity of a computer suite must be controlled by air conditioning or fans to maintain a comfortable working environment. A computer suite can become overly hot as a result of the heat generated by computers and CRT screens. For many people, radiation emitted by devices can result in physical discomfort. For example some people suffer headaches because of the ultraviolet glare from VDUs. Flat screen monitors do not emit radiation and take up much less space. Even the type of carpet must be considered, as static electricity can build up in carpets with a high proportion of synthetic material. An anti-static mat will earth a person and reduce the chance of painful shocks, or damage to sensitive equipment.

26.6 A Well-Designed User Interface

It is good practice for those who design ICT systems to seek to include the following elements in their systems to help create good user interfaces:

+ **An appropriate type of interface.** As described in section 26.3 different types of interface are available. It is important that the most appropriate interface is chosen for each particular situation.

+ **Consistency across the interface** of each package. Icons and menus should be in familiar, consistent locations on the screen to reinforce long term memory. The appearance should also be consistent between packages. Users will be more comfortable if a new application behaves like something they are used to.

+ **Screen design.** It is important to choose a screen design that is appropriate for the likely users: size, font and amount of text; use of colour; inclusion of graphics. Care should be taken to prevent cluttering the screen, and to choose images which are meaningful. Real world concepts, such as a scissors icon for cutting, will afford the purpose of the icons.

+ **Suit the needs of all users.** The interface should allow for both novice users, who will need guided through tasks, and expert users, who will want to use shortcuts and to be able to customise parts of the interface, such as toolbars.

+ **Input/output devices.** If possible, users should have a choice of input or output devices to aid with visual impairment, or personal choice, such as preferring keyboard shortcuts over a mouse. Good interfaces will be able to cope with disability tools such as spoken commands and larger screens.

+ **Error resistant.** It should be possible for a user to reverse an incorrect action. Actions with serious consequences, such as formatting a hard disk, should ask the user to verify that this is really what they want to do. Error messages should be meaningful and their message easy to understand, even by novices.

+ **Suitable help facilities.** Help should be context sensitive and appropriate to the needs of the user. Online help should be built into the software as well as being available from the Internet. Typically, it should contain an index of topics and a tutorial for beginners, and a place for typing in questions.

Good Design Versus Bad Design

Many programs with poor interfaces do not fail because of a single, overwhelmingly inept problem. Rather, a number of small annoyances build up to the point where the user begins to resent the system. For example, how often have you experienced one, or more of the following?

+ A new version of a frequently-used software package changes the layout of menus for no apparent reason, resulting in confusion.

+ Web sites that hide the purpose of buttons until a mouse-pointer is hovered over them.

- Word processors that re-format a document, for example by changing font size throughout, because the user did not de-select an option they did not know existed.
- Assistants that appear offering help with irritating regularity but with few instructions on how to de-activate them.

The key to understanding what constitutes good design is to look at examples of bad design. The easiest way to measure the success of an interface is to gauge the reaction of the target user, a group which is usually comprised of advanced users. For example, a lengthy form driven interface may appear tedious to an advanced user, but this may not be a fair judgement as it was probably not designed for them. To judge its effectiveness, it should be tested with the target, non-expert audience. To put it simply, if they get frustrated while trying to use the commands then it is a bad interface. If they feel the joy of achieving something, no matter how long it takes, then it is a good interface.

This process of assessment is ongoing. If, after several months, the user still has a satisfactory experience with the interface, instead of being bored because it is now too simple for them, the interface designers have done a very good job indeed. Users may have achieved this by learning shortcuts, or because the interface handles routine tasks well without presenting them as drudgery. A well designed interface will contain lots of power within the menus but these menus will be constructed so that novice users do not have to go near the powerful and potentially confusing material they do not need.

Many of these ideas are discussed in "Controlling Your Environment Makes You Happy'" by Joel Spolsky available via: http://tinyurl.com/4zgf

Questions

1. What is HCI? (4)
2. Give two reasons as to why human computer interaction is important in a typical information system. (4)
3. It is important that a system is 'user friendly'. What does this term mean? (2)
4. What is a command-line interface? (3)
5. Describe why advanced users may prefer a command-line interface over the alternatives.(2)
6. Describe why inexperienced users may not want to use a command line interface. (2)
7. Name and describe the four main features of a GUI. (8 marks)
8. Describe two differences between a command line interface and a GUI. (4)
9. What is a natural language interface? (2)
10. State the kind of user who would prefer to use a natural language interface. Give a reason for your choice. (2)

Questions

11. There are two main types of prompted-dialogue. Name and describe both, using a graphical illustration in your description. (3 each)
12. Identify and justify one suitable application for each of the following user interfaces (2 each):
   (a) command line (b) graphical user Interface (c) form-driven interface.
10. Describe two psychological factors that could influence human interaction with a computer system. (6)
11. Describe three ergonomic factors that could influence human interaction with a computer system. (6)
12. List and describe three factors that should be considered in the design of HCI. (6)
13. In the context of HCI, what is 'affordance'? (2)
14. In the context of HCI, what is 'familiarity'? (2)
15. State two reasons why different packages often have similar interfaces. (4)

CHAPTER 27
User Support and Training

27.1 Introduction

No matter how good a system is, it will not reach its full potential if it is not used properly. Many users adopt inefficient working methods simply because they do not know how to carry out a task in the system, or perhaps don't know that it can perform the task at all. For example, how many readers of this book have:

+ Created a table of contents by manually writing down the page number where each section of a document begins, then typing this up and repeating this process with each draft?

+ Fed numbers into a spreadsheet but calculated a total using a calculator?

It is easy to laugh at these examples but until a person is shown a more effective method to their existing one, they may not know that there is one. Some advanced users may simply tell others to "use the auto page numbers function", but unless they are shown how to do this, such advice will be useless. This chapter deals with the support and training available to both novice and advanced users.

27.2 Types of User Support

A variety of training methods are available to companies and to private individuals. These are chosen depending on the needs of the company or individual concerned, although not all methods may be suitable in all scenarios.

User Documentation

Most packages are supplied with user guides as part of their help functionality. Provided a user has a basic amount of knowledge, this is a useful first line of support. However, if the user's skills are very basic skills, a guide may be confusing, particularly if the documentation uses a number of technical terms. User documentation generally falls into the following categories:

+ A brief **'getting started'** or **installation guide** to help users get a new system up and running. This is a small booklet that provides an overview of hardware requirements, and basic instructions on installing a system. It details the main features of the software while referring users to the full manual where appropriate.

+ A **user manual** or **reference section** explaining how to use each feature of the system. This will generally include step by step instructions on performing all tasks along with appropriate examples of input/output screens and menus. User manuals may be supplied in printed form though are more commonly in electronic format, which is easier to search. Electronic manuals usually take the form of a PDF document which is included on the installation disk.

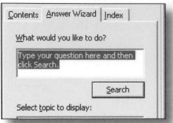

Figure 27.1: A Help system consisting of a searchable index. The user types in details of their problem and click 'Search' to be shown relevant Help topics.

Figure 27.2: Example of a step by step tutorial in Microsoft Word.

‹ **A searchable index**, included in the software itself. Such a system usually contains both an indexed set of help materials and tutorials (see next point). When the user has a problem, they click on the Help button (or otherwise activate the Help system) in order to bring up a window where they can type in details of the problem (see example in figure 27.1). The system will then present a list of topics that they can scroll through and select from. The help is usually context-sensitive, ie appropriate to what the user is doing at the time. It is also much easier to find topics with such a system than with a printed manual.

‹ **Tutorials**, usually included with electronic Help systems, take the user step by step through common tasks in order to teach them how to operate the system. Figure 27.2 shows a tutorial from Microsoft Word, in this case teaching users how to create a watermark.

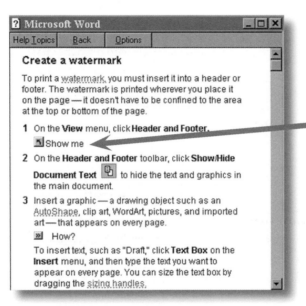

Clicking here highlights the header/footer of the document you are working on.

‹ **Troubleshooting facility**. This gives examples of common problems and error messages that may be displayed and what action should be taken to resolve the problems. Troubleshooting may take the form of a list of Frequently Asked Questions (FAQs), a document containing details of the most common queries associated with the system, and the solutions to these queries.

‹ **Tip Of The Day**. When some applications start up, a random tip is displayed on the screen (figure 27.3) often telling the user about features they might not have previously used. This is a form of pre-emptive error prevention.

Telephone Help Desks

These may be called by users who are experiencing difficulties and who wish to speak to an expert user. The operator has access to the same system as the user and may guide them through a solution by describing the process in detail. An improvement of such systems allows the operator to access the user's desktop via the Internet, which is particularly useful if the user cannot explain the problem

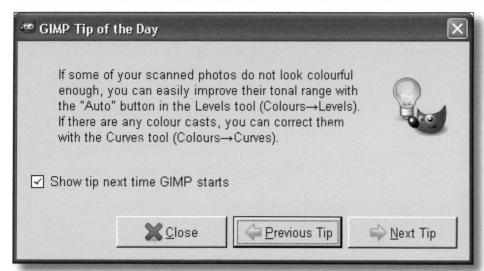

Figure 27.3: An example of a Tip Of The Day, displayed when starting GIMP, an open-source graphics program.

properly or if they are not adept at using the system. A major advantage of this approach is that users can describe their problem to someone who probably has seen it many times before, knows precisely how to help, and works on a phone line that is available 24/7. However, frustration may develop if the help desk is permanently busy, if there are multiple menu options given by an automated switchboard, or if the operator does not understand the user's description of the problem.

Switchboard Roulette?

By the way...

Callers to automated systems may sometimes feel like they are playing roulette: when they are offered a list of options, it can seem as if sheer luck determines whether or not they will 'win'. However, if the switchboard system is properly designed it will assist the caller by directing their enquiry to someone who can help them. For example, the recorded message *'Press 1 to place an order, press 2 to ask about an existing order, press 3 to return goods, press 4 for any other enquiries'* is helpful because the fourth option puts the caller through to a human being. Compare this with the message *'Press 1 for orders, 2 for existing orders, or 3 for returns'*. Here, the purpose of commands 1 and 2 are unclear, and there is no option for users whose request is not contained within the menu offered.

Other positive design aspects may use a caller's telephone area code to route them to an operator in their area, such as a pizza delivery firm who advertise a single phone number for the whole UK, but automatically redirect calls to the shop closest to the caller (or perhaps to an automated message saying, 'Sorry, we don't deliver in your area').

Although such systems have come into widespread use during the past decade, the first **Automated Call Distributors** went into service during the 1970s. Modern **Interactive Voice Response Systems** detect touch tones and perform simple speech recognition: for example the caller could read out a parcel's tracking number to a courier's automated system.

Online User Groups

Many programs have unofficial groups of users who help each other via online forums (figure 27.4) or through an e-mail distribution list. These provide personal contact between experienced and new users, and somewhere where members can post requests for help with particular problems. Archives of old material are often available on the Internet. On busy groups, a query is often answered within a few hours or even a few minutes. Many companies encourage the presence of user groups, viewing them as a valuable information source. Those who benefit from groups in turn often answer other queries, as a way of repaying the help that they were freely given.

Figure 27.4: MVPs.org, the web site of the "Microsoft Most Valuable Professional" program, offering community-based forums and advice to users of many Microsoft applications.

The process of learning a new system can be made easier for new users through good user interface design. This topic is included with the material on user interfaces in Chapter 26 but, in summary form, good interface design includes the following elements:

+ An appropriate type of interface;
+ Consistency across the interface of each package, and between packages;
+ Good screen design;
+ Suit the needs and skill levels of all users;
+ A choice of input and output devices;
+ Error resistant;
+ Suitable and adequate help facilities.

27.3 ICT, Training and Re-Skilling

As previously discussed, there are a number of ongoing costs involved in maintaining an effective computer system after it is first installed. As ICT is a constantly changing industry, an organisation must commit to regular training and updates if it wishes to remain effective. The following issues should be addressed before installation and before training methods are chosen:

+ **Training**. Employees must have the requisite skills if they are to do their job efficiently. Staff who are appropriately trained are better prepared to take on new challenges than those who are unsure about what they are doing. As ICT becomes increasingly important to daily working life, existing employees will require more and more training to keep up with developments.

- **Cost**. Depending on the method of training and the number of staff who require it, the cost could be substantial. An outside provider may have to be paid, which means that there may be transport and accommodation costs if training takes place off site. A business may also need to hire temporary replacements for staff who are absent, or pay existing employees to work overtime. If training takes place on site, there is the cost of resources such as CD-ROMs and DVDs.

- **Time**. A significant amount of time will have to be allocated to ensure thorough training or re-skilling. Although this is necessary to improve long-term productivity, short-term productivity is affected.

- **Willingness**. Busy employees may resent training, disregarding it as a disruptive waste of time. There are those who fear they will find it too difficult, and will be left behind or made to look 'silly'. Employers have to consider their employees' attitudes towards training when planning staff development days, and ensure they remain co-operative.

- **User needs.** Training must meet users at their point of need. There is no point putting novice or nervous users into an advanced course where they may not possess the prerequisite knowledge and be intimidated by the ability of others. Likewise, it would be inappropriate to expect an advanced user to benefit from a week of training aimed at novices.

- **Impact on ongoing work**. If employees attend training, they will not be able to complete their normal work. If it is reassigned to someone else, the other person may first need to be trained to understand the first person's tasks. If employees are making a transition between the two systems, such as during a phased or parallel implementation, there may be inefficiencies or duplication for a time.

The pace of change in the ICT industry is such that many people who were previously involved in other industries have decided to change career and re-train to enter ICT. For example, the decline in heavy engineering in Northern Ireland in the 1980s and 1990s resulted in many people from this industry choosing to re-skill in the field of ICT. In a similar way, many people within ICT choose to re-train in new, emerging areas of ICT.

27.4 ICT-based Training Resources

ICT can be used for training purposes, not only in the field of ICT itself, but in many other areas of work. Below are some examples.

Computer Based Training

This extends the idea of the tutorials found in many software packages. They add a separate program that replicates aspects of the software that a user is being trained to use. The tutorial, accessed via a network terminal or presented on optical disk, is interactive. It demonstrates a series of steps in using software that are reinforced through having the user work through exercises themselves with a test at the end. Demonstrations typically include multimedia elements (sound, animation, video) to show the user exactly what they should be doing: in the same way that a teacher would demonstrate before writing before asking students to repeat a task.

Computer based training allows many people to be trained at the same time, but at a pace that suits their own learning needs. This may also be cheaper than sending off many staff on a training course, as the materials would represent a single one-off payment as opposed to the ongoing cost of employing specialist trainers and associated travel costs. However, the training may prove ineffective if it does not force the user to repeat what they have been shown: the user may just skip through it. Also, a user's progress may be monitored by their supervisors to ensure a satisfactory pace is maintained and to give the user support in difficult areas.

Such systems may be accessed via CD, but it is also possible to design systems that are accessed via the Internet. The business subscribes to services provided by a specialist training organization. The services provided may include different levels of training (depending on a user's prior experience), a tailored study program that keeps track of the learner's progress and online assessments at the end of each training module. Support from a (human) tutor may be available via e-mail, video conferencing, telephone, or online forums.

Organised Training Courses

Dedicated providers may run training courses in their own premises, although this may not suit an organisation that needs its staff to be available at short notice. Large firms may therefore provide **in-house** training. In this approach, a group within the company has the responsibility of providing training courses for all staff. This has two main advantages: the courses are designed to exactly match the company's requirements, and it is conveniently located.

However, it is possible that the expertise needed will not be available internally. Both small and large organisations without the necessary expertise may therefore **outsource** their training. If a company is the only one using a particular course, it can be tailored to their precise needs. A company may arrange for selected employees to be sent for intensive training for a few days or even a week. Employees returning from courses may be in turn expected to train their own colleagues (sometimes referred to as **cascade training**). This is often expensive but has the advantage that an 'expert' is present within the organisation.

Many colleges offer part-time courses in ICT, teaching everything from courses for complete novices to advanced courses in specific packages. Although this training must be paid for, many people find it to be a worthwhile investment. Some people use these courses simply to gain experience in unfamiliar software. Others seek to gain formal qualifications, such as **OCR** word processing or the **European Computer Driving Licence** (ECDL). While private individuals may use such courses, many companies also recognise the value of them and fund those employees who wish to complete formally recognised courses in their own time.

Whether organised internally or externally, any course should be delivered by staff who are proficient in using the system. The tutor should be flexible enough to adapt the course to meet the needs of users, whether they are novices or experienced users. The tutor will usually demonstrate tasks via a PC and multimedia projector, before allowing students to work through related exercises at their own pace. These courses may be supplemented with CD or printed resources to recap key points of the lesson. In a course, users benefit from the support of an experienced tutor who can answer their questions as well as comparing their learning experiences to those of others. The experience is improved by the fact that they take place away from workplace distractions.

While many users benefit from such formal classes, others will prefer one-to-one training with a tutor to ensure they move at a pace that suits their needs.

Video Training

The advent of high capacity storage media, such as DVDs, allowed the development of affordable interactive video training products. DVD-based exercises are explained by an actor or tutor. Although the user can rewind and replay material, there is no opportunity for questions. Unlike computer based training, there is less scope for evaluation of a user's progress as exercises are not simulations of the application that are built into the training DVD. Rather, the user carries them out in the applications package they are learning.

With the growth of high bandwidth Internet connections, many video providers began to make their services available online to private users for whom the expense and/or use of DVDs may be impractical. A quick search on the Internet will reveal online training videos for most popular applications. While this may be of benefit to reasonably competent users, novices may benefit more from full computer based training.

| Investigate the support and training methods discussed in this chapter, and any others you may be aware of. What are their relative strengths and weaknesses? | **Task** |

---

1. Name and describe three methods of support that may be available to software users, along with a related advantage and disadvantage of each. (12)
2. Describe two ways in which the user interface of an information system can be designed to assist new users. (4)
3. Describe three implications for training as a result of the increasing use of ICT. (6)
4. State two reasons why some employees may resent training courses. (2)
5. Describe three different ways in which training could be provided for the users of a new software system. (6)
6. The training requirements of users may differ. Summarise the training and support methods that would be particularly suitable for:
   (a) an office worker with some ICT experience who is being introduced to an accounting package;
   (b) a network administrator with ten years' experience doing the job;
   (c) a person who has bought a PC, having never used one before. (6)

Questions

CHAPTER 28
Legislation

28.1 Introduction

Like any other area of life, there is a great deal of legislation that governs our use of ICT. Because ICT is a relatively new medium within our society, it was necessary to write a number of new laws to reflect its use and abuse. These laws have serious implications for our use of ICT, such as the handling of intellectual property and censorship.

Some of the material that comes under the category of "Legislation" is covered in earlier chapters. Therefore, it is **essential** that the student reads this chapter in conjunction with the following chapters:

+ Chapter 11, which details how ICT has affected society.

+ Chapter 12, which describes the various laws and acts that relate to ICT, and their implications for organisations, employees and the public.

28.2 ICT Legislation and Their Implications

Any new technology can lead to fresh opportunities for crime. It is often the case that these are not adequately addressed by old laws. For example, in the early 1980s hacking was not illegal within the UK simply because existing legislation did not make provision for it. The law had to be adapted to make provisions for this purpose.

There are four main laws governing the use of ICT. These are described in detail in Chapter 12, but a summary is provided here for convenience:

+ **The Data Protection Act (1998).** This Act governs how personal data can be used by defining the rights of both data subjects (people whose data is stored) and data users (people who store and/or use the data).

+ **The Copyright Designs and Patents Act (1998).** Although it covers a wide range of areas, within ICT this Act defines a series of offences for actions such as illegally copying software, using illegal copies, running software on more machines than licenses have been acquired for, modifying software without the copyright owner's permission and downloading or uploading illegal copies of software.

+ **Computer Misuse Act (1990).** This Act defines as offences any attempts to gain unauthorised access to a computer system (whether or not it is secure), gaining unauthorised access with the intention of committing or facilitating a crime, or for causing unauthorised modifications of the contents of a computer.

+ **Health and Safety (Display Screen Equipment) Regulations (1992).** These regulations set out the requirements that employers must meet to ensure the health and safety of employees that use computer equipment in work.

You should be able to describe these laws, together with their implications for an organisation, its employees and members of the public. These implications are discussed along with the relevant legislation in Chapter 12, while the more general implications of ICT on organisations, employees and the public are discussed in Chapter 11. However, a summary of the implications of ICT legislation is provided here for convenience:

+ Organisations that use personal data are required to register with the Data Protection Commissioner stating who they are, what data will be used, and where it is to be used. Data used for payroll processing is exempt, as is data that is related to national security or crime prevention.

+ Individuals who use data for personal reasons, such as Christmas card lists, are also exempt from registering with the Data Protection Commissioner.

+ Data users must adhere to eight defined 'principles' when using data. Data subjects have the right to see data held, and request that errors be fixed.

+ All businesses and private individuals must ensure that they have valid licenses for all software they use, and processes in place to ensure this remains true.

+ Businesses must take steps to secure data and access to computer systems, and ensure that one single member of staff cannot commit fraud alone.

+ Computer users should install appropriate firewalls and anti-virus software.

+ Businesses are responsible for the health and safety of employees, in areas such as eyestrain, repetitive strain injury, back problems, stress and radiation.

Crime and ICT

While mass processing of personal data was time consuming in the era before computers were widely used, it is now very easy to copy millions of individuals' personal data to portable media. Because of this, and the potential for abuse, there is a need for strict data protection legislation. Although companies require the freedom to process customer information relating to purchases and promotional material, customers need protection against the abuse of their personal details. This is vital, as many people do not take their online privacy seriously. The potential for identity theft is very real.

One consequence of the ease of copying digital media is that clear distinctions relating to what is and what is not theft are becoming blurred. A number of companies have attempted to enforce **Digital Rights Management** (**DRM**), but the inconvenience this causes for innocent users has prompted a number of firms to rethink the use of this technology. Paradoxically, there are people who would never think of stealing goods from a shop or a CD from a friend may not see any moral objection to downloading illegally copied music or buying a fake sports shirt.

28.3 Ownership and Intellectual Property

The use of computers and the Internet has posed a number of problems for the definition of **ownership**. In the conventional sense, property theft leads to the victim having less than they had before the theft took place. For example, if John steals Alan's CD, Alan no longer has that CD. However, if someone illegally downloads or uploads MP3s, nobody suffers from a reduced CD collection. Likewise, if somebody uses the Internet to watch sporting events without paying subscription charges, or to download a copy of an expensive software application, nobody has less property than they had before.

The counter-argument, however, is that engaging in this kind of activity results in somebody losing money that they otherwise would have earned. For example, if enough people download the latest album by a popular band instead of paying for it, it will cause that band to lose income that they are legitimately due. Digital data can be thought of as **intellectual property**, and making copies without the owner's permission is therefore intellectual property theft.

The arguments here are not new: they have been going on since at least 1842, when Charles Dickens campaigned on behalf of himself and others. He demanded proper recognition in America for the copyright of foreign authors whose works hitherto sold in huge volumes without a penny being paid to the original writers.

Patent and Copyright laws were created to prevent the reuse of other peoples' ideas. These laws offer a compromise between the need for inventors to make a living and the reality that an approach that is too heavy-handed stifles further innovation which often proceeds by refining and combining diverse ideas. This book, for example, benefits from the reuse of ideas:

+ It was written on word processors which copy ideas from other word processors;
+ The word processor is installed on a computer with an operating system that borrows ideas from many other operating systems;
+ The computer sits on top of a desk that borrows many features from various furniture designers.

Despite the fact that the debate is not new, the Internet has made crime, including copyright theft, more efficient for the perpetrators. There are many web sites (for example, *AllOfMp3*, based in Russia and which has subsequently been closed down) that distribute music without paying anything to the original artists. Further, the details of many other goods are regularly transmitted to the Far East, where replicas are made to be sold back to the West. The ability to easily transmit the details of football shirts, watches and designer clothes has undoubtedly aided the worldwide trade in counterfeit goods.

Setting up a web site in a country with a liberal approach to copyright is fairly easy in today's environment. The user does not even need to be physically in the same country as the servers, or the country in which the domain name is registered. Consequently, preventing and prosecuting criminals requires a high degree of co-operation between police forces across many countries.

The consequences of a widespread erosion of the concept of copyright are far-reaching in society. If consumers become used to the idea that ownership applies only to tangible objects, then they will become accustomed to downloading whatever software they want from online pirate sites or wearing counterfeit clothes.

Schools and universities have also become involved in the debate, as a growing number of students are being accused of plagiarising coursework. Despite the fact that the purpose of coursework is to honestly appraise a student's abilities, some of these people appear to see no ethical or legal problems with downloading coursework from the Internet. These people may go on to fake information on their CVs, running the risk of being sacked, or even prosecuted, if their dishonesty is later discovered.

> **Task**
>
> Split your class into two groups and hold a debate on the assertion:
> "*This house believes that it is acceptable to copy and share music and software.*"

> **By the way...**
>
> **These news stories cover topics related to ownership and ICT:**
>
> "File 'sharing' or 'stealing'? The semantic debate over whether copyright infringement is theft", LA Times, 18 February 2008, http://tinyurl.com/2n7czt
>
> "Pirate Bay Waters Get Choppy", BBC News Online, 31 January 2008, via http://tinyurl.com/39mbuw

28.4 Censorship and Surveillance

The Internet has become a serious obstacle for any government that wants to censor information, but also presents a golden opportunity for those who want to carry out surveillance on what people are doing. In this sense, it is just the latest battleground in the ongoing war between those who want to allow all information to flow unhindered (free speech) and those who want to control it in some way (censorship).

A generation ago, the older technology of Short Wave radio broadcasts allowed the BBC *World Service* and *Radio Free Europe* (among others) to be heard in Eastern Europe against the wishes of the Communist authorities there. In even earlier generations, there were those who printed controversial magazines, pamphlets and booklets, and those who tried to prevent the publication of what they regarded as subversive documents.

There are many reasons why governments may suppress information:

+ Dictatorships may want to prevent an exchange of political ideas that could lead to revolution and loss of power;
+ Democratic regimes may want controversial information silenced if it could threaten to destabilise the Rule of Law;
+ Governments may also seek to suppress information that would jeopardise a criminal investigation, or lead to a threat to security. For example most maps

published in Northern Ireland over the past forty years have omitted details of the buildings within military and police facilities (showing them as fields);

+ During a time of war, information that could damage troop morale or national confidence may not be reported. Letters sent home by soldiers may also be censored to prevent details of military operations falling into enemy hands;

+ In the world of entertainment, anything that is deemed unsuitable for a particular audience, such as a film with extreme violent or sexual content, may be edited or have its circulation restricted.

Censorship as it is carried out within the UK is often regarded as being less sinister than censorship in many other countries. During the World Wars, the British government suppressed information that may have been useful to the enemy. There is a striking difference between the environment of the first World War, during which material was restricted lest it should fall into the wrong hands, and that of today's society, which allows camera crews to broadcast live from a battle zone or soldiers to write blog entries about their experiences. There is always a need for authorities to encourage responsible reporting since the opposing forces can read material online just as easily as their families. Soldiers writing whenever they are tired or anxious might inadvertently give the impression that their troops are losing the war, and the media may be tempted to over-sensationalise a story just to gain more viewers or readers. These approaches do not take into account the effect that negative reporting can have on a country's morale.

This area of the specification examines how the Internet has impacted upon censorship, rather than simply addressing the debate that is being waged over the issue of free speech on the Internet.

The *Golden Shield Project* is a well-known example of state-managed censorship and surveillance. Nicknamed 'The Great Firewall of China', this project was organised by the country's Communist leadership to monitor and control the

By the way...

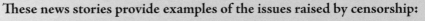
These news stories provide examples of the issues raised by censorship:

"Manhunt 2 Wins Battle for Release", BBC News Online, 14 March 2008, via http://tinyurl.com/27v4zp

"Did the Internet Get Away With it?" BBC News Online, 28 March 2008, via http://tinyurl.com/2qx9su

"Army Pulls Harry out of Afghanistan", The Scotsman, 29 February 2008, via http://tinyurl.com/2h6jjg

"Britain is a 'Surveillance Society'", BBC News Online, 2 November 2006 via http://tinyurl.com/wjl7y

"Phorm fires privacy row for ISPs" The Guardian, 6 March 2008, via http://tinyurl.com/2vtc58

"Dutch Islam Film Website Shut", BBC News Online, 23 March 2008, via http://tinyurl.com/2on8pt

BBC News Online "Interview with Sir Tim Berners-Lee", 17 March 2008, via http://tinyurl.com/368euz

people's Internet usage. A significant element was the ability to block those web sites that the Chinese police authorities considered to be dangerous or politically incendiary. The long list of restricted pages has included the *BBC News* site, *YouTube*, *Wikipedia*, the image hosting site *Flickr* and various blogs. Although Chinese law on this issue is not as stringent as it once was, many sites remain forbidden, including daily news sites, discussion forums, file hosting services and anything relating to the region of Tibet. This decision to censor information, and to arrest and torture those who break the law, is an ongoing concern, particularly to those organisations campaigning for human rights.

In countries with a more liberal tradition, suspect or illegal material is difficult to control. For example, documents promoting terrorism that may breach the British legislation on inciting violence can be published abroad and accessed from computers in the UK. A concern for parents is that, apart from totally banning their children from using computers, there is no foolproof means of preventing them from accessing unsuitable material. Any discussion on the pros and cons of freedom of speech must address the question "what if a child stumbles across content of a highly sexual or violent nature?" Despite many advances, Internet Service Providers are still unable to reliably take account of the age of the person accessing data.

An issue closely related to censorship is **surveillance**. In countries such as China, the authorities can monitor and censor the information that an individual is accessing on the Internet. While there are those who argue that innocent people have nothing to fear, it is nonetheless a concern to many that the UK is among the most monitored societies in the West. There are those who argue that the increasing use of ICT in everyday life, such as closed-circuit television systems, electronic traffic enforcement cameras and commerce on the Internet is leading to a situation where the government has an increasing ability to carry out surveillance which could, under unscrupulous leadership in the future, be used to exercise more control over people's lives.

28.5 Health and Safety Issues

It is important that users consider the long-term effects of computer equipment on their health. Long-term improper use of a PC can lead to serious and permanent health problems. Employers have a duty to consider those who work for them and not place them at unnecessary risk. To this end, there is legislation covering health and safety (see Chapter 12) that ensures employers take their responsibilities seriously. However, users also need to be aware of their own responsibility to take steps to protect themselves. Some of the more common health and safety issues related to ICT are described below. These topics were introduced in Chapter 12, but are described in more detail here.

Repetitive Strain Injury (RSI)

RSI is caused by repetitive physical movements which can, over time, cause damage to muscles, tendons and nerves in the arms and upper back. For example, long-term intensive typing at high speeds on a keyboard without a wrist rest or a lack of regular breaks combined with the constant use of pointing devices can both contribute to RSI. The symptoms of RSI include pain or numbness in the shoulders, neck, upper back, wrists or hands, and it can lead to long term disability. According to the Chartered Society of Physiotherapy, almost 450,000 UK workers had upper limb RSI in 2007, while between 2003 and 2004 about 4.7 million work days were lost to RSI, with affected workers taking an average 18 days sick leave.

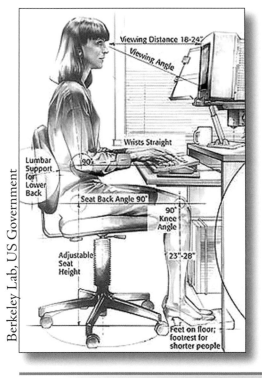

Figure 28.1: The ideal seating position at a computer involves a number of elements that affect all parts of the body.

Berkeley Lab, US Government

The risk of RSI can be minimized by:

+ **Taking regular breaks,** for example five minutes hourly to stretch.

+ **Using a wrist rest** to support the wrists.

+ **Switching to an ergonomic keyboard** which is moveable and separated from the screen (see section 2.2). When using any keyboard it is important to only tap the keys lightly.

+ **Adopting the correct posture**. The user should be able to sit straight and should not have to stretch to touch the keys or read the screen. A comfortable viewing distance is generally 50-60cm with the top of the monitor screen at eye level. Elbows should be kept close to the user's sides at an angle of least 90 degrees. Wrists should be in a neutral position ie not bent and slightly lower than the elbows while typing or using the mouse. Figure 28.1 shows the ideal position.

+ **Using a height-adjustable seat**, with a backrest which is adjustable both backwards and forwards as well as up and down so that the user's eyes are level with the screen. The chair must be stable and capable of swivelling. Feet must rest flat on the floor: if necessary a footrest should be used.

+ **Reducing the need for typing** and use of the mouse by using voice recognition as an alternative method of input.

+ **Positioning a document holder** between the monitor and keyboard to avoid twisting the neck to view source material.

By the way...

RSI is a real issue! RSI doesn't just affect people who slouch in front of their computer, as the following stories show:

Squeaky Mouse to Tackle RSI, BBC News Online, 10 May 2000, via http://tinyurl.com/333gu4

A new touch-sensitive mouse promises to make life on-line easier for millions of computer users. The mouse prompts a computer to squeak when the user presses it too hard. This could help reduce the risk of repetitive strain injury (RSI). Michael Macaulay, one of the creators of the new device says: "Studies have shown that the more anxious you are... the harder you are likely to press the mouse..." Bunny Martin, an RSI consultant, says there is a real risk as we increasingly click on mice and tap on keyboards. "If you wiggled a piece of electrical wire up and down, over and over again... it starts to fray and break... The difference between a computer and a human being is that we're not robots and I can't unscrew your arm and re-wire your wiring."

RSI Danger from Excessive Texting: BBC News Online, 9 June 2006
via http://tinyurl.com/pxsre
Experts have warned of the dangers of overuse of mobile phones and game
consoles in children after a young girl developed repetitive strain injury [she]
noticed pain in her fingers and wrists after sending up to 30 text messages a
day. RSI is normally associated with office workers who spend hours hunched
over a computer keyboard. But the condition is becoming common in children
addicted to technology... Sending text messages can lead to RSI because mobile
phone users tend to hold down their shoulders and upper arms when pressing
the buttons, cutting off blood to the forearm. Physiotherapist Bronwyn Clifford
who helped develop the guide said: "Excessive texting and prolonged use of the
buttons and dials found on an array of modern hand held gadgets, including
MP3s, Blackberry devices and portable games consoles, can contribute to
hand, wrist and arm problems. "The small, definite, repetitive movements used
to manoeuvre controls on these tiny handsets can begin to cause pain over
time. The thumb, while good for gripping, is not a very dextrous digit and is
particularly susceptible to injury."

Back Problems

Many computer users suffer serious back problems. This is often due to a poor
posture while sitting at a computer. Back problems can be minimised by:

- **Positioning the monitor and chair properly** (as described above).
- **Using a footrest** to ensure that feet are properly supported, and in turn
  supporting the back.
- **Having the correct posture** (as described above). It is important not to slouch.
- **Taking regular breaks** and changing position. Prolonged, static posture can
  also contribute to back pain.

Eyestrain

Users of computer monitors (VDUs) can suffer from eye problems such as
eyestrain, irritated eyes or blurred vision. This can often be caused by working
for long periods of time without interruption, with screens that flicker, or where
there are reflections on the screen from bright windows. Some research has also
suggested that work with VDUs may increase the risk of seizure in those suffering
from epilepsy provoked by flashing or flickering light.

To reduce eyestrain:

- The VDU should have a stable, flicker-free image and be capable of being
  tilted. It should have easily adjustable brightness and contrast controls, and
  have a swivel base.
- The VDU should have an anti-glare panel fitted, although many users also
  have an antiglare coating on their spectacles. LCD screens on laptops can only
  be used at certain angles without the colours becoming distorted.
- Users should regularly take their eyes off the screen and focus on another
  object, preferably a distant one, as well as taking hourly breaks.

- Users should undergo regular eye tests.
- The VDU should be placed in a position to avoid reflections from lights or windows. Reflections can be reduced by avoiding brightly painted or shiny white walls and fitting adjustable blinds to windows.

Emissions

VDUs emit relatively low levels of electromagnetic radiation when they are operating. Most of this radiation is given out from the back and the sides of the VDUs. Since radiation levels fall rapidly with distance from the VDU, it is advised that users should sit at least 50cm from the screen. Despite concerns that miscarriage or birth defects may occur when pregnant women work for long periods at a VDU screen, several recent studies have failed to find evidence to support these fears.

Recent research has also focused on concerns over the use of Wi-Fi networks, mobile telephones and laser printers. For example, scientists have discovered that some laser printers can emit potentially dangerous levels of toner into the air, damaging lungs in much the same way as smoke particles from cigarettes. The evidence that radiation from mobile telephones can damage health is inconclusive, with concerns generally limited to those who hold phones for extended periods next to their skulls. However, no published research has yet identified a definite health risk associated with Wi-Fi.

To reduce the amount of potentially harmful emissions:

- Peripherals such as printers should be located in a separate room to minimise airborne toner (and to reduce noise in the office).
- Wi-fi networks should only be switched on when required.

By the way... This story gives additional information on the concerns around emissions: "Wi-fi health fears are unproven", BBC News Online, 21 May 2007, via: http://tinyurl.com/29jx84

Stress

Some people find that working with computers can cause stress-related illnesses. Many people fear that the introduction of ICT into the workplace can lead to them being made redundant or that they will be unable to use the hardware or software and appear stupid. The constant need for re-training to keep up with technological advances can add further strain. Recent research reveals that employees are suffering from 'e-mail stress' and find it difficult to cope with the constant need to check and read the many e-mails that arrive in their inbox.

Some organisations may also use ICT to monitor the performance of their staff, for example a supermarket may analyse the speed at which an employee at the checkout can scan products and process a sale. Some supermarkets request that warehouse employees wear a computer on their wrist to allow orders to be transmitted directly to the employee. The computer can also calculate the time an employee should take to complete a task and identify staff who take unauthorised breaks. All of these uses of ICT can contribute to a person's stress level.

In today's society, we have become accustomed to rapid responses with no delay. We are used to sending an e-mail and expecting a response within the hour. If a news story is breaking in America, we are frustrated if we cannot read a news story only a few minutes after it happens. For many workers, this immediacy has been translated into an increased expectation that they can be contacted while away from work. For many office workers, the 9-5 day now starts when e-mails are checked at home, at 7am, continues on a laptop PC on a train and extends into the early evening with the same electronic devices. This loss of freedom can lead to mental problems, such as feelings of being 'out of control' or imprisoned in a technological jungle from which there is no escape.

As the dependency on ICT grows both in the workplace and home, stress levels can intensify when systems fail, for example if a computer or network develops technical problems and important work is lost. Stress in a person's life can manifest itself through a number of symptoms and may lead to more serious mental and physical health issues such as inability to sleep, headaches and increased susceptibility to illness. Stress may lead to long periods of absence from work.

To reduce stress:

+ Hardware and software should be of an **appropriate standard** to meet user needs. For example if multiple programs have to be open, then the computer should have sufficient RAM.
+ **Backups** should be performed regularly to avoid data loss and stress in the event of technical problems.
+ **Training opportunities** should be taken and user support contacted to get advice when a difficulty arises.
+ Employees should be encouraged to **keep work within working hours** and turn mobile phones off when they go home.

By the way...

These news stories cover topics related to stress and ICT:

"E-mail Stress, the New Office Workers' Plague", The Observer, 12 August 2007, via http://tinyurl.com/39fmll

"Firms Tag Workers to Improve Efficiency", The Guardian, 7 June 2005, via http://tinyurl.com/35z6sv

Questions

1. Summarise the main features of legislation relating to ICT. (5 each)
2. Describe two implications for an organisation as a result of each of the following legislation: (a) Data Protection Act (b) Copyright, Designs and Patents Act (c) Computer Misuse Act. (4 each)
3. Describe two implications for an individual as a result of each of the following legislation: (a) Data Protection Act (b) Copyright, Designs and Patents Act (c) Computer Misuse Act. (4 each)
4. Give three reasons as to why information may be suppressed. (3)
5. Describe how the Internet makes censorship of information difficult. (2)
6. Describe how the Internet has changed the definition of ownership. (3)

Questions

7. What is RSI? How can it be minimised? (3)
8. Poorly designed workstations can lead to health and safety issues. State three features of a well designed workstation, and for each feature outline the health and safety problem(s) that will be avoided. (6)
9. Identify four steps that should be taken to minimise eyestrain. (4)
10. Identify three causes of stress. (3)

CHAPTER 29
Professional Issues

29.1 Introduction

The *Concise Oxford English Dictionary* defines ethics as "The moral principles governing or influencing conduct". Ethics, as an academic discipline, has strong links to the development of both philosophy and religion. It is a much wider area of study than could be contained within a single chapter of this book. But whether or not they have formally studied the subject, most people have ethical views on many topics. In other words, most people have a view on whether activities such as copying CDs, plagiarism, taking drugs, hacking etc are 'right' or 'wrong'. For many people, regardless of their legal, religious or philosophical beliefs, these views are not entirely rigid, but can be influenced by the context.

This chapter discusses the ethical issues that you may face as an ICT professional. It also outlines the ways in which companies may attempt to pre-empt unethical practice and ethical dilemmas. For many of those working in ICT, their ethics are influenced by professional bodies such as the *British Computer Society (BCS)* or the *Association for Computing Machinery (ACM)* in the USA.

Ethical Dilemmas - Grey Areas?

Consider the following ethical dilemmas. Some are typical ICT-related situations while others are dilemmas often posed to students of ethical philosophy. In each situation, what would you do?

Task

+ You are the points operator for a railway company. You receive a phone call to tell you that a landslide has caused rocks and debris to fall onto the track. A train full of passengers will reach that point in one minute, most likely derailing and killing everyone on board. If you switch the points, the train will take a safe route but will hit some railways engineers who are working on the second line. You have no way to warn the engineers or the train driver in time. What do you do? Would your decision be different if you were told that the passengers are young children on a school trip? What if you were told that they are all OAPs?

+ You work for a large global ICT firm whose motto is 'Don't Be Evil'. You believe in freedom of speech and have liberal political views. However, the largest expanding market in the world has a government whose political philosophy contradicts much of what you believe. The government is known to take severe action towards opponents or anyone who acts in a way that opposes the state's official position. You have the opportunity to expand your search engine's operation into that country, creating new jobs, but only if you agree not to display results relating to human rights abuses in that country or to political dissidence. What do you do?

Then read "Google Move 'Black Day' For China", BBC News Online, 25 January 2006, via http://tinyurl.com/7fs6f

---

+ You work for a large Internet firm based in the West, and value freedom of speech. A national government considered by many Westerners to be intolerant of criticism asks you to pass on details that will identify an anonymous blogger. The blogger is extremely critical of the government's actions, and it is possible that he will be tortured if he is arrested. Yet the country's laws require you to pass on the information if you operate there, and the business be severely penalised if you do not. What do you do?

Then read "Yahoo In Second Chinese Blogger Row", The Times Online, 9 February 2006, via http://tinyurl.com/2q8h5p

The purpose of these tasks is to demonstrate that in ICT, like all areas of life, there are often no clear answers to ethical dilemmas.

29.2 Ethics and ICT

In any organisation there are many opportunities for employees to abuse their position. For example:

+ A postman may steal cash and credit cards out of envelopes, or open parcels to check them for valuables;
+ A checkout operator may fail to properly record sales, and steal the money the customer thinks they have paid to the shop;
+ An office worker may take paper or other stationery home for personal use.

ICT has its own particular ethical dilemmas, but the underlying ethical issues are common to all areas of life and work. A-Level students are expected to show an understanding of ethical practices that may affect their future career as ICT professionals. One common debate within ICT relates to the activities of one or two very large software companies, which may be perceived by some to be anti-competitive, but by others to be examples of successful business models. However, this part of the course is not intended simply to teach students about the opinions people have on the ethical behaviour of particular companies. Rather, the student is encouraged to understand the wide range of ethical issues that an ICT professional may meet, regardless of the products they use or the environment in which they work, so that they can judge ethical dilemmas for themselves.

ICT professionals have many opportunities for practices that may have an ethical or legal dimension. Examples of such practices include:

+ **Use of unlicensed software.** This may include a business knowingly buying insufficient licenses for a product (and hoping not to be caught); using the business software at home, outside the agreed license; or distributing unlawful copies of the business's applications software (such as, selling CDs of an office suite).

- **Improper use of rival's data**, to benefit the company. In 2007, the McLaren Formula 1 team faced severe penalties when they were deemed to have used technical data that an ex-Ferrari employee brought with him when he joined McLaren. While a Ferrari employee has access to much data that would benefit rivals, it is considered unethical for him to breach his former employer's confidence in such a way. In many firms it is common for senior staff to have several month's 'gardening leave' when they resign to go to a rival: they are effectively paid to sit at home and forget as much as possible, while missing out on new developments and innovations in their former firm.

- **Improper use of personal data** which the company may nevertheless have legitimate access to (eg details of private communications or finances). This may include passing sensitive data to third parties or using private data for blackmail (such as threatening to reveal a person's private details to prospective employers, or threatening to divulge financial details to others).

- **Plagiarism** of material, for example from the Internet, in place of proper research. While it may be tempting to cull material from web sites when faced with deadlines, this leads to a lack of thorough knowledge of material and will be detrimental in the long-run. If such material is published, it may lead to embarrassment for the firm and potential lawsuits for breach of copyright; Many companies clarify grey areas with strictly-enforced **Acceptable Use Policies**, (see section 29.3) that outline what is and what is not an acceptable use of company ICT systems. In addition, the professional bodies that many ICT professionals are expected to belong to have clear codes of professional conduct that members are expected to adhere to, with little tolerance given to those who bring the profession into disrepute.

The Need For Ethical Training

From a legal perspective, it may be a company's directors who are ultimately held accountable for their subordinates' malpractice if they have not instigated proper procedures to prevent unlawful acts. These procedures may include training courses, agreed codes of conduct and monitoring of employees' activities.

Companies may have a responsibility to ensure that employees understand the difference between what is deemed to be right and wrong. This is particularly important in our modern society, where morality is often viewed as being relative to an individual's situation, rather than being based on an agreed universal standard. As we have seen, many people feel that it is acceptable to make unlawful copies of software, music CDs or DVDs for their personal use, even though they would never consider shoplifting. There is a danger that this sense of moral relativism will be carried into their professional duties, hence the need for ethical training.

For example, workers may feel that it is acceptable to use unethical practices to benefit the company, such as the use of pirated software or 'hacking' into rival firms' computer networks. While workers may feel that unethical activity is fine at home, where there is a reasonable chance that they may get away with it, such practices are not tolerable in a professional environment because of their many far-reaching consequences. Such consequences include creating a climate of dishonesty or illegal behaviour which may spread through the firm, and possible legal action that could cripple the company (the collapse of Enron being a notable example).

29.3 Acceptable Use Policies

Many organisations expect their employees (or, students) to sign an **Acceptable Use Policy** (or **Employee Code of Practice**) before they are given access to company ICT facilities. At first glance, this may seem strange as ICT equipment is often the only type of equipment that is singled out for this special treatment. However, in a climate of widespread misuse of ICT and the legal procedures that may follow from it, many companies have been left with no option but to take this route. An Acceptable Use Policy (AUP) is designed to make users aware of what is regarded as acceptable use of ICT, within the company's aims, and to give examples of misuse. No AUP can be exhaustive, however, so staff are expected to use their professional judgement (and their professional body's guidance) in deciding what is and is not an acceptable form of research, proper business communication and use of time.

AUPs may draw inspiration from professional bodies' codes of conduct (see section 29.4) and may be incorporated into a company's training and disciplinary procedures. For many users, the first part of an Acceptable Use Policy that stands out is the provision that allows management to log all network activities. Users may wonder if agreeing to the AUP is effectively giving management a 'licence to snoop'. However, effective managers will remind employees that data logging also protects them, in the event of allegations of wrong doing and that employees whose conduct is appropriate have nothing to worry about. After all, if an employee does not send potentially libellous e-mails, and doesn't spend work time playing online games then there is no cause for worry. At the same time, most managers will see certain grey areas here. For example, a manager who decides to discipline a staff member for a single personal e-mail or using a work computer to book a flight (as opposed to conducting extensive holiday research) is likely to face a staff backlash.

The typical contents of an Acceptable Use Policy are as follows:

+ A statement of the **purpose of the AUP**: usually, to encourage effective use of ICT in order to support business objectives, while protecting the organisation and its employees from misuse of ICT;
+ A description of **what is regarded as an appropriate use of ICT**, in relation to the organisation's objectives;
+ A description of **what is regarded as appropriate personal use of ICT**, so long as this does not conflict with the organisation's objectives and ethics. Typically this may include:
  + A statement that personal use of the Internet, provided it is during working breaks, is acceptable;
  + A statement that personal use of company ICT must not be for personal

financial gain;

+ A description of **what is regarded as inappropriate use of ICT**. This may include:

    + Accessing certain web sites, for example sites that work colleagues or clients may find offensive (such as adult sites) or sites that are considered a distraction from work (such as chatrooms);

    + Installing software that is not clearly authorised by network managers, to restrict the likelihood of unlicensed software or malware being installed;

    + A restriction on the use of portable storage devices or data that can be carried on laptops to minimise the likelihood of accidental data loss, or wholesale transfer of data to rivals;

    + Sending personal e-mail from a work e-mail address. Legally, e-mail is on a par with communication on the company's headed notepaper and the company can be prosecuted for anything defamatory sent via a work address;

    + A restriction on the use of portable entertainment devices. If unlawfully copied MP3s are allowed to be in use in the office, who is legally responsible: the employee, or the employer who turns a 'blind eye' to many staff accessing pirated music?

Amoeba and Acceptable Use of E-mail

At Amoeba, Paul is having a bad day. He writes an e-mail to a colleague:

From: pwhite@amoebaantinques.com
Message: *Jane Smith is such a moaner, she is always complaining! She never pays her bills on time, yet expects...*

He could have instead printed out the message on company letterhead:

AMOEBA ANTIQUES (and logo)

Jane Smith is such a moaner, she is always complaining! She never pays her bills on time, yet expects...

He could even have put an article in the company newsletter, under the headline:

JANE SMITH IS A MOANER

Jane Smith is *such a moaner, she is always complaining! She never pays her bills on time, yet expects...*

This may seem like a facetious example since most people would never print out messages like this. However, the same people may very well consider sending the message by e-mail within the firm, or even outside the firm. Amoeba's managers are aware that, odd as it may seen, there is no legal difference between any of the three messages above. Libel is the publication of falsehoods about a person, regardless of how it is published. This is why Amoeba's Acceptable Use Policy is clear that such messages must never be sent, even by e-mail.

VNU Net reported on what is thought to be the first legal action involving libel-by-e-mail, in October 2000, accessible via http://tinyurl.com/yuboe3

Task

Within your school, there may well be an Acceptable Use Policy. Discuss:

+ What aspects of it benefit students?
+ What aspects of the AUP seem pointless?
+ What does the AUP ignore, that should be included?
+ What aspects of the AUP can be abused by staff?
+ If you were Head of ICT, what would your AUP contain?

29.4 Professional Bodies

To promote standards of professional behaviour within the ICT industry, bodies such as the **Association for Computing Machinery (ACM)** and **British Computer Society (BCS)** have drawn up ethical codes that members are expected to adhere to. Members who are found to be working in a manner that is not compatible with these codes may face expulsion or a loss of rank within the organisation. For many ICT professionals, membership of a professional body is an important part of career development and may help in establishing links with new employers or clients: expulsion would therefore be damaging to any career.

Ethical codes such as these may be incorporated into companies' usage policies or training. As well as outlining a need for responsible use of ICT (such as not pirating software or unlawfully gaining access to others' data), these codes also describe general good working practices such as honesty and good workmanship. As with the need for ethical training, these documents originate, in part, from professional bodies' realisation that not all professionals automatically consider ethical behaviour as their 'default' position.

Regardless of the ethical code a person is working to, a general pattern is seen of:

+ General moral standards of honesty and fairness;
+ Duties as an ICT profession: to use one's knowledge for the betterment of society and not to take advantage of those without your knowledge; not to behave in a way that brings the wider ICT industry into disrepute;
+ Ongoing personal development: the expectation that an ICT professional will remain abreast of changes in the technology he or she may encounter, in order that clients and subordinate staff benefit;
+ Leaders acting as role models and examples to their subordinates;
+ Responsibilities to clients: to deliver products of as high a standard as possible that meet the client's requirements, without gaining through taking advantage of others' lack of technical knowledge;

Professional bodies exist to further the interests of members as individuals and of the wider professional community they represent. By encouraging appropriate behaviour, and by saying to employers that "Our people can be trusted because they all adhere to a particular set of standards", the profession is viewed in a better light and appropriate standards can be maintained.

The ACM Code of Ethics

The Association of Computing Machinery's full *Code of Ethics* can be viewed on their web site at www.acm.org/about/code-of-ethics It consists of 24 main points, formulated as statements of personal responsibility. Each point is expanded in the full document and identifies the elements of each commitment. The points are:

1. General Moral Imperatives.

As an ACM member I will ....
1.1 Contribute to society and human well-being.
1.2 Avoid harm to others.
1.3 Be honest and trustworthy.
1.4 Be fair and take action not to discriminate.
1.5 Honor property rights including copyrights and patent.
1.6 Give proper credit for intellectual property.
1.7 Respect the privacy of others.
1.8 Honor confidentiality.

2. More Specific Professional Responsibilities.

As an ACM computing professional I will ....
2.1 Strive to achieve the highest quality, effectiveness and dignity in both the process and products of professional work.
2.2 Acquire and maintain professional competence.
2.3 Know and respect existing laws pertaining to professional work.
2.4 Accept and provide appropriate professional review.
2.5 Give comprehensive and thorough evaluations of computer systems and their impacts, including analysis of possible risks.
2.6 Honor contracts, agreements, and assigned responsibilities.
2.7 Improve public understanding of computing and its consequences.
2.8 Access computing and communication resources only when authorized to do so.

3. Organizational Leadership Imperatives.

As an ACM member and an organizational leader, I will ....
3.1 Articulate social responsibilities of members of an organizational unit and encourage full acceptance of those responsibilities.
3.2 Manage personnel and resources to design and build information systems that enhance the quality of working life.
3.3 Acknowledge and support proper and authorized uses of an organization's computing and communication resources.
3.4 Ensure that users and those who will be affected by a system have their needs clearly articulated during the assessment and design of requirements; later the system must be validated to meet requirements.
3.5 Articulate and support policies that protect the dignity of users and others affected by a computing system.
3.6 Create opportunities for members of the organization to learn the principles and limitations of computer systems.

4 Compliance With The Code.

As an ACM member I will ....
4.1 Uphold and promote the principles of this Code.
4.2 Treat violations of this code as inconsistent with membership in the ACM.

The BCS Code of Conduct and Code of Good Practice

The British Computer Society (BCS) have a *Code of Conduct* that *"sets out the professional standards required by the Society as a condition of membership. It applies to members of all grades... The Code governs your personal conduct as an individual member of the BCS and not the nature of business or ethics of [your employer/client]. It will, therefore, be a matter of your exercising your personal judgement in meeting the Code's requirements."*

The Code is summarised below. The BCS have also issued a much lengthier *Code of Good Practice*, that gives practical advice on how to work as an ICT professional, including developing professional relationships with clients, maintaining one's professional knowledge and training and ensuring a professional standard of workmanship. Both of these documents are available, in full, from the BCS web site via http://tinyurl.com/34r9qm

The Public Interest

1. In your professional role you shall have regard for the public health, safety and environment.
2. You shall have regard to the legitimate rights of third parties.
3. You shall ensure that within your professional field/s you have knowledge and understanding of relevant legislation, regulations and standards, and that you comply with such requirements.
4. You shall conduct your professional activities without discrimination against clients or colleagues.
5. You shall reject and shall not make any offer of bribery or inducement.

Duty to Relevant Authority [Employer/Client/Educational Establishment]

6. You shall carry out work or study with due care and diligence in accordance with the relevant authority's requirements, and the interests of system users. If your professional judgement is overruled, you shall indicate the likely risks and consequences.
7. You shall avoid any situation that may give rise to a conflict of interest between you and your relevant authority. You shall make full and immediate disclosure to them if any conflict is likely to occur or be seen by a third party as likely to occur. You shall endeavour to complete work undertaken on time to budget and shall advise the relevant authority as soon as practicable if any overrun is foreseen.
8. You shall not disclose or authorise to be disclosed, or use for personal gain or to benefit a third party, confidential information except with the permission of your relevant authority, or at the direction of a court of law.
9. You shall not misrepresent or withhold information on the performance of products, systems or services, or take advantage of the lack of relevant knowledge or inexperience of others.

Duty to the Profession

10. You shall uphold the reputation and good standing of the BCS in particular, and the profession in general, and shall seek to improve professional standards through participation in their development, use and enforcement.

11. You shall act with integrity in your relationships with all members of the BCS and with members of other professions with whom you work in a professional capacity.

12. You shall have due regard for the possible consequences of your statements on others. You shall not make any public statement in your professional capacity unless you are properly qualified and, where appropriate, authorised to do so. You shall not purport to represent the BCS unless authorised to do so.

13. You shall notify the Society if convicted of a criminal offence or upon becoming bankrupt or disqualified as Company Director.

Professional Competence and Integrity

14. You shall seek to upgrade your professional knowledge and skill, and shall maintain awareness of technological developments, procedures and standards which are relevant to your field, and encourage your subordinates to do likewise.

15. You shall not claim any level of competence that you do not possess. You shall only offer to do work or provide a service that is within your professional competence.

16. In addition to this Code of Conduct, you shall observe whatever clauses you regard as relevant from the BCS Code of Good Practice and any other relevant standards, and you shall encourage your colleagues to do likewise.

17. You shall accept professional responsibility for your work and for the work of colleagues who are defined in a given context as working under your supervision.

Ethical Dilemmas in ICT

Task

Discuss the following issues that many ICT professionals face. Go beyond a simple "Yes I would" or "No I wouldn't" answer and examine the issues from as many angles as possible. In all these scenarios, assume that resigning from your job is not an option.

- You work within a small family firm with a limited budget. All office computers are using a special edition of Microsoft *Office* that is intended for students, but is much cheaper than the full version. It was bought by your manager, who claimed it was for his daughter's laptop PC. You are a member of the BCS and are aware of their ethical codes. What do you do? Is your response affected if the company is a multi-national firm? What if the company is a small firm of solicitors, whose manager does not see a problem?

- You volunteer for a small charity who have been given four old PCs to use in their administration. While the PCs are old, they will run *Windows 98* and old office software, that meets the charity's needs perfectly well. You happen to have CDs for those products, licensed for personal use. What do you do?

- You are the Head of ICT in a school with a limited budget. While you have sufficient PCs with office software, you intend to use Adobe *Dreamweaver* with a number of GCSE and A-level classes, and would like students to have access to it at home. However, your budget only allows you to buy licenses for a few PCs. You know the skills taught through *Dreamweaver* are very useful in both study and work. What do you do?

- You are a student member of the BCS, studying Computing at University. As part of your course, you are expected to develop software with professional development tools. Unfortunately your University computer laboratories have limited access times. You are offered a CD from a fellow-student, for five pounds, with software that normally costs several hundred pounds. What do you do?

- You are the ICT manager in a company. A senior Manager asks you to install unlicensed software on his laptop PC. He is aware that you are a member of the BCS and that you strictly monitor licensing procedures: he also expects you to turn a blind eye in this instance. What do you do?

- You are a junior member of a company's ICT department and discover that your manager, also a member of the BCS, has knowingly been installing unlicensed software throughout the firm for several years. What do you do?

Questions

1. Discuss the social, moral and ethical issues for a professional working within the industry that might arise as a result of the introduction and use of information and communication systems. (9)
2. What is the purpose of an acceptable use policy? (3)
3. Outline the typical contents of an acceptable use policy. (4)
4. Explain the role that professional bodies play in promoting standards within the ICT industry. (3)
5. Outline three clearly different ethical dilemmas that an ICT professional may face. Present the counter-arguments for each. (6)

CHAPTER 30
Implications of ICT

30.1 Introduction

ICT has had many effects on how employees carry out their jobs and communicate with each other. This section explores these impacts in more detail, both in terms of employees and in terms of the organisations they work for. Some concepts, such as the development of e-mail, have already been discussed elsewhere in this book. **Teleworking** is discussed in this section for the first time, but the reader should ensure that they are already familiar with the underlying technologies, such as the Internet, upon which it relies.

30.2 Information Systems and the Service and Manufacturing Sectors

Good use of information systems results in an efficient flow of data throughout a modern organisation, allowing people at all levels to have better access to data needed for their daily jobs and planning the future. To understand the effect information systems have had on organisations it is worth considering the example of Amoeba Antiques, a modern organisation, and exploring how they would operate with and without information systems.

Today, communications between warehouse and stores, and the data processing at head office, is almost instantaneous. Indeed, many transactions are processed automatically and only considered by a human if an exception report indicates that something unusual is happening. A few years ago, it was normal for an order to be processed after a few days. Today this would be unacceptable.

Orders are either phoned to Amoeba's call centre, sited many miles from the warehouse, or placed online. They are then automatically transmitted to the warehouse for processing. The warehouse managers can see a continually updated list of pending orders. Meanwhile a customer can view the status of their order online or by phoning the call centre, and can make changes to their order up until the order is about to be dispatched. As stock levels fall, manufacturing facilities are automatically alerted and can operate without requiring a human to manually report to the factory. Management can view summaries of what is currently happening in the company and view historical data, details of current trends etc. All this is possible because of the way transaction data is processed and stored.

Now, consider how this would have operated in 1969, not 2009. Orders would be placed either by phoning an office at the warehouse, or by writing a letter. The order would be passed to the warehouse on paper, and making later changes

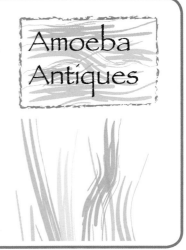

Amoeba Antiques

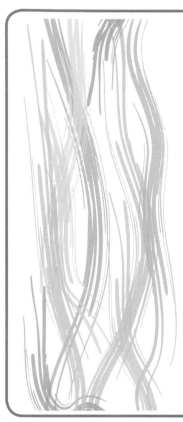

to the order would be difficult as someone would have to visit the warehouse to find it. A customer enquiring about the status of an order could phone with their query, though they may have had to wait a few hours for someone to phone back with the results. Management had no way to analyse trends easily as this required several people to process records manually. Suppose a manager was wondering when customer orders for Christmas goods usually started arriving at the warehouse: he would have to ask somebody in his department to go through a series of filing cabinets and copy out and summarise the necessary data. His query would be answered hours, or even days, after it was first made.

The intervening years have seen many changes in the way goods move around Amoeba's warehouse. Today, when an order is being processed in the warehouse, a bar code on each item is scanned at each step. When this was first introduced warehouse staff were sceptical, since they felt they could tell simply by looking, where things were. But this system allows analysis of how items move and where bottlenecks exist within the warehouse, information that would have been tedious to gather before. This data also allows customers to view the status of their order online, without being in touch with any warehouse staff. However, the use of bar code scanning in Amoeba is due to be replaced with **Radio Frequency Identification (RFID)** which uses tags (tiny integrated circuits) containing information about the product they are attached to and capable of transmitting this data to transceivers within the warehouse. RFID tags can be used to record where each item is automatically.

At the operational level, the automation of data gathering has fed the development of information systems. Data that was too time consuming to collect forty years ago can now be gathered instantly. The instant gratification afforded by information systems reflects many other aspects of 21st century culture: today people do not expect to wait in a restaurant or a shop and expect call centres to answer their queries immediately. The lengthy waits that management experienced forty years ago were part of a wider culture that many people today are not used to.

Manufacturing

The manufacturing industry depends on a factory taking some raw materials, putting them through a process and shipping a product. In the past human intuition and experience were used to estimate quantities of raw materials. The layout of the factory was based on the assumption that human experts would not order too much material to fit in the warehouse, or let finished stock build up and use up all the storage space. It was vital to estimate demand correctly: if the experts under- or over-estimated production, the company might lose money and not be able to correct the problem in time. Successful companies thus depended on human experts accurately predicting trends in the marketplace. These human experts had access to only a fraction of the data now available through information systems. Effective use of information systems today can remove a great deal of uncertainty from decision making.

Information systems assist manufacturing in the following ways:

- Planning for the future is much easier today because historic and current trends in the marketplace can be accessed with great ease.

- The difficulty in assessing quantities of raw materials is removed. Historical data of exactly how much raw material is consumed on each product, including wastage, can be analysed. Indeed, if several production lines make the same product, each line can be analysed separately to look for excessive wastage in one area.

- If a new product is to be made, CAD/CAM systems (see section 11.8) configure tools automatically and report the amounts of raw material required to factory warehouse and ordering systems. Once a designer is finished, advanced CAD/CAM systems can configure themselves and transmit orders for materials directly into suppliers' databases (which may be part of a chain of automated ordering and manufacturing systems going back to mines or quarries). Little human interaction may be required until the finished product is taken off the production line.

- Communications between suppliers and customers today is much more than the ordering of goods and subsequent invoicing. Some companies allow each other to access their systems to allow data to be transmitted seamlessly between them. For example, a warehouse system could transmit re-orders for raw materials without humans even having to notice that stock levels are falling, or a courier could be automatically informed that goods are ready to be picked up.

Service Sector

The service sector is that part of the economy principally made up of insurance, tourism, banking, retail and education. This sector operates in a different way from manufacturing but has also benefited through information systems. As with manufacturing, the use of information systems allows for analysis of trends and forward planning. The following paragraphs summarise the impact in each sector.

Task

All businesses rely on others to some extent. The use of information systems in each type are only briefly discussed below. For an area of your choice, and based on your knowledge of information systems *and on further research*, prepare a report describing how information systems are used in this area.

Insurance: Today people can take out insurance policies against all sorts of events occurring, such as a motor accident or household robbery. People pay a premium to the company and, if the event occurs, the company makes a financial payment back. It is vitally important for insurance companies to be able to evaluate the risk associated with each client to determine how much the client should pay. If certain events happen a lot to certain people, the cost of being insured against these events rises. In simple terms, if a person is deemed a 'bad bet' by the insurance company they either pay an increased premium or may not be offered insurance. For example, people living in certain areas are more likely to be the victims of flooding, while drivers of certain social groups (such as young men) are statistically more likely to have a car crash, so they pay more for car insurance. Insurance companies share data about their customers to detect fraud and to make better informed decisions about risks faced in particular geographical areas and social groups.

Task Investigate how insurance companies use information systems for forward planning, sharing data, and minimising their losses.

Tourism: In a tourist area, account must be taken of the impact that tourism has on public transport, communications, shops, events, hotels and restaurants. All of these organisations depend on each other. For example, entertainments depend on hotel space being available while the hotels need the entertainments to attract people. Shops depend on car parks and the local roads, and so on. Information systems help managers assess these interdependencies.

For example in 2008 planning permission was being considered for the redevelopment of a Tesco store in the centre of Coleraine, with a new multi-storey car park nearby. Because such a development could have significant impacts on traffic, and hence have effects on tourism in the town, information systems could be used to predict the effect on car parking and trade both during construction, and upon completion. This information could be used by road planners to alter the phasing of traffic signals and perhaps use brown tourist signage to direct tourists around local retail bottlenecks.

Task Investigate a tourist area or resort and the use of information systems by managers within the areas listed above.

Banking: Banks do much more than look after people's money. Investments may be in a simple deposit account with little interest, or customers may choose to invest a sum of money for a fixed term for a guaranteed return: eg £2000 for 2 years with 8% interest guaranteed. Appropriate steps must be taken to ensure the bank does not promise what it cannot deliver, and indeed the banking crisis of 2008 proved that in some cases these steps were insufficient, requiring government intervention.

As well as investing on behalf of customers, banks lend money to individuals and businesses and this money is paid back in a number of ways. For example, a car loan is usually payable over a few years at a fixed interest rate while a mortgage is often over 25 years at a variable rate. A business could borrow £1 million to build new premises, payable over a fixed term for future negotiation depending on how the business performs. In either case the bank must ensure they not only make a profit, but also that the loan is likely to be repaid (as with insurance, they ask if a customer is a 'good bet'). Information systems are a key tool in determining whether or not a loan should be made, and the likely return. Banks can use the Internet to instantaneously check the credit rating of any customer and contact their head branch to download details of the latest loan and investment products.

Task Investigate how a bank uses information systems to decide what products are suitable for domestic and commercial customers, and other ways information systems are used to guide decisions within the bank's operation.

Figure 30.1: Years of planning, predictions of consumer demand and models of traffic flow were carried out with information systems before even the foundations of Belfast's Victoria Square shopping centre were laid. The designers were able to ensure optimal access for pedestrians, and upgrade the local road network in time for the opening in 2008.

Retail: The success of a retailer depends on a number of factors including the popularity of goods, price of goods, location and the infrastructure surrounding it. Assessments of what people will want and what they will pay must be taken well in advance of them going on sale because goods must be designed and manufactured. Successful retailers have to keep predicting consumer demand month after month. When a new store is built, its location is no accident (figure 30.1).

Investigate a well-known retailer and detail how information systems are used to plan and manage the business.	**Task**

Education: Decisions are made at a variety of levels in school. For example, departments will invest in textbooks each year, basing decisions on subject growth or decline, while school management and education authorities make long term decisions relating to staffing and school infrastructure. Long term decisions may also take account of the environment the school is in, for example, population change due to declining birth rates or immigration.

Investigate how a school and/or educational authority uses information systems, considering activities at operational, tactical and strategic levels.	**Task**

30.3 Information Systems and Society

The development of many pieces of technology, such as television or radio, can be traced back to a single event or series of events as the moment that particular technology started making inroads on people's daily lives. Many people with even a passing interest in computers can identify code-breaking machines such as the World War Two *Enigma* machine, and later devices such as the original *Apple Macintosh*, which were monumental in the development of devices we now take for granted.

However, there is no single event that people easily point to and say "That's when information systems came into our lives." Rather, the use of information systems has come about with the gradual development of computing. Because of the gradual evolution of databases and transaction processing systems the eventual appearance of information systems was often unnoticed and regarded by many as simply an improved computer system. However, the unheralded existence of information systems does not diminish their importance. Any large organisation we deal with uses information systems for forward planning and depends on them to a large degree.

Consider the following scenario, typical of western countries, which shows how a person will be in contact with information systems throughout their lives.

1. A woman becomes pregnant. Consequently, her shopping habits change slightly. Her supermarket loyalty card statistics allow her to be targeted with advertising for baby products. From the moment it is conceived, a child has registered within an information system.

2. A boy is born. His details are recorded within a hospital system. Silently, those details eventually appear on educational authority systems.

3. A local authority health visitor finds out about the birth, the baby's details having been communicated by automated systems.

4. The child's parents are reminded by automatically generated letters to have their child vaccinated and registered with a school.

5. School authorities have details of how many children are being born in their area and can plan future school capacity.

6. Other local authorities pay attention to this birth (albeit as part of an aggregate figure), so they can plan housing, sewage, electricity supply, etc.

7. As the child grows, he is represented by data on a variety of information systems: educational authorities, health authorities, supermarkets, banks, etc. To some, his personal details matter while to others he is a statistic.

8. The boy grows up and applies to universities in Scotland. Although he has grown up in Northern Ireland, Scottish banks and public transport companies are able to target him with advertising within days of his exam results being known.

9. While studying, the mobile phone company he uses builds a transmitter near his halls of residence to improve coverage. Even though there are no 'permanent' residents for some distance, the company has statistics for the quantities of calls made in that area and at what times of year they are made.

10. Within days of graduating, his bank offers him a 'graduate' account and a finance firm offers him loans for cars and holidays.

11. His supermarket stops targeting him with vouchers for instant noodles and baked beans, replacing them with advertisements for steak and expensive wine. They have noticed he is suddenly spending more money.

12. Throughout life, his data is processed in a variety of systems. When he goes to his GP with an illness, his details are transmitted to a hospital consultant and an appointment made.

13. Even in death, his details continue to be processed for several years. Statistics of causes of death are processed so that the effectiveness of health campaigns can be evaluated. Undertakers and local authorities want to plan ahead to maintain cemeteries and crematoria.

Information systems have thus impacted on every aspect of society and every aspect of a person's life. They are obvious to those who work with them every day, and millions more who interact with them on a daily basis. While the above examples may suggest information systems run our lives, the opposite is true. Information systems are only tools, albeit very powerful ones, that have gradually transformed many aspects of business and society.

30.4 Impact of ICT on Employee Work Patterns

The advent of the Internet has allowed employers and employees to explore new models of working which do not require the employee to by physically present in an office or factory to carry out some or all of their duties. The two principal technologies that allow this are **video conferencing** and **teleworking**.

Video Conferencing

Video conferencing is a system that allows people in different locations to talk to and see each other at the same time using modern telecommunications. Video conferencing was discussed in detail in section 10.3, but a brief summary is provided here for convenience.

Video conferencing systems are able to link people on several continents for a meeting, where in previous years they would have had to meet in person involving time consuming, costly and environmentally damaging aeroplane journeys. Users view their remote colleagues through monitors, while sitting in front of cameras themselves. It can impact upon working patterns by:

+ Allowing employees to work from home or outside the office.
+ Reducing the need for employees to travel to distant locations, thus reducing time from home or the office.

The advantages of video conferencing are not limited to workers. Facilities offered to the general population (such as those offered by *Skype*) allow people to keep in touch with family in more enjoyable ways than they would be able to with traditional telephone calls.

Teleworking

| Definition | **Teleworking** is the use of ICT to enable people to work at a considerable distance from their conventional place of work. |

There are four main forms of teleworking:

+ **Home-based telework** or **telecommuting**, in which an employee works at home instead of travelling to business premises.

+ **Mobile telework** or **nomadic telework**, in which executives, professionals or service staff use ICT to enable them to spend more time with customers and deliver a range of services 'on the road' that would have previously involved office-based staff or visits to the company offices. ICT can allow employees to access their office via connections in the customer's premises; via the growing number of wireless 'hotspots' in railway stations, airports, etc; or via a 3G mobile telephone network.

+ **Telecentres**, providing local office facilities for people who prefer not to work at home but wish to avoid the cost, time and inconvenience of commuting. The advantage to the employer is that office space usually costs less at these telecentres when compared with the main location of the business. Telecentres are usually shared between a collection of companies, but can be wholly owned by a single company. A **telecottage** is a smaller, more rural version of the telecentre. Both telecentres and telecottages provide communities with high-performance ICT, local employment, and the more social aspects of work that may be missed by a worker based at home.

+ **Call centres** are derivatives of telecentres. These are used mostly for customer support. As there is no specific requirement for a particular geographical location, these call centres are based in areas where it is cheap to rent office space and where the necessary skills exist. For example, one of British Telecom's main call centres for UK customers is in India. They are usually equipped with high performance ICT systems and are linked into the main ICT infrastructure of the business.

A worker wishing to telework needs a number of pieces of equipment. First of all, they need a computer with a high speed telecommunication link such as broadband to enable the employee to collaborate with co-workers. For example they should be able to access the Internet or the company's intranet or database. It is important that the employee can make use of the company's e-mail system and online bulletin board. If they are using video conferencing, they will need a webcam, speakers, microphone and video conferencing software. They may also require a fax machine, or a PC with fax software permanently connected to a telephone line. They will need storage media such as CD-RWs, memory sticks or portable hard disks

iStockPhoto.com

Figure 30.2: A call centre often employs many people hundreds or thousands of miles from the people whose calls they are answering.

to perform backups of data they hold, if they have not had a chance to upload it to company webservers. Teleworking equipment must be kept secure from intruders by way of firewalls, anti-virus software and encryption software.

The advantages of teleworking for employers are:

+ Cost savings, such as the costs of premises and labour.
+ Increased productivity due to reduced travel time and stress, and fewer interruptions.
+ Improved motivation as employees respond well to the signal of trust that being allowed to telework gives them.
+ Skills retention since employees who might otherwise leave the job may be able to stay. For example, if another family member has to move because of a conventional job move, the teleworking employee can move too. Employees who take a career break can continue working part time and remain up to date with the business. Employees who start a family can work from home, or a combination of home and office to suit their parental responsibilities.
+ Organisational flexibility allows the creation of teams which represent the best mixture of skills and experience for a particular project, regardless of geography and time zones and with a minimal need for extra travel.
+ Resilience in the face of external disruption, such as transport strikes, severe weather, natural disasters or terrorism. For example, after September 11, 2001, global finance company Cantor Fitzgerald was able to survive, despite the loss of its headquarters in New York's *World Trade Center* and 658 of its employees, by re-focusing its operations at one of its regional centres within a matter of days.

The advantages of teleworking for employees are:

+ Reduced travel time, costs and stress. Although, in contrast to the 'relaxed lifestyle' image often painted by the media, many teleworkers use part of this time to get more work done.
+ Improved work opportunities since people are not confined to applying for jobs that are within a reasonable commuting distance.
+ Less disruption to family life since the teleworker is at home more often and there is a reduced need to move house when relocated by work.
+ A better balance of work and family life, since work can be organised around the family, rather than the other way round. For example, a parent can return to work whilst simultaneously looking after a young child.
+ Participation in the local community by being able to take part in community activities at a time when commuters are still travelling.
+ Flexible hours suiting a person's daily 'rhythm'. Some people are at their most productive in the early morning, some late at night. A person can work at a time that suits them, which is not necessarily the traditional 9am to 5pm.

The advantages of teleworking to society are:

Figure 30.3: Traffic congestion wastes thousands of hours every day. Teleworkers can avoid the rush hour, saving time and money.

+ Reduced traffic congestion (figure 30.3). Studies for the UK Department of Transport show that even on days when teleworkers do commute, they tend to choose off peak times that suit their flexible hours, hence avoiding traffic jams. In Belfast, a city with few teleworkers, it can take up to an hour to travel along the M1 motorway into the city at peak times.

+ Reduced total travel and consequent pollution. Studies also confirmed that teleworkers generate a worthwhile net reduction in total car travel.

+ Wider employment/work opportunities. Telework has the potential to give people in an area of high unemployment access to work opportunities that arise anywhere in the world. Notable examples of this are areas of Canada and India whose economic programs involve selling themselves on a world-wide level as desirable locations for foreigners to set up call-centres, a policy which has been very successful.

+ Access to employment opportunities for people with specific needs. For example, those with disabilities that make it difficult to travel to work or endure a normal working day; single parents; carers with responsibility for an elderly or sick relative.

+ Economic regeneration in areas with high unemployment, thanks to government incentives for the location of telecentres.

The disadvantages of teleworking are:

+ An organisation may have less control over their employees. Management may find it more difficult to monitor the work rate of employees.

+ Some people lack the motivation to work alone, and need the discipline provided by set hours and a managed environment. If a person is new to a job he may need this discipline while he settles into his role. For some people, physically going to work is an important part of their lives, which separates work from their personal lives or provides a place to make friends and develop their social skills and contacts. Telecentres may address some but not all of these issues.

+ The place that a teleworker uses may be badly equipped for some kinds of telework. For example, even the most highly motivated individual could have problems focusing on complex tasks in a small apartment with children underfoot and noisy neighbours. Or the person's home may lack the proper telecommunications infrastructure for efficient contact with the office. Telecentres would be more appropriate in such cases.

+ An organisation will have a greater dependence on technology to facilitate communication between employees thus increasing costs. The use of telecommunications can leave an organisation more vulnerable to security risks such as hacking or viruses.

+ An organisation may not be well adapted to the flexibility that telework can provide. This may be due to a lack of the necessary technology or management not trusting staff to work effectively on their own.

+ The work itself may not be appropriate for telework. There are many tasks that require the close interactions of a team working together in one room. Examples include some kinds of design or other creative work, where the atmosphere of the studio or research setting is an important part of the creative process. In some activities there is an advantage to the team spirit and internal motivation generated by leaders and managers sitting with the teams and 'leading from the front'. In addition, some jobs such as distribution or manual labour, clearly have little or no potential for teleworking.

The Rise of the Teleworkers

Government figures show their numbers have more than doubled in the last eight years. And there are now nearly 2.4 million of them... Typically teleworkers are male, older, self-employed and likely to work in the building and construction industry. According to the latest data from the Office for National Statistics,.. they are also likely to be managerial, technical and professional staff.

"Working from home has remained an important element of teleworking," said the ONS, "but developments in electronic networking now make it possible for people to work in other remote locations, such as neighbourhood centres, Internet cafes, hotel rooms, clients' premises, on trains and in cars."

BT has been issuing some of its telephone engineers with PDAs so they can see the job schedule at home and drive straight to the first job of the day, instead of clocking in at a depot first.. And the London Borough of Sutton has been piloting the use of PDAs and hand-held printers by its social workers. The innovation has helped cut the length of time necessary for their clients to receive their benefits from 12 weeks to just two...

According to the ONS, the big increase in teleworking has been driven by more people working in different places but using home as their base. They far outnumber those who simply stay at home to do their work... It remains unclear whether the surging numbers are people who are simply doing the same jobs as before but with the aid of mobile phones and computers - or, instead, doing work that they would never have contemplated before.

BBC News Online, 6 October 2005, via http://tinyurl.com/j6czg

By the way...

Task

Assess the opportunities that teleworking provides for each of the following people:

+ A single mother who wants to work but does not want to leave her children with a child minder for long periods of time.
+ A manager in an IT company whose wife (a doctor) has been relocated to a hospital 100 miles away from where they currently live and work.
+ An unemployed person in Delhi, India, who has learned to speak English.
+ An electrician who specialises in installing wiring in new-build houses.
+ A person who has a medical condition that requires that they be linked to a medical machine every two hours for treatment.
+ A manager who is frustrated that she has to travel over an hour from Coleraine to her work in Belfast and home again each day in heavy traffic.

Amoeba Antiques

Amoeba and telework

Amoeba are eager to adopt new technologies where this will benefit their staff. Consider the following examples.

Sales representatives: until a few years ago, sales representatives were expected to be physically present at their local Amoeba office on a regular basis – if only to drop off and collect paperwork. The use of ICT means these people use a laptop computer and connect to Amoeba's network regularly via a mobile phone connection. This allows orders to be sent directly to Amoeba on the day they are placed with the sales representative and for him or her to receive feedback immediately. Any necessary paperwork is usually handled via post.

Software developers: not all of the members of the software team were at their physical peak at 9.00am. The use of telework has allowed the 'night owls' to work at home, at night. Many of their peers who prefer to work through the day have also opted for the telework option. The use of a broadband Internet connection allows full access to Amoeba's network. This has also negated the need for some meetings because many issues that need discussed can be handled via internal discussion forums.

Staff returning from maternity leave: many office-based staff are reluctant to return to work after the birth of a child because of the associated costs of child-minding. While Amoeba have an on-site crèche this is not practical for children who are very young or for those who have to travel a significant distance. The use of teleworking allows the parents of these children to do their work and keep an eye on their children at the same time. Teleworking also allows parents to stay at home to look after sick children without missing work or to collect children from school without having to work part-time.

A graphic designer: one of Amoeba's leading graphic designers has always preferred to work alone rather than with a team. In recent years all his work has been done using computer tools. When the option of running a B&B in County Kerry came up, he and his wife could not resist the challenge. From Amoeba's perspective little has changed – he always worked alone, whether on-site or off-site. Through high-speed communications links, he remains in touch with the office and drives to Belfast once every few months.

For teleworking to succeed, a number of related issues have been considered.

Teleworking problems: whether they are 18 year old office 'juniors' or 22 year old graduates, a lack of discipline is often a problem for younger employees who may not be used to working for 8 hours per day. Hence the temptation for these people to develop a 'slack' approach has resulted in Amoeba's managers deciding not to make teleworking available to people who have been with the company for only a short time.

This not only affects young employees – there are older employees who tried teleworking but were too easily distracted at home, for a variety of reasons (family, daytime television, housework). Also, some people missed the social interaction of work. Teleworking has been particularly successful with people who had large distances to travel.

Teleworking developments: the 'brain drain' towards big cities has left many areas, such as the west of Ireland and the north of Scotland, lacking in younger residents who have often left to seek work. Amoeba realise that in such areas, property (and hence, wages) often costs less than in the cities. Consequently a new call-centre for their telephone sales-line has been sited in the west of Ireland to take advantage of an available, cheaper, workforce. The use of ICT allows calls to Amoeba's sales line to be diverted to these people who take details from the customers and enter them into Amoeba's sales system. The record of the sale is forwarded immediately to the appropriate warehouse.

30.5 Impact of ICT on Work

ICT has had many impacts on the lives of individual workers, not all of them good. On one hand, it has freed many people from dull, repetitive tasks, but on the other hand, people who are not trained to do skilled work may now be unemployable or have few career options. In general though, good use of ICT has far more benefits than drawbacks. This section discusses the main areas in which ICT has affected individuals, rather than their employers.

There is no doubt that the introduction of information systems often results in redundancies because there is a reduction in the number of jobs which require basic manual skills, and in the number of people required to run an organisation. However, many of the remaining jobs are less labour intensive and have different degrees of automation. As fewer workers are now required to do the same work, the economy can expand with more goods produced by the same number of workers.

Look at the table which shows some statistics on Vauxhall's Luton car factory for two different years. Computer Aided Manufacture was introduced to the factory between these dates. What do these figures tell us about the impact of ICT on (i) factories (ii) their employees (iii) their customers?

Task

Year	1959	2001
Number of Employees	20,000	2,000
Cars Produced	100,000	107,000
Average car price (2004 equivalent)	£15,000	£14,000

Employees now spend less time manually collecting and recording information as it can be input automatically into the information system. For example transactions in stock control applications can be recorded using bar code scanning. This will make employees more efficient and productive. Employee efficiency is also improved by the fact that there is no longer a need to use manually paper-based records. Summary reports or calculations will be compiled automatically and presented to employees in an accurate and appropriate format to employees. This will allow the employee to make more accurate decisions and allow operational staff to respond to customer queries more efficiently. Increased efficiencies may allow some employees to work part time or flexible hours. Some may be able to choose teleworking (see previous section).

Information systems enable management to closely monitor the performance of staff. For example in a sales environment the system could record and analyse the number of sales made by each member of staff per day or month. While staff may dislike the pressure that this creates, it may make them more productive.

When a new information system is introduced, old skills may become redundant and staff will have to undergo training because of new computer equipment. Different levels of staff in an organisation (strategic, tactical and operational) will have different training needs. For example in a shop, operational staff will have to be able to use the bar code scanner to record purchases and returns as well as able to query the MIS to answer customer queries in relation to stock availability. There is no guarantee that all unskilled workers will find a place for themselves in a 'knowledge based' society. Hence most western governments place a high level of importance on educating their young people in the use of IT.

A-Level and GCSE level textbooks written in the 1980s predicted that less time would be spent on work while more time would be spent on leisure (or **personal** use of information systems). To an extent this has become true: ICT is used for games, relaxation and booking holidays. However, the use of ICT has also resulted in the phenomenon of **information overload**, where people are unable to cope with the rate at which they are presented with information. In this sense, therefore, ICT has also had negative effects on people's ability to relax. Some of the more positive ways in which ICT has impacted leisure are discussed in the next section.

30.6 Impact of ICT on Leisure

ICT has changed the form of existing leisure activities as well as creating new ones. The average person now spends 50 hours per week on the telephone, using the Internet, watching TV or listening to the radio. More than 75% of 11 year olds have their own television, games console and mobile phone. Some of the areas in which ICT has affected leisure are discussed below.

Reading: eBooks, digital versions of conventional printed books, can be downloaded from the Internet and read on eBook readers or computers. Amazon's *Kindle* eBook reader lets users instantly receive newspapers and magazines they have subscribed to via Amazon, and displays documents that are sent to a personal *Kindle* e-mail address. Unlike conventional books, eBooks take up little storage space with the potential of hundreds of books being stored on a computer or eBook reader. People who have difficulty reading printed books can change the text size and font to suit, while audio versions can be downloaded onto a computer or portable media player. Once downloaded, audio books can be played anywhere and other tasks can be completed at the same time. This suits people with impaired vision as well as those who are to busy to sit down and read. When the writers of this book studied GCSE Computer Studies their textbooks predicted that within a few years newspapers would be electronically delivered to PCs overnight, to allow the owner to print only the material they were specifically interested in. While it may have seemed far-fetched, this is not too far removed from what has actually happened.

Radio: The British public continues to listen to the radio but ICT has allowed them to explore new ways to listen. 41% of the population listen to radio with their digital televisions, 24% listen over the Internet, and 8% use their mobile phones. A growing number of radio listeners regularly use **podcast** services (see section 10.4). Digital radio allows listeners to choose from a wider range of stations, receive better sound quality with no interference, do without manual tuning and receive extra information (such as pictures or text describing the program). Some digital radios let the user pause, rewind and record live radio programmes. In order to receive the digital radio broadcasts a **DAB radio** (Digital Audio Broadcasting) is required and the listener must live within a DAB coverage area.

Watching Television: Digital television can be received through an aerial, satellite, cable or phone line. In order to watch it, a user needs a **set-top box** or a TV with a built-in **decoder**. As well as extra channels, digital television provides improved reception quality, electronic programme guides and interactive features ('the red button') as well as incorporating television and radio services in a single receiver. According to recent research, digital television is now installed in 85% of UK homes with the average viewer watching 3 hours and 36 minutes per week. The majority of children between 8 and 15 years of age watch television every day. **High definition television**, or **HD TV**, offers sharper, clearer pictures and better sound, but new equipment is required in order to access these HD services. Data projectors are also a popular alternative for viewing films or games on a big screen without purchasing a large TV.

By the way...

Improved Reception

All television and radio broadcasts suffer from interference. Any listener to football commentary on Medium Wave broadcasts is used to the sound of commentators fading away at crucial moments, just as TV viewers have seen pictures break up during poor weather. Analogue receivers have no way of knowing if the received signal is what was actually broadcast or if it has been corrupted, so the viewer/listener has a less-than-ideal experience of the broadcast. Digital transmissions use **checksums** within each packet of data, so that a corrupted signal can be detected. Additional data sent with the signal allows errors to be reversed and the correct signal re-created. Hence, users see either a perfect picture or none at all.

Television on demand: The traditional concept of scheduled channels and television programmes is evolving into personalised ones matched exactly to our interests. **Personal video recorders (PVRs)** record digital television directly onto hard drives. They let the user pause, rewind and replay live action on screen whilst simultaneously recording a programme. This gives viewers newfound flexibility to watch programs at the most convenient time (and to fast forward through adverts). PVRs have built-in programme guides, making it easier to choose what to record. Some models let users automatically record all episodes of a favourite programme, or all programmes on a specific subject. Examples of PVRs include the popular *Freeview+* and *Sky Plus*.

BBC, Sky, Channel 4 and ITV all launched rival video-on-demand services during 2007 which allow the user to view television programs and films in real time over a broadband connection via a set-top box, or on a computer with a broadband

Internet connection. A device called the *Slingbox* enables users to view their recorded television programmes from anywhere in the world via the Internet. Video-sharing services such as *YouTube* allow users to share their own videos, and access material they would otherwise be unavailable, such as obscure television programmes from many years before. Many file-sharing services also allow users to illegally watch programs that are normally restricted to pay-TV services.

DVDs: Users have long been able to purchase video on DVDs. Because DVDs are cheaper to manufacture than tape, and require less storage space, a number of television and film companies have released entire series' of television programs from many years ago or re-released movies to accommodate people moving from VHS. Customers benefit from reduced storage space and better picture quality. However, there is an environmental cost of this process, since households will discard functional, but obsolete, equipment as newer devices, such as Blu-Ray players and LCD televisions, become available.

Figure 30.4: There are concerns about the effects of excessive computer gaming on health and well-being.

Computer Games: More than £1.52bn in revenue was taken from sales of computer games in the UK during 2007. Modern games come in a variety of forms, depending on how they are to be used: on PCs, consoles or handheld devices. At the time of writing the Nintendo *Wii* has successfully expanded gaming out of its traditional niche and introduced gaming to new audiences. Games are available for even very young children, with people in the 6-24 age range most likely to play. Nevertheless, the average age of the UK gamer is actually 28 (see BBC UK Games Research, via http://tinyurl.com/3bc5hb).

The growth of broadband has increased the popularity of multiplayer games with people all over the world participating in the same game. For example in June 2007 more than 9.3 million people were playing *World of Warcraft* with the average player completing 17 hours of play per week. Even game consoles, such as *Xbox 360*, *PS3* and *Wii*, can access the Internet and allow users to participate in multiplayer games. Concerns over computer games relate to the fact that people's health can suffer if they play for too long without exercising; and the effect that introducing children to violence in games could have (figure 30.4).

Task Find out how much exercise the average person is recommended to have each day. Why is this exercise important? Do you, personally, get the recommended minimum amount? Do you think ICT has contributed to a reduction in people's general health and fitness?

Music: The idea of portable digital music is not new, but formats such as **MP3** have proven popular since they do not take up much storage space (typically 1MB per minute compared to over 10MB per minute for a CD) and large numbers of songs can be saved onto a single portable device. Their popularity has been improved by the creating of online music stores, such as Apple's *iTunes* store, where people can download a track for less than £1. A number of home stereo systems are also available which can link to a PC and allow the user to listen to their entire music collection in any room.

Surfing the Internet: As of 2007, more than 50% of households in the UK had broadband Internet. The average user spent 36 minutes online in 2006, and while more than half of all children surf the Internet regularly, it is the over 65 age group that spends the most time on the web. One of the reasons for the popularity of the Internet is that it offers something of interest to all age groups. It is possible to communicate with people from all over the world via e-mail, Instant Messaging, etc. Online social networks such as *Facebook*, *MySpace* and *Bebo* allow people to interact with other people around the world, and are hugely popular with young adults. The Internet has allowed the development of online shopping, with many people choosing to shop from organisations in other countries from the comfort of their own homes. Price comparison web sites (such as *PriceRunner* and *Kelkoo*) allow users to compare the price for a single product on many competing web sites and choose the best.

Online virtual worlds, such as *Second Life* are becoming popular, causing concerns that people are going to ignore 'real life'. Other concerns about the Internet are the risks to young people of people who claim to be somebody they are not. The Internet also suffers from a lack of quality control: material on a given web site may be inaccurate, offensive or even illegal. Despite huge advances in search engine technology, people still find it hard to sift through the huge amount of information on the Internet.

In-Car Technology: ICT has done much to transform the driving experience. Rear-seat entertainment (including DVD players, games consoles and music systems), air conditioning and climate control create a pleasant environment for drivers and passengers alike. Satellite navigation systems are becoming a vital tool for motorists, both as an alternative to an atlas and as a tool for avoiding congested routes (although they have been known to direct lorries down narrow country lanes!). Ford has introduced a **Voice Control System** operated via Bluetooth which allows the driver to control their music, satellite navigation system and mobile telephone calls without lifting their hands from the steering wheel.

ICT is also being used to improve safety. Safety features such as **ABS (Anti-lock Braking System)** and air bags have been long available. Systems can now use lasers and radar to interpret the road ahead and give visual and audible warnings if a dangerous situation presents itself, and intervene and activate the car's brakes automatically if the driver fails to brake in time. Lasers can scan the road surface ahead, preparing the suspension to react to the terrain. Automatic headlamps, rain-sensing wipers and car parking sensors are also offered by many car manufacturers, while some luxury cars now have ability to parallel-park themselves at the touch of a button.

Fitness Machines: Instead of simply rowing or cycling, fitness machines are equipped with many features to help users meet their exercise goals. Consoles enable users to choose their training program based on time, distance, calories to be burnt, resistance level etc. The user's heart and pulse rate can be measured to provide feedback as to their performance during the workout. While exercising, an LCD screen will display live statistics on the user's performance.

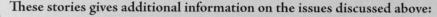

By the way... These stories gives additional information on the issues discussed above:

"Britain Enjoying Digital Boom", BBC News Online, 23 August 2007, via http://tinyurl.com/2gyqav

"Digital TV in 85% of homes as switchover start begins", Ofcom press release, 2 September 2007, via http://tinyurl.com/38elbz

"Video Games Make History in 2007", BBC News Online, 31 December 2007, via http://tinyurl.com/26m2q3

"Digital Play Digital Lifestyles" (PDF), BBC, December 2005, via http://tinyurl.com/3bc5hb

"Online Games Battle for Top Spot", BBC News Online, 26 December 2006, via http://tinyurl.com/2sp75q

"At a Glance: UK Digital Boom", BBC News Online, 23 August 2007, via http://tinyurl.com/374low

"Dimming down: How the brainpower of today's 14-year-olds has slipped 'radically' in just one generation", Daily Mail, 25 October 2008, via http://tinyurl.com/6nk3dc

Questions

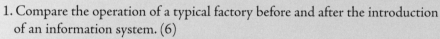

1. Compare the operation of a typical factory before and after the introduction of an information system. (6)
2. How have information systems impacted on the daily routine of a typical middle-manager? (4)
3. Consider a large organisation, with manufacturing and retail facilities:
   (a) State and describe three ways in which information systems have been a benefit to the company as a whole. (6)
   (b) State and describe two ways in which the manufacturing areas of the company have benefited through information systems. (4)
   (c) State and describe two ways in which information systems have been a benefit to customers. (4)
4. State and describe three ways in which information systems influence the daily life of an average member of the public. (6)
5. Define teleworking. (2)
6. State and describe three different types of telework. (6)
7. For each of (a) employees, (b) employers, (c) society at large, state two advantages of teleworking. (2 each)
8. For each of (a) employees, (b) employers, (c) society at large, state two disadvantages of teleworking. (2 each)
9. What is video conferencing? (2)
10. Describe two ways in which video conferencing can impact upon working patterns. (4)
11. Describe three ways in which ICT has impacted upon leisure time. (6)
12. Evaluate whether the overall effect of ICT on leisure activities has been positive or negative. (6)

CHAPTER 31
Managing Change

31.1 Introduction

The uses and capabilities of ICT are constantly changing. Readers of this book have already seen many dramatic changes in technology during their lifetime, eg:

+ The development of the World Wide Web;
+ The introduction of Digital Television;
+ The widespread use of GUIs;
+ Miniaturisation of technology, leading to a modern handheld device combining the capabilities of a desktop PC, MP3 player, camera and telephone.

While changes to people's lifestyle on this scale have occurred before (such as during the Industrial Revolution), they generally occurred over a longer time frame, and never have they moved with the same speed as recent advancements. One of the consequences of the rapid progress of technology in our current era is that the readers of this book inhabit a world that is radically different from the one in which their parents grew up. Further, it is likely to be as different again from the one in which their children will grow up.

This means that skills must be constantly refreshed, so that ICT professionals remain in touch with an ever-changing industry. For ICT end users, this means that today's 'cutting edge' is tomorrow's 'dinosaur'. The **technological graveyard** is full of obsolete gadgets and software that were once considered top of the range (*Windows* 95, VHS recorders, analogue television, Laserdisc, MiniDisc players etc) but now may well be as extinct as a Tyrannosaurus Rex.

31.2 The Changing Use of ICT

In our current environment, ICT has taken on a role imagined only by science fiction writers a few decades ago. In fact, a glance at an early episode of *Doctor Who* or *Star Trek* reveals that the writers were not ambitious enough. During the 1960s, fans of the very first series of *Star Trek* were wowed by the idea that in the 23rd Century people would have palm-sized personal communicators on which they could speak to each other across long distances, and that paper documents would be replaced by LCD screens that could store hundreds of pages. Of course, today's society has been using similar devices for some time, and many are much more advanced than anything operated by Captain Kirk and his colleagues.

These series also imagined a future where entire civilisations could be connected through a massive computer network. Little did they know that in the not-too-distant future users would be able to use such a network to send messages, transfer files, watch films, download music, book flights or even buy their groceries.

The point of these observations is to show that we have become so accustomed to the wide variety of technology available to us that we perhaps take it for granted without realising how much it has affected our lives. Consider what your life would be like if you could not:

+ Take, send and receive photographs using your mobile phone, digital camera and computer;
+ Play video games online against people all over the world;
+ Chat with friends using instant messaging services;
+ Store thousands of songs on a single MP3 player rather than owning a bulky CD collection;
+ Mount a flatscreen television on a wall as if it were a painting.

By the way...

Electronic brain implants?!

If you were able to tell one of the Science Fiction writers from the 1960s about the technology that they could expect to see in the future, they probably would not believe you. Similarly, our society often dismisses many current technological suggestions as far-fetched. For example, the idea of electronic implants in the human brain, for medical purposes or otherwise, might sound ludicrous, but think for a moment how you would have responded if you had been told that you would one day be able to surf the Internet wirelessly using a cordless telephone. Certain concepts always seem silly until somebody actually invents them. See www.kevinwarwick.com (Professor of Cybernetics at the University of Reading).

Hardware and Software Factors Influencing Change

A typical GCSE Computer Studies case study from the 1980s may have asked students to investigate how computers were making their way into their homes. In such an exercise, students would have learned that their television, washing machine and microwave oven each contained a **microprocessor**, a small, self-contained controlling computer. These microprocessors were dedicated to running a single program and were mass produced cheaply.

In contrast, the general purpose **microcomputers** such as a *ZX Spectrum* or a *Commodore 64* were owned by only a few students and were very expensive. The students who did own one were expert users by today's standards. Hardware limitations meant that modern intuitive GUIs were not practical. Therefore, the typical modern end user, who points and clicks with no idea of where data is coming from and who has limited problem solving skills, would not have been very productive on older machines. However, it was necessary for the few computer users there were in the 1980s to understand how the underlying hardware functioned. Many of these users are now in positions of technical support or ICT management.

As with any mass produced device, the cost of making computers fell, leading to increased sales and freeing up money to go into research and development. This led to major improvements in hardware that was smaller and more powerful than its predecessors. Improved systems also meant that more capabilities could be added to devices.

A major turning point for home PC users was the release of Microsoft *Windows 95*. The GUI took the ease of use of *Apple Macintosh* software to a wider public as it ran on a wider variety of (often cheaper) hardware. This resulted in disgruntled Apple users displaying the slogan '*Windows 95 = Macintosh 89*' on bumper stickers and tee shirts. However, whether or not this was a case of 'copying' is in some ways irrelevant, since the growing Microsoft user base in turn led to:

Figure 31.1: A mobile telephone from around 1995. The device was state of the art at the time, but obsolete just a few years later.

+ Falling prices;

+ A greater range of applications;

+ More investment in the development of increasingly powerful, smaller devices.

While students in the 1990s could see a clear distinction between a general purpose computer (PC) and a specialist device (music player, telephone, radio, television etc), the current trend is that many specialist devices have evolved into general purpose computers in their own right. Modern mobile phones perform many of the same tasks as a personal computer, such as browsing the Internet, sending e-mails, storing a database of contacts etc. For example, Apple's *iPhone* is an MP3 player with an in-built Internet-enabled computer and telephone (or is it a telephone with an in-built music player and Internet access?).

The following trends can be observed in modern ICT devices:

+ **A continued shrinkage of hardware.** For evidence of this, compare mobile phones from the 1980s with those of today. Shrinkage allows many devices to be combined within one single unit, eg a *Blackberry*.

+ **Many users replace perfectly functional equipment** to keep up with changing trends, some on an annual basis, and others even more frequently. Therefore, some manufacturers are less concerned with the long term durability of a product, as this adds to manufacturing costs. Instead, they mass produce cheap units that only have to last for a few years (figure 31.1).

+ **An explosion in the number of mobile devices in use**, such as telephones and MP3 players. The field of mobile telecommunications has benefited from the shrinkage in hardware and also from developments in rechargeable battery technology as manufacturers fight for customers who want to avoid changing batteries or recharging their equipment every few days;

+ **Development of RAD (Rapid Application Development) tools** and increasing software complexity. In the 1980s it was possible for a single person to understand all aspects of a large system. It was considered good practice to re-use modules from existing programs where possible, which explains the similarities between most parts of Microsoft *Office* (for example, the toolbar at the top of various *Office* programs which has the options for File, Edit etc). Decades of code reuse, combined with the size of projects that make use of new hardware capabilities, have resulted in massive systems that no one person could understand completely. For example, Microsoft *Windows Vista* (2006) has around 50 million lines of code, around ten million more than *Windows XP* (2001) and ten times as many as *Windows NT* (1993). Some of this code was written more than a decade before and originally used in *Windows NT*, and some was even written by other companies and incorporated directly into *Windows*. The complexity of so many modules means that security issues and other bugs can be very difficult to locate and eradicate and large amounts of time and money are required to maintain them.

+ **Many 'specialist' devices are actually made of general purpose hardware** that is given a purpose by the software running on it. For example, it is cheaper to produce ten thousand **PROM chips** or hard disks and program them for a task, than it is to have equipment purpose-built for that task. Since many devices share mass produced hardware components, cost savings can be passed on to consumers, who become increasingly demanding with their expectations. One example of the drop in costs is Sony's mass produced *Playstation 3*, which has eight processors and cost a few hundred pounds. It exceeds the capabilities of a 1980s supercomputer that filled a room, needed dedicated air conditioning and was built in low numbers for millions of pounds.

Task

Read the following news story: "Police Probe Theft of MoD Laptop", BBC News Online, 19 January 2008 via http://tinyurl.com/2kjgn3 With reference to this, or another similar news story, assess the risks to personal data that recent changes in ICT have created, and discuss how such risks can be minimised.

+ **A widespread increase in portable storage devices** and laptop computers which poses a variety of security risks. For example, viruses or data theft. A couple of decades ago, anyone who wanted to steal data would have had to conceal floppy disks which were easily damaged, thus corrupting the information stored on them. Nowadays, a suitably equipped mobile telephone or MP3 player can be connected to a PC to transfer data.

+ **The role of ICT management** is affected by the capabilities of new technology. Twenty years ago, a large company's network would have been restricted to PCs and servers. Now it is much more complex, thanks to a combination of:
  + PCs;
  + Users wanting mobile access to e-mail via PDAs;
  + Users wanting access from their home PCs;
  + Interfacing with partner networks.

It is no wonder that many firms have resisted a move away from *Windows XP* to *Windows Vista*, *MacOS X* or *Linux*. What they currently have is adequate and is already understood, whereas a mass migration to another operating system, together with any unforeseen problems it may cause, is not seen as beneficial.

31.3 The Effect of Technology on ICT Management

The benefits of ICT to large companies are as numerous as they are for private individuals and small businesses. From the introduction of simple data processing computers and fax machines through to today's e-commerce environment, the business landscape has changed immensely. Any corporation that attempted to revert to manual data processing, typing pools and sole reliance on traditional post would have difficulty succeeding. The use of ICT has brought increases both in the speed of data, and in the time it takes to make it available, thus raising the expectations of workers and clients exponentially:

+ For media firms, the 10pm printing deadline of previous decades has turned into a rush to update news web sites as soon as the stories break, which in turn forces an increased reliance on digital media in research.

+ For software developers, it is no longer sufficient to make sure a program works on a single PC. Today, users expect to be able to access help forums and download regular program updates.

+ Hardware vendors are expected to make manuals available online as well as in printed form.

+ Customers do not find it unreasonable to expect that their orders will be processed immediately by a warehouse and received within 48 hours. The days of waiting for posted orders to arrive and be sorted, and the widespread disclaimer 'please allow 28 days for delivery', are long gone.

All of this has drastically changed the role of ICT management. On one hand, an ICT manager may be responsible for a network that functions perfectly well. On the other, users have high expectations and will demand:

+ Increased connectivity with the Internet or external WANs;

+ Network-orientated capabilities built into the everyday software that the business uses in order to facilitate data sharing. This in turn demands the installation and maintenance of other programs such as Microsoft's *.NET Framework* or Sun's *Java EE*;

+ Easy access to corporate servers hundreds of miles away from the company's offices.

Unfortunately for ICT management, users are often unaware of the underlying complexity of their system. In many firms, users may not understand why, two years after it was released, *Windows Vista* was still not being used in their offices when their twelve-year-old son at home had it on the computer in his bedroom. The same users may be baffled to learn that even two years after it was released, *Vista* was still impractical for many offices as it was not compatible with certain printer drivers and software.

The technological environment in which we live and work is changing rapidly. It is a combination of all of these influences on the use of ICT, the attitudes and abilities of the people who use the technology, and the quality of company planning that dictate whether a new system will succeed or fail.

31.4 The Success or Failure of an Information System

According to research, 25% of IT projects are deemed to be a success, and 25% a failure. The remaining 50% have some degree of both success and failure (source: KPMG 2006, see http://tinyurl.com/3ajsal). In another poll 57% of those questioned said that fewer than half the projects they were involved with were successes. In 67% of cases, the functionality of the proposed system was reduced, in 45% of cases more money was allocated and in 31% lower quality and performance were accepted (source: HP 2007, see http://tinyurl.com/22s3pv).

When introducing a new information system the key **reasons for failure** discussed below should be addressed in order to ensure the success of the information system, as a successful system results from much more than good design and programming. The order in which they need to be addressed depends on the method of implementation adopted and other circumstances unique to the company.

+ **A poor investigation at the analysis stage** with little consultation with the customer and end users may lead to a system that does not meet requirements. This may result in an unworkable design, obsolete features or even the project's cancellation. It is also important that users are involved in the development of the system, so that they are less resentful or apprehensive about the introduction of a new computer system. A system that does not do what is expected or required to do may have an adverse effect on existing systems – or it may be hated by users. See section 15.3.

+ **Inadequate testing.** For an information system to be reliable it must be tested thoroughly at all levels. This necessitates a large volume of test data and different types of test data. The end users should be involved in acceptance testing before the system is signed off it does not contain bugs. Companies must take adequate measures to ensure that operations and data are not compromised if errors manifest themselves. This includes making multiple backup copies of data and using redundant systems that duplicate everything the main system does. See section 15.6.

+ **Employee problems** are often the most difficult to solve. Employee attitudes must be considered and addressed as it is essential that they are supportive of a new information system. It is certain that their jobs will change in some way. While some employees will be glad to get rid of mundane tasks, others will want to hold onto theirs because they are comfortable with them. Employees may view a new system as either the solution to their problems, or a needless replacement for one that worked perfectly well, brought about by a manager who they think does not understand their situation. Such a negative attitude may affect other employees and the way in which they regard the new system. In addition, if the people behind a new system are already unpopular within the firm, there may be a deliberate effort by certain employees to jeopardise it. Good management seeks to understand why certain people will resist change: whether it is to deliberately cause problems or because they are concerned about their own position.

+ **Data incompatibility.** Employees may have to access data from the old system and therefore it is essential that hardware and software are compatible between systems. If data is not properly imported, or the system's design is inefficient, users will quickly become frustrated. Consider the irritation a *Windows* PC user may experience in switching to another operating system (or vice versa) because the tasks they used to perform with ease are now extremely difficult. Add to that the frustration of data from one package not importing into another. While data compatibility may seem like a trivial issue, when it goes wrong it can make the user's working life tiring and stressful. New systems are often hampered by design decisions that were taken decades before, such as Microsoft's choice to develop their *OOXML* format (used with *Office 2007*) instead of adopting the ISO standard *ODF* used by their rivals (note: a modified form of *OOXML*, not actually used in any commercial products, has since been accepted by ISO). This is in part due to a need to retain access to old formats that came into being because design decisions in the 1980s / 90s did not fully account for users on many different platforms twenty years later. Any firm with decades' worth of data is in a similar position. Designers of a new database written today for fast hardware have to consider the problems that designers of the old system face on slow 1980s hardware.

For a discussion on the problems created by various complicated file formats, see "Why are the Microsoft Office file formats so complicated?" by Joel Spolskey, via http://tinyurl.com/2ez8ju

By the way...

+ **Inappropriate method of changeover.** The choice is direct, parallel or phased, the method of changeover must be chosen carefully to suit the users. For example, a company moving from one office package to another may decide to give users six months to migrate from one place to another at their own pace while training is organised. Other companies may do the opposite and force users to change systems overnight. If the new system is not satisfactory some staff may stop working and complain that the system is faulty. See section 15.7.

+ **Insufficient training for staff.** Staff must receive adequate training at an appropriate time before the system is implemented. This will ensure that the information system is used to its full potential, to avoid critical errors which could lead to failure. Support, such as user documentation or a helpdesk, could also be made available once the system is operational. However, busy employees may resent training, viewing it as a disruptive waste of time. Therefore, training must be presented to employees as something that will benefit both them and the company. It can be seen that the attitude of employees contributes to a system's failure or success. However, if employees are treated in a sensible and respectable manner, many potential problems can be avoided.

+ **Poor budgeting.** For an information system to be successful, accurate budgeting must also be in place. Any new system must be completed according to the budget agreed by management at the start of the project. However, costs are often underestimated and can soon spiral out of control, resulting in the project's failure.

+ **Poor maintainability.** At all times, a system must be maintainable, ie relevant to the company's mission, environment and people. If a system fails to adapt, it may soon be rendered useless and the company's business will suffer. Systems may even fail before they are implemented because of unforeseen changes in requirements. See section 15.9.

Task

IT Failure 'Causes £130m Arrears' - BBC News Online, 2 July 2008

"Rates arrears of £130m accrued because an expensive computer system is not up to the job, the Northern Ireland Audit Office has revealed. The Rate Collection Agency's £10.5m system was last year unable to send out final notices, the auditors found. Landlords received prompt-payment discounts totalling £5m, whether or not they had paid on time.

"The Department of Finance said major moves had been taken to address the problem and the debt was down to £85m. One of the many problems found by the Audit Office was an incident where the computer calculated Disabled Persons Allowance of £2.9m for a single ratepayer. The error was only detected and payment stopped as part of a manual supervisory check. Less significant errors could go unnoticed by manual checks, the report said. Auditors said record-keeping was so poor, the existence or accuracy of some figures could not be verified.

"Introduced in October 2006, the Abbacus IT system was aimed at improving rate collection and housing benefit payment. Inadequacies in the original specifications were blamed in part and an additional sum of more than £1m has already been paid to the installers for improvements."

Full story at http://tinyurl.com/5f77am

Using the above news story and the material in this section, assess the factors that can result in an IT project suffering from failures.

Questions

1. Describe two hardware developments which are changing the way in which ICT is being used. (4)
2. Describe two software developments which are changing the way in which ICT is being used. (4)
3. Describe three benefits of ICT for management. (6)
4. Identify and describe three factors that can influence the success or failure of an information system. (9)

Index

Bibliography

Books referred to:

BCS (2008), *BCS Glossary of Computing and ICT* (12th Ed), BCS, 9781906124007

Foster & Kesselman (Eds) (2003), *The Grid 2: Blueprint for a New Computing Infrastructure*, Morgan Kaufmann, 1558609334

Pressman & Ince (1994), *Software Engineering: A Practitioner's Approach* (European Ed), McGraw-Hill, 0077079361

Silberschatz, Galvin & Gagne (2005) *Operating System Principles*, John Wiley & Sons, 0471694665

Somerville (2004), *Software Engineering* (7th Ed), Addison-Wesley, 9780321210265

Somerville (2000), *Software Engineering* (6th Ed), Addison-Wesley, 9780201398151

Tanenbaum (2002) *Computer Networks*, Pearson, 0130384887

Web sites referred to:

About.com	http://home.about.com/compute/index.htm
Fundamentals of Communications, Alcatel	http://www.ind.alcatel.com/fundamentals
Build a Computer	http://www.build-a-computer-guide.com
Software Management Guide, Business Software Alliance	http://global.bsa.org/usa/policyres/admin/gsmus.pdf
A relational model for data for large shared data banks, Codd	http://www.acm.org/classics/nov95/toc.html
Creating a Development Dynamic Digital Opportunity Initiative	http://www.opt-init.org/framework/pages/2.2.1.html
DTI Telework Guidance	http://www.dti.gov.uk/er/individual/telework.pdf
Free Online Dictionary of Computing	http://www.foldoc.com
Better management for software projects, Murthi	http://www.developer.com/mgmt/article.php/1450361
Practically Networked	http://www.practicallynetworked.com
Protocols.com	http://www.protocols.com
Resource Directory Network	http://www.rdn.ac.uk/casestudies/eevl/ict/case3.html
Search Networking	http://searchnetworking.techtarget.com
Webopedia	http://www.webopedia.com
Wikipedia	http://www.wikipedia.com
How Stuff Works	http://www.howstuffworks.com
Teach ICT	http://www.teach-ict.com
JISC Legal Protection	http://www.jisclegal.ac.uk
Federation Against Copyright Theft	http://www.fact-uk.org.uk

Disclaimers and Copyright Information

URLs:

Colourpoint has no control over the web sites mentioned in this book. The web sites whose URLs are given were checked at time of writing, but the ownership or content may have changed subsequently. Teachers and parents are advised to check web sites before letting children view them.

CCEA Specification and Examination Questions:

All references to the CCEA A Level ICT specification were correct at time of going to press (2009) but may change. Always consult the latest specification first. Examination questions are reproduced by kind permission of CCEA.

Trademarks:

The following tradenames and trademarks are owned by their respective copyright holders: Adobe Acrobat, Pagemaker, Photoshop; Altavista; AOL; Apple Appleworks, iBook, iTunes, iPod, Macintosh, Mail, Newton, OS 8, OS X, Quicktime, Safari; AT&T; AVG Anti-virus; BBC; Belfast NewsLetter; Ceefax; Cisco; Computer Weekly; Corel WordPerfect; Daily Telegraph; Digital Vax, VMS; Filemaker; FreeBSD; Google; Hewlett Packard, HP-UX; IBM; ICab; ICQ; ISO/OSI; ITN; Linux; Lotus WordPro, 1-2-3, Freelance, Smartsuite; Lynx; Macromedia Flash, Dreamweaver; Mastercard; Microsoft Access, DOS, Excel, Hotmail, Internet Explorer, Mail, MSN, Office, Office Assistant, Outlook, Outlook Express, Paint, Paint Shop Pro, Powerpoint, Publisher, Scandisk, Windows 2000, Windows 3.1, Windows 95, Windows CE, Windows Explorer, Windows ME, Windows Media Player, Windows NT, Windows XP, Windows 7, Word; Mozilla; NCSA Mosaic; Netscape Navigator; Novell Netware; Nintendo Wii, OpenOffice Calc, Impress, Writer; Opera; Palm PalmOS, Pilot, Tungsten; Pegasus Mail; PsionOS; Real One; Sun Solaris; Teletext; Tiscali; Trillian; Unix; Visa; Wanadoo; Websense; WinZip; XNews; Yahoo!, Yahoo Companion, Yahoo Instant Messenger; Zigbee.

Copyright:

Some screen shot(s) reprinted by permission from Microsoft Corporation. Screens from Pegasus Mail ©1990-2009 David Harris: used by permission. Screens from Trillian ©1999-2009 Cerulean Studios: used by permission. Novell screens ©1990-2009 Novell, Inc. All rights reserved. Used with permission. Novell and NetWare are registered trademarks of Novell, Inc. in the United States and other countries. Images of BBC Ceefax and BBCi and quotes from BBC News Online ©2000-2009 BBC and appear with permission. Material from the *Guide To Software Management* appears with the permission of the Business Software Alliance. *The Data Protection Act 1998, The Copyright, Designs and Patents Act 1998* and the *Computer Misuse Act 1990* are Crown Copyright. Crown copyright material is reproduced with the permission of the Controller of HMSO and the Queen's Printer for Scotland. Material relating to the Data Protection Act from *The Information Commissioner's* web site ©The Information Commisioner. Material from the Free On-Line Dictionary of Computing is reproduced with permission. ©1993-2009 Denis Howe http://www.foldoc.org.